CONSCRIPT NATION

PITT LATIN AMERICAN SERIES

CATHERINE M. CONAGHAN, EDITOR

CONSCRIPT NATION

COERCION AND CITIZENSHIP IN THE BOLIVIAN BARRACKS

ELIZABETH SHESKO

UNIVERSITY OF PITTSBURGH PRESS

Chapter 4 draws on material from "Mobilizing Manpower for War: Toward a New History of Bolivia's Chaco Conflict, 1932–1935," *Hispanic American Historical Review* 95, no. 2 (2015): 299–334. Several other chapters draw on material from "Constructing Roads, Washing Feet, and Cutting Cane for the *Patria*: Building Bolivia with Military Labor, 1900–1975," *International Labor and Working-Class History* 80 (Fall 2011): 6–28.

Published by the University of Pittsburgh Press, Pittsburgh, Pa., 15260
Copyright © 2020, University of Pittsburgh Press
All rights reserved
Manufactured in the United States of America
Printed on acid-free paper
10 9 8 7 6 5 4 3 2 1

Library of Congress Cataloging-in-Publication Data

Names: Shesko, Elizabeth, author.
Title: Conscript nation : coercion and citizenship in the Bolivian barracks
  / Elizabeth Shesko.
Description: Pittsburgh, Pa. : University of Pittsburgh Press, [2020] |
  Series: Pitt Latin American series | Includes bibliographical references and index.
Identifiers: LCCN 2019053604 | ISBN 9780822946021 (cloth) alk. paper | ISBN
  9780822987383 (ebook)
Subjects: LCSH: Draft--Bolivia--Social aspects. | Civil-military
  relations--Bolivia. | Bolivia. Ejército--Recruiting, enlistment, etc. |
  Sociology, Military--Bolivia. | Bolivia--History, Military--20th century.
Classification: LCC UB345.B5 S54 2020 | DDC 355.2/23630984--dc23
LC record available at https://lccn.loc.gov/2019053604

Cover image: Walter Murillo, during his year of obligatory military service in 1940. From the personal collection of Rosa Marina Murillo
Cover design: Melissa Dias-Mandoly

CONTENTS

Acknowledgments

vii

INTRODUCTION

Conscription's Deep Roots

3

CHAPTER 1

Conscription without Citizenship

16

CHAPTER 2

Life and Labor in the Barracks

42

CHAPTER 3

Clientelism and Conscript Insubordination

64

CHAPTER 4

Mobilization for the Chaco War

86

CHAPTER 5

Good Sons and Bad Fathers in the Postwar Period

111

CHAPTER 6

Soldiers and Veterans but Still Not Citizens

129

CHAPTER 7

What Difference Did a Revolution Make?

151

EPILOGUE

The Military's Restorative Revolution of 1964

170

Notes

175

Bibliography

231

Index

251

ACKNOWLEDGMENTS

The research for this book began when I first approached the imposing gates of La Paz's Estado Mayor in 2008. Over the decade that I have lived with this project, I have accumulated many debts and been lucky enough to work with incredible people. First and foremost, I am grateful for John French, who is the model of a generous and engaged adviser. This book would be a far inferior product without the long hours he spent reading my work and debating its implications.

I count myself privileged to be part of an amazing cohort of Bolivianists who have turned renewed attention to this country, so much of whose history remains to be written. Nicole Pacino, Sarah Hines, Kevin Young, Bridgette Werner, and Molly Giedel from our Bolivianist writing group provided thought-provoking comments on the introduction and final chapter. I look forward to a career of continued exchanges with them and with Tasha Kimball, Carmen Soliz, Thomas Field, Matt Gildner, Luis Sierra, Elena McGrath, Nancy Egan, Chuck Sturtevant, Ben Knobbs-Thiessen, Hernán Pruden, and Andrew Ehrinpreis. I have also profoundly benefitted from the brilliant work and mentorship of the Bolivianists who blazed the trail for us, illuminating important parts of the country's history and politics before it was in fashion. Gabi Kuenzli, Robert Smale, Brooke Larson, Erick Langer, Laura Gotkowitz, James Dunkerley, Ann Zulawski, Rossana Barragán, Nancy Postero, Krista Van Vleet, and Marta Irurozqui have all contributed to more than just the bibliography of this book, whether they know it or not. Waskar Ari's ongoing advice and assistance on research, introductions, housing, and linguistic and cultural translations have been invaluable.

The community of social and cultural historians studying military life also profoundly enriched this work. Michelle Moyd put together a stellar conference about global military labor, and Reena Goldthree helped organize a workshop and an AHA panel on military labor in Latin America and the Caribbean. The conversations resulting from these events were formative to my thinking. Peter Guardino, David Carey, Zachary Morgan, René Harder Horst, Hendrik Kraay, Stephen Neufeld, Nico Sillitti, Leith Passmore, and Paul Johstono have influenced me and offered critical feedback. Putting together an edited volume is a thankless job, and Bridget Chesterton did an important service by bringing together historians of the Chaco War. Peter Beattie kindly commented on several conference papers and the introduction; his work has been an inspiration. And Jonathan Ablard has been with this project almost as long as I have, serving as a key collaborator. Dirk Bönker assisted me in my crash course in military history and worked with me to understand what stands out about the Bolivian situation.

Historian Luis Oporto has been an important supporter of this project's development. I owe him a crucial debt for his guidance in pursuing access to the Ministry of Defense archives. The staff there, led by Lic. Berta Lecoña and Colonel Carlos Gonzalo Arzabe at the Central Archive and Colonel Adolfo Colque, Lieutenant Colonel Hugo Quiroga, and Major Gonzalo Leytón at the Territorial Registry, kindly assisted with this research. I am also thankful to Colonel Simón Orellana, Sub-Official Luis Mamani, and the rest of the staff at the Historical Archive of the Estado Mayor for facilitating my work with their priceless archival holdings. Dr. Rossana Barragán and her crack staff at the Archive of La Paz provided knowledgeable assistance in navigating their extensive holdings. The then-director of the Arturo Costa de la Torre Library, Ivica Tadic, gave me a warm welcome and helped me sort through years of military journals. And the staff at the Archive of Bolivia's Plurinational Legislature were unfailing in their assistance with my research on legal, congressional, and periodical sources.

The Sánchez family in Asunción took me in when the vagaries of Bolivian visas threatened my research fellowship. Evelyn especially offered guidance and friendship. Colonel Néstor González and his staff at Paraguay's Ministry of Defense's Historic Institute helped me sift through their rich holdings to find hundreds of photographs and documents related to prisoners of war. Lic. Adelina Pusineri at the Andrés Barbero Museum and Archive was more than generous with her time and archival expertise. Marie Morel provided company and introduced me to the holdings of the Archbishopric Archive.

None of this research in Bolivia, Paraguay, the United Kingdom, and the United States would have been possible without the support of the US Department of Education, the Mellon Foundation, the Tinker Foundation, the Duke Foundation, the Duke Graduate School, the Duke History Department, and Bowdoin College. A summer FLAS allowed me to study the Aymara language with Miguel Huanca. During my research trips, Amy O'Toole, Marina Murillo, and Alicia Dinerstein kindly opened their homes in Bolivia to me, providing far more than just a place to sleep. The day I met Nely Canqui at an archivists' congress was a lucky one. She not only supported my work but became a close friend. Heather Joffe and Alicia Dinerstein made my stays in Bolivia feel like home. I could not have asked for better friends with whom to travel.

Janice Joffe at Bowdoin College taught the gateway Spanish course that started me on this trajectory and has encouraged me along the way. Fascinating courses with Matt Lassiter got me interested in history, and Enrique Yepes's intellectual generosity first exposed me to the rigor of academic writing. Allen Wells mentored me throughout the process. The year I spent back at Bowdoin in his office surrounded by his books was a privilege and inspiration. Kelly Kerney's wit and friendship was by far the best thing I gained from college, however.

At Duke and UNC, Pete Sigal, Jocelyn Olcott, Orin Starn, Diane Nelson, and Kathryn Burns complicated my understandings of identification and difference and deepened my questions about how local politics and power relations articulate with broader structures. I also benefitted greatly from the insights and patience of Jan Hoffman French. Bryan Pitts, Kristin Wintersteen, Katharine French-Fuller, Jeffrey Richey, Reena Goldthree, Erin Parish, Caroline Garriott, Vanessa Freije, David Romine, Corinna Zeltsman, Anne Phillips, Jeff Erbig, and Rachel Hynson forged an unparalleled intellectual community and support network of Latin Americanists. Alumni like Alejandro Velasco, Ivonne Wallace Fuentes, Mark Healey, Tom Rogers, and David Sartorios gave valuable advice when I hit walls. Julia Gaffield, Mitch Fraas, Orion Teal, Anne-Marie Angelo, and Bryan Pitts have offered unwavering friendship over the years. Only graduate school could bring such wonderful people together only to then scatter them to the ends of the earth.

My colleagues at Oakland University have provided a supportive environment for me to grow as a researcher and instructor. Sara Chapman Williams and Derek Hastings gave sage advice that I too often failed to follow. The administrative expertise and friendly faces of Janet Chandler and Johanna McReynolds are unparalleled. Kevin Corcoran has been the model dean, which you do not hear much in academia. Dante Rance in ILL has done more for this project than he will ever know. I have come to depend upon the friendship of Dan Clark, James Naus, Alison Powell, Erin Dwyer, and Yan Li and thank them for helping to make Michigan home. Mike Huner's dedication to organizing a regional history workshop for Latin Americanists has introduced me to a new group of engaged colleagues.

Josh Shanholtzer at University of Pittsburgh Press shepherded this first-time author through the publication process with efficiency and grace. Alejandro Velasco, Tasha Kimball, and Marc Becker were generous with their advice as I nervously approached publishers. Oakland University's URC fellowship funded the time and data analysis that made chapter 6 possible. The anonymous reviewers of this manuscript as well as of my HAHR and ILWCH articles pushed me in new and fruitful directions. This book could not have been completed without the assistance of Marina Murillo, who was constant in her pursuit of the proper permissions and TIFs. Her willingness to share family photographs and history added a rich layer to the manuscript. The first pages of this book benefitted greatly from Bryan Pitts's smart criticism and keen eye for language. George Milne generously created the book's maps, helping me bring my vision to life and ensuring that he will never get lost in La Paz. Marilyn Shesko was unstinting with her time and proofreading skills.

Having played a key if unwitting role in this project's genesis, Adam Wallace has put up with it and outlasted it, making sure I never took myself too seriously. He's accompanied me in a relationship that has seen us living across six states and three countries—no easy task. I cannot imagine this journey without him. Our children, Rebecca and Grant, significantly delayed this book's completion but have made my life far richer by pulling me away from my screens to play in the sunshine and read stories. My grandmother, Marian Markovich McIlvin, helped set me on this path, instilling in me the family traditions of travel and photography. Above all, I thank my parents Gregory and Marilyn Shesko for supporting me over the years and for raising me in a world of books, words, and storytelling. I am especially grateful for the borrowed time with my father that has allowed him to see this book to completion.

CONSCRIPT NATION

INTRODUCTION

CONSCRIPTION'S DEEP ROOTS

In his inaugural address at Tiwanaku in 2006, Evo Morales promised to complete the revolutionary struggles of Túpac Katari and Che Guevara by refounding the nation through a Constituent Assembly that would finally "end the colonial state."[1] After more than a decade of social mobilization, Morales's historic election marked the emergence of a new, indigenous-inflected nationalist project in a country whose indigenous majority had long been marginalized by the white and mestizo elite. His revolutionary 2009 Constitution went so far as to rename the country. It promised that the new Plurinational State of Bolivia would be "based on respect and equality for all, on principles of sovereignty, dignity, complementarity, solidarity, harmony, and equity in the distribution and redistribution of the social wealth, where the search for *buen vivir* [a harmonic life] predominates."[2]

Everything had changed in Bolivia. Or almost everything. Amid these radical transformations in what it meant to be Bolivian, one thing remained strikingly similar—the requirement of male military service. In fact, four separate articles of the 2009 Constitution reiterated the duty of all men to serve.[3] Article 108 identified sixteen separate obligations of Bolivians. Alongside their duties to protect natural resources in a sustainable way and "care for, protect, and help their ancestors" was the only gendered duty: "to give military service, which is obligatory for men."[4] The article that boldly restricted public service to those who speak at least two of the country's thirty-seven official languages also mandated that male candidates complete military duties.[5] The repetition of this obligation raises a question: Why did this new foundation for Bolivian governance and society take such pains to recommit the nation's men to serving in the military, a violent and coercive institution that has long promoted assimilation into a mestizo national cultural ideal?

By analyzing military service from its establishment in the early twentieth century through the changes wrought after the 1952 revolution, this book explains the history of Bolivians' paradoxical embrace of conscription by arguing that this coercive state project evolved into a pact between the state and society. This pact was not negotiated on equal terms, nor did it create a unified nation devoid of hierarchy. But conscription was constitutive of citizenship and state formation in Bolivia. It was not only fundamental to establishing bureaucratic structures throughout the national territory but also the primary mechanism for efforts to instill a sense of national identity in indigenous and working-class men. Yet the Bolivian state lacked the coercive power to impose it through force, the bureaucratic power to impose it administratively, and the ideological power to impose it through nationalism. So it combined the coercive structure of conscription with arbitrary impressment while working to negotiate consent. I argue that many Bolivian men, especially from the lower classes, participated in military service (and pressured others to do the same) because it was a way to ascend the social ladder, forge patronage relationships, prove adulthood and manliness, and make claims on the state.

MILITARY SERVICE IN CONTEMPORARY BOLIVIA

The construction of a classed and gendered identity on the basis of military service has led this practice to thrive in Bolivia as it is being eliminated in some other parts of Latin America and the world. Since the 1970s, scholars have been discussing the decline of conscription as militaries have adjusted to an era of limited and unconventional warfare that often has only tenuous connections to national borders.[6] The originators of the modern system of universal male military service, France and Germany, have ended or suspended the obligation. Although heightened geopolitical tensions in the 2010s have sparked some renewed interest in compulsory service, it is certainly no longer the norm. By the 1990s, notes military historian George Flynn, "the conscript's day was over."[7]

In Bolivia, however, twenty thousand young men enter the barracks as conscripts each January, with newspapers reporting on long lines outside of the most prestigious units and publishing pictures of the tents pitched days in advance by eager recruits.[8] Men need military service documents (see figure I.1) to vote, run for office, or hold public employment. Having these documents has become "synonymous with being mature and responsible"; indigenous respondents to a 2002 survey presented this documentation as "indispensable" to their personal lives.[9] As is true for many systems of supposedly universal service, they can obtain this paperwork without dedicating a year of their lives to the barracks. Twenty-thousand secondary students annually elect to complete pre-military training on weekends to earn their service documents, and those who want and can afford to forgo training altogether can pay a fee of three thousand bolivianos (about $430, which would be out of reach for most working-class Bolivians).[10] And many others simply go without these documents.[11] The conscription system in place today effective-

FIGURE I.1. Military service booklet of Hugo Murillo, 1941. Personal collection of Rosa Marina Murillo, La Paz. Used with permission.

ly staffs the ranks with men who choose to be there. They cannot be called volunteers, however, because of the legal compulsion that structures their military service. But their collaboration establishes them as patriotic citizens who have answered the call to defend the nation.

These young men enter the barracks because they understand the experience of military service to be a meaningful one for social, cultural, political, and gendered reasons. It has become embedded in the fabric of Bolivian society, at least for men from the working classes, especially in some rural communities. Although the obligation to perform military service is still explicitly male, the armed forces offered 180 conscript spots for female volunteers for the first time in 2018.[12] Opening up this experience to young women, even in this very limited way, suggests that many Bolivians see military service not as an onerous duty to be avoided but rather as one that carries prestige.

The term "conscript" has gendered, class-based, and nationalist meanings in today's Bolivia. When campaigning for president in 2005, Evo Morales prominently invoked his time in the military as proof of his patriotism, pointing out that his opponent, who had called him an indigenous separatist, had never donned a uniform or taken the conscript's oath to the flag.[13] In April 2017, Vice Minister of Decolonization Félix Cárdenas advocated that all candidates for president, vice president, and the legislature be required to speak an indigenous language and, if male, have entered the barracks as conscripts. "In Bolivia, the only president who has done obligatory military service is called Evo Morales, all the others were *omisos*, none of them went to the barracks."[14] Conscription has become a marker of pride and nationalism for non-elite men.

FROM LIBERALISM TO REVOLUTIONARY NATIONALISM

This book tells the story of the militarization of Bolivian politics and society in the era prior to the rule by generals (with brief civilian interludes) from 1964 to 1982. Following Maya Eichler, I define militarization as "any process that helps establish or reinforce a central role for the military in state or society."[15] In Bolivia, these processes had two threads, the interrelation of which this book teases out. The first is the intermixing of military and civilian cultures through conscription during times of both war and peace. The second is the role of military officers (and sometimes even conscripts) in high politics, despite the institution's constitutional mandate to be "a fundamentally obedient institution" prohibited from political participation (*deliberar*).[16]

This study of conscription thus analyzes politics and belonging during Bolivia's periods of liberalism (1900–1936), reform and reaction (1936–1952), and revolutionary nationalism (1952–1964). Before 1952, Bolivia severely limited formal citizenship, which was defined as the right to vote and be elected.[17] Although the discursive use of the term "citizen" was far less rigid, referring to a general sense of belonging, nationalism, and rights that applied far beyond the limited pool of voters, this broader definition still encompassed only a limited proportion of those living within the national territory.[18] A substantial number of men in the barracks were thus what I call noncitizen soldiers, meaning they had neither formal citizenship rights nor a strong sense of duty and belonging to the Bolivian nation.

Although masked by the language of inclusivity, the project of obligatory military service in fact originated as part of an attempt to limit indigenous communities' sense of belonging to Bolivia. After defeating Conservatives in an 1899 civil war, Liberals worked to restrict the power of the indigenous allies who had made their victory possible. The military service law contributed to these efforts by making conscription obligatory for all men, which ended previous exemptions for tribute-paying Indians. Drawing on congressional debates, War Ministry records, and Prefecture records, the first chapter of this book shows that military conscription in the early twentieth century was structured by Bolivia's persistent and pervasive racism and thus reinforced racialized hierarchies.

The second chapter, however, takes readers inside the barracks to argue that the experience of military service was never within the control of the liberal state that instituted it as part of its nation-making project. Throughout the twentieth century, soldiers cultivated their own countervailing cultural practices within a larger military culture, both investing in and contesting the norms, punishments, labors, and living conditions imposed by their officers. Fundamentally different concepts of legitimate authority clashed in the barracks as Bolivia haltingly transitioned from an army based on impressment to one based on patriotic service.

The fracturing of the Liberal Party after 1914 created a new atmosphere of fear and suspicion in the barracks as officers engaged conscripts in plots to bring favored civilians to power. Formally educated conscripts had long drawn on patron-client ties to complain about the barracks, claiming that the institution had failed in its obligations to them. However, in a time of heightened partisan conflict, authorities interpreted the expression of these grievances as politically motivated mutinies that might signal the next coup. Chapter 3's analysis of four conscript-led mutinies in La Paz between 1920 and 1931 shows that literate and politically engaged conscripts were emboldened by the factionalized context to bypass the command structure and use the idea of citizen soldiers to make demands about the conditions of military service. Instances of rebellion and insubordination thus haunted the Bolivian army as tensions grew over the border in the Chaco.

The 1932–1935 Chaco War with Paraguay was the deadliest interstate conflict in twentieth-century Latin America.[19] After mobilizing an unprecedented number of men, Bolivia suffered losses proportional to those of European nations in World War I.[20] Drawing on military-justice testimony, the fourth chapter argues that recruitment processes and the treatment of deserters were remarkably flexible and that accommodations did not always correlate to men's social status. Archival sources from Bolivia and Paraguay show that frontline soldiers were far more diverse than previously recognized and included volunteers, draftees, and men violently impressed into the ranks. Military and diplomatic mistakes quickly turned the war into a disaster for Bolivia, as its soldiers suffered the ravages of not only combat but also disease and dehydration. Yet this mass participation and shared suffering led to increased investment in military service and laid the foundation for Bolivia to become a conscript nation.

Economic crises, coups, strikes, and uprisings characterized the postwar period as reformist and revolutionary parties challenged the traditional elite. Although the military should have emerged disgraced by the war, it instead dominated the country's labyrinthine politics, with officers holding the presidency for eleven of the next sixteen years. Some of these leaders had been part of the high command during the war, but others were junior officers who saw themselves as representing the noncitizens who had fought. These reformers challenged the established order and called for profound societal change. They promised to forge a new Bolivia, redeemed and united by veter-

ans' sacrifice. Detailing the increased engagement with the state that resulted from efforts to reward veterans and punish evaders, chapter 5 argues that
veterans, including some from rural areas identified as indigenous, assumed
a new authority and expressed a rhetorically powerful sense of belonging to
the Bolivian nation. The postwar era thus added a new form of distinction to
Bolivia's deeply rooted hierarchies.

Conscription thrived after the war due to the increased importance of
military service documents, the state's capacity to devote more resources to
recruitment, social pressure from peers and veterans, and individuals' power
to use service to make claims on the state.[21] However, most of the men who
had served on the front lines in the Chaco and who filled the barracks in the
1940s still lacked formal citizenship rights, as the 1938 Constitution explicitly retained literacy restrictions on suffrage. The reformist administrations of
Toro (1936–1937), Busch (1937–1939), and Villarroel (1943–1946) proved
unwilling to break from entrenched notions of hierarchy. However, the nation they imagined to have been forged in the Chaco and in the barracks
included only those willing to assimilate and participate in their version of
nationalism. Despite this continuity, chapter 6 shows that mass participation
in a failed war and the circulation of new ideologies did affect attitudes and
cultural norms in the military.

Wartime service had exposed a generation of young elite and middle-
class men to the indigenous masses that made up the bulk of the Bolivian
army. Already familiar with the revolutionary and reformist ideologies based
in Marxism that were circulating in the 1920s and 1930s, these men returned
from the front convinced that Bolivian society needed to change profoundly.
Seeing themselves as allied with and speaking for the masses, they formed
new political parties during and after the war to oppose the oligarchy. One
of these new parties was the Revolutionary Nationalist Movement (MNR)
led by Víctor Paz Estenssoro. After participating in the reformist military
government of Major Gualberto Villarroel from 1943 to 1946, the MNR attempted to take power by force several times. Although Paz Estenssoro won
the majority of votes in the 1951 presidential election, a military junta sent
him into exile.

Supported by miners, factory workers, and the *carabineros* (militarized
police force), the MNR staged a coup on April 9, 1952, that soon became a
revolution. During its first sixteen months in power, the party made suffrage
universal, nationalized the three largest tin mines, and enacted far-reaching
agrarian reform. The revolution threatened the survival of the military,
which had long supported the oligarchy by repressing strikes and uprisings.
Antimilitary sentiment proliferated after the revolution; the MNR slashed
the budget, shuttered the Military Academy, purged the officer corps, and
drastically reduced the number of conscripted troops. Symbolizing a pro-

found shift in power, militiamen in the mines and rural areas, many of whom had already served as conscripts, proudly wielded army rifles to protect their revolutionary conquests and the new administration.

However, key MNR leaders believed that the institution could be remade to serve party goals as the "Revolution's Army." The military's long-standing claims to embody the nation and prepare its youth for citizenship resonated with the MNR's nationalism. Chapter 7 explains the institution's survival after 1952 and its return to power after 1956, charting continuity and change in the conscript experience. Although the assimilatory purpose of military service remained, as did the violence and hierarchy of barracks life, new rhetoric about conscripts and their labor indicates that the new state no longer dismissed them as noncitizen soldiers but actively sought their support as citizens of the revolutionary nation.

CONSCRIPTION IN A GLOBAL CONTEXT

The growing scholarship on Latin American militaries has moved away from Miguel Centeno's pathbreaking work, which argued that limited wars in Latin America led to limited states that tended to be despotic and have a weak institutional capacity.[22] Instead, historians have examined military service in terms of gender, race, and social mobility. A large literature looks at the role of military service in non-elite nationalism, especially during the long nineteenth century. This vein of research has examined how indigenous and Afro-Latin people both shaped armies and were shaped by their participation in them.[23] These works begin to present military service as more than simply coercive but rather as a balancing act between state and individual needs.

Much more limited, however, is work on the systems of supposedly universal male conscription that spread throughout the region in the early twentieth century. Although its origins can be traced to the ancient world and the French Revolution, the modern form of obligatory military service dates to the mid-nineteenth century, when extensive peacetime conscription became the norm in Europe and spread throughout the world.[24] Between 1896 and 1916, every South American country except Venezuela and Uruguay passed conscription laws along these lines. These laws sought to replace armies based on the arbitrary and forcible recruitment of the poor (the *leva*) with ones made up of honorably conscripted citizen soldiers.[25]

Instead of a few men serving for long terms, conscript armies featured quite limited service by the masses in order to ensure that a significant portion of the male population had experience in arms and could be called up in case of international conflict. Putting what were essentially civilians in uniform necessarily led to changes in military culture. Spreading conscription to the masses also affected society, as states had to make and fulfill promises to get and retain men in the military. The coercive force of poverty led to the barracks' becoming a site of social mobility.[26] And the exclusive recruitment of men meant that conscription served to legitimize authority over women and became a marker of violent and dominating versions of masculinity.[27]

Universal male military service has long been associated with the ideal of citizen soldiers who have a stake in their own defense. This concept constructs soldiering as honorable because true citizen soldiers fight out of a sense of nationalism rather than for material benefit or out of fear of physical punishment. In theory, the military thus becomes an organic representation of the people rather than an institution with its own interests.[28] In Bolivia, this rhetoric elided the fact that property and literacy requirements barred many soldiers from enjoying formal citizenship rights.

In many Latin American countries, internal reasons for instituting compulsory military service trumped the geopolitical ones that had principally motivated European states. As neighbors turned toward conscript armies, border concerns were certainly part of the Latin American calculus. However, these states passed conscription laws more to assert control over the national territory, strengthen bureaucratic systems, gain access to labor, and nationalize and improve the population through a soft form of eugenics. Despite using liberalism's language of universality, governing elites, often over the objections of military officers, targeted for conscription men they viewed as most in need of discipline and instruction in literacy, public health, and nationalism.[29] Yet fear of race war also undergirded these conscription projects, as elites moved to militarize the very men that their armies were so often called on to repress.[30] Work on conscription thus supports Centeno's contention that Latin American militaries were organized around fighting internal enemies "defined racially, along class lines, and by critical ideological struggles."[31]

Although states adopted obligatory military service for similar reasons, implementation and communities' responses varied widely at both the national and subregional levels.[32] In Argentina, mass immigration, an ideologically charged atmosphere, and the unlikelihood of international conflict led to strongly coercive administrative methods, which produced comparatively high levels of participation. Unlike in Bolivia, Argentine conscripts secured the right to vote (without any literacy or property restrictions after 1912) through military service, and this association provided a rationale for denying women suffrage.[33] Work on Chile is more limited but suggests that the conscription system struggled with widespread exemptions and evasion.[34] Although Peru might be the most analogous country to Bolivia, no work has yet explored conscription in the early twentieth century except to suggest that discharged conscripts became peasant leaders.[35] Focused more on the late twentieth century, the scholarship on Ecuadorian conscription shows that the country did not actively pursue indigenous participation in military service until the 1940s.[36] And when Mexico experimented with a universal male draft in the 1940s, it produced limited results and led to significant physical, bureaucratic, and discursive resistance from both conscripts and the local authorities responsible for implementation.[37]

Many of these works have productively focused on competing narratives of masculinity surrounding barracks life. They tend to agree that states used gendered narratives to attract men to obligatory military service, promising "domination over women in exchange for fealty to the state and the social order."[38] Yet defining military service as the masculine honor of protecting the nation conflicts with the widespread use of humiliating physical punishments to discipline soldiers and the feminized nature of barracks work.[39] Different ideas about masculinity thus developed and clashed in the barracks, often resulting in an aggressive form of machismo based on physical dominance.[40] Working-class and rural men sometimes came to use a militarized masculinity gained in the barracks to question the manliness of the elite men who dominated society.[41]

Guatemala and Brazil offer the best cases for comparison due to the state of the scholarship on conscription and the existence of similarly racialized divides. Guatemala included indigenous people in the conscription system around the same time as Bolivia, whereas Brazil needed the geopolitical impetus of World War I to overcome the context of federalism and the fear of military interference in politics.[42] Brazil's system focused on the "'honorable' urban poor" and led to the "emergence of urban populism."[43] Although Bolivia's system was also disproportionately urban prior to the 1950s, in the 1910s and 1920s it produced a significant number of educated and middle-class conscripts who invoked the ideal of citizen soldiers to make demands and object to the conditions of service.

Guatemala, on the other hand, mostly used impressment to conscript rural indigenous men. Like their Bolivian counterparts, Guatemalan elites used conscription as a tool of integration and indoctrination as part of a modernizing state project.[44] Yet work by David Carey shows that during Jorge Ubico's administration in the 1930s, Guatemala incorporated indigenous men into the nation explicitly as Indians, embracing ethnic markers in the barracks—something that would have been quite unthinkable in Bolivia.[45] As was the case in Bolivia, however, many Kaqchikel conscripts experienced empowerment through military service, gaining confidence and concrete skills in the barracks.[46] The two countries diverged due to the 1954 coup and subsequent civil war that devastated rural Guatemala, which led indigenous people to successfully demand the end of conscription in the 1990s rather than embracing it as many Bolivians did.[47]

This scholarship on the mechanisms and experience of obligatory military service in Latin America consists of several isolated case studies, which limit the explanatory power of comparison. Only Peter Beattie's work on Brazil has the breadth and depth of sources comparable to this book. Although extensive work exists on Paraguay's wartime experience, scholars have yet to explore peacetime military service. More case studies are thus needed to clarify comparative aspects, but Bolivian conscription stands out in several respects. First, Bolivia was the only country (other than its opponent, Paraguay) to fight a large-scale, external war in the era of obligatory military service. This effort mobilized not only reservists but also many men without prior military training. It produced a generation of veterans from a variety of regions and social classes, all of whom had a clear avenue for claims-making based on wartime service. Veterans' relationship to the military institution and to the Bolivian state was essential to spreading awareness of and compliance with the obligation. Second, the 1952 revolution made all conscripts formal citizens and brought to power a government that needed their support at the polls and in the streets. Finally, Bolivia's particularly weak and localized state apparatus allowed for considerable individual and local manipulation of the obligation, experience, and meaning of conscription. Although conscripts throughout the region and world have co-created military service, affecting the institution and creating their own military culture, Bolivia appears to be an extreme case in that this process was so extensive that "conscript" became a term of pride.

INDIGENEITY AND STATE FORMATION IN BOLIVIA

The military has received little scholarly attention in spite of its fundamental role in Bolivia's history. Over the course of the twentieth century, the armed forces shaped the political system, drew people into the state through annual conscription and armed conflict, served as a school for citizenship, claimed to incarnate the nation, and helped define dominant masculinities. The military and military service are crucial to understanding some of the scholarship's biggest concerns: state formation, indigenous identity, revolutionary nationalism, and dictatorship. Yet because of the devastating consequences of the Chaco War and the Cold War dictatorships that took over after the fall of the MNR, the literature on the Bolivian military has been disproportionately focused on the details of campaigns, the actions of specific leaders, and officers' intervention in politics.[48] These works address a limited set of concerns, seeing the military in terms of leaders, battles, and tactics. Soldiers thus become merely bodies following orders rather than diverse subjects of state engagement.

Understanding the military as constructed through its relationship with conscripts, my work assimilates the lessons of operational and political military history but asks questions about military culture, soldiers' experiences, and the impact of the military and conscription on broader society. Narrating the goals and experience of military service over six decades, this book builds on the foundational work of Bolivians and Bolivianists who have parsed out the changing legal framework of conscription, helped explain how conscription functioned in the 1910s and 1930s, and explored men's wartime experiences.[49]

Existing work overwhelmingly focuses on military service as the machinery of an oppressive state that has perpetuated "colonial-type relations" by encouraging passive citizenship and teaching conscripts that indigeneity "was a worthless and stigmatizing cultural sign."[50] This is, of course, true. Designed to make conscripts less indigenous, the physical and cultural violence of military service played an active role in Bolivia's fluid and situational classificatory matrix, which is based on shifting sociocultural markers such as dress, hairstyle, language, diet, surname, schooling, occupation, region, residence, and income.[51] My work deepens this line of scholarship by showing how entrenched hierarchies structured who served and under what circumstances. More importantly, it explains how military service obscured the role of race and class in these hierarchies, instead expressing difference in terms of ability, honor, and patriotism.

But this book depicts consent as more than just complicit or opportunistic submission. Recent Bolivianist scholarship has productively focused on indigenous mobilization and citizenship, looking at the acculturative goals central to modernizing projects and the equivocal ways that the leaders of indigenous communities both engaged with and resisted the state.[52] Yet those who opted to assimilate, internalizing the stigma placed on indigeneity, have received less attention, which is why this book focuses on both coercion and consent. It also moves away from the study of indigenous activists to look at the daily interactions between the central institution of the Bolivian state and ordinary Bolivians from across lines of region, race, and social class. Because the state lacked the power to compel military service except through arbitrary impressment, it worked to negotiate consent. Multiple layers of claims-making, negotiation, and accommodation therefore characterized the state formation built around military service. I argue that conscription was embraced from below because it provided a space for Bolivians from across divides of education, ethnicity, and social class to negotiate their relationships with each other and with the state.

Internal military records drive this new interpretation of Bolivian state formation. Materials from Bolivia's Estado Mayor Archive depict the inner workings of the military institution and the practice of conscription. Informed by rich testimony from mutiny, abuse of authority, and desertion proceedings, the book takes readers inside the barracks and narrates con-

FIGURE I.2. Brass band playing at Gran Poder festival, 2006, La Paz. Photo by the author.

scripts' experiences of labor, insubordination, punishment, and homosocial camaraderie. I also draw on thousands of service records from the Ministry of Defense's Territorial Archive to elucidate the background of individual soldiers and chart the changing face of conscription across the national territory during the 1940s and 1950s.

Perhaps the ubiquity of brass bands in Bolivia encapsulates the unintended and unexpected effects of obligatory military service. Anyone who has been to Oruro's Carnaval, La Paz's Gran Poder, or any number of local festivals in neighborhoods and villages throughout Bolivia recognizes the central role of the brass bands that accompany the costumed men and women dancing the *morenada, tink'u,* or *caporales.* Anthropologists have commented on the importance of these *entradas* to affirming a "sense of common belonging" and expressing a Bolivianness "composed of multiple regional and ethnic identities."[53] Individuals identifying as indigenous participate in, and indigenous communities host, such festivals, but they are expressly Bolivian rather than exclusively indigenous. Yet they are still associated with indigeneity. As Roberto Albro notes, urban people use these costumed dances to maintain an "active connection to their indigenous heritage."[54] The brass bands that provide the beat for these dancers have their origin in the military bands that played at festivals for patriotic celebrations, raised soldiers' spirits during long marches, and convoked men to war.[55] Former conscripts, many of whom learned to play these instruments in the barracks, appropriated this and other aspects of military service and invested them with new meanings. Over a half century, they forged a conscript nation that was still hierarchical and divided by profound differences but was never simply an assimilatory project.

CHAPTER 1

CONSCRIPTION WITHOUT CITIZENSHIP

In 1905, Bolivian Lieutenant Colonel Carlos Nuñez del Prado sought to rescue the heroism of the common soldier from the "deep abyss of indifference and obscurity."[1] Printed in Bolivia's first official publication for military officers, his fictional depiction of an Aymara soldier named Quilco appeared at a dramatic moment in the army's history. The newly triumphant Liberal president, who had won power with Aymara support, ended military exemptions for tribute-paying Indians while putting his former indigenous allies on trial. His successor began implementing conscription laws and worked to professionalize the military. Published in the *Revista Militar*, Nuñez del Prado's story reflected a shared belief among reformist officers that a modernized army would save Bolivia by rising above partisan politics and training its people to be patriots.[2] In his fable, military discipline proved capable of transforming a "poor shepherd" into a "son, always faithful to the *patria* [nation]."[3]

Set fifty years in the past, the article vividly described Quilco's forcible impressment when a battalion passed through his "isolated hamlet in the mountains" en route to suppress one of many revolts against President Manuel Belzu (1848–1855).[4] The drama of the story lies in the contrast between Quilco's "placid and serene" life as a *colono* (tenant laborer) and the physical and cultural violence of military service. Nuñez del Prado described Quilco as "kidnapped from among his sheep and llamas" and disciplined by "a crack of the whip, dealt by an energetic and skillful hand." The soldiers cut off his braids and stripped him of his woolen pants and "his beautiful new poncho that had inspired the envy of his fellows."[5]

Nuñez del Prado criticized a military system in which a soldier "invested all national sentiment in a *caudillo* [strongman] rather than the *Patria*, sacrificed himself for the man rather than the Nation."[6] This framing of the issues allowed Nuñez del Prado to portray Quilco as a hero. The moment of patriotic transformation comes when Quilco, not having received orders to stand down from guard duty, refused to allow his battalion to exit the barracks to join the forces backing a *caudillo*. The author hailed Quilco for shooting his perfidious lieutenant colonel; in the aftermath, the other soldiers bayoneted and trampled Quilco, leaving his dead body to become a "vigorous protest against murderers and horrible anathema to traitors."[7]

As an officer who preached respect for hierarchy, Nuñez del Prado might be expected to condemn Quilco's killing of his superior. Yet oddities abound in this account. The author criticized corporal punishment but did not entirely repudiate it. In fact, brutality was precisely what produced Quilco's obedience to orders. Although the author celebrated Quilco's trampled body as the emblem of an apolitical army, he did not attribute this heroism to patriotism. Rather, Quilco acted patriotically because he faithfully—if stupidly—followed his corporal's orders not to "allow anyone to enter or leave the barracks, not even the Everlasting Father."[8] Nuñez del Prado could not break with ingrained prejudices about the natural subordination of indigenous Bolivians by portraying Quilco as an independent actor with motives beyond thoughtless obedience. In a moment when a new army was being built, this reformist officer rejected the army's past but reproduced attitudes toward the indigenous majority long characteristic of Bolivia's ruling elites.

The Quilco fable has little to do with indigenous life—other than acknowledging violent methods of domination. Rather, it reveals officers' belief that military training could transform conscripts. Like Nuñez del Prado, the Liberal politicians who led Bolivia into the twentieth century renounced a military past marked by abuse of soldiers, repeated coups, and humiliating defeats to neighboring nations. They envisioned a new army that would avenge Bolivia's recent territorial losses, establish control over the countryside and mines, and nationalize the country's multiethnic, multilingual, and regionally diverse population. Not acknowledging the potential tensions among these goals, Liberals asserted that European-style professionalism and effective legal norms for conscription would erase the army's anarchic past and allow it to create a modern Bolivia.

The law instituting universal male conscription was an aspirational effort that could be effectively implemented only by a muscular and interventionist state. The Bolivian state had no such capacity and instead depended on often unreliable local partners. But despite substantial financial, administrative, and geographic constraints, Liberals mounted a sustained effort to implement the law, balancing coercion, inducement, and concessions to establish conscription as a fundamental part of national life. As was common with Liberals throughout Latin America, a wide gap developed between ideologies of equality and racialized practice. Deeply ingrained hierarchies of culture, race, and class thus structured who would serve in the army as men avoided obligatory military service through patron-client connections, exemptions, evasion, and the lottery.[9] Officers and legislators tended to overlook the evasion of formally educated men, and the burden of military service fell primarily the *indígenas* and artisans they believed would most benefit from the civilizing power of the barracks. Yet my research reveals a wide range of responses to the law and a surprisingly flexible relationship between the state and its conscripts (both indigenous and non).

THE ORIGINS AND PROVISIONS OF THE 1907 CONSCRIPTION LAW

When discussing nineteenth-century Bolivia, it is "somewhat misconceived," in the words of historian James Dunkerley, "to refer to the army rather than armies."[10] National in name only, these armies better resembled the personal forces of *caudillos*. Yet they consumed between 40 and 70 percent of the national budget, which was primarily derived from indigenous tribute. They were also top heavy with officers: as late as 1876, the army consisted of 384 officers, 637 noncommissioned officers (NCOs), and only 825 troops. The duty of men to serve in the army had existed on paper since independence, but conscription laws had always provided for replacements and exemptions, including for all tribute-paying Indians. In practice, Bolivia's nineteenth-century army recruited mostly through impressment. Despite the long terms of service prescribed by law (five to eight years), regiments experienced rates of turnover as high as 75 percent per year due to desertion.[11]

As a landlocked country that had recently suffered substantial territorial losses, Bolivia watched with concern as its neighbors brought in European military advisers and instituted obligatory military service. The nation had lost its Littoral department in the War of the Pacific (1879–1883), during which Chile battled Bolivia and Peru over nitrate-rich lands. Bolivia fought only in the first year of this war, unable to continue recruiting and funding its locally organized regiments.[12] The war brought intra-elite disputes into relief, producing the Liberal and Conservative parties in 1883 and 1884. Although the two parties both adhered to more or less conservative variants of European-style liberalism, Liberals concentrated in La Paz advocated re-entering the conflict to preserve Bolivia's territorial claims, whereas Conservatives in Sucre sought to maintain lucrative commercial ties to Chile.[13] The divisions over the Catholic Church, which in other countries marked the differences between the two sides, played only a minor role in Bolivia due to the church's weak position dating back to 1826 when President Antonio José de Sucre took control of tithes, confiscated the church's mortgages and private estates, eliminated *cofradías* (religious brotherhoods), and closed smaller monasteries.[14]

After winning the 1884 election, Conservative governments pursued liberal policies of eliminating corporate privileges and developing the export sector. Their efforts to restructure tribute and implement the 1874 Disentailment Law, which privatized communal lands, met with significant indigenous resistance. However, the power and reach of the central state grew considerably as Conservatives kept taxes on mining low while investing in transportation networks, financial institutions, and isolated projects to colonize border regions.[15] Following a regional trend, they took the first steps to transform the military into a modern bureaucratic institution by replacing *rabonas* (female camp followers) with institutionalized meal service in 1888, founding a military academy in 1891, and establishing the Quartermaster Corps in 1899.[16] The legislature also passed a conscription law in 1892 that substantially revised the 1875 precedent; however, neither the Baptista (1892–1896) nor the Alonso (1896–1899) administration seriously attempted to implement it.[17]

The crash in the silver market that followed international adoption of the gold standard shifted the balance of economic power from Conservative Sucre to Liberal La Paz, which was at the center of the new tin industry.[18] Stymied at the ballot box by electoral interference, Liberals and key Aymara leaders formed an alliance based on a platform of Federalism, tax abatement, and the return of communal lands. When the Liberals of La Paz rose up in December 1898 under then-Colonel José Manuel Pando, the situation seemed to favor President Sergio Fernández Alonso, given his control of the national treasury and army. The Liberals, on the other hand, relied militarily on indigenous allies led by Pablo Zárate Willka, Juan Lero, Lorenzo Ramírez, and Feliciano Condori. Battles occurred in four of Bolivia's nine departments as the war subsumed local conflicts and expressed them in partisan terms, with massacres and abuses occurring on all sides. In early March 1899, one such episode occurred in Mohoza (Inquisivi, La Paz) when Aymaras under Ramírez killed over a hundred Federalist cavalrymen, thus revealing the limits of Pando's power to command his indigenous allies.[19] In pursuit of victory, Pando continued to fight alongside Aymara forces despite these incidents.

After the war's end in early April, however, he quickly moved to dissolve indigenous forces and arrest their leaders, whom he accused of massacring Liberal troops at Mohoza and landowners in Peñas (Paria, Oruro). The subsequent Peñas and Mohoza trials ran from 1899 to 1902, and appeals extended into 1905.[20] Resulting in the execution of dozens, these trials publicly reconfigured Aymara participation in the 1899 conflict as a violent "race war" rather than a political alliance. Historians E. Gabrielle Kuenzli and Forrest Hylton have analyzed the trial transcripts and press coverage to argue that this trope facilitated Liberals' drive to exclude their Aymara allies from the fruits of victory while criminalizing this population and deepening racial divides.[21]

Liberals soon welcomed the defeated Conservatives back into the fold as reinforcements for the social order. The former rivals shared an orientation toward Europe, a broad adherence to certain liberal tenets, and a desire to incorporate Bolivia fully into international markets.[22] Liberals fulfilled the promise to move the seat of government to La Paz but shed Federalism and their commitment to regaining Bolivia's coast. They also took up Conservatives' project of military professionalization by establishing a school for noncommissioned officers in 1900.[23] More importantly, President Pando nullified provisions dating back to 1838 that prohibited the recruitment of tribute-paying Indians.[24] This gesture of inclusivity seemed to conform to liberal ideals of legal equality but also sought to ensure that they would never again form autonomous irregular forces.

The drive for military reform also gained steam from events in Acre on the northern border with Brazil. Rising rubber prices had caused the area's population to balloon—with Brazilian settlers. When they declared this Amazonian territory an independent republic in April 1899, Bolivian troops could not get there until December due to the distance from La Paz. Soldiers quelled the revolt, but Liberal leaders decided to rent the territory to a foreign-owned rubber company. Citing concerns about imperial encroachment, Brazil responded by sending forces to the region. After several years of skirmishes, Bolivia and Brazil signed the Treaty of Petrópolis in November 1903, which ceded 191,000 square kilometers to Brazil in exchange for two million pounds and a promise to build a railroad.[25]

Pando's successor, fellow military man General Ismael Montes, sought to depoliticize the army, insisting it would finally adhere to the clause included in every constitution since 1831 that prohibited officers from even discussing political matters (deliberar).[26] To that end, no one drawing wages from the military, from the lowest conscript to the highest general (even including retirees drawing pensions), could vote or run for office. This would supposedly make them "neutral and rigorously impartial in politics."[27] Montes contracted with a small French mission under Colonel Jacques Sever in 1905 to reorganize the army and take charge of officer training.[28] In this, Montes followed the lead of Chile, Peru, and Argentina, which had engaged European missions in 1886, 1896, and 1899.[29] His stated goal was a professional army characterized by civilian control, professional training, and merit-based promotion. The new army would be a unitary institutional actor and would banish the specter of factionalism, military coups, and interference in partisan elections. Active-duty officers and troops were therefore denied suffrage and the right to run for public office.[30] No longer would troops serve a particular party or caudillo, as Quilco's battalion had done in the 1850s.

With Sever's help, Montes also set out to operationalize the existing framework for military conscription.[31] These efforts culminated in the 1907 obligatory-military-service law, which, with minor changes, regulated conscription in Bolivia for the next half century.[32] The 1907 law mandated that eighteen-year-old men register for the draft in August or September by personally presenting at the local registration table.[33] The authorities who registered these men were to note each one's name, parents' names, place of birth, profession, address, level of education, skin color, and distinguishing features. These data would be sent to the prefect and the minister of war to compile an annual military census and be crossed-checked with lists of men born that year furnished by parish priests. Each registrant would receive a certificate proving his compliance with the law.[34]

On paper, the law set out to mark the distance from the *caudillo* era, when men could buy a replacement, by defining service as a personal and inescapable obligation with exceptions granted only to the physically and mentally unfit. Clauses entitling men to a three-month term of service if they supported children or elderly parents aimed to win popular sympathy by ensuring that no family shouldered an overly harsh burden. After registering, men seeking exemptions, postponements, or reductions had several months to petition the departmental prefect. Unless they could prove absolute poverty, men granted exemptions or reductions had to pay a tax ranging from twenty to two hundred bolivianos, depending on individual circumstances.[35] By December 15 of the next year, all men not granted official exemptions were to travel to their provincial capitals and then on to the department capital. If their number exceeded the department's quota, the prefect would hold a lottery.[36] Those whose names were drawn (*sorteados*) would serve for two years; the rest would receive three months of training before being discharged. Men who missed the lottery became *omisos* (draft evaders) along with those who had failed to register. Reformers needed to make soldiering respectable, even a source of pride, in order to convince citizens to send their sons. To refigure service as a privilege rather than a punishment, the new law banned the enrollment of vagrants and other delinquents. Such men were instead supposed to work on the harsh frontier for the duration of their military service.[37]

The law contained provisions designed to ensure compliance and prevent corruption: the military registry had to be well advertised and open during fixed hours, particular authorities had to be present for registrations, lotteries were to be public events, and unbiased physicians had to certify exemptions.[38] Men would receive documents to certify their observance of the law. These papers would be necessary to gain employment, to conduct official transactions, and to protect oneself from impressment. Regulations mandated that each new soldier be photographed and issued a military service booklet to record his personal information, training, promotions, discharge, and subsequent reserve service. The law decreed that these booklets be verified before men could vote, receive a university or professional title, enter a monastery or be ordained, attain a mastery, or hold a government position.[39] These provisions directly threatened the position and citizenship rights of men from Bolivia's upper classes and thus pressured them to comply with the law.

FIGURE 1.1. Altitude map of Bolivia with current borders. Map by George Milne.

Liberals also worked to assure these populations that military service was an honorable pursuit. Following a regimented exercise program and receiving instruction in military theory and civic obligation would prepare conscripts physically and mentally to fulfill their duties. After learning to march in formation, use weapons, and guard installations, they would swear allegiance to the flag and participate in war maneuvers to prepare them to defend Bolivia.[40] Authorities promised that self-disciplined conscripts would replace violently impressed troops whipped into submission, as Quilco had been. The power to transform the population through military service depended on a rigid but fair hierarchy that would teach conscripts to obey authority figures without question. Liberals thus vowed to eliminate corporal punishment and make military service "pleasant or at least bearable with patriotic compliance." Discipline, the minister of war argued, must be achieved through the "moderate and gentle treatment that should be given to soldiers, who, fulfilling a legal obligation, selflessly serve the *patria*."[41] General Sever expressed the role of honor in this injunction by expressly prohibiting humiliating acts.[42]

In its ideal form, obligatory military service would mold Bolivia's population according to a model of modernity adopted from Europe, strengthening the state and serving multiple objectives of the Liberal government. Having recently ceded over six hundred thousand square kilometers, legislators first emphasized that conscription would protect "our threatened borders" by ensuring that the entire male population had military training.[43] Secondly, conscript labor would also be used to build Bolivia's infrastructure, construct border posts, and staff military colonization projects in peripheral regions.[44] Obligatory military service would also teach the indigenous population, even the potentially dangerous Aymaras, not only to be obedient, as with Quilco, but also to identify with and serve the nation. In this imagined egalitarian system, the sons of Indians, artisans, and privileged families would share in the duty of defense since all were theoretically equal before the law. Finally, conscription functioned as a legibility project for social control, a means by which the state collected information about its population and initiated residents into a documentary regime.[45]

BOLIVIA'S POPULATION AND GEOGRAPHY

A wide gap existed, however, between the law's aspirational provisions and its actual implementation. Immediately after coming to power, Liberals conducted a national census that laid bare the challenges they faced in implementing the 1907 law. While the lowlands remained largely unexplored, much of the population lived at high altitude in a terrain marked by mountainous peaks, thirty of which soared to over nineteen thousand feet.[46] Nascent transportation and communication networks reached only a fraction of this large but thinly populated territory. And Bolivia's population was listed as 50 percent indigenous, 75 percent rural, and more than 80 percent illiterate. However, as shown below, even these results overestimated Bolivia's territory, population, urbanity, and literacy rates while underestimating its indigenous population. The challenges to implementing compulsory military service would be even greater than these statistics suggested.

According to the census, Bolivia had three regions: the western altiplano, the valleys of the central region, and the eastern lowlands.[47] Defined by mountainous terrain, high altitudes, and a cold climate, the altiplano (see figure 1.1) extended over three of Bolivia's eight departments (La Paz, Oruro, and Potosí). This zone supported llamas, sheep, potatoes, barley, and quinoa and contained mineral deposits that represented the nation's primary exports.[48] Covering parts of Cochabamba, Chuquisaca, Tarija, La Paz, and Potosí, the temperate valleys and humid *yungas* of the fertile central region provided wheat, corn, coffee, cacao, coca, fruits, vegetables, and quinine. The lowlands spanned the Colonias (now Pando), Beni, Santa Cruz, Tarija, and northern La Paz, making up almost two-thirds of Bolivia's territory. This region included diverse habitats such as savanna, pampas, Amazonian rainforest, and the dry scrub forest of the Chaco. The areas bordering the central region had settlements devoted to cattle ranching, sugarcane, and rice, but the rest of the region drew interest only with the discovery of exportable commodities, such as rubber and oil.[49]

The census account of Bolivia's transportation and communications networks reflected these geographic challenges. Telegraph lines connected only a third of the country's one hundred postal offices.[50] Rains made many of the 2,297 kilometers of roads impassable for several months a year. And almost half of the 1,129 kilometers of railroad tracks claimed in the census lay on soil lost to Chile during the War of the Pacific. Oriented toward export routes, the two major lines connected the city of La Paz to the port of Guaqui on Lake Titicaca and the mines of Oruro and Potosí to Antofagasta, by then a Chilean port.[51] Administratively, Bolivia consisted of eight departments and a northwestern territory. In this highly centralized system, the president appointed the prefects who governed each department and nominated the subprefects charged with running the departmental subdivisions—called provinces. The subprefects, in turn, nominated the *corregidores* who administered each of the provinces' cantons and vice-cantons.[52]

Claiming an area of 1.82 million square kilometers and population of 1.816 million, census officials calculated Bolivia's population density at 0.99.[53] Noting that this was the lowest in South America, they bemoaned the "complete depopulation" of fertile lands.[54] Similar concerns emerged from statistics on rural and urban dwellers. Despite the definition of an urban area as any settlement with over two hundred residents, census takers still designated a mere 25 percent of Bolivia's population as urban.[55] This would make conscription procedures difficult. Administrators would have to travel long distances into the countryside to raise awareness of this obligation, and young men would have to do the same to register and report for service.

Statistics on education also signaled a potential barrier. Those lacking formal education would be less likely to learn about the conscription law and would need assistance to read newspaper or handbill notifications about the duty to serve. Only 16.6 percent of those over the age of seven who participated in the census had even minimal literacy skills. Discounting women raised this figure only to 19.5 percent.[56] Even these statistics overestimated the population's level of schooling by including only the 1.6 million people formally counted in the census. Whereas most educated people probably participated, those missed by census takers were the most likely to be illiterate.

The census identified eighty different sociolinguistic groups, which together formed the indigenous "race." Census takers divided the population into the following races: indigenous (50.8 percent), mestizo (26.82 percent), white (12.75 percent), and black (0.22 percent).[57] Looking forward to the 1950 census, which categorized 63 percent of the population as indigenous, Erwin Grieshaber has convincingly argued that the 1900 census counted only tribute payers as indigenous rather than relying on other sociocultural markers such as language and dress.[58] Based on this method of calculation, the officials who conducted the census expressed the belief that the indigenous population had been "mortally wounded" by drought, famine, pestilence, and alcoholism and thus predicted the "slow and gradual disappearance of the indigenous race."[59]

These words represented ruling elites' fondest hope for Bolivia. Their path to modernization depended on the eventual assimilation and disappearance of indigenous peoples, whom they viewed as alcoholic and uneducated. These beliefs lay behind almost every section of the census. Not surprisingly, this document effaces the existence of *ayllus* (Andean communal groupings) and other indigenous communal structures. Lamentations about sparse population, illiteracy, and the predominance of rural living were in essence complaints about indigenous "backwardness." For example, when classifying people as urban or rural, officials expressed concern about the "quality" of many of those being counted as urbanites: "Some have opined that any town where the indigenous element is predominant should not be considered an urban population."[60] No progress would be possible, they believed, in places where indigenous ways of life predominated.

These ethnocidal ideologies of assimilation and whitening motivated legislation that officially eradicated communal structures, imposed obligatory military service, and would later create educational reforms.[61] By removing indigenous men, even if temporarily, from their rural environs, these institutions would introduce them to "civilized" ways of living. Officers and legislators spoke reverentially of the barracks as an educational space where conscripts would learn literacy skills, discover the importance of hygiene, and be exposed to the benefits of modern living. Military service would thus address many of the obstacles noted in the 1900 census.

IMPLEMENTING OBLIGATORY MILITARY SERVICE

Bolivia's geography and demography would pose a significant challenge to implementing the 1907 conscription law. Would the population, the majority of which was indigenous, illiterate, and rural, know about and understand their obligation? Would they be able to document their precise age, register for the draft, and understand their entitlement to exemptions or reductions of service? Could they feasibly travel the distances involved during the time allocated? And would the government be able to feed, house, clothe, and pay every nineteen-year-old man, even if only for three months? Most importantly, how would the government enforce this law among those who failed to register or present for service?

Despite all the barriers, the 1907 law produced surprisingly successful, if somewhat limited, results in its initial years. In 1910, Minister of War Andrés Muñoz wrote hopefully that obligatory service had "already become a habit, representing our youth's best school for education and for national unification."[62] A successor in the position gleefully proclaimed five years later that so many conscripts had presented that only 37 percent could serve the full term.[63] Despite these optimistic pronouncements, the small size of the standing army meant the majority of men still avoided conscription through ignorance of the law, willful disregard, exemption, or the protection of patrons. Military authorities thus found their ambitions limited by the inability to punish most evaders and control the inefficient and recalcitrant provincial authorities responsible for local implementation.

President Montes's successor, Eliodoro Villazón (1909–1912), remained deeply committed to military professionalization. The officer corps, however, was divided between Francophiles and advocates of German training.[64] When its contract came up for renewal in May 1909, the French mission fell victim to this dispute as Villazón decided that German methods would be "more appropriate for our army."[65] Major Hans Kundt arrived in La Paz in early 1911 with three captains, one lieutenant, and thirteen sergeants from the Prussian army, thus initiating a volatile relationship between Kundt and the Bolivian political elite that would stretch into the 1930s.[66] Kundt soon took Sever's seat as chief of staff and began churning out regulations for training, salutes, physical education, and barracks regimen.[67] The army not only adopted the Prussian goosestep and uniform style but also imported five million marks worth of equipment and arms from German vendors.[68]

This period also saw the consolidation of conscription procedures: men registered for service, petitions for exemption flowed into the prefectures, and lotteries determined how long each conscript would serve. The Quartermaster Corps printed military service booklets, sewed uniforms, and cobbled shoes for each contingent. Army photographers had even developed portraits of 2,731 soldiers by August 1908.[69] Upon presenting for service, conscripts received medical exams and smallpox vaccinations.[70] Those designated for three months of training were discharged in February or March, while the rest remained until October of the next year; all received military service booklets attesting to their compliance with the law.[71] Thus, many of

TABLE 1.1. Conscription Statistics, 1908–1913

Year	Army Size	Men Registered	Conscripts Presented	Lottery: 2 Years	Exempted	Reduced Service	Postponed Service	Tax Collected
1908	3,200	4,124	1,754	680	452	386	-	-
1909	3,000	8,110	945	578	199	155	14	-
1910	2,953	5,450	1,279	934	228	258	73	-
1911	3,430	4,257	1,336	801	278	294	36	6,225 bs.
1912	3,750	6,281	1,239	-	329	129	65	-
1913	4,150	-	2,319	1,439	332	144	124	8,380 bs.

Sources: Ministerio de Guerra, *Boletín militar, Memoria de Guerra*, and *Anexos*; the yearly laws that regulated the army's size. Dashes indicate unavailability of statistic in these sources. However, these sources offer several figures that differ, especially for statistics regarding exemptions, reductions, and postponements. When these contradictions occurred, I chose to use the number offered in the Minister of War's August report to Congress.

the mechanisms set forth in 1907 had been put into effect, albeit in a limited fashion.

The *Boletín militar* portrayed conscription as a transparent bureaucratic process by publishing the acceptance or rejection of every petition for discharge, exemption, reduction, and postponement; these notices sometimes even included the amount of tax paid.[72] For example, Clodomiro Aparicio from San Lorenzo (Tarija) received an exemption in 1908 after paying the maximum tax of two hundred bolivianos and submitting documentation that proved his age, his registration for the draft, and that he suffered from chronic bronchitis.[73] Although the vast majority of successful petitions came from professionals with Hispanic surnames, at least one identified the petitioner as indigenous—rural laborer Benigno Vasquez. Hailing from Aquerama (Cochabamba), he produced documents that proved him the only support of impoverished parents and thus entitled to serve only three months in 1908. After showing his "utter poverty," Vasquez was exempted from paying any tax.[74] Although obligatory military service did not reach into every household, Aparicio, Vasquez, and the thousands of other men whose names appear in the *Boletín militar* show that it had been established as a functioning bureaucratic system.

As shown in table 1.1, thousands of men registered for service, hundreds paid the prescribed tax after receiving exemptions or reductions, and over a thousand presented each January 1 to participate in the lottery. These statistics demonstrate not only the existence of a functioning bureaucratic system but also that the army's needs for manpower were more than met by those who chose to present. In fact, the conscription system would have been totally overwhelmed if every nineteen-year-old man had indeed appeared.

The funds annually allocated by Congress to feed, house, and pay conscripts would not have covered even their expenses for travel to departmental capitals, and the one army surgeon sent to each center to verify their physical fitness would have thrown up his hands in despair.

Historian Luis Oporto notes in his study of conscription in the mining district of Llallagua that men belonging to the working class of artisans and miners registered religiously but usually failed to present or fled if chosen in the lottery.[75] The national-level statistics presented in table 1.1 support this conclusion: almost half of the men who registered for service neither presented nor arranged for an exemption, resulting in over eight thousand evaders during the first six years of the new law. This number did not include the thousands of men whose names never graced a military register. Extrapolating from the age statistics reported in 1900, each cohort of nineteen-year-olds consisted of approximately thirteen thousand men, which meant that only 30 to 60 percent registered each year.[76]

Along with these statistics, exceptions granted by political authorities reinforce the aspirational nature of the law. Issued in December 1908, the first of these exceptions suspended the capture of indigenous draft evaders and gave them a ten-month extension to register. The decree attributed this measure to the many petitions "received from *indígenas* in diverse regions [that] express[ed] a failure to comply with the current regulations due to ignorance of the laws."[77] These petitions successfully mobilized assumptions about indigenous backwardness to obtain this concession. At least in one case, the prefect of La Paz diligently followed this decree: after eleven captured draft evaders from Caupolicán arrived in La Paz in January 1909, the prefect sent Mariano Mento, Manuel Chipana, and Andrés Anco home, citing this extension.[78] These exceptions for indigenous men allowed the minister of war to portray the central government as a forgiving father, whose duty was to help "the indigenous class, [who,] for their lack of education and social conditions, has not been able to precisely comply" with the law.[79] Similar windows of exception were granted to all evaders in 1910 and 1918 but only to indigenous evaders in 1913 and 1916.[80] These decrees attempted to coax all Bolivians—but especially indigenous Bolivians—into following the law, rather than punishing them for noncompliance. Such exceptions to bureaucratic procedure acknowledged that obligatory military service depended upon individual acceptance of this duty.

Implementation of the law also relied on the subprefects that administered provincial capitals and the *corregidores* of cantons. Successive ministers of war repeatedly enjoined these authorities to do everything in their power to ensure that all men registered for the draft; however, the frequency of these pleas indicates the limits of these officials' willingness or ability to accomplish the task. Memoranda quoted the pertinent legal passages and threatened severe sanctions for noncompliance. In particular, the minister of war counseled local authorities regarding the obligation to register indigenous men, suggesting that they enlist parish priests to "make the indigenous race understand their obligation to register and serve in the Army." He also recommended that they threaten legal action against property owners and indigenous communal authorities who "hamper[ed] in any way the enrollment of their *colonos*" and community members.[81] Yet the reliance on local authorities to implement conscription meant that if an individual *corregidor* decided it was not worth his effort to negotiate with local power brokers over conscripting their workers, he could ignore or deflect military requests. It also allowed individuals to maneuver in the gap between theory and practice, relying on luck, negligence, and personal relationships to save them from military service.

The subprefect of Ingavi, for example, replied in 1913 that the registration of Indians in his region was impossible because the "Indian, suspicious and distrustful by nature, avoids indicating the number of people in his family" and disappears as soon as he realizes that a census has begun.[82] Another such authority, the *corregidor* of Cohoni, wrote of the hundreds of men living on haciendas who, "supported by their *patrones*," willfully disobeyed the law.[83] Evidence suggests that some local administrators even altered the documentary record to help men avoid service. In one case, the *corregidor* of Italaque denounced his substitute for registering twenty-four-year-old Jacinto Riveras as if he were only eighteen. This act of patronage provided Riveras with a registration certificate he could apparently use to obtain a government post "without first fulfilling his sacred duty to the *Patria*."[84]

Instituting the use of military service documents was a similarly dependent and uneven process. In theory, these documents would provide their holders with opportunities, and their absence would make men unemployable and vulnerable to impressment. To put this theory into practice, the minister of war and departmental prefects repeatedly ordered local authorities and police to demand and inspect military service documents.[85] Mining companies even received orders in 1913 to demand military conscription booklets before hiring men.[86] These constantly reiterated instructions indicate both the determination of government officials to enforce the law and their inability to do so. As Luis Oporto notes, many miners enjoyed de facto dispensation from military service, as mining companies used their political sway to protect their labor forces.[87] Yet evidence does suggest that these documents were beginning to be recognized as necessary, especially for men who traveled away from their communities. Juan Postigo, a rubber-industry worker from Apolo passing through La Paz in 1909, begged the prefect to certify his registration for the draft, stating, "I fear the patrols in the street."[88]

Since the number of conscripts who presented always exceeded the limits set by Congress, the army did not have to expend scarce resources scouring the countryside for evaders. Yet this did not mean they never entered the ranks. Records from the La Paz prefecture show that departmental authorities sent at least 142 evaders to military units between 1908 and 1919.[89] However, their capture and manner of transmission again depended almost exclusively on the decisions of local authorities. In one particularly striking case, the *corregidor* of Laja (Omasuyos) ordered ten men, who self-identified as rural indigenous laborers, to escort twenty evaders to La Paz. According to their erstwhile guards, the captives chose a "solitary place" near the Huañaahuira River, where they "collectively rose up and, armed with rocks, began to run, so that we had to fight them." After recapturing thirteen, they finished the journey to La Paz. The *corregidor*'s decision to commission a small group of unarmed (and almost certainly unpaid) men to escort the evaders had allowed seven to fight or bribe their way to freedom.[90]

Even though the 1907 law did not produce a conscription juggernaut, many indigenous *colonos* and *comunarios* (those living in communities) followed state procedure in registering and presenting for service. Some may have done so voluntarily or even "with great enthusiasm," to quote the quartermaster of Viacha in describing five indigenous conscripts from San Andrés de Machaca (Pacajes, La Paz).[91] The province of Carangas (Oruro) offers an especially instructive example. In 1910, Minister of War Muñoz lamented the "laziness of the authorities in the province of Carangas, where it is known that, up to now, there has not been even one enrollment in the military register this year."[92] Yet, only three years later, the prefect of Oruro noted with surprise that more than a hundred young men from Carangas had reported for service.[93] His successor in 1914 described the 225 conscripts from Carangas as "robust soldiers and enthusiastic to carry out their patriotic duties."[94] In this traditionally Aymara region where indigenous communities controlled virtually all of the land, indigenous men may have embraced military service as part of a pact of reciprocity with the state whereby they expected to receive recognition of their land claims in exchange for labor.[95]

The implementation of the conscription law demonstrates the Bolivian state's dependence on indirect rule through local authorities.[96] Despite the fact that they directly owed their positions to the central state, most apparently had few incentives to comply and instead made decisions based on their own loyalties and agendas. This resulted in the uneven spread of military service across the national territory. Financial, geographical, and practical constraints meant that the central state could neither ensure universal awareness of the law nor enforce it by capturing those who failed to comply. Obligatory military service in early twentieth-century Bolivia could not be imposed through effective bureaucracy nor through domination; it instead depended on individual and communal acceptance. Rather than uniformly punishing noncompliance, state agents added flexibility to the law by decreeing periods of exception during which men of all ages could present without penalty. This tactic served multiple ends: it maintained the pretense of state control, communicated the state's benevolence, and attempted to draw more people into the conscription system. In the absence of imminent international conflict, the small size of the standing army meant that state agents could hope that conscription would take root without resorting to mass, arbitrary impressment to fill the ranks. Successive ministers of war could thus express satisfaction with the law's results even as they registered concern about recalcitrant local authorities and the ever-multiplying number of evaders.

"ODIOUS PRIVILEGES": CONSCRIPTION'S UNEQUAL APPLICATION

Liberal rhetoric emphasized that obligatory military service would be a sacred duty shared by the population as whole, thus forging a unified nation in the barracks. The Liberal press romantically presented the barracks as a site "where the tycoon's son gives up his courtly airs upon coming into contact with the artisan and the Indian and realizes the democracy and the love owed to all social classes, having mixed with them and suffered the same fatigues and hardships of service."[97] However, legal loopholes, fraud, favoritism, and the punishment of evaders with extra years of service meant that little cross-class mixing occurred in the barracks and that poor and indigenous Bolivians shouldered much of the burden. Legislators, caught in a contradiction between the ideal of service to country and the realities of the nation's "best sons" spending two years in uncomfortable barracks, refused to close loopholes and even attempted to lessen the obligation. Most formally educated men who did enter the barracks became NCOs or served in the more prestigious cavalry or artillery regiments. The new hierarchies built around military service thus expressed racial- and class-based hierarchies in the meritorious terms of ability, morality, and patriotism.

Despite Liberals' professions of equality, debate over the 1907 laws reveals that one of its foremost goals was the transformation of Bolivia's indigenous population through positivist social hygiene.[98] The army would convert the country's Indians into disciplined soldiers who spoke Spanish, willingly obeyed authorities, and were unfailingly loyal to a national-level *patria*. Deputy Aurelio Gamarra argued that conscription would "awaken" the Indian "from his ignorance.... It is the solution for an entire social problem for us, of civilizing the *indígena*."[99] Minister of War José S. Quinteros made use of what would become a persistent metaphor when he invoked the "sacred interests of the Republic" to justify the state's right to demand "sincere collaboration" with conscription.[100] Liberal rhetoric thus elided the fact that the majority of the men eligible for service would be noncitizen conscripts, at least in the formal sense of meeting property and literacy requirements for suffrage. Yet this rhetoric does suggest what Liberals imagined indigenous conscripts would receive in return for their service: an entrée into the "modern" world and salvation from their communities' backward practices. They might not become citizens with voting rights, but they would fall within the discursive use of the word "citizen," developing a sense of belonging and duty to Bolivia.

Regulations implementing the conscription law reflected the liberal ideal of unmarked citizens and thus expressly prohibited the officials from recording racial identity. Yet indigeneity lay at the center of the 1907 law, which would modernize Indians and make them Bolivians. Indigenous status thus morphed from race to class as the minister of war demanded that registrars note conscripts' social class, suggesting "*indígena*, artisan, *cholo*, [and] gentleman" as possibilities. Obviously uncomfortable with the proximity of these categories to racial ones, he offered assurances that these data would serve only to prevent the confusion of men with similar names. Registration guidelines instructed officials to record each conscript's skin color but explicitly stated that they must judge this factor based on only the hue of his face, "without taking race into account under any circumstance."[101] Tellingly, this order asked them to ignore racial identity while still assuming that races were easily identifiable categories. Such admonishments, however, were routinely violated by officers and government officials, who, while they may have subscribed to the liberal ideals that motivated this policy, lived their daily lives in a society defined by racial hierarchy. Thus, of the ninety-six deserters reported to the prefect of La Paz between 1911 and 1916, almost 70 percent were identified as belonging to a particular race.[102]

Prohibited from recording racial identity but seemingly unable to omit indigeneity, statistics on conscripts used *indígena* as an occupational rather than a racial category, including it as equivalent to artisan, student, and lawyer.[103] These statistics show that illiterate artisans and *indígenas* constituted an overwhelming majority of conscripts. For example, 72 percent (see table 1.2) of the cohort that presented in 1910 fell into these two categories. Including the next largest professional category (*comericante*, which encompassed both storekeepers and petty traders, some of whom almost certainly would have identified as indigenous) brought this statistic up to 87 percent. Successive ministers of war explicitly described the majority of conscripts as belonging to the lower classes of society and indigenous groups.[104]

The 1900 census classified the majority of the population as rural and illiterate. However, this majority consisted precisely of those men whom authorities struggled to register for service. They resided farthest from departmental capitals and most likely did not need military service documents, given that they would not be running for public office or seeking degrees.

TABLE 1.2. Conscripts by Department and Profession, 1910

Profession	Chuq.	La Paz	Cocha.	Oruro	Potosí	Tarija	Santa Cruz	Beni	Total
Lawyers	2	2	3	2	0	0	3	0	12
Accountants	1	3	3	2	0	0	1	0	10
Professional Students	6	14	17	4	4	2	8	3	58
Secondary Graduates	3	9	6	2	3	2	3	0	28
Secondary Students	2	11	14	2	1	1	7	0	38
Telegraphists	0	3	1	1	3	0	2	0	10
Clerks	0	0	0	0	1	0	1	1	3
Photographers	0	3	0	0	0	0	1	0	4
Traders/ Storekeepers	14	53	33	19	34	12	22	4	191
Artisans (Illiterate)	62	128	211	65	138	18	51	9	682
Indígenas (Illiterate)	21	42	31	19	46	25	46	7	237
Total	111	268	319	116	230	60	145	24	1,273

Source: Ministerio de Guerra, *Memoria de Guerra* (1910), clvii.

While most *ayllus* had leaders who kept themselves abreast of the state's laws, this information was often filtered through many layers before reaching the average eighteen-year-old. And these leaders were just beginning to forge ties with *colonos* during the early twentieth century.[105] Many rural men thus remained (or at least could claim to be) ignorant of both the duty to serve and the procedures for obtaining a legal exemption. So what could account for their robust representation in the army? In short: other groups' use of exemptions to avoid service and the extra years in the ranks imposed on draft evaders.

Obtaining exemptions and reductions in service required more than a passing familiarity with the law. For example, when Isidro Quispe from Pomani (Sicasica, La Paz) petitioned for reduced service in 1908, he found that a clerical error had misidentified his age, which meant he was already considered a draft evader. He attached testimony proving he had not yet turned eighteen and was the only support of a widowed mother; his petition stated, "Through our condition as *indígenas*, both my mother and I are utterly poor." However, the minister of war denied his petition because it had not been filed at the proper time.[106] Thus, although Quispe should have been entitled to reduced service, he would legally have had to serve four years as a draft evader.

As shown in table 1.1, over three thousand men received exemptions, reductions, or postponements of service between 1908 and 1913. Quispe did not typify these petitioners. Statements by the minister of war indicate the "tendency of the upper social classes to evade service" by faking illness, studying abroad, or obtaining temporary employment with exempt industries.[107] Year after year, the minister of war decried the "odious privileges" provided by unscrupulous physicians who certified fraudulent medical conditions.[108] He repeatedly condemned laws passed in 1910 and 1911, which, ostensibly to facilitate progress, granted telegraph, telephone, steamship, and railroad employees exemptions from military service upon payment of the required tax. He begged Congress to limit medical exemptions, force men studying abroad to serve when they returned, and change the provision that allowed many students to serve only three months.[109]

Although these pleas resulted in some practical and legal changes, they produced only minor victories in an unwinnable war. For example, a March 1911 resolution prohibited railroad companies from hiring eighteen-year-olds, but the companies simply ignored the law, at least according to the war ministry's annual reports in 1913, 1914, and 1918.[110] Although medical exemptions had to be approved in person by military physicians after 1914, ministers of war in the 1920s still complained of educated men faking illness.[111] In 1921, Minister of War Pastor Baldivieso bewailed the fact that the upper and middle classes attempted to wheedle exemptions not only for their "sons and close relatives but also *compadres, ahijados,* and even servants."[112]

Many Bolivians privileged enough to call in favors, understand loopholes, or bribe officials thus obtained military documents without entering the barracks. Although draft evaders in spirit, they did not usually face legal consequences. Their possession of valid documents ensured that the new social category of *omiso* would not apply to them. This term comes from the Latin root *omissus*, meaning remiss or negligent, and translates as draft evader or shirker.[113] Describing those who failed to register or present for service, *omiso* status left men vulnerable to immediate impressment.

Although budgetary and administrative factors limited the ability to capture the average *omiso*, this vulnerability made the conferral of *omiso* status a particularly attractive tactic for pursuing private vendettas.[114] Individuals involved in land disputes and authority figures hoping to rid themselves of troublemakers could report their enemies as *omisos* and perhaps have them banished to the army. Evidence from the 1910s and 1920s indicates that this occurred in at least nineteen cases in just the department of La Paz.[115] For example, Asthenio Miranda claimed that Major Astigueta was using the pursuit of *omisos* as a pretext to capture "*indígenas* who would not submit to his service because the property was in litigation."[116] Several petitions show that nonliterate actors also made use of this strategy. In a particularly striking case, four indigenous men from Ichoca (Inquisivi) successfully convinced the minister of war to order their *corregidor*'s capture as an *omiso*.[117] This, however, may not have been quite the coup it initially seems. *Corregidor* was effectively an unsalaried position often held by local landowners or members of the indigenous elite; not all were fully literate.[118] One of the whistle-blowers in this case may well have been a candidate to take over the post. Most *omisos* certainly did not live in constant fear of capture, but the existence of the category could serve as a powerful tool for people from many walks of life.

Within the barracks, *omiso* was a stigmatized social category used to distinguish honorable conscripts from men who had failed in their patriotic duty. Documents explicitly noted which soldiers had entered as *omisos*, indicating the importance of this status. Some lawmakers even expressed the belief that the state did not owe *omiso* soldiers dignified treatment. For example, after passionately describing the horrific conditions suffered by soldiers marching to the eastern border, Deputy Mariano Saucedo from Santa Cruz argued that these circumstances were "perhaps justified for the *omisos*" but were appalling for "those who faithfully comply with the law of military conscription."[119]

Since the vast majority of *omisos* were rural indigenous men unaware of the law's provisions, this status provided an excuse for their differential treatment. In 1912, for example, the subprefect of Ingavi captured Simeon, Francisco, and Juan Limachi of Tiahuanacu along with Mariano Quispe and Domingo Tonkoni of Tiripucho for failing to serve. Four days later Major Alfredo Richter reported the desertion of "these Indians" and complained about their very presence in the Machine Gunners Battalion, calling them "completely useless for this combat arm." His description of their escape indicated their exclusion and markedly different status. Ostensibly due to lack of space, they had been sleeping in a storeroom next to the stables and were thus able to bore a hole in the wall.[120]

Richter's comment about the Indians' unsuitability for machine gunnery points to the hierarchies used by military authorities to assign soldiers to particular units. Geographical considerations and prejudices that equated formal education with ability ensured that different social classes would seldom mix in the barracks. In order to minimize transportation costs, conscripts typically served based on where they reported for service.[121] Residents of La Paz therefore usually remained near their families, whereas conscripts from the departments of Santa Cruz and Tarija staffed garrisons on the harsh frontiers.[122] More significantly, administrators primarily assigned illiterate soldiers to infantry regiments, reserving space in cavalry and artillery units for conscripts deemed more capable.[123] The literacy rates of two units garrisoned in the La Paz department in 1917 offer an instructive example: over 86 percent of the men in the Abaroa Cavalry Regiment were literate as compared to fewer than half the conscripts in the Campero Infantry Regiment.[124]

Even within units, military hierarchy explicitly benefited formally educated soldiers based on the idea that they were a civilizing force that would regulate and elevate their countrymen. These conscripts thus served as the NCOs responsible for much of their peers' daily drilling and discipline. They played an indispensable role in military training, serving as the "framework through which conscripts are broken in."[125] The 1907 guidelines for promotion to NCO valued formal education and moral conduct above physical ability, guaranteeing that men from wealthier families would rapidly regain the social status that had supposedly been erased by "the democratic equality in military service that does not recognize the odious distinction of social class." Affirming that the only hierarchy in the military was one of "competency and morality," these promotion guidelines reframed social class as an earned rather than inherited status.[126]

Modifications to the 1907 law affirmed the use of education to establish hierarchies among conscripts. Legislative projects in 1916 and 1917 debated the article that provided reductions in service for men who would earn a university degree or professional title during the term of service. Despite the minister of war's plea to eliminate this privilege, the legislature proposed extending it to all literate men. Although this project failed, a 1917 law postponed and limited all students' service. Proponents argued that due to their "extensive scientific and moral preparation," such men acquired military training at a faster rate and had thus "worked twice as much" in a shorter period.[127] This argument worked to recode preferential treatment based on social class as merit based.

A fundamental ambivalence about the project of universal military service lay at the heart of these promotion guidelines and efforts to limit the service of formally educated men. Legislators discursively constructed the barracks as the cradle of the nation, yet they were aware of the sacrifice of time, comfort, and physical well-being that service entailed. While acknowledging that all Bolivians should share in this duty, they had trouble imagining their own sons serving in far-away barracks alongside unlettered Indians. Demographics and legal forms of evasion ensured the majority of the troops would be drawn from the ranks of artisans and rural laborers. Assignment methods, promotion requirements, and omiso status then worked in combination to reinforce social divisions while delinking them from factors such as race. Differences in economic and cultural capital were thus reconfigured as differences of honor and morality, making hierarchies in the barracks appear to occur based on factors such as patriotism rather than education, skin color, and financial means.[128] A far cry from the egalitarian ideal promulgated in

1907, the structures that formed around conscription served to legitimize and reproduce hierarchical justifications for domination.

CELESTINO COICO AND THE BURDEN OF MILITARY SERVICE

These discussions of the law and battles over implementation reveal very little about how people, especially from rural areas, perceived this obligation. Lacking the funds and political will to impose the 1907 law through violence and domination, Liberals hoped that awareness of the law would spread as former conscripts returned home. They would act as disciples, converting friends and family to the idea of military service as a sacred duty to the national-level *patria*. Later cohorts would thus consent to conscription. In practice, understandings of this duty differed based on communal norms. Many indigenous men may truly have been "anxious to serve," as one US observer reported in 1928.[129] Others, whose communities lay far from trade routes, likely remained unaware of this duty.

The in-depth analysis of one 1924 case indicates not only a complicated understanding of the law and the obligation it imposed but also the existence of a budding industry to process exemption petitions and even provide fraudulent military service booklets. Celestino Coico's 1924 petition for exemption from military service identified him as an *indígena* from the ex-community of Guairiu (Yungas, La Paz).[130] Dated January 7, the petition was submitted long past the statutory limit of September for exemptions. Coico, in fact, had already traveled to La Paz for the lottery. His petition mobilized a combination of legal, moral, and logical arguments to plead for exemption:

> In conformity with the requirements of the Military Conscription Law, I now appear to declare that I am unfit for the following reasons. Article 15 of the Military Service Law exempts the physically unfit and I am among those, as much because I suffer from a chronic illness, which is obvious at first sight, that the indigenous people [*naturales*] [call] *Sextite*, which is a rash on the genitals [*orgános húmedos*] that does not allow me to work, much less move in violent and unnatural ways. Unluckily abandoned by my parents, who have died, by necessity I had to contract matrimony six months ago so that I could be cared for, and I beg that I also be exempted from service according to what is established by Article 17 Subsection 4 of the aforementioned law. Also, as a contributing *indígena*, I recognize my obligation to pay the territorial contribution, which I would not be able to do in the barracks and which would defraud the State. For that and for regular conduct and prerequisite report of the Señor Commander, I ask for a medical exam by a chief physician, so that it can convince him of the obstacle that makes me unfit

for service and result in exempting me from the service, which we all must
complete, but that, unfortunately, I cannot for being physically impossible.[131]

The first argument of physical unfitness leads to the second argument, which
invokes an article that actually says that married men with children should
serve three months. Perhaps Coico or his scribe misunderstood this clause
since the petition cites only his marriage without mentioning children. Yet
even these legal arguments slip in and out of a professional voice, adopting a
language of pathos to describe his illness and orphanhood. The third argument draws on a very different logic from the liberal idea of military service
as a universal duty that would civilize and incorporate the indigenous population. "Territorial contribution" invokes the corporate logic that had previously exempted certain indigenous populations from recruitment because
of their tributary status.[132] Coico was not alone in professing this exemption
long after its abolition: Bacilio Pillco's 1911 petition for discharge similarly
invoked "my condition as a tribute payer" to explain his unsuitability for service.[133] These petitions indicate the continuation of a tributary logic and its
use in combination with newer legal provisions.

Such petitions must be understood in terms of composite or co-
authorship rather than read as the direct expressions of indigenous people.[134]
Coico's first petition carried the signature of Benjamín Choque, and Pillco's
was signed for him by someone with the surname Crespo. Illiteracy was fundamental to the matrix of social, racial, and cultural factors that determined
an actor's indigenous status at the time. Thus nearly all documents in the
early twentieth century that identified an indigenous petitioner were signed
"for the presenting party" by the notaries, scribes, tinterillos (untitled legal
intermediaries), or lawyers who translated petitions into official writing. Although these men were integral to indigenous people's interactions with the
state, the relationships, processes, and interactions that produced such petitions remain obscure.

Written in the first person, Coico's petition presents itself as his own
words. Yet the signature of Choque at the bottom of the page and the petition's use of stock legal language points to a more complicated authorship.
What was the relationship between Coico and Choque? In what language did
the interaction that produced this petition take place? Did Choque charge for
his services? What changes did Choque make in the process of translating
Coico's request into terms that would be legible to the state? The petition's
confusing construction, grammatical errors, and multiple arguments point
to at least two possibilities: either Choque was not making much of an effort
or he was not highly qualified.

The minister of war quickly denied this petition based on a report from
the recruitment commission stating that Coico had been declared fit for ser-

vice after being "extensively examined by the Commission's surgeons."[135] Coico then pled for reconsideration, this time in a petition signed by a different person, whose signature is illegible. His second petition altered strategy, making a claim based solely on physical unfitness for service. It opened by cleverly reinterpreting state rhetoric about the sacred nature of defense in personal rather than national terms:

> The right to defense is sacred, even more so if it means the defense of personal health. I have seen, Señor Minister, the report of the military commission and regrettably it has declared [me] fit for service, which, if it were true, I would aspire to and the resolution assuredly has been confirmed. I regret that a detailed exam, on which the existence of a citizen or *indígena* depends, has overlooked my bad state, not by pretext, but rather to present to the Surgeon General . . . and sent me to ask your respectable Minister for the examination of the ulcers, which are not only visible but also spread out on the body, that, if it wouldn't offend your respectable authority, I would beg that you see them and measure them, like they examine and give reports, in order to make up the guardians of order. For that reason, I ask you to order that the Surgeon General of the Army perform a personal exam of my anemic state and of the gangrenous ulcers I have all over my skin and, seeing that, deign to reconsider the resolution.[136]

While offering a token acknowledgment of the state's vision of military service, the petition primarily makes a graphically personal appeal. It repeatedly cites the sores on his skin in an attempt to persuade the minister of war of his agent's error in declaring Coico fit for service. After implying that if only the minister could witness this bodily evidence, he would be persuaded of the error, the petition insists that the surgeon general of the army personally examine Coico. This petition also indicates an understanding of a pact whereby "a citizen or *indígena*" presents for service and receives from the state a thorough medical exam to ensure that unfit men do not further ruin their "personal health" through military service. When this petition was immediately denied, Coico enlisted one Dr. Molina to write a final appeal, in which he claimed to be "prostrate in [his] bed with pain."[137]

None of these petitions provided Coico with an exemption. After he sent an unnamed "advocate" to the lottery on January 18 rather than presenting personally, the minister of war ordered his capture as an *omiso*.[138] Three weeks later, the Chulumani (Yungas, La Paz) police fulfilled this order.[139] Coico then testified to spending eight days in La Paz as a conscript and paying Dr. Néstor Molina nine bolivianos to advocate for his freedom. When he could not get "a favorable military service booklet" through Molina, he paid Dr. Donato Millán 37.50 bolivianos. Millán, Coico reported, "succeeded in getting [his] freedom, giving [him his] release booklet."[140]

This case indicates not only the success of the 1907 law but also the immensity of the challenge of achieving mass acceptance. The conscription system functioned in that some authority in the Yungas ensured that Coico registered and presented for service. However, far from viewing conscription as a sacred duty with which he was honored to comply, Coico apparently understood it as a burden from which he should seek liberation. The case also provides evidence of professional intermediaries who composed petitions and perhaps also bribed officials or falsified military service booklets. The growing importance of these documents becomes apparent in a military commander's statement that Coico had returned "armed with said booklet."[141] Far from being outside of state structures, this man from a rural indigenous community was part of the conscription system and had even engaged with the state by submitting petitions that reinterpreted obligatory military service through not only a personal but also a corporate relationship with the state.

In a short time, Liberals' efforts to implement the 1907 conscription law filled the ranks of Bolivia's standing army and convinced many men to obtain military service documents. Less easily achieved was the goal of an egalitarian system that would bring men from all social classes together in order to form a unified nation. In fact, daily practice in recruiting stations and barracks constantly contradicted liberal notions of equality. Even as legislators pontificated about creating a modern nation of equal citizens, they were unwilling to part with the benefits of living in a hierarchical society dependent on racialized differences. Nor was incorporating indigenous Bolivians on their own terms thinkable; they would have to change their way of life in order to join the nation. Military and political authorities thus focused on making Indian men modern by eliminating markers of indigeneity through military service.

Comparing Coico's experience with that of Quilco, the fictional Aymara man with whom this chapter began, offers a way to evaluate Liberals' attempt to form a conscript army based on consent and legal norms rather than violent coercion. Coico, unlike his fictional counterpart, had some understanding of military service as a pact under which both the state and conscripts had duties and rights. Although both men viewed soldiering as a form of captivity, documents rather than the whip kept Coico in La Paz. Only after he was "armed with said booklet" did he return home. However, the forms of fraud that developed in conjunction with the 1907 law meant that conscription was less effective at keeping Coico in the ranks than the brutality that had transformed Quilco into a soldier.

In that he presented for service, Coico did not represent the average Bolivian of the period. The law created approximately forty-four thousand *om-*

isos in just the first five years. In the coming decades, the number of men who presented for service grew, but the number of *omisos* only multiplied.[142] The vast quantity of *omisos* points to the fiction of centralized authority. Corruption appears to have been rampant on all levels, as authorities ignored orders, helped friends, and collected bribes to grant extraofficial exemptions.[143] Evidence from prefecture archives does show, however, that many conscripts like Coico did present for service, sometimes walking for weeks to reach the departmental capital. For example, ten men from the Muñecas province (La Paz) presented in March 1913 after traveling from "the remote rubber regions." Despite the late date, the subprefect implored the minister of war to treat them as conscripts rather than *omisos*, given the long and difficult distances they had voluntarily traversed.[144]

Yet this plea points to a contradiction inherent in the 1907 law. Military service could never be honorable if extra time in the barracks was being used as a punishment. Nor had the system achieved anything close to the ideal of universality: Bolivia had neither the budget nor the need for a large standing army. Most of the men who evaded—whether as *omisos* or through legal exemptions—would not suffer any consequences. The process of bringing men into the barracks thus had both successes and shortcomings. Through an examination of soldiers' experiences in the barracks, the next two chapters will evaluate the other factors by which, according to the law's goals, it must be judged: creating an apolitical force above partisan politics, banishing violent coercion from the barracks, and "civilizing" indigenous conscripts by teaching them not only Spanish and literacy skills but also obedience and allegiance to a national-level *patria*.

CHAPTER 2

LIFE AND LABOR IN THE BARRACKS

Colonel Alfredo Richter's 1921 political tract-cum-memoir opens by recounting the dark days of his time as a young officer when many of "the bad habits of the older systems" still reigned. Comparing soldiers to criminals attempting to break out of jail, Richter draws a bleak portrait of officers combing local bars for missing conscripts, sleeping with their men on the "foul" barracks floor to discourage desertion, and dreading the weekly trip to wash underclothes in the river because of the sheer quantity of soldiers attempting to flee.[1] He vividly portrays a disciplinary system that imposed authority through harsh physical punishment and humiliation, reporting that the band would play a joyful tune as NCOs stripped the offender of even his underwear, subjected him to lashes, and then filled his wounds with "an infusion of salt and urine."[2]

Richter wrote these lines from jail, as a political prisoner suspected of conspiring against the Republican regime that took power in a July 1920 coup.[3] As an officer during the Liberal era, Richter translated and wrote military textbooks and regulations, most prominently the *Soldier's Catechism*, which was used in basic training.[4] A principal intellectual of military reform, Richter bitterly lamented his beloved institution's support for the Republican coup and blamed the ambitions of undisciplined junior officers for the disaster. Richter invoked a shameful history of desertion and abuse precisely in order to argue that the coup had halted the military's steady march to progress and had inaugurated a return to the dishonorable past. His bleak narrative of life in the barracks played on societal fears that associated military service with political interference, forced labor, unhealthy living conditions, and the enactment of violent and deeply personal punishments on troops' bodies.

The transition from an army based on impressment, where brutality served as a motivator, to one based on patriotic service was not easy, especially given the pervasive authoritarianism and racism that characterized Bolivia's diverse and divided society. Efforts to reform military culture were thus only partially successful and resulted in an institution that reflected the nation's hierarchies of race and class. Under the new system, legislators understood military service as a pact between the state and its residents, recognizing that if the living and laboring conditions of soldiers were not at least bearable then men would neither respond to the call nor feel compelled to remain in the barracks. However, the ideal of citizen-soldiers' learning to respect, serve, and defend their *patria* was often stymied by fiscal constraints and individual decision-making. Some conscripts thus received tattered uniforms, ate rotting food, slept on the floor, endured vicious punishments, and performed nonmartial labor to the detriment of preparing for war. And commanders routinely failed to follow established procedures, revealing an imperfectly professionalized officer corps lacking the capacity or willingness to implement the strictly hierarchical and bureaucratic regime for which Colonel Richter yearned.

The prevalence of negative images of barracks life makes the widespread acceptance of obligatory military service in the decades following the 1907 law quite striking. This chapter details life and labor in the barracks in order to understand what service might have meant for the men who participated. Interpersonal ties, patriotic discourse, and a bureaucratic system that discouraged noncompliance combined to inspire men to present for service. Experiences of barracks life helped form conscripts' sense of exclusion from or belonging to a particular company, regiment, and sometimes even nation. The quotidian happenings of drill, punishment, horseplay, and teasing were thus the fundamental building blocks of a conscript nation as soldiers developed their own traditions and cultural practices in the barracks. The state and even officers had surprisingly little control over these experiences and the meanings invested in them.

THE SOCIAL LIVES OF CONSCRIPTS

Each January, a new set of conscripts entered military service in the regiments that dotted Bolivia's cities and frontier. From that moment on, the bugle would wake them in the early morning and call for silence each night. A new conscript ideally received a uniform and basic equipment, including shoes or sandals, gaiters, underwear, shirt, pants, belt, handkerchief, cap, canteen, water jug, soap, towel, comb, and blanket.[5] He would be subject to periodic inspection of these items and faced garnished wages for any loss or damage.[6] During his first days of service, a conscript learned how to dress in uniform, maintain personal hygiene, keep the dormitory clean, salute, and address a superior. Officers warned him, for example, not to brush off his clothes indoors, "put underwear between the cot and mattress," lie down with his boots on, smoke or eat in bed, or spit outside of spittoons.[7]

Some conscripts lived in the model barracks built in Oruro (c. 1908), Viacha (c. 1913), the Miraflores neighborhood of La Paz (c. 1914), Guaqui (1916), and Corocoro (c. 1922), whereas others slept in jails, churches, and rental properties barely worthy of the name "barracks." In 1909, for example, the Loa Battalion bunked in the penitentiary and the Campero Battalion was quartered in a rental space so inadequate that one night it "rained more in the rooms used as dormitories than in the patios."[8] Although administrations intermittently invested in building and repairing barracks, they could never keep up. In 1920, the director of military health pointed out the following flaws in the barracks in Caraguichinca (a sector of the city of La Paz): small and insufficient rooms holding up to 56 beds, lack of ventilation, and only 4 bathrooms for 340 people.[9] And although the Loa, Camacho, and Abaroa Regiments had updated barracks in 1925, the Sucre Regiment resided in an old convent, part of the Pérez Regiment slept in space rented from the municipal government, and the Ballivián Regiment occupied two private residences.[10]

Statistical data on soldiers' ethnicity, profession, level of education, and community of origin have yet to be found for years after 1911, but officers and other observers in the 1920s consistently averred that indigenous men made up the majority.[11] Most barracks were quite multilingual spaces.[12] Some officers and NCOs spoke enough Aymara or Quechua to effectively train monolingual conscripts, allowing the minister of war to credibly brag in 1914 of frequently meeting "Indian conscripts who do not even speak the national language well" but still have a "comprehensive knowledge of handling weapons and their role as elements in a company."[13] Although urban and formally educated soldiers tended to win assignments in the more prestigious cavalry and artillery regiments, men from different ethnicities and social classes still mixed within units. Saturnino Alsuarás, a literate trader from Guaqui (La Paz) serving in the Ballivián Cavalry Regiment, noted, "There are all types of people in the barracks."[14]

For breakfast, lunch, and dinner, conscripts lined up to receive their rations—usually a heavy soup and bread.[15] These communal meals had been prepared by fellow conscripts and paid for by the regiment with funds garnished from each soldier's daily wage.[16] The absence of a centralized provisioning system left each regiment to purchase its own foodstuffs, leading to corruption and abusive extractions.[17] Many noted that food in the barracks was "very bad in quality but abundant in quantity."[18] Soldier Roberto Camacho particularly objected to the type of food served in the Ballivián Cavalry Regiment in early 1932, complaining about "a period in which we were subjected to quinoa and *lakua* [a thick soup made with corn flour]."[19] The disdain with which he refers to these foods typical of the altiplano suggests that Camacho, a secondary-school graduate from Cochabamba, thought himself above such fare.

During the first three months of service, infantry, cavalry, and artillery regiments were supposed to share a routine of classroom instruction in the theory of combat and weapons use, practical training in the same, and physical-fitness programs that emphasized endurance and precise obedience to orders. Prior to receiving a rifle and bayonet, each conscript was to learn the name of and how to clean every part of the weapon. He was also supposed to attend lectures that explained trajectory, line of fire, and range before ever setting foot on the training grounds. After three months of theoretical and practical instruction, the combat-training programs split: cavalry soldiers learned to manage their mounts as a squad and perform reconnaissance, artillery soldiers transported and manned cannons, and infantry soldiers drilled at the company, battalion, and regimental levels in shooting, marching, building fortifications, and field service.[20] In all the branches, officers assigned soldiers to guard duty on a rotating basis. Regulations dictated that these sentinels must stand at the ready, their rifles armed with bayonets, and prohibited them from "talking, sitting, reading, singing, or distancing themselves more than twenty steps from the sentry box."[21]

A perpetual shortage of professional NCOs meant that certain conscripts received promotions to private first class or even corporal after just six months of training. Although the criteria for promotion prioritized university or professional education over military prowess, Richter's *Catechism* offered it as a reward for any conscript who showed "skill in shooting, dexterity in physical training, vigor and good conduct, personal hygiene, dress, and self-abnegation in service."[22] All of the NCOs who testified in military justice proceedings were at least semiliterate. Most identified as students, but quite a few claimed trades such as cobbler, barber, tailor, mechanic, carpenter, bricklayer, or even rural laborer.[23] These NCOs learned their duties on the job and thus replicated patterns set by those who preceded them, leading to persistent gaps in training.[24] Even if not promoted to NCO, every conscript who completed his first year of service became an *antiguo*, who had the privilege of seniority over the novices entering the barracks and oversaw much of their training.[25] The power given *antiguos* made the arrival of new conscripts a situation ripe for hazing that often included gendered taunts and physical abuse.[26]

Not surprisingly, the barracks hemorrhaged soldiers, who lied, ran, or jumped over walls to escape from the ranks.[27] Desertion fundamentally shaped the social structure of regiments since officers rightly feared that it, like an infectious disease, could quickly decimate their army. In addition to posting sentries, they used threats and social ties to discourage such behavior. During training, they insisted that deserters would forever wear "the black shroud of cowardice."[28] Such statements transformed an affront to the nation (as represented by the military institution) into a cause for personal and familial shame. Officers also fostered godfather relationships between conscripts, making the more experienced personally responsible for their charges and ensuring that potential deserters knew that their godfathers might also suffer for their sins.[29]

In spite of these measures, determined soldiers could always find a means of escape. Typical of deserters at the time was Santiago Aguirre, described in military records as a twenty-four-year-old indigenous farm worker from Callapa (La Paz) garrisoned at Uyuni (Potosí). Only months after entering service in 1914, he faked illness and fled as a fellow soldier escorted him to the hospital.[30] Others simply drifted out of military service. For example, the Loa Infantry Regiment lost conscripts Concepción Mamani and Valentín Murillo one Sunday in 1921 when they failed to return from an afternoon off in Oruro. Murillo, an illiterate agricultural laborer from Tumusla (Potosí), turned himself in a month later. When asked why he had deserted, he invoked the bonds of family, framing desertion as a logical reaction to the many months he had been away from his wife and children, leaving them "abandoned." That Sunday, he testified, "I got drunk in the city, and in that state, remembering my family, I bought a train ticket and left."[31]

Many soldiers, however, passed up such opportunities to desert and completed their terms of service. Even the most recently constructed barracks were not formidable fortresses. In fact, security was so limited in the Aviation School that conscript Hugo Tapia could drunkenly wander out of the El Alto barracks around one in the morning and spend the night at his aunt's house.[32] Tapia returned of his own volition the next day, as did the many conscripts who left the barracks to mail letters or run errands.[33] Nor did most soldiers desert when spending Sunday afternoons outside of the barracks visiting family, sauntering around the *plaza de armas*, or drinking with friends at local establishments.[34]

These soldiers chose to return for patriotic, personal, or professional reasons. For some, the barracks offered the opportunity to learn basic literacy skills. The Loa Regiment, for example, reported 152 literacy students in 1912 and 229 in 1916.[35] Nor were these simply administrative fictions: several conscripts testifying in military justice proceedings spontaneously mentioned literacy classes; one even noted that a particular officer "always made sure that they [illiterate conscripts] attend their classes."[36] The form of this training varied, with Murillo officers receiving orders to spend an hour each day on primary education but those in the Sucre Regiment only being offered weekly classes.[37]

Officers especially emphasized indigenous conscripts' enthusiasm for literacy classes.[38] Articles in the *Revista Militar* drew on tropes that portrayed rural indigenous people as children who, after centuries of cruel neglect, responded positively to the tender guidance of compassionate officers. For example, Lieutenant C. Bleichner wrote of having gained the confidence of three indigenous soldiers after discovering them in the forage storehouse "attentively reading their syllabaries and drawing letters on the ground." Fearing punishment for studying when they should have been cleaning their rifles, the conscripts told him of their disappointment with the literacy instructor and their desire to "learn to read and write in order to send some alphabetic characters to their parents, giving them a pleasant surprise." Instead of meting out punishment, Bleichner assigned two formally educated conscripts to teach these men, explaining that this would make them dedicated soldiers and better Bolivians: "From that day on, they gave maximum effort in their daily work, always trying to please me. These soldiers grew fonder of the barracks, of their officers, and were grateful to the *patria*."[39]

The idea of using kindness to build loyalty and win converts to military service commonly appeared in the *Revista Militar*, as its editors attempted to persuade officers that building personal ties through benevolent but strict behavior would produce better soldiers than verbal and physical abuse. Captain Alfredo Peñaranda presented such an argument in a story published in 1926 about fictional indigenous conscript Andrés Quispe's time in the barracks. After three days, Quispe considers deserting to escape from "the rage of the wicked sergeant." Yet the following day, Lieutenant Enrique Indaburo takes over their training. According to Peñaranda, the soldiers saw him as "a ray of sunshine on a cold winter's morning" after he learned their names, asked if any were ill, and played sports with them. Under this leadership, Quispe became a model soldier and grew to love Indaburo as a father figure.[40]

Written by officers for other officers, these stories featuring Indaburo and Bleichner modeled the ideal officer who would nurture indigenous conscripts, guiding them to put forth their best effort and become "good citizens, respectful of authority and conscious of their duties."[41] This idea of loyalty to the Bolivian nation was the first lesson conscripts were supposed to learn. They were to memorize phrases professing their duty to love and serve the *patria*, which Richter defined as "our common mother" and even "all that we have and all that we can be."[42] Such statements assert soldiers' unconditional love for the *patria*, but these stories show that officers recognized the importance of interpersonal bonds in forming dedicated soldiers. They hoped that soldiers' eagerness to please a favorite officer would eventually translate into the more abstract sense of national identity and loyalty to the *patria*.

All conscripts publicly performed an act of belonging to the Bolivian nation, though perhaps without sharing or understanding it, when they participated in the patriotic ritual of swearing an oath to the flag.[43] Bedecked in their finest uniforms, conscripts ritually intoned, "Yes, we swear," as military bands played the national anthem.[44] Although the precise text of the oath varied in the early years, it always expressed the conscript's willingness to sacrifice his life for the nation.[45] The language set in 1924 and subsequently printed in each conscript's military service booklet repeated this theme and

FIGURE 2.1. Sixth Company, Sucre Infantry Regiment, 1924. *Revista Militar* 35–36 (1924): 93, Biblioteca Patrimonial Arturo Costa de la Torre, Gobierno Autónomo Municipal La Paz. Used with permission.

added a profession of obedience: "Swear before God and the *Patria* to defend your flag even to the sacrifice of your life, never to abandon those who command you during war, and to apply yourself to superiors' orders."[46]

Outside of this idealized patriotism, some soldiers participated in military service because it represented an opportunity for sociability and building interpersonal bonds. Men forged or strengthened friendships as they worked side by side and slept in communal dormitories. During rests from marches and free time in the barracks, soldiers often sang tunes typical of their region in Spanish, Quechua, or Aymara.[47] They invented nicknames for one another and developed strong opinions about their fellows' personalities, describing one as calm and a jokester and another as "repudiated for unfriendliness to his *compañeros*."[48] As several conscripts in the Loa Battalion noted, "the intimate life of the barracks" produced deep relationships and created inseparable friends who lived like brothers.[49] The intimacy of these friendships even appears in posed photographs like figure 2.1, which depicts forty conscripts, three officers, and four civilians (including a woman who was presumably the company's *madrina* [godmother, sponsor]) from the sixth company of the Sucre Infantry Regiment in 1924.[50] The two men in the front left of the photograph sit close together, one with his arm casually slung over the other's shoulder.

Officers promoted such connections, recognizing their role in mission effectiveness. When writing the *Soldier's Catechism*, Colonel Richter praised camaraderie as an "indispensable . . . bond that unites men who work together for a common cause."[51] Officers thus encouraged conscripts to socialize through athletics, organizing soccer matches and Olympics-type tournaments.[52] Other forms of sociality were more furtive, like the soldiers who played cards in the dormitory and quickly hid the evidence when their captain entered.[53] One conscript even attempted to help another pass inspection by shedding his pants as soon as he was inspected and passing them to his friend, whose own pants were presumably ripped, lost, or otherwise out of regulation.[54]

Although the rules prohibited drinking in the barracks, alcohol was a mainstay of conscripts' lives.[55] Alcohol even facilitated breakdowns in military hierarchy, as when a professional NCO such as Subofficer Castor of the Ballivián Cavalry Regiment shared a bottle of pisco with his soldiers or a junior officer such as Lieutenant Jiménez of the Technical Battalion drank with the troops while on guard duty, "fell asleep completely drunk in the bed of a soldier," and then borrowed some aspirin from a conscript the next day.[56] These were not the uniform relationships of a strictly controlled bureaucracy; experiences of military service depended on personal relationships.

The intimacy of barracks life could also lead to exclusion and conflict. For example, Antonio Rosell, a painter from Cochabamba, lamented his lack of friends in the Murillo Regiment, and several conscripts in the Camacho Regiment complained of Aurelio Achá's tendency to gossip and scheme.[57] Language, region, and social class played important roles in determining friendships, with those who spoke the same language often banding together.[58] One conscript even testified to feeling left out of plans made by his fellows "in Quechua, since [he did] not understand."[59] And an indigenous soldier from Estancia Jiscajarana (Pocoata, Chayanta, Potosí) mobilized (albeit unsuccessfully) his ignorance of Spanish in an attempt to secure a discharge, arguing that being monolingual in the Loa Battalion "[made] it impossible for [him] to learn military service and [had] caused as much suffering for [his] superiors as for [him]."[60]

In contrast to the numerous discussions of drunkenness, these sources remain silent as to soldiers' sexual lives, even though anthropological accounts emphasize the importance of sex workers to the late twentieth-century conscript experience.[61] Statistics on venereal disease do suggest that many conscripts were sexually active. Out of an army of approximately 4,000 men, health officers reported 203 cases of venereal disease among conscripts in the first half of 1911 and 438 cases in 1913, suggesting that about 11 percent of troops suffered from these ailments.[62] Armed men roaming the countryside also presented opportunities for rape, yet this crime appears only twice in my sources; indigenous women were the victims in both cases.[63] Officially silencing this crime, the military penal code did not contemplate rape as an offense against military laws or discipline, and, if prosecuted at all, offenders were apparently referred to nonmilitary courts.[64]

Because they were spaces for men to forge homosocial relationships with both officers and other conscripts, the barracks were also a key site for learning, negotiating, and performing what it meant to be a man. Conscripts frequently offered evidence that their fellows had invoked a particular version of masculinity that equated bravery with manliness in order to pressure them into action. For example, Corporal Bernardino Fernández, a student serving his second year in the Loa Infantry Regiment, accused several fellow NCOs of using gendered insults to provoke him into joining their mutiny. He testified that when he refused to get out of bed, they had called him "a fool [cojudo]" who "should put on polleras [skirts worn by indigenous and chola women]." These taunts were quite effective, at least according to Fernández, who testified, "I had to get up out of pure self-respect."[65] In this and similar cases, conscripts mobilized these insults while testifying in military justice proceedings as part of attempts to excuse their own participation in acts of mutiny, insubordination, and desertion. They apparently expected that the military magistrate would understand the power of insults that questioned their manliness by challenging their bravery and comparing them to women and that he would consider these insults to be mitigating factors. Defining bravery as a willingness to challenge authority, this masculinity worked against the idea that being a good man meant serving the patria through obedience to officers.

Yet officers also contributed to the construction of an oppositional masculinity. For example, Sublieutenant Olmos reported that a conscript in 1930 had resisted his use of exercise to punish the company. The way he told the story is that after twenty minutes of complying, Vicente Rodríguez "stayed standing when I ordered him to kneel. Then I approached him and gave him a kick[;] I should [be able] to punish [them] without giving them any explanation."[66] Rodríguez responded to the kick by arming his bayonet. Olmos, rather than immediately quelling this blatant act of insubordination, chose to face Rodríguez as equals in order to defend what he seemed to have perceived as a threat to his masculinity. He reportedly yelled that "if he [Rodríguez] was a man, he should come [and] we'll duel with our fists, and if [not then] he is a coward, even if he has a loaded rifle."[67] Although masculinity is often seen as a way of encouraging discipline in the military, the form of masculinity expressed by Olmos and the conscripts who used gendered insults to encourage insubordination served to violate rather than impose discipline and hierarchy.

Each October or November, the regiments discharged the conscripts who had completed their term of service.[68] Administrators acknowledged an institutional responsibility to arrange for their journey home, providing, at least officially, travel allowances and railway vouchers.[69] Some regiments marked the end of service with an official ceremony in which conscripts stood at attention while commanders thanked them "in the name of the Nation, for having fulfilled, with loyalty and abnegation, the military duty imposed by law."[70] Participants then reiterated their oath to sacrifice all for the *patria* and hugged their fellow conscripts as the band played patriotic tunes.[71] They left the barracks with military service booklets in hand that documented their completion of this duty and that could set them on a path to citizenship. Some carried other tangible mementos of their service, such as badges that displayed their proficiency in military skills.[72] All left with memories of negative and positive experiences in the barracks, where they had worked, trained, suffered privations, expanded their social networks, and perhaps even changed their views of Bolivia. Many likely felt a mix of relief, accomplishment, sadness in leaving friends, and anticipation of returning to their families, communities, and girlfriends. Officers publishing in the *Revista Militar* wrote hopefully of the "thousands of Indians who have passed through the army's ranks" and who, returning to "their huts, communities, haciendas, or *ayllus*, are the best proponents of military service" and cause a "geometric progression each year in the percentage of indigenous conscripts."[73]

MARTIAL AND NONMARTIAL LABOR

A lieutenant writing in a 1924 issue of the *Revista Militar* idealistically referred to the barracks as "sacred grounds" where "men are made." He then added, "The barracks is not a correctional site, nor is it a group of men required to do forced labor."[74] Yet, taken together, the compulsory nature of military service, the illegality of refusing orders, the social status of most conscripts, and the nonmartial quality of many tasks indicate the opposite. The realities of a weak state in a thinly populated territory meant that conscripts often deployed to guarantee elections and break strikes as well as perform nonmartial labor such as building roads, harvesting crops, and serving officers. Pervasive fears of "race war" likely reinforced this orientation since many rural elites felt profoundly ambivalent about militarizing indigenous conscripts. Arming them with the tools of work rather than the weapons of war provided a convenient solution.

Although draped in words like duty, service, and sacrifice, soldiers' tasks are nonetheless work.[75] Conscription is a form of coercive labor that fills the ranks by combining a discourse of patriotic service with a bureaucratic system that discourages noncompliance. Bolivian conscripts and officers certainly thought of their daily activities as labor; they consistently referred to the "labors of the troops" and to the work of drilling and weapons training.[76]

To make sense of the diversity of conscripts' labors, I define all activities they performed under superiors' orders as labor. I distinguish, however, between martial and nonmartial labor. Under this framework, martial labor consists of tasks directly related to defending the national territory, including fighting international wars, repressing internal unrest, protecting state installations, patrolling borders, and the training necessary to prepare for these eventualities. Martial labor thus comprised not only battles and maneuvers in the field but also quotidian tasks such as guard duty, weapons training, and maintaining armament.

Repressing rural uprisings and mining strikes also falls under the rubric of martial labor, yet these tasks were more controversial.[77] In the correspondence that constantly flowed to government offices, prominent figures professed themselves desperate to preserve their lives and property from "being cruelly and brutally victimized by these Indians."[78] Conscripts thus marched into indigenous communities and rural properties at least forty times between 1911 and 1925 in just the department of La Paz.[79] They also repressed mining strikes in 1912 (Pacajes), twice in 1919 (Corocoro and Huanani), and in 1923 (Uncía).[80] Although military administrators usually agreed to send troops, disputes over these repressive measures sometimes arose. Minister of War General Fermín Prudencio routinely denied petitions by landowners and subprefects, dismissing appeals as "matters of mere personal interest," in which "the Army, made up of only conscripts" could not interfere because training had to take priority.[81] However, after losing his post, he did not hesitate to personally request that the new minister of war send armed forces to "subdue the rebellious *indígenas* on his property called Achuta."[82] Officers in command of such missions also voiced objections to these labors. Captain Samuel Alcoreza described his troops' repressive labor as arduous and futile. Responding to an urgent appeal from the Mallea Balboa family in 1915, he led thirty artillery soldiers on "a full night's trek through paths full of water and mud, in which the troops have suffered the indescribable" only to arrest "defenseless Indians who were sleeping" in their homes. Alcoreza reported that there had been "no attempted uprising" and bluntly accused the landowner of "intimidating the Indians with armed forces."[83]

Such requests, denials, and concessions were an arena in which power played out, as military administrators attempted to balance obligations and personal connections with their ambition to create a professional military devoted to armed training. The small number of soldiers deployed for these missions suggests tacit acknowledgment that the goal of these martial labors was intimidation in the service of powerful individuals.

Similar disputes about the institution's priorities occurred surrounding conscripts' nonmartial labor, as administrators attempted to balance martial training against fiscal constraints and the urgent need for national infrastructure. I define nonmartial labor as tasks also commonly performed by civilians that were not directly related to defense. Of course, the labors of soldiers throughout the world have always included nonmartial tasks in support of martial ends. Domestic work, such as cleaning, washing, and food preparation, ensured a productive workspace and healthy soldiers.[84] Conscripts assigned the role of auxiliary nurse became responsible for transporting medications and for basic first aid.[85] Some conscripts served as the mechanics who maintained vehicles and the drivers who transported troops. In cavalry units, soldiers also cared for the mounts, cleaned stable troughs, and carried fodder.[86] These and other nonmartial tasks were essential to garrisoning, training, and fielding an army.

Some conscripts had additional nonmartial duties as "assistants" to officers. For example, conscript Juan Chuquimia, a mechanic from La Paz, used the "moments that [he] had free from service" to carry out "the duties that, as an assistant, [he] had to do" for Lieutenant Casto Soria.[87] Internal regulations limited assistants' work to "the washing of garments, the cleaning and training of horses;" mandated that officers pay them a defined monthly salary; and insisted that these soldiers were not domestics.[88] Even if precisely followed, these rules provided for assistants to take on work that would otherwise be performed by family members or presumably better-remunerated servants, allowing officers to maintain the lifestyle of a higher social class. Assistants' work was thus part of life in the barracks but was less clearly connected to martial ends than some other nonmartial labors.

Conscripts' nonmartial labor assignments often led them outside of the barracks in service of both martial and nonmartial ends. They prepared land for colonization; populated border regions; logged forests; built and repaired roads, barracks, ports, wells, dams, embankments, irrigation channels, public pools, schools, hospitals, and stadiums; manufactured items; grew foodstuffs; extorted low prices from townspeople; and even followed orders to steal goods. These nonmartial labors were physical tasks that ranged from the dangerous to the banal, some of which were legal and others illegal but sanctioned by officers.

Soldiers in units primarily devoted to manual labor tended to be less educated, more indigenous, and less likely to speak Spanish. For example, the members of the 1921 Technical Battalion assigned to build new barracks in the windswept western reaches of the copper-mining district of Corocoro were, according to one formally educated conscript, majority indigenous.[89] Dominant ideas about the correlation between ethnicity and ability likely meant that conscripts who fell toward the indigenous end of the spectrum disproportionately performed nonmartial labor of the more abject sort.

The earliest evidence of soldiers' nonmartial labor outside the barracks comes from accounts of frontier units in the 1910s and 1920s. Principal among Liberals' goals was protecting Bolivia's claims to vast and sparsely populated border regions, especially given recent territorial losses to Brazil and Chile. Despite various schemes for settling these lands with European immigrants or Bolivian families, Liberals soon determined military colonies to be the most practical option.[90] Small detachments of soldiers thus established outposts in the vast savannahs of the east, in the scrubland of the Chaco, and on river ports in the dense rainforests and pampas of the north and northeast, staffing at least fifty different forts, garrisons, and colonies between 1910 and 1928.[91]

Because the state had little infrastructure in these regions and few towns from which to provision the troops, these soldiers had to be self-sufficient. These conscripts were as likely to hunt monkeys, plant manioc, or cut swathes in the jungle as they were to stand guard, march, or clean their weapons.[92] One officer lamented this fact, reporting that the "training demanded by military regulations has not been properly fulfilled because much of a soldier's time must be devoted to working the land."[93] Conscripts assigned to these units traveled long distances, suffered from excessive temperatures and torrential rains, performed fatiguing labor, risked exposure to disease, and faced formidable natural obstacles. Frontier conscripts were thus more likely to perish during service or return with diminished capacities.[94] Two discharged soldiers from the Montes Battalion, for example, petitioned the prefect of La Paz in 1908, begging for help returning to their homes since they were "gravely ill, attacked by sicknesses that we contracted" in the "deadly territory of Acre."[95]

Closely connected to the frontier initiative was the use of military laborers to build roads between these regions and population centers. Evidence indicates that at least some conscripts in sapper units followed a modified service schedule, receiving infantry instruction from January until June and then exclusively working on roads during the dry winter months that stretched from June to October.[96] Soldiers in the Juana Azurduy Infantry Regiment, for example, hewed a road between Sucre and the Chaco in 1928, using picks and dynamite to break apart solid rock.[97] This work could be just as dangerous as brandishing a loaded rifle, as shown by a writer's portrayal of these conscripts "inclined over horrifying abysses, levering apart the rocks with their crowbars, placing quarried blocks from considerable heights."[98]

Far from being concealed, nonmartial labors on the frontier and building roadways were conspicuously celebrated in the military press. Especially in the 1920s, the *Revista Militar* commonly published articles that documented in words and images the diverse labors of frontier service. The inclusion of images of robust conscripts and pristine barracks perhaps endeavored to persuade officers, troops, and their families that frontier service was not only safe but also bringing much-needed progress to Bolivia's hinterlands.[99] Photographs of sapper labor similarly characterized the army as the principal motor of progress. In these images, partially completed roads and bridges appeared before backdrops of dense forests, impenetrable mountains, and rapid rivers, thus portraying conscripts as conquering nature's challenges with not only wheelbarrows and shovels but also dedication. Although these photographs depict men performing taxing and decidedly nonmartial labor, their uniforms, the orderly manner of work, and the presence of an officer calmly overseeing their performance remind viewers that these are conscripts serving their *patria*.[100]

Although the daily labor of frontier and sapper conscripts was distinctly nonmartial, this work fell to the army for strategic reasons: populating the frontier and connecting Bolivia's disparate regions would secure borders, achieve food security, and facilitate the transportation of resources. In fact, mainstream journalists used militarized language to describe this labor, arguing that soldiers were "conquer[ing] with hoe and machete what has not been done with sword and rifle."[101] However, the connection to national defense was significantly more abstract than for guard duty and weapons training.

These diverse labors on the frontier laid the intellectual groundwork for using urban soldiers for similar tasks even if they lacked a logical link to national defense. As it became acceptable for uniformed labor to build highways, it was less of a conceptual leap to ask soldiers to repair urban roads. If soldiers on the frontier were planting seeds, why not make centrally located units more self-sufficient? If soldiers in border units were building their own barracks, then urban soldiers could build schools. Conscripts stationed in population centers thus began to perform manual labor on public works projects like wells, levees, schools, hospitals, and stadiums. For example, when the telegraphs director could not find workers in Pelechuco (La Paz) to install lines in 1913 due to fears of an indigenous uprising, he called on military labor to finish the job.[102] And Technical Battalion soldiers stationed in Corocoro (La Paz) reported spending their days excavating stones, building irrigation channels, leveling land, and carrying water in 1921.[103]

The obligatory nature of military service allowed the state to furnish itself with a labor pool compelled by law to work for low pay. Although the government had to invest funds in order to pursue deserters and recruit, discipline, transport, house, and feed troops, it paid conscripts only cents a day.[104] The very term used to describe these wages— *socorros* (aid)—indicates they were seen not as remuneration for labor but rather as an allowance provided by a benevolent state. Put simply, "the salary received by a conscript is better thought of as a bonus to cover his necessities."[105] Yet officers could garnish this "bonus" to replace lost or damaged items. Soldiers serving in a 1931 infantry regiment complained of additional involuntary garnishments to purchase copies of the *Soldier's Catechism*. They added that they had to use their "reduced *socorros* to acquire shoes, sandals, and underwear" since their officers had failed to issue them these items.[106]

Bolivia's turbulent economy weighed heavily in decisions to assign conscripts nonmartial tasks. Liberals had effectively bought off the opposition
with massive public works and positions in the expanding bureaucracy, both
of which were funded through international loans secured by booming tin
exports. However, dependence on foreign trade for state revenues meant that
slight fluctuations in the world economy could threaten Bolivia's ability to
service its growing debt. Slowing exports caused a short but profound crisis
in 1913–1914, which ultimately led to the fracturing of the Liberal party and
the emergence of the opposition Republicans. Although the economy recovered in the wake of the World War I, another short depression threatened
debt payments in the early 1920s. Bolivia was one of the first countries to
feel the effects of the Great Depression as tin prices plummeted 60 percent
between 1927 and 1932.[107]

Although nonmartial labor was already prevalent prior to the economic
crises of the 1920s, these assignments were often contested by members of
the military establishment, who argued that they harmed military prepared-
ness. In the 1910s, the institution sometimes even followed through on this
rhetoric by contracting with civilians to build barracks rather than using the
labor of conscripts.[108] The atmosphere of budgetary constraints, however,
clearly affected military rhetoric and practice. Ministers of war repeatedly
complained that economic woes prevented the military from achieving its
goals, be they the staging of annual maneuvers, the training of reservists, or
the construction of hygienic barracks.[109] In the 1920s, the minister of war's
annual reports to Congress began to read like laundry lists of troops' nonmartial tasks, perhaps in order to stave off looming budget cuts. To cite just one
example, in 1928, he boasted of work by the Azurduy Infantry Regiment on
a road from Sucre to Cuevo, the Sixth Division on one from Guayaramerín
to Cachuela Esperanza, and the Padilla Engineering Regiment on roads and
colonization in the Chapare.[110] In the face of increasing deficits, the minister
of war issued orders in 1931 that soldiers repair their own barracks "in order
to economize for the national treasury."[111] The commander of the Colorados
Infantry Regiment accordingly ordered each company to make 2,500 mud
bricks per week.[112]

Although the labors they performed often resembled those of their civilian peers, soldiers who made oral, written, or physical attempts to better
their working conditions were deemed mutineers, arrested, and judicially
processed. Thus mutinies that resemble strikes dot the military history of
twentieth-century Bolivia; some soldiers even used the language of work
stoppage to express their demands and defend their actions. In 1906, for
example, soldiers abandoned Puerto Heath on the Peruvian border citing
excessive work, having served double the promised tour, and their com-
plaint that "our *Patria* pays us poorly."[113] And various groups of conscripts in

the 1920s were formally accused of mutiny for objecting to, in their words, "working like donkeys" and doing "excessive work, day and night."[114]

Martial visions of military service meant that nonmartial labor experiences could become a subject of debate from below, especially when formally educated soldiers were ordered to perform work they viewed as unbefitting their status and uniform. At least one officer reinforced this sense of entitlement to the martial labor of training by threatening his conscripts with roadwork in the Chapare if they misbehaved.[115] Nonmartial labor thus became a punishment rather than part of their sacred duty. In one particularly striking case from 1931, a group of formally educated soldiers from the Colorados Regiment invoked this idea of what constituted appropriate military labor to complain about superiors who made "us complete work that does not correspond to military service, like making mud bricks."[116] Nonmartial labor thus became an arena of contestation as the gap between theory and practice opened a space for dissent and different ideas about the nature of military service clashed.

The social status of the majority of conscripts likely influenced ideas about the acceptability of assigning soldiers to nonmartial tasks in agriculture, on public works projects, or as officers' assistants. Because most of the men entering the barracks were miners, artisans, and rural agriculturalists rather than students or urban professionals, military administrators and officers were perhaps more comfortable picturing them as wielding shovels rather than rifles. This hypothesis raises a question about the differences between obligatory military service and other contemporaneous forms of labor extraction, such as *postillonaje* (mail service) and *prestación vial* (obligatory road tax/work).[117] Whether conscripts understood military service as an onerous labor tax or as an honorable rite of passage varied by individual. Unfortunately, since illiterate conscripts from rural areas rarely testified in military justice hearings or registered their thoughts about military service in writing, we cannot know whether nationalist rhetoric affected their opinions about this labor obligation. Some perhaps perceived a substantive difference between work done in uniform for the state and work done in the home and fields of the *patrón*.

Some conscripts certainly saw donning a uniform to defend their *patria* as an honorable duty and would have rejected any comparison between obligatory military service and institutions like the colonial *mita*.[118] Student-turned-conscript Ricardo Pacheco, for example, expressed the pride that he and his fellow conscripts took in having "come to the barracks to serve our *patria*."[119] A journalist writing in *El Diario* in 1930 suggested a similar sense of pride among Aymara men in the community of Sajama (Carangas, Oruro). He reported that former conscripts used "reservist" as a title that marked accomplishment, writing phrases such as "Manuel Choque, Re-

servist of the Campero Regiment" on the entrances of their homes.[120] One
image of conscripts working on a road in the Chapare in 1924 brings these
questions into relief. Not a rifle in sight, the men are shown digging drainage ditches by the side of the road. Several of those in the foreground appear
not even to be wearing a military uniform. Little distinguished these soldiers
from coerced laborers unless they, as Pacheco and Choque perhaps did, saw
themselves as different, as laboring to build their nation and as becoming
men who honorably served their *patria*.

INSOLENT CONSCRIPTS AND TYRANNICAL OFFICERS

If men were to serve because of a sense of duty to the *patria*, their treatment
in the barracks had to be appropriate to that end; soldiering had to be honorable. Policy makers thus officially banned violent physical punishment.
However, the idea of discipline that replaced it was riddled with internal contradictions, as seen by the carefully worded definition offered in Richter's
Catechism: "Discipline is complete submission to all military regulations
and absolute obedience to all commanders. *It is not an imposed servility but
rather the duty of a free man to the army as a national institution*" (italics in
original). This definition betrays anxiety over how to reconcile the need for
soldiers to obey all orders without question with the idea of filling the ranks
with thinking citizens. Discipline, he argued, had to be freely given by patriotic soldiers rather than imposed. He encouraged conscripts to self-regulate,
asserting that discipline and punishment should ultimately be antithetical;
punishment only existed for those "who stray from their duty and do not
want to adapt to the demands of discipline."[121] Tellingly, even in his optimistic formulation, punishment still played an important role in achieving
military discipline. The text implied that men would subordinate themselves
to military hierarchy; those who failed to self-regulate would have discipline
physically imposed upon them.

High-level policy makers had attempted to prohibit violent punishments
since at least 1893.[122] In 1916, the army officially regulated sanctions for minor infractions by conscripts and NCOs. A list of twenty-seven offenses such
as carelessness in physical hygiene, "tepidness in service," and petty theft
could be punished only through extra cleaning duties, confinement, and
plantón (forced standing) for a certain number of hours.[123] All more serious
offenses had to be referred to military justice, which had long been restricted
from meting out physical punishments.[124]

Despite official policy, punishment in the barracks was typically a personal rather than a bureaucratic process. Evidence from seventeen military
justice proceedings from 1917 to 1932 indicates that officers and NCOs used
both legal and illegal forms of punishment to ensure compliance with orders.

Rather than being bureaucratically administered according to military regulations, many of these punishments were arbitrary and often deeply personal. Granted the power by military hierarchy to exercise personal control over conscripts, some superiors used public humiliation and the performance of gendered domination to maintain relations of authority that ideally would have been established through respect for rank and uniform. Commonly associated with premodern forms of statecraft, this type of punishment as a public spectacle served to prove, in a highly visible and theatrical way, the direct power of one individual over another.[125] These experiences likely affected conscripts' understanding of authority. Rather than establishing a legitimate right to rule, certain officers and NCOs enacted a personalized regime of physical dominance that used ideas about sexuality and masculinity to dominate and control conscripts.

Officers often used exercise as a legal way to punish those who erred in military training or barracks comportment. This type of punishment produced bodily pain and proved officers' power over their charges. Troops typically had to jog and do pushups to the point of exhaustion.[126] These punishments could also take more creative forms: disappointed with his soldiers' "lethargy" and failure to maintain alignment during training in close-order formation, one sublieutenant in 1930 corrected them various times and then, still not satisfied with their performance, ordered them to repeatedly run, throw themselves on the ground, crawl, and then kneel.[127] Also requiring strength and endurance was the punishment of forced standing, during which soldiers had to stand at attention, sometimes holding weights, for a period that could range from twenty minutes to several hours. This was the most common punishment mentioned in military justice records from the period, occurring in thirteen of the seventeen cases. Offenses provoking this punishment included not only severe breaches such as insolence, insubordination, and drunkenness but also minor faults.[128]

In many cases, officers resorted to not-so-legal beatings if they could not successfully impose exercise or forced standing, were dissatisfied with the manner in which conscripts performed these punishments, or lost control of their own rage. Witnesses in military justice proceedings routinely told of kicks, beatings, saber blows, and even whippings. To cite just one example, conscripts serving in the Train Battalion in 1919 alleged that Lieutenant Armando Ballón had tweaked the ears of one of their number for responding incorrectly to a question, made another's tooth fall out by hitting him with the butt of a rifle for errors in positioning during target practice, and kicked a third while saying, "I'm going to make you march well."[129]

These were not just allegations made by disaffected soldiers. The officers who testified in these proceedings usually admitted to dealing out such punishments. Sublieutenant Natalio Pereira, for example, almost boasted in a 1917 report about taking a cavalry conscript "by his chest" and "making use of [his] saber, [punishing] his insolence" until "[he] made him obey."[130] Officers consistently argued that physical violence was necessary to prevent conscripts from, in the words of one officer, "making a mockery of my authority."[131]

Some incidents also had strong overtones of sexual dominance: Pacífico Arce, a student from Cochabamba serving in the Ballivián Cavalry Regiment in 1931, accused Sublieutenant Anibal Cusicanqui of placing a saddle on him, mounting him, and using spurs on him in front of his fellow soldiers.[132] Another conscript alleged that his NCOs had forced soldiers to stand naked for two hours.[133] And at least two soldiers reported being kicked in the testicles.[134] How or why these disputes became sexualized remains unclear, but since Cusicanqui admitted having punished Arce but roundly denied the saddle incident, I suspect that at least this type of overtly sexualized punishment exceeded disciplinary norms. Indeed, these conscripts may have formulated such accusations anticipating that they would gain more traction than stories of forced labor or beatings.

While these cases may represent particularly brutal behavior, evidence suggests that other factors (such as the specter of mutiny, political conflict outside of the barracks, and the personal connections of individual conscripts) allowed them to enter the historical record. Similar disciplinary methods were likely widespread, especially with illiterate conscripts assigned to outlying units who did not have the skills or connections necessary to contact the press, inform a politician, or pressure a commander to investigate. Conscripts' social status was clearly a determining factor in these cases. None of the thirty-four conscripts involved in these documented cases of violence were Aymara- or Quechua-speaking agriculturalists. In fact, most of them served in the more prestigious cavalry and artillery units, and at least 85 percent (twenty-nine of thirty-four) were fully literate. Pursuing occupations such as bakers, barbers, cobblers, and mechanics, the majority belonged to the urban artisan class. Also among their number, however, were four university students, an accountant, a telegraph operator, a typesetter, and a white-collar employee.[135]

Largely absent from the historical record is the treatment of rural conscripts, especially those stationed outside of urban centers. Accustomed to hacienda and mining overseers who often used whipping, beating, and sexual abuse to maintain authority, these actors were likely less inclined to blatantly challenge their officers.[136] They probably chose more subtle forms of resistance, such as foot-dragging or feigned misunderstanding.[137] And if they did assault an officer or plot a mutiny, the incident likely remained unreported, with officers personally handling infractions rather than relying on military tribunals, which were reserved for formally educated conscripts and high-profile incidents.[138] Yet we can still be sure that less-privileged conscripts also suffered brutal treatment—probably to a greater extent than their urban counterparts. In fact, one conscript from Oruro justified his superior's unsanctioned use of "the stick or the whip," saying that legal disciplinary methods only worked with "other elements, more intelligent and better educated than the *indígenas* who make up a large percentage of the Technical Battalion."[139]

These cases reveal a profound ambivalence among military authorities toward the changes in their institution. They theoretically agreed that the exercise of legitimate authority in the barracks should depend on a fair and uniform disciplinary regime that treated conscripts as honorable citizen-soldiers. Prohibiting such punishments was thus fundamental to making soldiering honorable and to instituting a model whereby men would remain in the barracks willingly, out of respect for their officers and fearing the stigma of desertion more than the bodily consequences of defiance. Yet, in practice, officers and even some administrators were unwilling to completely depart from older forms in which ultimate authority resided in the individual officer rather than in bureaucratic regulations. Not all troops, they argued, deserved respectful treatment, and maintaining discipline easily trumped regulations prohibiting violence. The failure of governmentality led to physical assaults that both soldiers and officers perceived as challenging their honor and masculinity.[140] The new disciplinary norms of Richter's *Catechism* and the 1916 regulations thus regularly came into conflict with the established habitus of the officer corps.[141]

Despite the prevalence of violent punishment, nonmartial labor, inedible meals, and unsanitary barracks, ideas about soldiers' honor and rights still spread among certain sectors of society, as shown by the eagerness of some conscripts, especially those linked to powerful patrons, to report perceived violations. Julio Rendón, for example, convinced fifteen of his fellows to abandon the Technical Battalion barracks in 1921 to report the deplorable conditions, unbefitting honorable soldiers of the *patria*, that they had suffered under the command of Captain Melitón Brito. They complained of hard labor, intolerable cold within the barracks, and the legendary temper of their commander.[142] Rendón, a student from a well-connected family in Sucre, decided to report these violations directly to General Pastor Baldivieso, the current minister of war and a personal friend of his grandfather.[143]

Relatively privileged conscripts like Rendón brought to the barracks their own ideas about legitimate forms of punishment and the labor appropriate for soldiers. These ideas brought them into conflict with officers, especially those accustomed to training less privileged troops. One group of formally educated soldiers serving in 1931 felt so confident of their rights that they sent a letter to the divisional commander in which they complained about forced labor, unfair salary deductions, abusive punishments, and being denied Sunday leave. They even offered a definition of discipline that implied a reciprocal relationship between the state and its soldiers: "The obligations imposed by military discipline are bilateral; the soldier must comply with superiors' orders that conform with regulations, and the superiors, principally, must not exceed their authority; they are not permitted to impose inhuman punishments, on the contrary, they should, without relaxing discipline, care for their subordinates, giving them the consideration due to all rational beings." These soldiers asserted the primacy of bureaucratic regulations and their own right to assess the legitimacy of orders based on whether they conformed to these regulations. They further limited their superiors' power based on an idea of "natural rights that cannot be trampled on, not even under the pretext of military discipline."[144] Their words were a far cry from the definition of discipline in Richter's *Catechism* and certainly from officers' insistence on strict obedience to military hierarchy.

The clash between fundamentally different concepts of legitimate authority and the army's purpose resulted from the recent turn to universal male conscription and thus constantly resurfaced in the barracks, military tribunals, the press, and even the legislature. In theory, soldiers were honorable citizens who eagerly presented for duty, and officers were professionals who treated their soldiers fairly, earning respect because of their training and experience. In practice, however, soldiers existed on a spectrum that included those violently impressed, reluctantly conscripted, and eagerly volunteering. And each officer acted according to his own individual personality and previous experience with conscripts. Some men thus entered the barracks with ideas about their own honor based on their social status, whereas many of their officers believed that this honor had to be earned through daily action and strict respect for authority. Although violent punishments by officers and NCOs affirmed their immediate physical power over conscripts, they ultimately called its legitimacy into question, since their illegality opened a space for dissent. The very fact that these grievances were recorded shows that dominance was not absolute and that there was ample room for both official and more hidden forms of resistance.

As part of a liberal project to instill patriotism and extract labor, conscription reproduced and reinforced many of Bolivia's inequalities. Officers often drew on traditional hierarchies based on sociocultural markers such as language, income, and education when promoting conscripts and allocating labor assignments, thus ensuring the continuation of social and racial divides in the barracks. However, even given these privileges, the barracks were not a segregated space: formally educated young men did serve alongside noncitizen conscripts, including Aymara- and Quechua-speaking agriculturalists and artisans. Conscription not only reproduced hierarchies but also reshaped them by adding the completion of military service to other long-standing distinctions. Moreover, some conscripts could improve their social position after having entered the barracks, worn a uniform, worked for the state, handled weapons, and maybe even learned Spanish, gained literacy skills, or built patron-client ties to an officer. In fact, Carter and Mamani argue that by 1932, young men in one Aymara community considered "going to the barracks and complying with obligatory military service to be acts of prestige."[145] In some ways, conscription did begin to create the nation of which Liberals dreamed. However, the state never controlled this process: officers continued to exercise unsanctioned forms of authority, and conscripts began to construct their own norms, social ties, and exclusions. In so doing, officers and conscripts joined a host of actors who were negotiating the terms of service and even the very purpose of conscription in the press, military tribunals, and barracks.

CHAPTER 3

CLIENTELISM AND CONSCRIPT INSUBORDINATION

On July 12, 1920, Bolivia experienced its first coup of the twentieth century when officers and conscripts with ties to the Republican Party took La Paz's Plaza Murillo and installed a civilian junta. This coup marked the failure of the Liberal project to forge a professional and nonpartisan army. Over the subsequent decade, periods of heightened fear and suspicion punctuated life in the seat of government as civilian administrations declared states of siege and exiled enemies in hopes of staving off the next coup. In the army, the era was characterized by instances of rebellion throughout the national territory as officers plotted regime change. This decade would also see repeated investigations into acts of mutiny led by small groups of literate conscripts. Although the mutineers attributed their actions to quotidian grievances about military service, we cannot understand these mutinies and the reactions they provoked without the larger political context of instability and clientelism. Nor can we understand this period of Bolivian politics without accounting for the claims-making of these literate and often politically engaged conscripts.[1]

The emergence of the Republican Party in 1914 inaugurated a period of civil and military unrest centered in La Paz, which housed the president, legislature, main arsenal, and Quartermaster Corps, not to mention over one hundred thousand inhabitants.[2] Those in power assigned multiple regiments to La Paz during periods of political uncertainty to increase the likelihood that plots would be discovered and to ensure that a single commander could not overthrow the government. Belonging to these strategically important units, the leaders of the mutinies hailed from the minority of conscripts who were already citizens. Many were the students and professionals who made up the emerging middle class and would have an important impact on national politics over the next decades. Although other participants held occupations such as mechanic, carpenter, or tailor, their claims to literacy made them citizens and distinguished them from the disenfranchised majority. The implications of political upheaval were particularly profound for literate conscripts stationed in the nexus of partisan action. This situation stood in stark contrast to the *caudillismo* of the nineteenth century, when foot soldiers did not usually come from the literate classes and were often outnumbered by officers.[3]

During this decade, a crisis in constitutional politics arose out of and fueled a crisis of authority in the military. The 1920 coup shifted the balance of power in the barracks; the loyalty of conscripts suddenly mattered deeply and thus was subject to intense scrutiny during periods of upheaval. Rather than remaining within the barracks walls, the grievances of literate conscripts became linked to larger political movements. Although not all mutinies were tied to partisan politics, they entered the documentary record because of such fears. Despite professions to the contrary, these conscripts were clearly political subjects with patron-client ties to officers and civilian politicians. Focusing on La Paz, this chapter analyzes four such mutinies in light of the turbulent politics of the period, arguing that a culture of insubordination had developed among this subset of soldiers that was directly related to ideas about their rights and duties as Bolivian citizens.

PARTISAN EXPLOITATION OF CONSCRIPT GRIEVANCES

Members of the Republican Party attacked Liberals' administration of obligatory military service as part of their efforts to break Liberal dominance. In refounding the army, Liberals had sought to banish the specter of nineteenth-century *caudillismo*, characterized in Bolivia by frequent coups and the proliferation of private armies calling themselves national forces.[4] These earlier armies served as an explicit foil to what Liberals were trying to build: a new, unified, and strictly hierarchical military that submitted to a civilian government and followed bureaucratic procedures. Liberals seemed to have achieved these goals as officers received professional training and conscription took root despite the often-brutal treatment of soldiers. The appearance of an apolitical force subordinate to constitutional authority was easy to maintain in the climate of economic and political stability that prevailed during a decade of unopposed Liberal rule. Republicans, however, began to crack this veneer by attacking the Liberals' army as no different from the nineteenth-century force in its humiliating and brutal treatment of conscripts.

Liberals faced no organized opposition between 1904 and 1913, when Ismael Montes tried to push through unpopular monetary policies during a period of economic crisis. Lawyer Bautista Saavedra seized on the opportunity, convincing independents and disaffected Liberals to unite under the amorphous banner of the Republican Party.[5] Most prominent among those Saavedra recruited to the Republican cause were Senator Daniel Salamanca and General José Manuel Pando, a well-known war hero who had served as the first Liberal president. These leaders organized a national convention for August 1914, but President Montes declared a state of siege, sent forty Republicans into exile, and closed opposition newspapers just days before the convention was to take place.[6]

The legislature inaugurated its annual cycle of sessions in this context, which led members of the opposition to elevate conscripts' grievances onto the national stage in order to attack the government. Republican Deputy Rafael de Ugarte, for example, inveighed against the "cruel and inhuman treatment" of conscript Gerónimo Santalla. Raising this incident in successive sessions, Ugarte gave impassioned speeches that Bolivia must not return to the disastrous times of the nineteenth century, when tyrannical officers regularly administered "barbarous punishments." Ugarte further threatened that he would prefer that "the Army disappear before the conscript who fulfills his duty is tortured."[7] Accusing Liberals of neglecting soldiers, Republicans also harped on the army's failure to feed conscripts properly. Deputy Abel Iturralde of La Paz claimed that three soldiers from the Loa Infantry Regiment had fainted due to undernourishment after being served "a meal of revolting *harina* [unprocessed corn flour] that was not even cooked, and the soldiers hurled the food in disgust."[8] Since raw *harina* was commonly served to dogs, Iturralde's description of this institutional failure implicitly accused the army of dehumanizing the soldiers who patriotically fulfilled their duty to Bolivia.[9] Accusing officers of abuse and corruption, these politicians undermined military hierarchy and encouraged conscripts to voice their grievances through the Republican Party.

When Montes lifted the state of siege in December 1914, the Republicans immediately organized a convention for January 1915. The new party, officially led by Senator Daniel Salamanca, issued a platform that called for free elections, decentralization, and limits on executive power.[10] With the Republicans running a full list of candidates in 1915, 1916, and 1917, a system emerged based on patron-client ties and structured electoral violence. Local leaders on each side funded election-day violence to prevent the opposition from entering the main plaza to vote. With an electorate of only sixty thousand and no secret ballot, these measures often determined elections.[11]

The reemergence of partisan conflict shattered the illusion of a professional military above the political fray. Liberals, having written the legislation and provided the funds that made the post-1899 army possible, expected the institution to subordinate itself to their authority. An apolitical army, in their view, would maintain internal order by guaranteeing their election and suppressing unrest in the cities, mines, and rural areas. Yet the political situation had so deteriorated by 1918 that, despite explicit prohibitions to the contrary, officers were openly debating politics in the barracks and Liberals were accusing Republicans of "seducing officers with bribes and the promise of promotion and foreign travel."[12] These conditions meant that Montes could no longer count on the army's unconditional support. He thus formed a paramilitary force called the Guardia Blanca (White Guard) to deliver the 1917 presidential race.[13] Although Montes successfully orchestrated the election of José Gutiérrez Guerra, the first months of the new administration were characterized by violence and political wrangling.

Perhaps in attempts to win the loyalty of La Paz–based regiments, both sides hailed conscripts, whether as heroes of the nation or victims of mistreatment. Liberals praised the work of soldiers in repressing "the unconscious masses" who had taken to the streets to support the Republican cause. *El Diario* lauded conscripts' performance as evidence that Liberals had built an outstanding army that instilled a sense of duty and taught loyalty to the constitutional order, which they would continue to protect, the organ implied, from uneducated mobs trying to bring down the government.[14] These words simultaneously served to woo formally educated conscripts to the Liberal cause and to persuade them to carry out their duties as soldiers by siding with the forces of order rather than the opposition.

The opposition responded by intensifying its attacks on Liberals' administration of obligatory military service. *La Verdad*, a La Paz–based newspaper owned by Republican Abel Iturralde, launched a concerted campaign to undermine the Liberal Party by exposing the conditions suffered by conscripts in the barracks. An April article reported allegations attributed to soldiers in the Murillo Regiment, who wrote, "The *rancho* [communal meal] is worse than for a dog. . . . There are nights that we don't eat because [the food is] raw, awful, and without seasoning." The letter closed by rhetorically asking whether "we are slaves of a hierarchy or servants of a free and independent *patria*."[15] This and similar articles in the Republican *La Razón* used descriptive language to depict an institution that dehumanized its soldiers. These conditions would neither promote national unity nor inspire men to identify with the *patria*. Instead, they asserted, Liberals' failures were dooming universal male conscription and destroying the very fabric of the army.

Republicans' wooing of conscripts and dissident officers was part of a quest to gain power by cultivating those marginalized by Liberal rule. Republicans had begun to gain widespread support among the working classes in urban areas and the mines, with Bautista Saavedra hailed as a savior and patron.[16] Many highland indigenous communities opposed Liberal rule since prominent party members had been the principal purchasers of communal lands under the 1874 Disentailment Law.[17] Saavedra thus maintained ties with the Cacique Apoderado movement, whose leaders were seeking legal support in their efforts to reverse the expropriation of communal land and the persecution of indigenous leaders. The indigenous communities and workers' groups to whom Republicans had turned for support grew increasingly restless toward the end of the decade as the government deployed troops to break strikes among mining, railway, and telegraph workers in 1919 and 1920.[18] Adopting incendiary language in the press and legislature, Republicans fanned these conflagrations in order to further erode Liberals' hold on power.

In February 1920, Republicans seized another opportunity to grandstand against Liberals' corruption of the armed forces and exploitation of indigenous communities. On the floor of the Chamber of Deputies, Abel Iturralde and Bautista Saavedra accused powerful Liberal landowner Benedicto Goitia and his son-in-law Lieutenant Colonel Julio Sanjinés of using the Abaroa Cavalry Regiment in Guaqui as a personal police force to repress their indigenous enemies.[19] Announcing that indigenous leader Prudencio Callisaya had died in the Abaroa barracks, the Republicans demanded an investigation.[20] Callisaya, as *apoderado* (representative) of the Sullkata *ayllu*, had been filing petitions and lawsuits against Goitia's land claims for at least six years when the local police arrested him on February 4, 1920, and then transferred him to the Abaroa Regiment. Around eleven o'clock the next morning, a soldier found Callisaya dead in his cell. Military officials claimed that he had hung himself from a beam with his sash, but Callisaya's family testified to having seen cuts on his corpse and his mouth filled with blood.[21] In making Callisaya's death a national scandal, Republicans positioned themselves not only as the defenders of indigenous communities' property claims but also as the restorers of an apolitical army that would protect the people rather than the politically connected.

During six years in opposition, Republicans cultivated allies among conscripts, workers, and indigenous groups as part of their quest for political power. In the process, they sought out and amplified soldiers' grievances. In a different political climate, incidents such as Santalla's beating and Callisaya's death may have appeared in military justice records or *apoderados'* petitions but would not have been debated in the press or the halls of the legislature. Partisanship gave these episodes a heightened visibility and transformed them into public scandals. Republican politicians promised to better serve the army by dismissing corrupt officers, focusing on national defense rather than internal repression, and ensuring that conscripts received the treatment they deserved as honorable soldiers of the *patria*.

BAUTISTA SAAVEDRA AND CONSCRIPT MUTINIES

Shaking the army's hierarchical structure, conscripts were active agents in the 1920 coup that ended Liberal rule and installed a junta led by Bautista Saavedra. Intense political conflict marked the ensuing months, which also saw the prosecution of mutiny charges against two groups of La Paz–based conscripts due to suspicions that their actions had been politically motivated. Although both groups made service-related demands, they sought to resolve grievances through direct contact with patrons outside of the military, which was, by definition, overt insubordination. The demands they voiced suggest a sense of entitlement to dictate the terms of service. The new administration intensely scrutinized these conscripts' actions and political ties because their loyalty to particular officers or political groups could mean regime change.

The son of a minor government functionary and a mother characterized by contemporaries as of "American blood," Bautista Saavedra had an accent characteristic of Aymara speakers and was known as a *cholo*.[22] Yet he was clearly a member of the intellectual class, having attended the prestigious Colegio San Calixto and earned a law degree at the Universidad Mayor de San Andrés.[23] Convinced of the impossibility of electoral victory due to fraud, Saavedra had been cultivating military contacts since 1918 but was unpopular with much of the officer corps—unsurprising, given his intense criticism of the army's administration. However, he eventually recruited Lieutenant Colonels Gumercindo Heguigarre and Andrés Valle, who swayed several other officers.[24] Saavedra's campaigns on behalf of the popular classes had already won the support of many among the rank-and-file troops—so many that Republicans writing the history of the 1920 "revolution" could claim that "there wasn't a conscript who didn't show ardent enthusiasm for the future triumph of the Republican Party."[25] The night of July 12, Colonel Valle, along with Colonel Juan J. Fernández and two captains, went to the Campero Regiment's barracks, stripped the officer on guard of his weapon, and woke the troops with orders to arm themselves. Valle delivered a rousing speech and then marched the 780 conscripts to the city center; en route, they reportedly yelled, "Long live the great Republican Party! Down with the doctrinaire thugs!"[26] Separating into companies, they quickly took 230 police officers prisoner in their barracks and convinced the NCO School and Colorados Regiment to join the coup, encountering only minor resistance from some Military Academy cadets.[27]

As part of efforts to secure his rule, Saavedra formalized the status of an armed group of supporters that would come to be called the Republican Guard. The day after the coup, he placed his steadfast ally Colonel Valle in command and assigned several loyal cadets to this unit, which quickly grew to a force of 750 men.[28] In a dramatic projection of power, Saavedra established its headquarters in the La Merced church, only a block from the presidential and legislative palaces in Plaza Murillo.[29] The September 1920 *La Razón* article announcing the creation of the Republican Guard declared that it would consist of former conscripts, be subject to military discipline, and primarily serve a policing role. Few were convinced by claims that the force was apolitical and that "Republican" in the name was unrelated to the party.[30]

Despite the creation of the Republican Guard, the national army was still a powerful force, and the majority of high-ranking officers had strong ties to Liberals.[31] However, Saavedra had widespread support among the lower ranks, with many conscripts expressing a sense of personal loyalty to him.[32] He cultivated this relationship by directly addressing the troops the day after the coup to thank them for their "noble sacrifice."[33] Shaped by the electoral violence of the past five years, many conscripts entered the barracks with partisan leanings. Once there, they also developed patron-client relationships with the officers who trained them. Interwoven with these factors were the ties of friendship and rivalry among soldiers that could also affect each man's decisions. Saavedra's attempt to consolidate power created situations in which conscripts' multiple allegiances could come into conflict. Discontent smoldered as their officers received new postings and many favorites were banished to frontier units.

Within weeks of the coup, however, prominent Republicans expressed discontent with the junta's membership and decision-making, laying the groundwork for a vicious battle to lead the party.[34] To ensure the continued support of the regiments in La Paz, Saavedra placed trusted followers among the ranks to "watch the commanders, officers, and troops as spies" in August 1920. Some of these men had completed their obligatory military service and become NCOs through reenlistment (rather than professional training); others who had not yet finished their initial term of service also received promotions. One of these spies, twenty-three-year-old tailor Miguel Carreón, testified that he and his fellows routinely visited Saavedra's home to ask for payment of the promised salary and to report on their findings.[35] The existence of Saavedra's spies among the troops likely did not remain secret and must have created a climate of fear among officers who did not know who was surveilling whom. The dual roles of these spies made a mockery of military hierarchy, unofficially placing subalterns outside of the command structure and asking them to monitor their superiors.

Trouble began in the Campero Regiment in October 1920 when a new commander took charge and several favored officers found themselves relegated to the frontier. Meeting in the dorms, guard room, and supply depot, soldiers and NCOs spread rumors about their new commander, Lieutenant Colonel Carlos de Gumucio, calling him a tyrant and hatching a plan to reject his command.[36] In clear acts of mutiny, the armed soldiers yelled in unison during combined exercises that they wanted to speak with their former commander, Major Ovando. When Ovando arrived, he scolded the soldiers for their indiscipline and assured them that Gumucio was "not as bad as they imagined him to be."[37] The soldiers complied with the punishment of forced standing for their insubordinate acts, but five of them later traveled to Bautista Saavedra's house to negotiate. Having fought on Saavedra's behalf in July, they made a direct and personal appeal that Ovando be reinstated and that orders assigning one of their sublieutenants, Manuel Heguigarre, to a frontier garrison be revoked.[38] Far from rebuking this blatant violation of military hierarchy, Saavedra received them graciously. He patiently explained that a regiment as important as Campero needed to be commanded by a lieutenant colonel rather than a major. Nor could their request regarding Heguigarre be fulfilled since he had "cheered for Montes and the Liberal Party," and there could not be "traitorous officers in the army." Despite refusing their requests, Saavedra attempted to retain their loyalty by encouraging them to visit him again if they had any concerns and even rewarding them with five bolivianos to "have a beer in [his] name."[39]

Neither Saavedra nor the three officers who mediated the troops' public act of mutiny reported these incidents up the command structure.[40] Saavedra's respectful treatment of the five conscripts suggests his conviction that the loyalty of the rank and file could keep him in power or facilitate his downfall. Saavedra and the officers likely chose not to report these incidents because they were each in the process of maneuvering for position—albeit at different levels—and hoped to manage these conscripts' demands to their own advantage. The actions of these conscripts suggest their confidence in their position as supporters of Saavedra.[41] Emboldened by their connection to him and their role in the July coup, these soldiers freely admitted to spreading rumors about their new commander, making collective demands about the regiment's leadership, and personally petitioning a member of the ruling junta regarding matters internal to the unit. Their low position in the military hierarchy seemed not to affect their sense of entitlement to make demands.

This episode occurred immediately prior to the election of delegates to the national convention that would reform the 1880 Constitution and elect the next president. Daniel Salamanca, José María Escalier, and Bautista Saavedra were all vying for the position. Divisions between these leaders were not only personal but also regional, with Saavedra supporters concentrated in La Paz, Salamanca backed by his native Cochabamba, and Escalier strongest in the south. Although Saavedra secured the presidency, this contentious convention led to a permanent split among Republicans, with Salamanca forming the Genuine Republican Party.[42]

Both displaced Liberals and dissident Republicans looked to the military to regain power. The first attempt to overthrow Saavedra occurred the same month he assumed the presidency—January 1921—when Lieutenant Colonel Juan José Fernández, who had been a principal supporter of the July 1920 coup, marched a battalion to Plaza Murillo with plans to force Saavedra into exile. Colleagues persuaded him to desist, but his actions proved that Saavedra rightly feared conspiracies among the officer corps.[43] Seeking to shore up his precarious rule, the new president began directly interfering in the

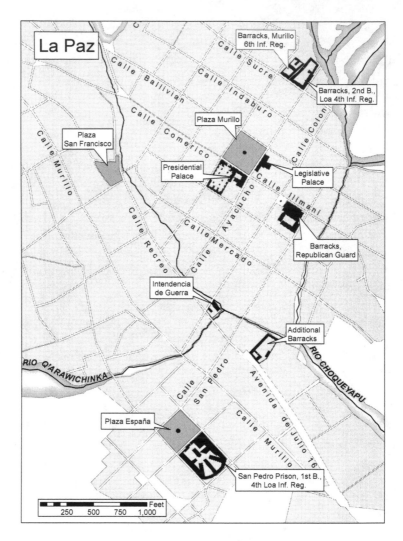

FIGURE 3.1. Street Map of La Paz, 1912. The NCOs were being held near Plaza Murillo. Map by George Milne, adapted from *La Paz, 450 años, 1548–1998*, 1:128.

military, to the extreme of personally dictating the movement of troops and asking loyal officers to disobey orders from the high command.[44]

In February 1921, Saavedra moved to contain dissident officers by appointing General Hans Kundt as chief of staff and expediting his application for Bolivian citizenship.[45] As leader of the 1911 mission, Kundt was on leave in Germany when the mission was recalled from Bolivia at the outset of World War I. In late May 1920, Kundt renounced his German citizenship and embarked for Bolivia as a private citizen to investigate business schemes.[46] France's delegation strongly objected to Kundt's assumption of a military post in Bolivia as a violation of the Treaty of Versailles, but British diplomats encouraged the move, arguing that he would "keep the army out of politics and prevent further disturbances."[47] On the contrary, Kundt would become essential to keeping Saavedra in power and looked to US military observers like the "pillar upon which rests the stability of the government."[48]

Kundt and Saavedra's ability to control the army faced an important test two months after he took office. With promises of discharge for *antiguos* (conscripts in their second year of service) left unfulfilled and rumors circulating that soldiers' wages would soon be cut by twenty cents, conscripts from the Murillo and Loa Regiments apparently planned a display of force for March 5 to air their grievances. However, a recently discharged conscript denounced it as a revolutionary plot, which led to the arrest of the conscripts serving as head NCO (*primero*) of each company on March 2. Hearing rumors that the captive NCOs were being abused and might be summarily executed, some of their fellows in the Loa Regiment went to bed clothed, rising at 12:45 a.m. to cut the barracks' telephone wires, arrest the officers as they slept, and break open boxes of ammunition with machetes.[49]

At least two hundred soldiers from the Loa Regiment's second battalion broke out of the barracks and went next door to the Murillo barracks (see figure 3.1), yelling, "Wake up *compañeros*." About ninety answered the call. They headed to the San Pedro Prison (el Panóptico) to awaken Loa's first battalion, which was garrisoned there. Bands of conscripts then wandered the streets, setting up machine guns at important corners. Awoken in their homes by the shots, officers made their way to the Loa barracks, freed the captives, and organized the remaining soldiers. The Republican Guard and companies from the Pérez and Reserve Regiments also participated in efforts to contain the uprising, aptly demonstrating why leaders stationed several different units in La Paz. Encamped in Plaza Murillo, where the NCOs were being held, the largest group refused to surrender until the president responded to their demands. The officers convinced them to name two representatives to go to Saavedra's house, where he apparently ceded to their requests. By 5:00 a.m., the soldiers had returned to the barracks and relinquished their arms. They were eating a breakfast of bread and tea when General Kundt arrived and spoke to the troops, followed by President Saavedra and Minister of War Pastor Baldivieso. The soldiers repeated their demands: that the NCOs be released, that wages not be cut, that *antiguos* receive a quick discharge, and that the Loa Regiment return to Oruro under its former commander.[50]

In a copious investigation that lasted three months, military courts recorded almost five hundred pages of testimony and asked detailed questions about political ties, civilian interference, and statements made during the mutiny. The results suggest a mixture of political and service-related motivations. More importantly, they show how the July coup and eight months of open struggle for control of the government and military had thrown these regiments into disarray and encouraged insubordination: these conscripts openly professed partisan allegiances, agitated for discharge, complained about labor conditions, and made personal demands on the president, minister of war, and chief of staff. The length of the investigation and the questions posed reveal a pervasive fear that individual conscripts might conspire with officers and politicians to overthrow the government.

Two conscripts testified that a major and two civilian legislators from Salamanca's Genuine Republican Party had instructed them to incite the troops as part of a revolutionary plot; however, they later retracted these statements, claiming to have lied after being "bribed and threatened by personages offering immediate freedom."[51] Whether or not these two Murillo conscripts participated in a plot to overthrow Saavedra, the roots of the uprising lay in the mutineers' social background and the ways that political upheaval had directly touched their lives. Not one of the mutineers who testified in the proceedings lacked the ability to sign his name, which suggests that the leaders hailed from the upper strata of Bolivian society. They likely were accustomed to making demands and participating in politics. In fact, testimony revealed that party loyalties had caused rifts among the ranks: several soldiers accused a peer of threatening to kill Saavedra because he thought that Salamanca should be president.[52] Others, such as nineteen-year-old conscript Domingo Peña from Santa Cruz, asserted allegiance to Saavedra's faction, professing to be "one of the most fervent supporters of the current cause."[53]

Yet the effects of the 1920 coup reached beyond conscripts who had strong partisan ties; political maneuvering had created service-related grievances that made the March mutiny possible. Conscripts in the Loa Regiment had been particularly affected. In February, someone (likely Saavedra) had ordered the unit's removal from Oruro due to evidence that some of its officers were plotting with Luis Calvo, the department's recently deposed prefect.[54] When the regiment arrived in La Paz, it was physically separated into two barracks, leading to rumors that the "President didn't trust the Regiment."[55] In the months leading up to the mutiny, then, political intrigue had caused the Loa conscripts to have an unfamiliar commander foisted on them, be drawn into a revolutionary plot, be uprooted from their barracks and separated from their fellows, and discover that promises of discharge were going unfulfilled. When rumors of wage cuts and the sudden imprisonment of their NCOs were added to this mix, their mutiny should not have come as a shock. The testimony of nearly every conscript involved suggests an atmosphere of general discontent among the ranks and widespread murmuring for the discharge of *antiguos*.

The mutineers' demands reflected a profound sense of privilege rather than the ideal of subordination. These men were products of the partisan conflict of the past five years and, more immediately, the political turmoil and plotting that had characterized their time in the barracks. Like the Campero soldiers four months before, these conscripts made demands about the conditions of service, expressed loyalty to particular officers, showed little respect for military hierarchy, and contacted political authorities directly. The two incidents differed in many ways, however. Whereas the Campero conscripts had a personal relationship with Saavedra and therefore likely felt untouchable, the 1921 mutineers were in a more precarious political position; their regiment was suspected of plotting with Calvo and at least one conscript was clearly against Saavedra. Perhaps for that reason they planned to take up arms in order to voice their complaints.

Unlike the Campero mutiny, that of the Loa and Murillo Regiments had major repercussions beyond the barracks. Too public to be concealed, the mutiny made headlines for months and was debated in the legislature.[56] Saavedra used the mutiny as an opportunity to exile suspect officers, which produced a standoff with his minister of war, who demanded their return and amnesty for all participants. Saavedra had to capitulate to stay in power and thus granted amnesty on September 1, 1921, to all officers and conscripts involved.[57] After this disappointment, he worked to weaken the national army while building up the Republican Guard as a force loyal only to him. Within a year of the mutiny, Saavedra and his supporters had slashed the military budget, reduced the length of military service, and cut the army from seven thousand conscripts to three thousand.[58] Rumor even had it that the weapons issued to army soldiers in La Paz were rendered inoperable.[59] By 1923, the Republican Guard was better armed, better paid, and larger than the regular army.[60]

SOCIAL REPRESSION AND THE 1930 COUP

During the remainder of Saavedra's presidency (1921–1925) and that of his successor, Hernando Siles (1926–1930), acts of conscript mutiny disappear from military justice records.[61] Although literate soldiers likely continued to act in insubordinate ways and call on the discourse of citizenship rights in order to express service-related grievances, political leaders were secure enough in their rule that such incidents were no longer perceived as politically motivated. Despite intra-elite disputes, the army successfully deployed throughout the period to subdue strikes and uprisings by mobilized workers in the mines and rural areas, demonstrating that the factions vying for dominance all shared a vision of the nation that did not include independent action from below.

Having gained the support of workers and highland indigenous communities during his rise to power, Saavedra soon revealed his alignment with the liberal project for the nation. Like his predecessors, he would not hesitate to use force to suppress political dissent and internal unrest; army units thus regularly deployed to the countryside and mines. The first major incident occurred just a week after the Loa mutiny disturbed La Paz. Approximately three thousand indigenous community members in Jesús de Machaca, located about fifty miles from the city, burned villagers' homes and killed the *corregidor*, his family, and sixteen others. This indigenous community had quickly recognized the junta after the July coup and had repeatedly denounced abuse by Liberal administrators and villagers. Saavedra responded forcefully to the rebellion, however, sending Colonel Vitaliano Ledezma in command of one hundred soldiers from the Abaroa Cavalry Regiment. Although estimates of these troops' destructive force vary widely, Choque and Ticona's measured evaluation has settled on around eighty deaths, the loss of thousands of livestock, and the destruction of hundreds of community members' homes. Seventy men were arrested as agitators and tried in La Paz.[62]

As shown by historian Robert Smale, miners also had high hopes for the Saavedra administration but soon learned that labor's victories after the July coup would not continue. After management fired twenty-six workers for participating in May Day celebrations in Uncía (Potosí), the government responded to workers' request for mediation by sending 220 soldiers from the Ballivián Cavalry Regiment in late May. The structure of this military deployment allowed management to court the regiment's sympathy by providing comfortable facilities and abundant food. These efforts were quite successful. In what became known as the Uncía Massacre, troops killed at least six miners on June 4 when they opened fire on a crowd demanding the release of union leaders and sympathizers. In Smale's words, Saavedra's open support for the mining companies effectively "smother[ed] the Central Labor Federation of Uncía's remnants."[63]

The struggle to control dissidence in the armed forces also continued. Accusing the two senior cohorts of military cadets of plotting a coup, Chief of Staff Hans Kundt dismissed them in August 1922 and made the remaining classes swear loyalty to Saavedra.[64] In February 1924, members of the opposition torched the Republican Guard's barracks and shot the unit's commander, Saavedra's loyal ally Lieutenant Colonel Andrés Valle.[65] Only a week later, Liberal General Óscar Mariaca Pando staged a border rebellion in Yacuíba (Tarija). Then, fanning the flames of separatism in Santa Cruz, Genuine Republicans with the support of five army colonels seized the provincial capital in July 1924. In personal command of a thousand soldiers, Kundt easily suppressed the first rebellion and was organizing to do the same in Santa Cruz when Saavedra brokered a political solution.[66]

The administration of Saavedra's successor, Hernando Siles, faced similar challenges from a divided military and mobilized populace. Most prominent was the July 1927 rebellion in Chayanta (northern Potosí), which began when three hundred community Indians occupied several farms, put the landlords on trial, and ritually executed several men. Given the national network of indigenous leaders, the rebellion spread rapidly; by the end of August approximately ten thousand Indians from four of Bolivia's nine departments had participated. Deploying troops from La Paz, Sucre, and Oruro, the army quelled the uprising by early September, killing more than three hundred rebels in the process. They arrested almost two hundred as instigators and took them to Sucre for trial. Although early reports depicted the rebellion as a communist threat, the government chose to deemphasize these links during the trial, instead blaming the uprisings on centuries of abuse by landlords, *corregidores*, and priests. Siles, constructing himself as a magnanimous father figure, granted amnesty in October 1927 to all of the Indians accused of leading the rebellion. In the amnesty decree, he denied the capacity of these men to be political actors, arguing that they were only reacting to abuse. Therefore, he concluded, the state should offer them protection rather than punishment "due to their inferior social condition." Despite the government's silencing of these ties, several of the indigenous leaders of the rebellion had had direct contact with radical artisans and intellectuals, with whom they had discussed the redistribution of wealth, the return of land to the *ayllus*, and the construction of rural schools. Some *ayllu* representatives had even attended the Third Workers' Congress in April 1927. Although historians differ over the importance of labor leaders' influence, they agree that Indian *comunarios* and *colonos* were the primary actors in and leaders of the Chayanta rebellion.[67]

Unable to control new ties among labor, student, and rural groups, Siles found himself facing mobilized opposition quite different from traditional partisan conflict. As part of plans to extend his presidency, he stepped down on May 28, 1930, leaving the government in the hands of a Council of Ministers, which included Kundt's allies Colonels Carlos Banzer and David Toro.[68] This move laid bare the factions in the army, with opposition officers objecting to Banzer and Toro's presence on the council as unconstitutional and General Kundt abandoning all pretense of impartiality to back Siles openly.[69] The main student group declared a strike on June 12 and organized a series of demonstrations in La Paz that culminated on Sunday, June 22, when riot police opened fire in Plaza Murillo, killing several students.[70] The coup everyone knew was coming started when the Camacho and Aroma Regiments in Oruro declared themselves in revolt on June 24 and their officers issued coordinated demands for a military junta under specific officers, all of whom had ties to the Liberal or Genuine Republican Parties.[71] The officers' justification was steeped in what Fredrick Nunn calls "professional militarism," a discourse that portrays the army as the incarnation and the ultimate guardian of the *patria*.[72] Their statement read, "Our duty guides us to save the *patria* at the cost of our own blood. . . . We very much regret that we are the only ones in the Army who understand our duty to the *patria* at this time. Our cause is completely apolitical, as proven by our appeal for a military government."[73]

Seeking to retain control over La Paz, Kundt attempted to expel various Military Academy cadets and two officers for seditious acts; in response, the cadets moved to take the city center, meeting with opposition from the NCO School and part of the Pérez Regiment. When ordered by Kundt to take the Military Academy early the next morning (June 26), a group of captains and lieutenants in the Pérez Regiment joined the rebellion, turning their weapons on the other officers in the regiment. Two hundred soldiers from the Pérez Regiment under the rebellious officers headed to the Aviation School in El Alto to coordinate the coup.[74] Kundt and Siles held out until the early morning of June 27, when they fled for various embassies to head into exile.[75]

Led by General Carlos Blanco Galindo, the new junta consisted of six officers, most of whom had suffered exile or forced retirement at some point in the previous decade.[76] The junta declared an end to military interference in politics, appointed a panel of civilian advisers, began preparing for elections, and encouraged the political parties to produce a unity presidential slate. The resulting ticket brought together former enemies from the Liberal, Republican, and Genuine Republican parties: it proposed the presidency of Daniel Salamanca with Ismael Montes and Bautista Saavedra as vice presidents.[77] However, renewed divisions soon emerged as Liberals used the economic pressures of the Great Depression to advocate for substantial reductions in the military budget. Junior officers vociferously objected to salary reductions, and Major Oscar Moscoso published an open letter threatening strife within the army if the administration followed through with the cuts.[78] The military was anything but apolitical, with officers openly participating in partisan conflict throughout the decade.

CONSCRIPT MUTINIES ON THE EVE OF THE CHACO WAR

The 1930 coup produced an atmosphere of political uncertainty in many ways similar to that of a decade before. As a result, military authorities again intensely scrutinized acts of insubordination by formally educated conscripts, fearing that they might be signs of a countercoup. These suspicions produced court martial testimony that helps to delineate the contours of a culture of insubordination that had emerged among this class of conscript. The actions and words of these soldiers, all of whom were literate men from capital cities, suggest a common sense of entitlement as citizens to dictate who would command them, protest how their superiors exercised authority, and demand their "rights" regarding food, labor, equipment, and wages.[79] They called on the discourse of honorable citizen soldiers to argue that the *patria* had not fulfilled its side of the bargain.

The first major incident occurred just two months after the coup, at a point when fears still ran high that Siles and Kundt's supporters might stage a countercoup.[80] For that reason, military authorities and even a member of the junta thoroughly investigated when ten conscripts stationed as guards at the Aviation School, located on the outskirts of La Paz in El Alto, took up arms against Sublieutenant Juan Antonio Rivera on Sunday, September 7. Although the examining magistrate repeatedly asked the accused and witnesses "if anyone outside of the School had influenced the insubordination," conscripts and officers alike asserted the internal nature of the incident.[81] To celebrate a birthday on Saturday night, the soldiers had bought a crate of beer, various bottles of wine, and the fixings for sandwiches.[82] Around ten o'clock the next morning, three high-ranking officers (including two members of the ruling junta) arrived to inspect the troops. They questioned Carmelo Menacho, a nineteen-year-old student from Santa Cruz who was the unit's *primero*, as to whether the troops had any ammunition, indicating their suspicions that something more than a party might have been afoot. Upon receiving a negative answer, they retired from the Aviation School, leaving in charge Sublieutenant Juan Antonio Rivera, who had accompanied them on the inspection.[83] Rivera, who had no previous relationship with this group of conscripts, later reported that he tried to discipline them after being told "in an insolent tone that they were still drunk."[84] The soldiers eventually complied with the punishment of forced standing that Rivera imposed, but when he ordered them to continue their punishment after lunch, they contested his orders, saying that this was abusive treatment; since it was a Sunday afternoon, they were off duty and wanted to sleep.[85] Rivera then hit soldier Raimundo Ríos with his saber. When he moved to hit Ríos a second time, the others rallied to defend their fellow, raising their rifles against the officer, taking his saber, and checking his pockets for weapons.[86] When the Aviation School's director, Major Jorge Jordán, arrived on the scene several hours later, the soldiers claimed to have armed themselves "against the commander of the guard, who has abused us." They turned over their arms and ammunition to Jordán, who arrested them for mutiny.[87]

Although records of the incident exist because of fears that it might have been politically motivated, the roots of this mutiny were located in ideas about social class, friendship, and the exercise of legitimate authority. The ten soldiers involved had entered the ranks eight months earlier, completed the initial training period, and been assigned to guard the Aviation School, presumably because they came from relatively privileged backgrounds. Hailing from the cities of La Paz, Oruro, Cochabamba, and Santa Cruz, they were all literate and claimed occupations such as student, clerk, telegraph operator, and mechanic.[88] These conscripts apparently enjoyed significant independence in the Aviation School and felt no compunction about bringing alcohol into the barracks and holding a party in the dormitory. They expressed no shame and offered no apology after high-ranking officers discovered their offense. And when an unfamiliar subaltern officer attempted to impose his authority, they repeatedly displayed defiance. Combined with their lack of respect for Rivera, their bonds of friendship, forged over alcohol but also during military training, hours of guard duty, and free time in the dormitories, compelled them to defend a fellow soldier against what they saw as abuse of authority.

The actions and attitudes adopted by these conscripts suggest a failure of military ideals of discipline and obedience. The mutineers' testimonies during the proceedings lack contrition and respect for rank; they do not even read as strategically sound statements calculated to appeal for leniency in a mutiny trial. After being indicted on the charges, the soldiers took the defiant step of writing a letter to the Liberal *El Diario* that emphasized Rivera's abuse and their own off-duty status.[89] In their letter and testimonies, these men actively claimed rights as soldiers that superseded obedience to military hierarchy. They argued, "We took this position due to the . . . bad behavior" and "abuses of Lieutenant Rivera, who prevented us from going to the city, despite the fact that we should have been off duty, . . . was trying to make us do forced standing again," and "insulted us" and "committed outrages" against Ríos.[90] In their reading of the mutiny, the fault lay with Rivera.

Even though the evidence suggests purely internal triggers for the Aviation School mutiny, testimony indicates that some of the conscripts were considering taking advantage of the situation to stage a general mutiny, perhaps with political overtones. Several soldiers in the NCO School who were visiting the Pando Regiment that Sunday afternoon later testified that one of the mutineers had entered the regiment to ask a Pando conscript for help "with the mutiny because they were treated badly." Witnesses reported that the Pando soldiers refused, citing the short period of time left before they would be discharged.[91] Had the mutineers found support, however, the incident might have triggered a larger uprising, as had occurred with the Loa Regiment in 1921.

The turbulent political climate so elevated this incident that rumors flew through La Paz that the soldiers had long been coordinating a mutiny.[92] The personnel appointed to the indictment process directed pointed questions to that effect and ferreted out dozens of witnesses to independently confirm the sequence and tenor of events. Despite the fact that the accused conscripts had admitted to actions that clearly fell under the legal definition of mutiny, the military tribunal, finding no evidence of political involvement, ultimately determined that their acts of insubordination against Rivera did not constitute a mutiny. The tribunal found them guilty of insubordination and drunkenness during acts of service. Pointing to Rivera's behavior as a mitigating factor, it sentenced the participants to three months' confinement, which would be doubled for Carmelo Menacho, who, as the ranking conscript, was considered the ringleader.[93]

This incident at the Aviation School took place as the country's financial and political situation was deteriorating. The unity ticket fell apart by the end of September 1930, and the junta rejected Saavedra publicly in a Liberal daily: "The Army is dissatisfied with the name of Señor Saavedra . . . The Army wants men who have already been tried in government not to act anymore."[94] Thus on election day in January 1931, Genuine Republican Daniel Salamanca shared the ticket with Liberal José Luis Tejada Sorzano and ran basically unopposed.[95] Characterized by anticommunism, the suppression of strikes, and expensive plans to establish forts in the Chaco, the Salamanca administration also saw increasing rifts within the army as officers joined opposing secret lodges of the type common throughout South American militaries in the period.[96]

In this context, the Colorados Infantry Regiment in the Miraflores neighborhood mutinied the night of September 10, 1931. Explosions and shots rang out around midnight, and soldiers poured from the barracks. When authorities entered, they found Sublieutenant Noel Ríos shot dead; the two sentries on duty reported that the men had risen up because they had been made to "carry mud bricks for some new buildings going up in the barracks" and because they had not been "paid the usual wage [*socorro*]." By 4:00 a.m., Military Academy cadets and the soldiers in the NCO School had rounded up all but five of the mutineers. *La Razón*, which supported Salamanca's Genuine Party, cast doubt on the service-related motives proffered by the mutineers and instead suggested that the roots lay in communist propaganda.[97] Military authorities' fear of political subversion among the ranks was so great that they dissolved the prestigious Colorados Regiment on October 9 for "grave offenses against military honor and discipline" and dispersed its soldiers throughout the La Paz regiments.[98]

Less is known about this incident than the other three because the indictment proceedings are not among the archives of the military tribunal. Records do exist, however, from a related investigation of abuse of authority that was convened at the demand of the seventeen Colorados conscripts accused of inciting the mutiny. In a petition to the divisional commander, they vigorously protested that "only the soldiers will be judged and that the trial will not include certain officers of the regiment" who were the "true perpetrators" of the mutiny because their abuse forced the soliders "to assume a certain attitude that was nothing more than a reflexive and instinctive move to defend human dignity." They then listed service-related complaints such as forced labor, poor food, the failure to provide sandals, and unfairly garnished wages paid with considerable delay. The incident that immediately precipitated the mutiny, they maintained, was the "mistreatment, in a shameful and denigrating manner," of Corporal Gilberto Camacho by a sublieutenant on the day of the mutiny.[99] The military magistrate investigated their complaints but ultimately determined that their issues with wages, labor, and equipment all stemmed from legitimate orders or financial constraints and did not constitute exploitation or embezzlement by their superiors. He did recommend that the sublieutenant in question face a disciplinary hearing for having kicked a soldier but concluded that his actions did not merit indictment for abuse of authority.[100] Whether or not the Colorados mutiny had political undertones, testimony during the military justice proceedings reveals a haphazard and financially troubled institution in which acts of indiscipline were common and even urban troops regularly went without pay and performed extra duties.[101] Such was the state of the national army as President Salamanca moved toward war with Paraguay.

All of Bolivia's major political actors professed their desire for an apolitical army that would build a strong nation capable of defending its borders rather than serving the exigencies of a particular party or strongman. Intense partisan conflict after 1914, however, quickly revealed the insincerity of this goal. The factions all used the army to serve elite interests by repressing working-class and indigenous unrest. Outside of this shared interest, politicians sought military allies to guarantee that elections would swing their way, support their coup, or shore up their rule. Despite prohibitions on voting while in military service, officers and literate conscripts were partisan actors who exacted pressure on the government and participated in coup attempts based on patronage ties.

This era saw two successful coups and many other failed or rumored ones, all of which involved military officers. Yet it should not be seen as a return to nineteenth-century *caudillismo*. This army had many viable claims to professionalism. Although it certainly had factions, it was structurally and bureaucratically one army rather than the multiple forces of previous decades. Unlike in the nineteenth century, officers did not seek to rule; both coups led to the election of civilians. Yet as partisan politics grew contentious, the reassignment and discharge of officers for political reasons again became habit, so much so that Dunkerley's observation about the 1860s that "uninterrupted incorporation into the *escalafón* [list of active officers] [was] the exception rather than the rule" could easily have been referring to the 1920s instead.[102]

Another major difference was the direct involvement of some conscripts as active decision makers in these intrigues. An important contingent of the rank and file in the 1920s had patronage ties to political parties and clearly saw themselves as citizens of the Bolivian nation. These conscripts made claims based on a sense of entitlement; they submitted to the duty of service and in return expected a certain level of treatment. They thus called on their patronage networks to right perceived wrongs in the barracks and sometimes used their place in the barracks to benefit patrons in the civilian world.

The July 1920 coup directly engaged certain La Paz–based conscripts in partisan politics, as they forged personal ties with Bautista Saavedra by first playing an important role in the coup and then serving as his spies. These factors severely undermined military hierarchy and conscripts' respect for rank, as shown by the Campero soldiers' direct petitioning of Saavedra. For that reason, the Campero mutiny in October 1920—even though it involved the least extreme actions—is the most important for understanding the culture of insubordination that was emerging among the ranks of literate conscripts stationed in the conspiratorial confines of La Paz. As with all aspects of barracks life, attitudes toward authority were likely transmitted by *antiguos* to new members of the regiment along with rules about how to wear a uniform, march, and operate a rifle. Thus, when the tinder box created by Saavedra's cuts to the army's prestige, size, and budget was lit by the match of the March 1921 arrest of the ranking NCOs, the mutineers refused to stand down until they spoke personally with the president, chief of staff, and minister of war.

The parallel mutinies that followed the 1930 coup had far more tenuous connections to partisan politics. This difference perhaps stemmed from the disillusionment produced by Saavedra's tenure and a tumultuous decade marked by uprisings and political intrigue. In contrast to 1920, the 1930 coup was officer driven; conscripts followed rather than conspired. The 1930 and 1931 mutineers appeared to lack personal relationships with ruling politicians; none of the conscripts who testified in these later proceedings seem to have had connections to or made demands on high-ranking officers or politicians. Nor did they openly profess partisan leanings as had their predecessors.

Yet something about these two political moments determined that these groups of conscripts would be prosecuted for their actions. Barring one 1906 frontier mutiny over poor living conditions, none of the extant military justice cases alleging rebellion, sedition, mutiny, or even insubordination occurred prior to 1920. But records survive from twelve such cases after the July 1920 coup and from four following the June 1930 one, with only three in the intervening decade.[103] The Loa (1921) and Colorados (1931) mutinies, in which armed conscripts broke out of their barracks and took to the streets in the middle of the night, would have been significant events in La Paz no matter what the political context. The other incidents, however, occurred within the confines of the barracks and likely became the objects of military justice investigations only because they occurred amid political instability. When similar incidents occurred outside of these periods, commanders likely opted against formal investigation, instead choosing to deal with such matters through disciplinary councils or informal punishment.

Although military magistrates attempted to ferret out any sign of political motivations, the conscripts involved averred service-related complaints. Years of contentious partisan maneuvering, during which national and institutional politics became completely interwoven, made literate conscripts more willing to press their demands and to evaluate and refuse orders. In all four mutinies, the conscripts rejected military procedures, found alternate ways of expressing service-related grievances, and implicitly argued that officers had violated their rights as citizens. Crucially, while many of the mutineers demanded discharge, none rejected the legitimacy of the state's demand for their labor. They sought to negotiate the terms (rather than the very basis) of obligatory military service.

The focus of these moments on open insubordination by conscripts who were already Bolivian citizens gives the erroneous impression that most conscripts serving in La Paz were from the literate classes. In fact, the evidence suggests the opposite: the majority of men stationed in the seat of government were disenfranchised, like the majority of male Bolivians, by illiteracy and poverty.[104] However, formally educated conscripts who were already part of the electoral system were more likely than their illiterate counterparts to have partisan commitments. They were also more likely to draw on the citizen-soldier discourse in order to express their grievances. Although indigenous and illiterate conscripts were certainly among the hundreds of soldiers from the Loa, Murillo, and Colorados Regiments who broke out of the barracks in March 1921 and September 1931, the officers in charge of the military justice proceedings failed to ask any of them to testify, likely assuming they had mindlessly followed their more educated fellows. In many ways, this disregard drew on the same logic as the amnesty granted the Chayanta rebels. Both measures depended on a conviction that men with insufficient linguistic and cultural capital were not actors in their own right and could only react to abuse or inducement. Fears of partisan conspiracy motivated these mutiny investigations; in that context, only the conduct of those deemed political actors mattered.

The energetic investigation of these cases indicates authorities' awareness that these troops were neither docile nor under the complete control of their officers. Conscripts' manner of collective action indicates a host of social bonds that differed from case to case: some brought partisan leanings with them to the barracks, while others mutinied for camaraderie, loyalty to a favored officer, or even regimental pride. Conscription was effective in fostering solidarity, at least among literate soldiers, but the institution failed to channel these energies as officers, knee-deep in partisan intrigue, modeled conspiracy rather than institutional respect for hierarchy. These investigations of conscript-led mutinies reveal the indiscipline and political paranoia at the heart of the military's hierarchical structure.

CHAPTER 4

MOBILIZATION FOR THE CHACO WAR

The 1932–1935 Chaco War with Paraguay has long been remembered as an unmitigated failure by a weak and poorly integrated Bolivian state. The common narrative tells how the politically vulnerable Salamanca administration unnecessarily provoked the conflict and then violently wrenched highland indigenous men from their homes to serve on the front lines. It evokes images of incompetent officers carousing in the rearguard while poorly provisioned soldiers deserted en masse, driven mad by interminable thirst in the Chaco's hot sands. While capturing key dimensions of the conflict, this seemingly definitive vision has obscured how little we know about who fought, how they were mobilized, and what their experiences were in the field.[1]

We still lack even the most basic statistics on the Chaco War, such as the composition of the troops and how many Bolivians fought, died, deserted, and were captured. To deepen our understanding of the changes wrought by the war, we need a grounded history that encompasses both the experience of Bolivians incorporated into the rank and file and the methods of the state that deployed them. This chapter begins to address this challenge through a focus on mobilization in the highlands and the disciplining of soldiers in the field. In the process, it calls into question the image of Bolivia's wartime army as disproportionately composed of impressed indigenous soldiers. The government's ability to raise four successive armies for deployment in the Chaco—while balancing the need for men on the front with continued production in the mines and agriculture—should be viewed as a success, albeit a tragic one, on the part of what is commonly dismissed as a weak and poorly integrated state.

The Bolivian state made many compromises to accomplish unprecedented mass mobilization, in which it sent to war more than twenty times the number of conscripts it had been training on a yearly basis.[2] Its impressment practices were both ruthless and racialized; however, the central state's mobilization policies repeatedly attempted (although with only limited success) to produce an army less rural and less indigenous than the nation as a whole. The central state's surprising success in mass mobilization did not, however, extend to its ability to effectively deploy and care for its soldiers in the Cha-

FIGURE 4.1. Chaco region with approximate pre- and postwar borders and maximum advances of Bolivian and Paraguayan forces. Map by George Milne.

co. Data drawn from 101 wartime desertion proceedings suggest similarities between how the state mobilized its soldiers and how officers dealt with their resistance in the face of mismanagement, deprivation, and demoralization. Civilian leaders in La Paz and military commanders in the field recognized the impossibility of formal adherence to their own laws, decrees, and orders and instead relied on implementation by their subordinates, producing results that could only seem profoundly arbitrary to those affected.

ESTIMATING THE ARMIES' SIZE, CASUALTIES, AND COMPOSITION

The dispute with Paraguay over the Chaco Boreal dated back to independence, but a series of conferences and unratified treaties had done little to fix the border. Although both countries remember the conflict as a proxy war between Standard Oil and Royal Dutch Shell for export routes and imagined oil deposits, little convincing evidence has emerged to support this narrative.[3] Tensions had been high for a decade as both nations sent small groups of soldiers to establish outposts in the disputed area. The region represented an opportunity for Paraguay to repair its economy and to prevent further ter-

TABLE 4.1. Estimates for the Chaco War

	Estimated Population	Men Recruited 1932–1935	Percent Recruited	Deaths	Percent Dead	Deserters	Money Spent
Bolivia	2,000,000 to 2,500,000	162,083 to 250,000	6.5 to 12.5	50,000 to 60,000	20 to 37	10,000	$228 million
Paraguay	900,000	140,000 to 150,000	15.5 to 16.7	36,000 to 40,000	24 to 29	No estimates given	$128 million

Sources: Dunkerley, *Origines del poder militar*, 167; Querejazu, *Masamaclay*, 482–84; Quintana, *Soldados y ciudadanos*, 54; Wood, *United States and Latin American Wars*, 95; Zook, *Conduct of the Chaco War*, 149, 240–41.

ritorial losses after a crushing defeat in the War of the Triple Alliance (1864–1870). For Bolivia, the Chaco offered the possibility of securing a navigable port on the Paraguay River and thereby obtaining an export route. However, the proximate cause of the war was more political than strategic: Bolivian president Daniel Salamanca faced a hostile Congress, vocal groups of radicalized students and workers, and an economic crisis.[4] He had witnessed the nation's uniting behind Hernando Siles after a 1928 Paraguayan attack on a Bolivian outpost and knew that patriotic outrage could distract from partisan contention. Confident that Bolivia's superior resources, larger population, and German-trained army would guarantee it a swift victory, Salamanca used Paraguay's ouster of Bolivian forces from a lake they had taken from Paraguay the previous month as an excuse to take three other outposts.

Early victories for Paraguay (September to November 1932) gave way to an offensive in which Bolivia recaptured its original outposts and took three of Paraguay's (December 1932 to April 1933). At this point, Bolivian forces were only a hundred miles from Asunción (see figure 4.1). Yet this marked the apex of the war for Bolivia; the ensuing months brought repeated retreats and mass surrenders of its soldiers, equipment, and weapons. These humiliating defeats brought down not only General Hans Kundt, the German officer recalled from Europe to lead Bolivia's forces, but also Salamanca, whom the military ousted in late November 1934. By that time, Paraguay's troops had reached populated areas near the Andean foothills, holding far more ground than their country had ever claimed prior to the war. Yet Paraguay had also incurred heavy losses, faced long supply lines, and exhausted loans from Argentina. Both belligerents were thus prepared for peace when they met in Buenos Aires in May 1935. The armistice signed on June 12 provided mechanisms for demobilizing the armies, exchanging prisoners, and fixing the border. Negotiations over these terms stretched until the July 1938 signing of the peace treaty. It determined a border south of the 1935 truce line but still awarded Paraguay three-quarters of the Chaco Boreal and left Bolivia with a swamp rather than the desired port in the northwest.[5] Diplomatic mistakes, strategic blunders, and infighting had left Bolivia with far less land than it had held before its leaders provoked the war.[6]

The vast number of Bolivians who fought, died, fell prisoner, and deserted is fundamental to understandings of the event's impact. Scholars invoke these numbers to support claims regarding the transformative nature of the war and refer to high rates of desertion to assert soldiers' mistreatment and lack of identification with the cause.[7] Yet a systematic examination of the origins of these statistics reveals the precariousness of the most basic facts. In fact, estimates vary widely (see table 4.1) because poor record keeping has been compounded by a lack of systematic research. For example, sociologist Juan Ramón Quintana cites a 1936 memoir that claimed that official records document the recruitment of 162,083 men; however, he prefers David Zook and James Dunkerley's estimates of 250,000.[8] Several other sources offer an alternate estimate of 200,000.[9] Citations for these numbers, along with figures for the dead, all trace back to works published between 1937 and 1944 by Colonels Aquiles Vergara Vicuña and Julio Díaz Arguedas, neither of whom offer any basis for their estimates.[10] Few have even bothered to guess how many were evacuated due to wounds or disease.[11] Nor do scholars have any grasp of the actual scale of desertion, instead relying on an unexamined estimate of 10,000.[12] Calculations based on the estimates available suggest that Bolivia mobilized somewhere between a low of 6.5 and a high of 12.5 percent of its total population and that between 2 and 3 percent of the total population died.[13]

Although Bolivia fielded more men over the course of the war, its soldiers in the region never outnumbered those of Paraguay until the final months of the conflict.[14] The existence of Chaco armies, in the plural, is therefore a more accurate way to think about a war in which the Bolivian government at first opted for limited mobilization. Of course, estimates of these armies' sizes and casualty rates suffer from the same deficiencies as those for the war as a whole. According to the best information currently available, approximately 15,000 Bolivians participated in the first phase from June to December 1932. Although only around 2,500 died, few remained in the field for the next wave of mobilization; the rest had fallen prisoner or been evacuated due to wounds or illness.[15] The second phase of the war comprised General Hans Kundt's year of command, over the course of which approximately 77,000 men left for the region, 14,000 died, 10,000 fell prisoner, 6,000 deserted, and 32,000 were evacuated due to wounds or illness. This left an army of 7,000 in the field because the other 8,000 were dedicated to rearguard services.[16] Kundt's successor, General Enrique Peñaranda, fielded a third army of 45,000 to 55,000, and another 30,000 to 50,000 men participated in the final six months of the war.[17]

The lack of empirical studies on who fought in these armies has meant that impressions of the war have been overly influenced by postwar novels' and campaign diaries' relentless focus on the plight of indigenous soldiers. Augusto Céspedes's 1936 novel movingly invoked the "long line of impressed Indians."[18] Jésus Lara even titled his 1937 campaign diary *Repete* in reference to the nickname that formally educated soldiers used to describe their indigenous fellows, who, speaking little Spanish, supposedly said *"yo repete"* (I repeats) to plead for second helpings of *rancho* (communal meals).[19] Drawing on typical tropes, this nickname characterized indigenous soldiers as motivated only by primal needs. Citing these very narratives as evidence, historian Herbert Klein asserted in 1969 that "conscription of Indians" was "universal," thus setting the still-prevailing historical narrative as to the composition of the rank-and-file troops.[20] More recent scholarly publications have claimed that "the equation between indigenous and frontline was virtually absolute" and that "Andean indigenous footsoldiers . . . were its main protagonists."[21] A consensus has thus developed that Bolivia's forces were overwhelmingly composed of rural indigenous men who had been violently wrested from highland haciendas and communities.

Although many of Bolivia's soldiers hailed from the lowland departments of Santa Cruz and Tarija due to their proximity to the zone of operations, this chapter focuses on the highlands because of the importance of these soldiers' mobilization to narratives about the war. Images of the hardships they endured have been fundamental to reformist and revolutionary movements over the decades, featuring prominently in the writings of young intellectuals who would go on to lead the reformist Revolutionary Nationalist Party (MNR), the Trotskyist Revolutionary Workers Party (POR), and the Stalinist Party of the Revolutionary Left (PIR). Combining nationalism, *indigenismo*, and variants of socialism, they argued that a corrupt oligarchy had failed to modernize while selling the nation's wealth to foreign imperialists and maintaining colonial-style relations with abject indigenous masses.[22] They asserted that indigenous men had fought for Bolivia on the front lines while elites cowered in the rear guard or profited from bogus exemptions. Although intended to condemn the oligarchy for failing to educate and integrate the indigenous population, these narratives also implied that rural indigenous men had made for poor defenders of Bolivia's territory. For example, after arguing that "the *campesino*. . . . was forced to serve as a soldier on the front lines, to defend something unknown or to which he had no ties," MNR leader Augusto Cuadros Sánchez noted that "the vast majority of the thousands of peasant soldiers did not know how to shoot their rifles or if they did, they shot in the air, covering their heads."[23] This line of thought would later lead military historian David Zook to argue that Paraguay owed its victory to the "individual initiative" taken by "the soldier of a free country," who vanquished Bolivia's "politically, socially, and racially submerged" conscripts.[24] After the 1952 revolution, the new state's raison d'être would thus be to "improve" this population by integrating Indians into the nation's life, culture, and economy.[25] Although the proindigenous movements that gained prominence after 1970 offered scathing critiques of assimilationist programs, they also emphasized indigenous suffering in the Chaco as part of their portrait of an internally colonial state.[26] This narrative risks depicting indigenous soldiers as no more than victims and implicitly blaming them for Bolivia's loss.

The idea of a uniformly indigenous army also renders invisible the frontline service of men from other regions and social strata, especially members of the popular classes who might not have identified as indigenous. While rural indigenous men were certainly the largest single group in Bolivia's army, this must be understood within the country's demographic context. Both the 1900 and 1950 censuses categorized the bulk of the Bolivian population as rural and indigenous, so the fact that they predominated among the troops should come as no surprise.[27] Moreover, both the indigenous-army thesis and the census data assume a simple and easily differentiated binary between indigenous and non despite the fluid nature of these categories. Once in uniform, many Quechua- or Aymara-speaking men from urban areas, mining communities, and the countryside who may or may not have self-identified as indigenous would have been seen as such by the urban intellectuals who later wrote memoirs of the war.

Attempts to quantify the social status of the troops are stymied by the lack of comprehensive recruitment records.[28] However, data on prisoners of war show that even the later armies included not only agriculturalists but also many miners, tailors, mechanics, typographers, and students from all parts of the country, only some of whom would have identified or been identified as indigenous.[29] The thousands of telegrams sent by upper- and middle-class Bolivian families to inquire after their sons and husbands held captive in Paraguay indicate that these men had been close enough to the action to be captured, even late in the war.[30] Many were officers and noncommissioned officers, but quite a few were identified as part of the rank and file. For example, Alberto Aramayo Zalles in Buenos Aires sent an appeal to the archbishop of Asunción in November 1935 to advocate for the repatriation of his brothers Guillermo, José, and Ricardo. He identified José as a sublieutenant but asserted that Guillermo and Ricardo were foot soldiers.[31] Similarly, an influential lawyer from Cochabamba named Daniel Beltrán imposed on the archbishop to provide his son Julio with letters of recommendation, clothing, textbooks, and substantial sums of money. Julio had been serving as a rank-and-file soldier in the Rioja Battalion. His father begged the archbishop to look after Julio, explaining that he was "twenty-three, white, and already sick

TABLE 4.2. Calls for Mobilization for Bolivia's First Army
(June–December 1932)

	Date	Cohort	Ages	Category
1	July 22, 1932	1930–1931	20–21	Trained reservists
2	August 5, 1932	1927–1931	20–24	Trained and untrained reservists from department capitals only
3	September 23, 1932	1923–1926	25–28	Trained reservists nationwide and untrained reservists from departmental capitals only
4	November 18, 1932	1923–1932	19–28	All (trained and untrained reservists plus those who failed to register or present for service)

Sources: Supreme decrees of July 22, August 5, September 23, and November 18, 1932; these decrees are transmitted and discussed in various communications from the general staff to the prefect of La Paz in nos. 1663-32, 2091-32, 3300-32, and 3542-32, Prefecture-Admin box 208, ALP.

with malaria and was waiting to be sent to the rear guard" when he was cap-tured in January 1934.[32] Paraguayan records also include a set of seventy-two telegrams sent by Bolivian prisoners to their families after capture; all went to men and women with European surnames living in Bolivia's major cities. While Paraguayan officials likely granted these prisoners this privilege due to their social and cultural capital, less than a quarter identified themselves as officers.[33] Most of the men subject to mobilization during the Chaco War were certainly noncitizen soldiers. Yet these noncitizen soldiers would not all have identified as indigenous. Nor were well-educated and relatively wealthy men absent from the rank and file.

EARLY MOBILIZATION

After developing an effective mechanism for limited conscription and invest-ing in foreign missions to reorganize and train the army, elites grew confident in the ability of these forces to defend Bolivia's sovereignty. But mobilizing an army for war in a region far from population centers would prove a far more difficult task than filling the barracks each year. Limited calls for mo-bilization between June and December 1932 produced Bolivia's first army, which memoirs and media sources have depicted as wealthier, more educat-ed, and far less indigenous than the three subsequent armies raised. Yet ev-idence from desertion records and published oral histories provides details as to literacy, language, profession, and ethnicity that show that many men who identified as indigenous farmworkers from the highlands also presented when called.

TABLE 4.3. Literacy of Deserters, September 1932–January 1933

Professed Level of Literacy	Illiterate	Able to read "a little"	Not asked about literacy, but able to sign name	Fully literate
Percent of Deserters	38.7	16.1	24.7	20.4

The signatures of those in the third category range from shaky lettering to fluid calligraphy, with the latter dominant. Data drawn from: DES-15-016, 15-018, 15-021, 16-001, 16-003, 16-006, 16-007, 16-008, 16-009, 16-010, 16-011, 16-013, 16-014, 16-015, 16-017, 16-020, 16-021, 16-023, 16-026, TPJM-AHM.

President Salamanca and the Bolivian high command issued the first call for reservists in July 1932. This and all subsequent mobilization orders were published in the press and distributed to departmental prefects. The prefects forwarded them to the provincial subprefects to send to *corregidores*, who were to disseminate the calls to rural landowners, indigenous communities, and mining areas. Local authorities thus carried the responsibility for informing the population, producing recruits, and facilitating their travel. As shown in table 4.2, the first call encompassed only men who had recently completed military training. The next two decrees expanded the cohorts of trained reservists mobilized and called up men who had reported for obligatory military service but had been immediately discharged due to quotas. These calls for untrained reservists applied only to those residing in departmental capitals, however. This restriction likely stemmed from an assumption that urban dwellers would not only be easier to conscript, transport, and train but also make better soldiers than men from rural areas. Only in November did the call expand to encompass entire cohorts of both rural and urban men, including those who had previously failed to register or present for obligatory military service.[34]

The 1932 mobilization orders should have produced an army that, in comparison with the population as a whole, was disproportionately composed of urban reservists. Data gathered during ninety-eight desertion hearings held during the first phase of the war support this supposition but also show a remarkable diversity among the accused, who hailed from over fifty cities and rural communities in all of Bolivia's departments except Beni. As shown in table 4.3, the majority were at least semiliterate, with about 60 percent signing their name or claiming they could read and write. This level of literacy was far higher than that of the country's population: the 1900 census reported a literacy rate of just under 17 percent, and that figure was only up to 32 percent in 1950.[35] Farmworker was by far the most prevalent profession (46 percent), but bricklayers, traders, cobblers, carpenters, smiths, miners, mechanics, electricians, typographers, and students also numbered among these deserters. At least 65 percent had already completed military service, and none were identified as *omisos*, who had failed to register, or *remisos*, who had failed to

FIGURE 4.2. Newspaper clipping of Manuel (left) and Raúl Murillo, c. 1933. Personal collection of Rosa Marina Murillo, La Paz. Used with permission.

present.[36] Even if students and urban professionals were overrepresented in early contingents, archival sources show that they were nowhere near the majority of those who responded to these first mobilization orders.

Why did these men present for service? This question is far easier to answer for soldiers from urban areas. During the first months of the war, patriotic nationalism ran at a fever pitch in cities, creating an atmosphere that pressured men to present.[37] Memoirs and photographs depict crowds of men and women from a range of social classes enthusiastically bidding farewell to reservists.[38] Archival sources also document men's willingness to leave their homes, schools, and jobs to serve. For example, two cousins from Cochabamba were so determined to go to war that they gave up their studies in July 1932. Too young to enlist, they volunteered as paramedics but soon found a way to take up arms and join the frontline troops in order to "fulfill [their] duty to the *patria*."[39] Men from humbler backgrounds were also eager to present. For example, Manuel Murillo Ávila (pictured in figure 4.2 alongside his brother Raúl in a newspaper clipping) volunteered over the objections of his father, Eulogio Murillo, a hatmaker in La Paz, who wanted him to wait until his category was officially drafted. Manuel was one of the many who died during the war.[40]

The volunteers and reservists described in these sources hailed from the literate classes of elites, professionals, urban workers, and artisans—the same types of men that had demonstrated rank insubordination during the 1920s and early 1930s. In fact, they probably responded to calls for mobilization for the same reason that they had been insubordinate: because they saw themselves as citizen-soldiers with both rights and duties. The service-related complaints that had sparked their insubordinate behavior stemmed from a belief that they deserved better treatment as honorable servants of the *patria*. This self-image is the same one that inspired them to fight in the Chaco and that would radicalize many after they witnessed the botched conduct of the war.

Why men from the provincial highlands, especially indigenous farmworkers, chose to report for service is more difficult to assess due to the limitations of archival sources and oral histories. Although correspondence in the archives of the La Paz prefecture indicates that *corregidores* and subprefects regularly sent reservists to recruitment centers throughout the war, they efface the mechanisms, compromises, and individual choices that produced these recruits.[41] Similarly, service documents and the volumes related to mobilization simply list the name and sometimes the residence of reservists.[42] Knowing that Benedicto Flores came from Morococala (Oruro) and traveled to the front in August 1932 with five hundred other soldiers as part of the Fifteenth Infantry Regiment reveals little about how or why he mobilized.[43] What looks like orderly mobilization in these records likely obscures a wide range of circumstances among diverse actors, including patriotic volunteers, reluctant or coerced reservists, and men not eligible or fit for service.

On the other hand, many oral histories of rural highland soldiers reflect a retrospective narrative of voluntary presentation. While influenced by a postwar atmosphere that diminished the likelihood of acknowledging that a local authority had forced one to present, we should take such claims seriously, evaluating them alongside narratives of violent impressment. For example, anthropologists working among Aymara speakers in the 1960s report that one community claimed to have voluntarily sent fifty-four of its young men to fulfill early calls for mobilization.[44] And six of the ten veterans from rural Chuquisaca and Potosí whose oral histories Arze includes asserted that they presented, whereas only one admitted to being impressed.[45] For example, Victoriano Nava, who worked in agriculture in Ravelo, Potosí (near Sucre), remembers presenting at the age of seventeen even though his cohort had not yet been called. When pressed as to his motives, he responded, "Because of my friends . . . of course I went early."[46] Similarly, Luis Michel, who self-identified as an illiterate *campesino*, acknowledges that many of his fellow farmworkers in Zudáñez, Chuquisaca, "had taken to the hills" but distinguishes himself from them: "We, through our choice [*nuestro gusto*], went to present."[47]

Nava and Michel attributed their decision to enlist to ties of friendship and personal pride. Others may have felt pressure from local authorities and determined that they would have to serve by force if they did not present. Still others, having completed a year or more in the barracks, may have assimilated the state's narrative of patriotic service and presented out of a sense of duty. While local authorities of the La Paz department did not hesitate to report draft resistance by rural men, they mostly wrote of the "delirious patriotic enthusiasm" that accompanied the departure of local reservists after the first mobilization order.[48] A September 1933 letter from the indigenous community of Ichoca (Inquisivi, La Paz) presented the mobilization of 218 men from its canton as their "contribution [*aporte*] of blood."[49] Whatever men's motives for presenting were, the fact that these authorities and soldiers could assert that they had done so voluntarily reflects the functioning of the mobilization system. Bolivia's first Chaco army thus consisted of reservists from diverse regions and social classes, who, at least in retrospect, represented themselves as voluntarily mobilizing for war.

MADRINAS DE GUERRA

Elite and middle-class women played an important role in facilitating mobilization by serving as the *madrinas de guerra* (godmothers or sponsors of war) who provided financial, practical, social, and moral incentives for men to present for service.[50] Describing women who wrote to often unfamiliar soldiers in order to boost their morale, the term *madrina de guerra* has been used throughout the Spanish-speaking world, most prominently in the Spanish Civil War.[51] In Bolivia, the concept of *madrinas de guerra* drew on the country's system of ritual kinship (*compadrazgo*).[52] Women of varied age and marital status served as *madrinas*, forming both horizontal and vertical ties with their *ahijados* (godsons). As noted in chapter 2, women served as *madrinas* of a particular company or regiment during the 1920s. But this social institution came to flourish during the Chaco War, with some *madrinas* sponsoring entire units and others forming relationships with individual soldiers.

Memoirs of formally educated soldiers describe horizontal *madrina* relationships in which both parties were unmarried, young, and from a similar social class. These texts depict *madrinas* within the constraints of familiar narratives of women and war. They construct these *madrinas* as potential romantic partners excited by the prospect of forging relationships with valiant young men as they set off for battle. Roberto Böhrt, for example, writes of meeting local *madrinas* while training in Viacha. They gave him cigars and other goods; one even granted him a "passionate kiss." As his unit made its way to the front, Böhrt acquired another "beautiful" *madrina* in Tarija and remembers stimulating conversations over wine with her and other *madri-*

nas at a local club.[53] Similarly, Carlos Pozo depicts *madrinas* as flocking to his unit, which was filled with professionals and students. After hard days of training, these soldiers apparently spent hours in the *madrinas'* homes, only returning to the barracks in time for curfew.[54]

Yet archival evidence also reveals non-romantic relationships between *madrinas* and their *ahijados* that more closely resembled the traditional tie between godmother and godson than a flirtation between social equals. Although gifts were a part of horizontal *madrina* relationships, the financial aspect was most important when women sponsored men from a lower social class. Señora Esther B. Pereira, for one, sent twenty bolivianos to the archbishop of Asunción for him to pass on to her *ahijado* Quintín Cuba in the Posta Ybyravo prisoner-of-war camp.[55] Soldiers were not the only beneficiaries of *madrinas'* munificence. In at least one case, the wife of a mobilized soldier expressed hope that his *madrinas* would help her: Osdulia de Mercado, whose husband Luis had been a cobbler in Santa Cruz before the war, sent a letter in November 1932 that pleaded with him to recommend her to his *madrinas de guerra* so that they would attend to her needs.[56]

Madrinas also served as intermediaries and used their social status to learn of *ahijados'* fate.[57] For example, José Castedo, who was himself illiterate, must have found someone else to write in December 1932 to Señorita Yolanda Landibar, his *madrina* in Santa Cruz. In a letter laced with misspellings, he carefully gave her the names of his parents in Lorito (Chuquisaca) and begged her to reassure them that he was well.[58] How he expected her to accomplish this task is unclear, given that his family lived four hundred kilometers from his *madrina*. Raquel Villavicencio in La Paz performed a similar role, asking the archbishop of Asunción to "reduce the suffering of a mother who unites her pleas" with hers by informing them whether Pastor Conteras was among the prisoners taken in Cañada el Carmen.[59]

Some *madrinas* served in order to express their own patriotism and claim a public space for their participation in the Bolivian nation. At least one married, wealthy woman, Alicia Aramayo de Cariaga of Tupiza, presented being a *madrina* as a duty of her social class, a sort of noblesse oblige. She also deployed this charitable work in order to exchange it for personal favors. In the process of asking the archbishop in Paraguay to ensure that her own son was included on the list of injured prisoners being repatriated, she reminded him, "I always accept or write to *ahijados de guerra*—almost always the poorest and most defenseless."[60]

Although Bolivian *madrinas* likely all came from the literate classes, their relationships with their *ahijados* varied widely, depending on differences between their ages, social classes, and even regions. Some, like Raquel Villavicencio, had ties to soldiers' families, while others, like Yolanda Landibar, lived far from their *ahijados'* homes. Some were almost girlfriends while others could be sponsors, confidantes, or go-betweens. All of these *madrinas* incentivized and facilitated men's participation in the war. They also aided in the construction of soldiering as not only patriotic but also sexually attractive and essential to masculine honor. Not associated with the military or the state, this social institution grew up around wartime mobilization, overlaying the relationship between the soldier and his *patria* with a gendered relationship to a woman who could potentially serve as his patron and personal ally.

THE TURN TO IMPRESSMENT

Even in the earliest phase of the war, the state struggled to disseminate mobilization orders and keep track of its soldiers' identities. Those captured as evaders could thus credibly claim ignorance. For example, after being taken on the road between Tupiza and Atocha, Ambrosio Chambi, a monolingual Aymara speaker from Acha Chilcani (a locality near Corque in the Carangas province of Oruro), claimed that he had completed military service but was unaware that his category had been mobilized: "I have my service booklet in order, and I didn't think that they had called up those who had already served but rather only *omisos*."[61] While Chambi may have feigned ignorance to avoid punishment, his audience treated this claim as plausible. Testimony that *patrones* had prevented reservists from presenting was apparently also quite credible. Invoking the system of *pongueaje* in which *colonos* performed unpaid domestic labor for their *patrones*, Ramón Julio Choque, an illiterate farmworker from southern Potosí, told the magistrate, "I knew of the call, but my *patrón* made me work in his store in Atocha, telling me that I could present later."[62] The difficulties of mobilization suggested by these testimonies in 1932 foreshadowed the enormity of the challenges that would lie ahead.

After the war took a disastrous turn for Bolivia, enthusiasm to join the ranks waned. By the end of 1933, mobilization orders came swiftly, calling up all men between the ages of eighteen and thirty-five (see table 4.4). Although some continued to present, the balance between willing and impressed soldiers shifted. If the Salamanca administration wanted to win, it would need to override resistance and recruit more and far less willing men. Those recruited into the second army (1933) under Kundt and the third (1934) and fourth (1935) armies under Peñaranda thus represented a spectrum that included those who had presented voluntarily, those who responded to a set of coercive structures instituted at the local level, and those violently wrested from thoroughfares and homes by patrols. Despite the pressing need for soldiers, however, the president and Congress granted a series of concessions to diverse interest groups, such as mining companies, banks, railroad compa-

TABLE 4.4. Bolivian Calls for Mobilization, 1933–1934

	Date	Cohort	Ages	Category
5	February 1933	1933	19	All
6	September 12, 1933	1934	18	All
7	October 5, 1933	1921–1922	30–31	All
8	December 12, 1933	1917–1920	32–35	All
9	March 17, 1934	1935, 1916	18 and 37	All for 1935; NCOs from 1916
10	Prior to March 28, 1934		19–35	30 percent of *indígenas*
11	May 3, 1934	1915–1916	37–38	All
12	December 9, 1934			General mobilization of all able-bodied men

Sources: Supreme decrees accessed at http://www.gacetaoficialdebolivia.gob.bo; Chief of Recruitment to Prefect of La Paz, no. 972, February 27, 1933; General Staff to Prefects, no. 2997, October 5, 1933; President of Recruitment Commission to Prefect of La Paz, no. 275, March 27, 1934; Corregidor of Italaque to Prefect of La Paz, March 28, 1934, all in Prefecture-Admin box 208, ALP.

nies, and rural landowners, that limited the vulnerability of their workers to recruitment.

Mobilization involves an active choice, albeit one structured by social and legal sanctions. Instead of presenting, those aware that they had been called up for service could seek legal forms of evasion, bribe an official, or hide in the countryside. Whether or not they were aware of orders, those impressed as evaders had no such choice. Bolivia's 1907 conscription law provided the legal framework for both mobilization and impressment: if men caught by patrols belonged to the cohorts already called and could not produce documents exempting them from wartime service, then they were legally vulnerable to immediate capture and enrollment.[63] Although mobilization and impressment are both coercive mechanisms, they are quite distinct in terms of state capacity. Impressment is profoundly violent and usually quite arbitrary; it is the recourse of a state unable to motivate soldiers to mobilize, either out of patriotic nationalism or the conviction that they would be forced to serve if they did not present. Local authorities may have relied on pressure and violence to enforce mobilization orders, but when they sent reservists to mobilization centers, it reflected the effective functioning of the state apparatus at the local level.

Although primarily associated with nineteenth-century recruitment, forcible enrollment had never disappeared from the Bolivian army. As shown in chapter 1, the 1907 conscription law provided for the capture of anyone who failed to register or present for service, inspiring diverse actors to report enemies as *omisos* so they would be forced to serve long terms in the ranks.

Local authorities may have set up checkpoints to inspect military documents and used armed detachments to capture *omisos* prior to the war, but no evidence suggests that anyone patrolled the countryside or inspected homes to pursue *omisos*. However, the Bolivian state at war needed far more men. Impressment, legally justified by the 1907 law, thus emerged as an organized practice during the war.

Sources have not yet emerged that document precisely when recruitment commissions began pursuing evaders in rural communities and patrolling thoroughfares to inspect documents. The need became clear, however, by the early months of 1933, when local authorities in rural areas reported marked resistance to the recent call-up.[64] No more than six months into the war, then, armed commissions began seeking out men who had evaded or were unaware of initial calls, many of whom lived in places where the state apparatus did not function properly due to societal resistance or local authorities' negligence.

The use of impressment produced powerful memories of wartime recruitment as profoundly violent, arbitrary, and forceful incursions into the daily lives of rural Bolivians. Drawing on Arze's work, several scholars have posited the existence of a "parallel war" in the countryside, provoked by recruitment efforts and individuals that took advantage of the war to appropriate soldiers' lands.[65] During William Carter and Mauricio Mamani's fieldwork in the 1960s, community members told tales of widespread panic when patrols arrived to capture conscripts who had not presented because they feared dying at the front.[66] And Taller de Historia Oral Andina's work shows that many indigenous women remember their husbands, sons, and fathers "being rounded up like llamas."[67] Military justice records support these memories, suggesting an invasive process wherein patrols violently and humiliatingly inspected travelers.[68] Local authorities also reported that the arrival of recruitment commissions caused rural indigenous men to flee en masse, abandoning their labors.[69]

In April 1933, as Bolivian forces appeared to be making progress in the Nanawa sector, prefects circulated an order that represented a dramatic shift in mobilization policy. Since November 1932, calls had applied to all men of a particular age, regardless of ethnicity or social status. Citing the disruption to food supplies and transportation being caused by recruitment commissions, this new order exempted from mobilization indigenous men living on haciendas and in independent communities: "The indigenous farmworkers included in the call for reservists should not present to recruitment centers but instead intensify their agricultural work in order to supply the army and civilian population."[70] Limiting the number of rural indigenous men going to the front, this order represented a return to the logic of the 1932 decrees, which had called up untrained reservists from only departmental capitals. In addition to promoting agricultural production, this decision likely stemmed from the conviction that *colonos* and *comunarios* did not make for dependable frontline soldiers. The intensity and persistence of rural resistance probably also played a role, as well as pressure from wealthy landlords and indigenous communities. This concession certainly did not mean that indigenous men would no longer fight in Chaco, however, since it did not exempt men who had failed to respond to earlier calls.

This policy was in effect for almost a year until several disastrous months at the front caused the government to again revise plans for rural mobilization. In order to staff the third army in early 1934, Bolivia instituted a quota system under which 30 percent of all eligible *indígenas* from each community or hacienda would be obliged to enlist.[71] The quota would be raised to 50 percent in 1935 for the fourth army's final defense of Villamontes.[72] Yet the Bolivian high command still attempted to keep as many rural indigenous men as possible from the front lines, ordering that mobilized *comunarios, colonos,* and day laborers preferably be used for rearguard labors, such as road work, because their "participation was questionable" in the zone of operations.[73]

The quota system represented a clear cession of state power to local actors, both public and private.[74] In exchange for producing soldiers, *corregidores,* hacienda administrators, and indigenous authorities gained control over issuing the paperwork that protected rural indigenous men from impressment. While the system was supposed to operate through an unbiased lottery, some landowners clearly used it to rid themselves of troublemakers.[75] For example, Manuel Mamani, a *colono* on the Poma Ayama hacienda, alleged that he had been included in the 30 percent quota due to the hostility of the *hilacata* (indigenous authority, likely handpicked by the *patrón*), who had administered the lottery.[76] Although the quota system did not eliminate the violence of recruitment patrols, it provided protection for many rural indigenous men who would otherwise have been subject to impressment.

It also encouraged favoritism, abuse, and manipulation. Finger-pointing and denunciations abound in the prefectural and military tribunal records. *Comunarios* reported their neighbors as *omisos,* denounced violence by recruitment commissions, and accused patrols and local authorities of fraudulently charging for military documents and extracting goods in the name of national defense.[77] *Corregidores* and subprefects in turn blamed the "defeatist campaign" of soldiers evacuated from the front for convincing others to flee rather than mobilize.[78] Their frantic missives demanded armed men to recruit among the *comunarios,* reported that powerful landowners were impeding the enlistment of their *colonos,* and denounced the violence of recruitment patrols.[79] And the leaders of the patrols insisted that local authorities were interfering with their work and exacting bribes to release captives or erase men's names from recruitment lists.[80] The fact that the prefect and military courts viewed most charges of abuse and corruption as credible enough to merit investigation indicates that the government had little faith in its agents.

Indigenous farmworkers were certainly not the only ones to avoid mobilization. On the contrary, the prevalence of elite evaders produced the stock figure of the wealthy *emboscado* (evader). These men took refuge in country estates, bribed officials to be declared unfit, purchased falsified documents, or fled abroad. These methods of evasion depended on bribery and personal relationships, as noted by the subprefect of Larecaja, La Paz, who complained in late 1933 that men in his jurisdiction must have benefited from "sponsorship [*padrinazgos*] or favors [*condescendencias*]" because they had returned from recruitment centers with exemption documents despite being in perfect health.[81] This was the same patron-client logic that had structured the favoritism that ministers of war had railed against in the 1910s and 1920s.[82]

Especially in the later phases of the war, the Salamanca administration and Congress spoke vigorously against these forms of avoidance, even passing a law in late 1933 ordering the return of those who had gone abroad to evade service.[83] Yet this decree had no enforcement mechanism beyond social sanctions and a likely empty threat to block remittances. Similarly toothless was an October 1934 decree that ordered men previously determined unfit to be reexamined.[84] White-collar professionals did have to present documentation proving their age or legitimate exemption, but no evidence suggests that recruitment patrols frisked them as they traveled.

In fact, the president and Congress repeatedly facilitated elite evasion despite their public condemnation of *emboscados*. Elected officials were exempted, as were many government functionaries.[85] And, in December 1933, Salamanca decreed that men who had already lost a brother in the war could be taken off the front lines to serve in the rear guard. The provision that petitioners had to prove that the brothers were legitimate (or, if illegitimate, had been legally recognized) betrayed the class bias of this exemption.[86] Although this measure was typical of contemporary armies, gossip at the front presented it as a maneuver to save one of Salamanca's sons from the front lines after the death of another son, Alberto, in service.[87] However, as Bolivia's position grew direr a month later, the decree was modified to spare only those with two dead brothers.[88]

The state also facilitated evasion by creating the new category "reservist on assignment," which provided a mechanism for men in particular industries to serve by staying in their current positions rather than by deploying to the front. This was a form of legally sanctioned evasion that, like the quota system for farmworkers, resulted from bargains struck between the government and interest groups in response to economic exigencies. This category had its roots in demands from the mining industry. Given that the financing of the war depended on loans from mining companies and emergency taxes on tin exports,[89] Salamanca's administration obliged by issuing a decree in September 1933 that declared miners with special skills reservists on assignment.[90] According to the logic of this category, the state was trading these reservists' labor on the front lines for their strategic labor to the benefit of the larger war effort. Later decrees granted the same status to men with "technical knowledge" working in banking, business, railroads, and other industries.[91]

As Bolivia's fortunes worsened, the administration ordered all reservists on assignment to pay 20 percent of their salaries to support the war and the companies sponsoring them to submit monthly lists of workers, establishing commissions to verify the legality of every transaction.[92] The Ministry of National Defense's archive has hundreds of lists attesting to salary deductions for reservists on assignment. They show, for example, that the Empresa Minera Negro Pabellón paid 237.13 bolivianos in February 1935 for the services of four reservists on assignment and that the Antofagasta Chile and Bolivia Railway Company had thirty-three of its employees declared reservists on assignment just before the war's end in June.[93] While reservist-on-assignment status was certainly a powerful mechanism for elite evasion, these sources also show that many rural workers benefited from this status as the military decided that their labor in agriculture, infrastructure, and transportation would bolster the war effort more than their soldiering.[94] For example, on March 13, 1934, the Office of Military Rations (Sección de Etapas) issued twenty-one-year-old Román Machuca of the Turobo farm in Montero (in Warnes, Santa Cruz) paperwork that granted him permission to "devote himself to agricultural work" rather than mobilize.[95] The same volume of bound documents shows the granting of this status to 239 other men from Santa Cruz and 124 from Tarija.[96]

Bolivians from diverse social strata sought ways for themselves, their sons, and their employees to avoid the front lines. Although the government responded by patrolling rural areas and passing laws to curb elite evasion, it also made significant concessions to several interest groups regarding the extent to which it would mobilize their clients. The contrast between the treatment of literate emboscados versus rural omisos and remisos was indeed stark, but the hierarchies of evasion were not always so predictable. Reservist-on-assignment status protected not only professionals but also many illiterate agriculturalists. And the decrees issued in 1933 and 1934 expressly set out to limit the participation of uniformed indígenas.[97] Ultimately, mobilization exceeded bureaucratic structures because it hinged on the local actors who checked documents, staffed patrols, and administered the quota system. Rather than precisely fulfilling orders, many of these men acted based on personal relationships and opportunities for enrichment when deciding which evaders to pursue and which to ignore. Wartime mobilization thus

opened a space for contention, creating new rifts among and within sectors
of Bolivian society.

COPING WITH WARTIME DESERTION

After mobilizing and impressing soldiers, the state had to not only transport,
clothe, feed, and effectively deploy them but also prevent them from deserting and mutinying, despite horrific conditions. These challenges began with
the long and arduous journey to the Chaco, which archival sources, memoirs,
and oral histories portray as marked by thirst and blisters as men lugged their
equipment hundreds of kilometers.[98] Carlos Escobar, for example, presented in Oruro in mid-September 1932. After a month of training, this literate
farmworker from Jayguayco (Cochabamba) departed for the Chaco on October 12. He would not reach Villamontes for another three weeks. His detachment walked for four days to Tarija, where they were issued rifles; walked for
another four days to Entre Ríos; and then finally advanced, yet again on foot,
to Villamontes.[99]

Some soldiers apparently enjoyed considerable liberty during this journey and were able to take advantage of the local establishments providing
food, alcohol, and likely sex that had popped up. Dozens of soldiers testified
to drinking themselves into oblivion after long days of marching.[100] Others
seized opportunities to desert. Described in military records as an illiterate twenty-three-year-old farmworker from Tupiza, Potosí, Manuel Farfán
summed up the complaints of many of these deserters: "It was better to desert
than to endure the lack of food and other privations on the journey. . . . As for
the food, I say that it was of bad quality, and our allowance [socorros] was not
paid to us punctually."[101] By the time most soldiers arrived in the region, they
were exhausted and likely doubtful of the army's ability to care for them.

The statements of several deserters drew on a contractual logic, citing the
army's or state's failure to care for them or their families as the motivating
factor in their decisions to desert. Benedicto Calisaya, for example, claimed
that he hid in the forest as his unit marched out of Ballivián because on the
trip there, they had no rations for four days.[102] Many others complained of
inadequate medical attention, accusing officers and doctors of ignoring their
infirmities.[103] Saúl Chávez expressed a widespread sense of frustration: "We
were sick and they did not attend to us in any way; moreover [we] also had
to sleep out in the open, which made my illness worse."[104] Other testimony invoked the bonds of family, suggesting that some soldiers had little faith
in the state's ability to care for their loved ones in their absence.[105] Several
statements, like that of Rosendo Cuentas, a thirty-year-old farmworker from
Caripuyo (Potosí), emphasized the "lamentable state" in which he had left
his wife and three children as the principal motive for desertion.[106]

Histories and memoirs of the war suggest that this inability to adequately provision and care for soldiers was widespread. Vivid portrayals of the horrors of combat and the desperation of Bolivian soldiers abound in the literature. For example, in his memoir, General Ovidio Quiroga describes his soldiers as tired, tormented by insects, demoralized, and resigned to death. The hunger of one group, he notes, was so desperate that they ate a putrid mule that had died on the path.[107] Soldiers testifying in desertion proceedings invoked similar hardships. They recounted marching for days in heavy rains, finding their fellows facedown in the scrub from thirst, and feeling "overwhelmed with fatigue" after fighting "day and night for more than a month, often without sustenance."[108]

These conditions, combined with a growing lack of faith in commanders' strategic decisions, produced minor mutinies. Soldiers refused to advance, turned weapons on their officers, and abandoned their positions.[109] On several occasions, commanders played the national anthem and gave stirring speeches before asking their men to take a step forward to show their willingness to continue fighting for the *patria*. Time and again, most remained behind as commanders inveighed against their cowardice and spit in their faces.[110] One soldier who did take a step forward, José Manuel Córdova, a miner from Potosí, described fighting for five days at *fortín* Castillo in September 1932. After two days' rest, his unit returned to the front, first following orders to join the right flank and then receiving new orders to double back to the left flank. This last order prompted the soldiers to sit down "in the road and start to mutter that they were not dolls, that they wanted to fight and not wander around tired all night."[111]

Most deserters lay beyond the reach of the military, having hidden in the countryside, fled to neighboring countries, or even presented at recruitment centers under different names. Deserters who turned themselves in or were captured received an arbitrary combination of lenience, humiliation, and exemplary punishment rather than systematic sentencing. The Military Penal Code provided for all rank-and-file deserters from the army on campaign to face military tribunals and be punished with four years' imprisonment, with an extra year if the desertion occurred in front of the enemy.[112] Despite the use of powerfully stigmatizing rhetoric, the army could not afford to lose frontline soldiers to mass imprisonment. Nor could it stage thousands of military justice proceedings. Informal procedures thus predominated. This informality, along with a general inability to keep track of soldiers, has produced military records so incomplete that scholars will likely never have a grasp on the actual scale of wartime desertion and mutiny.

Driven by a need for soldiers, reincorporation into the ranks appears to have been the most common method of handling deserters. For example, in July 1933, the commander of the 124th Oruro Detachment's First Company reported that Genaro Condori, Miguel Cuevas, and Carlos Flores, all of whom had been listed as deserters in May, had been reincorporated.[113] In fact, reports sent by officers often listed deserters who had recently joined the unit among the soldiers needing to be paid and fed.[114] Moreover, entire detachments of men departing for the front between February 1933 and the end of the war consisted solely of deserters, captured evaders, and men previously evacuated due to injury or illness.[115] The lists and reports indicating the reincorporation of deserters offer no rationale for these decisions.

However, at least 257 deserters and mutineers faced military tribunals, and at least twenty-three faced summary execution by firing squads, as military commanders used exemplary punishments to reassert their authority.[116] In March 1933, for example, soldiers at the Corrales outpost deserted en masse. General Kundt, upon learning of these desertions, instructed his officers to arrest the leaders (cabecillas), who should be "shot without any more formalities." However, he advised that repentant troops "who were seduced" should be reincorporated into their units.[117] This solution allowed the army to retain the vast majority of deserters while still demonstrating the severity of their crime. In the case of the Corrales desertion, Gonzálo Zambrana, described in the records as an illiterate farmworker from Santa Cruz, unwillingly provided the sacrifice that expiated the crimes of his fellows. In his testimony, Zambrana denied incitement charges and claimed that his only sin was having informed the captain that he and his fellows were "completely exhausted, without the courage or strength to continue fighting."[118] Despite testimony supporting his version of events, Zambrana faced a firing squad hours after giving his statement. Twenty-one other deserters attended his execution, thus converting his punishment into an instructive spectacle and ensuring that news of it would spread. When an official tribunal reviewed the case, it used forceful rhetoric to affirm the decision to swiftly execute Zambrana, arguing that it had been necessary in order to "energetically cut off the spread of an evil that threatened to disturb . . . the successful final outcome of [Bolivia's] armed forces in this war."[119]

Officers took similar measures to staunch the spate of izquierdistas. These soldiers were called "leftists" because they shot themselves in the left hand in order to escape the front line.[120] Lists compiled by the army named 720 izquierdistas over the course of the war and reported that firing squads had executed at least seven of them during a forty-five-day period in early 1934. This change in policy toward izquierdistas was quite effective: army records report a 93 percent decrease in this phenomenon after the executions.[121]

Without access to soldiers who had deserted over enemy lines, military leaders resorted to a different sort of exemplary punishment: publicly portraying deserters as cowards and traitors. Accusing Santiago García of deserting to Paraguayan forces and giving them information about his unit's position, General Kundt wrote to the head of military forces in García's home of Cochabamba, insisting that he "spread as much as possible, the name of this deserter, reporting the grave crime that he has committed."[122] On another occasion, Kundt attached a list of deserters and ordered that their names be printed in local newspapers under the headline "soldiers who, forgetting the glorious tradition of the Bolivian Army, passed to the enemy." He insisted that this publicity would prevent "the repetition of events so prejudicial and disgraceful for the entire nation."[123]

Many officers serving on tribunals employed a similar patriotic discourse to buttress their arguments for stiff punishments. Acting as a prosecutor in a set of fifteen desertion cases in mid-1933, Lieutenant Colonel Zacarías Inchausti urged the magistrate to reject recommendations for leniency and to "apply exemplary punishments that will curb all antipatriotic outbreaks." He insisted that "justice" would "raise the moral standard of the troops."[124] Another officer-prosecutor advocated "energetic and rapid sanctions" to protect "military honor and discipline and the nation's interests."[125] Desertion, they argued, threatened both the military as an institution and Bolivia as a nation. The punishment of errant soldiers would thus serve a moral purpose by instructing all conscripts and reservists in their duties to the nation.

Yet one military magistrate called on very different tropes in explaining his decision to excuse the desertion of two soldiers, indicating racialized ideas about Indians as children not fully responsible for their actions. Major Alcibiades Antelo recommended leniency because the accused had not received military training, "that is to say that they are not soldiers, and anyway they are pure Indians, ignorant."[126] The transcribed version of testimony in this case reported that one of the accused, a monolingual Quechua speaker named Valentín Mamani, had employed this very argument: he claimed to have thought that he was being released from military service when an officer took away his rifle and bayonet, saying that he did not need them due to his lack of military training.[127] While this might have been Mamani's interpretation of the situation, it could also have been an apparently effective strategy that called on stereotypes to present his desertion not as willful but as the result of misunderstanding.

The statements of another rural man combined claims of ignorance with patriotic declarations, perhaps hoping that one might help him escape punishment. After being picked up as a deserter because he was wearing an army-issued shirt, Manuel Ramírez made the following claim about his failure to report for military service: "because I believed that it wasn't a crime and because of ignorance of my duties since I am a poor farmworker who doesn't even know how to write. . . . Recently discovering that I am obligated to defend my *patria* . . . , I want to be taught how to use a rifle to go to the Chaco."[128] Ramírez's statement combined the tropes of patriotic duty with those of rural ignorance, blaming his failure in the former on the latter and implying that fault lay with the state for neglecting to educate and train him. Especially when combined with patriotic phrases, these claims may have found a receptive audience because they were legible within dominant narratives of race and social class.

Such patriotic professions were common in wartime military justice proceedings, as deponents drew on a predominant discourse of sacrificing all on the altar of the *patria*. For example, Froilán Navarro, identified as a twenty-five-year-old farmworker from Irupana (La Paz), claimed to have deserted due to illness and then presented again under another name. His testimony closes with his supposed desire to fight for Bolivia: "After everything, my deepest wish is to march to the front again, this time not to avoid but rather to face the enemy and fight on the front line to erase the affront that I have committed."[129] During certain proceedings, these patriotic declarations were so common that I suspect that prisoners were coaching each other in this discourse as they awaited trial or that the transcribing secretary began adding pro forma declarations after hearing them from so many deserters. When the prosecutor asked at the end of their statements if they had anything to add, many soldiers offered variations on what became a standard refrain: "I want to be incorporated in any regiment to return to the Chaco and comply with my duty to defend my *patria*."[130]

Some soldiers jailed in La Paz for desertion submitted impassioned pleas, perhaps written by lawyers, to return to the front. For example, a petition signed by Julio Rivas Arteche, who was described as a twenty-three-year-old farmworker from Charapaya (Cochabamba), displayed a remarkable fluency in the patriotic discourse that identified wartime self-sacrifice as the ultimate marker of national belonging: "As a good Bolivian, I beg to fulfill my duty, and I do not believe that I will be deprived [from participating] in this situation of pure Bolivianism." The petition further promised that he, "like a good soldier," was ready to "die, face to face [with the enemy], for the *patria* defending [Bolivia's] territorial integrity in the Chaco."[131] On the other hand, soldiers like Juan Cusi Mamani had not yet become so proficient in the use of this patriotic language, stating, "Rather than suffering in the brig, I want to be sent to the front to defend the country."[132] Far from professing that serving Bolivia was his fondest desire, Cusi presented it as preferable to incarceration. During a war in which the predominant method for dealing with captured deserters was reincorporation, soldiers tried for this crime had reason to believe that patriotic professions of their willingness to fight for a beloved *patria* might affect their sentences.

Many of those officially tried for desertion were eventually reincorporated into the ranks, sometimes even after a military magistrate had recommended jail time. For example, in October 1934, General Enrique Peñaranda closed a case that had been pending against fifteen deserters since September 1932. In explaining this action, he noted that he had not received any complaints or reports of bad behavior in the months since "the accused had been reincorporated into various units of the National Army."[133] Many of these deserters thus apparently went on to accumulate records of honorable service during the remainder of the war and, at its close, received discharge papers untainted by their earlier fault.

Just as the central state relied on local actors to implement its evolving mobilization policy, the treatment of deserters and mutineers ultimately depended on the decisions of individual officers. These men chose who would be labeled "deserter" or "mutineer" and whether these offenders would face firing squads or military tribunals. Most opted for reincorporation, giving soldiers tried for these crimes reason to believe that professions of their willingness to fight for the *patria* might affect their sentences. Holding facilities likely served as classrooms where deserters, perhaps with help from attorneys and notaries, tutored each other in using patriotic discourse to speak to the state. By the time they faced a military tribunal, soldiers like Manuel Ramírez and Froilán Navarro had learned to structure their speech according to norms considered valid by the institution and thus contributed to popularizing this language. Deserters could use this language to mark themselves as loyal or even to condemn the state for its negligence. However, unlike those that invoked parochial concerns of suffering, these statements called on the larger idea of the nation and thus also contributed to its construction. Boosted by these actors' interactions with state institutions during the war, this discourse served to teach the idea of patriotic duty.

Despite the generations that have passed since the Chaco War, understandings of the conflict and its impact on society still reflect the political narrative crafted in the war's aftermath. Even today, novels, campaign diaries, and essays such as Augusto Céspedes's *Sangre de mestizos*, Jesús Lara's *Repete*, and Augusto Guzmán's *Prisionero de guerra* (1937) are taught in Bolivian schools. Archival sources show that the conduct of the war was indeed characterized by manifest errors and criminal abuses, but these facts should not hide the remarkable success of the state in mobilizing its population, given the enormity of the challenge in a thinly populated territory with a multilingual populace. To have mobilized a similar percentage of the population as the US Civil War did can be described only as a triumph in terms of state capacity.

This triumph was achieved through a multipronged approach in which the central government ceded power to local actors to enact mobilization orders, negotiated with diverse interest groups to ensure continued production and protect particular men from recruitment, and relied on the brute force of impressment patrols to enforce a documentary regime. Practicality and uneven implementation also characterized the army's handling of deserters and mutineers in the zone of operations, leading to the reincorporation of most soldiers. Mobilization and discipline during the Chaco War is thus a story of indirect governance through accommodation and power sharing, as local authorities and subaltern officers had significant leeway to implement or even ignore orders.

The Chaco War touched all levels of society, bringing an unprecedented proportion of Bolivians into the military. While many of these soldiers were reservists who had already served as conscripts over the previous twenty years, many others had been excused through the lottery or exemptions or had never registered for service. Indeed, a significant number of the men who served had likely been unaware of their obligations under the 1907 conscription law. The Chaco War represented the largest single undertaking by the Bolivian state up to that point, as the central government and its agents balanced brute force, coercive structures, patriotic inducement, and concessions to various interest groups in order to raise not one but four armies. Rural indigenous men bore the brunt of the violence, but the state also tried to protect this population.[134] Mobilization policies in fact repeatedly attempted to produce an army less rural and less indigenous than the nation as a whole, likely due to doubts about this population's willingness and ability to fight for Bolivia. Official mobilization orders consistently sought to reduce the number of indigenous men vulnerable to impressment by limiting calls to departmental capitals, exempting indigenous farmworkers, and then instituting a quota system. The fact that so many rural folk served in the Chaco was thus a product of demographics and the state's dependence on often-unreliable local agents to enact its orders.

Although these archival sources cannot reveal individual motives for mobilization, they do show that men from different regional, class, and ethnic backgrounds presented in the first waves of mobilization and fought throughout the war. Most surprisingly, they show that the state's compromises and accommodations regarding recruitment and desertion sometimes favored indigenous men. Both civilian leaders in La Paz and military commanders in the field displayed a remarkable level of flexibility, combining energetic pursuit of those who evaded or deserted with concessions to individuals and various interest groups. Mass participation, extensive loss of life, and pointless suffering in the Chaco would lead Bolivia to become a conscript nation in which both veterans and young conscripts could make claims on the state and negotiate, both individually and collectively, the terms and meanings of military service.

CHAPTER 5

GOOD SONS AND BAD FATHERS IN THE POSTWAR PERIOD

Five years after the war's end, two evaders petitioned the Bolivian state to regularize their military status. Although written in the first person, these petitions are legal documents that follow a specific form and almost certainly were constructed by professionals. A masterful rendition of the language of patriotism, the first came from a property owner in the department of Potosí named Julio Barrera Acuña. It read, "The war . . . has sacrificed the lives and blood of the best sons of Bolivia. Conscious of their duty, they have given to the defense of the immanent rights of the nationality." Citing Barrera's malaria and duty to care for his elderly mother while his four brothers fought, the petition lamented, "I was deprived of the honor of giving personal service."[1] The second petition, from Alejandro Apaza, employed quite different tropes to explain his failure to serve. It claimed that he had not understood the wartime decrees since he thought that "one of them seemed to mean that *indígenas* on properties in the Yungas were exempt from participating in the campaign," so he "continued to work on the tasks of coca production."[2]

These petitions reflect a fraught process of postwar reckoning in which the Bolivian state, operating under severe financial constraints, sought to reward veterans and punish evaders. They also point to the vitality of Bolivia's hierarchies of race, education, and social class. These forms of distinction meant that Barrera and Apaza faced quite different expectations and might even be judged under different legal norms. Thus, like indigenous deserters during the war, Apaza or his notary played on ideas about indigenous ignorance to explain his failure to the state.[3] Yet the war also destabilized these powerful continuities by valorizing the social category of Chaco veteran, which could be claimed by many whom older hierarchies had relegated to inferior status. Veterans' discursive emphasis on patriotism and their own sacrifice allowed them to make claims on the state and forge a new space for themselves in the nation.

As reflected in Barrera's petition, the idea of sons became a popular way of expressing the relationship of veterans and evaders to the nation. Far from new, this familial metaphor had long been employed by state actors to justify military service. Bolivia, the *patria,* was the mother who nurtured her sons. Frontline veterans were her good sons, having loyally risked their lives to protect her integrity, whereas the evaders, deserters, and elites in the rearguard became bad sons. The unstated piece of the metaphor was the father, understood to be the politicians who led the nation and the military officers who trained the sons to defend their mother. Depicted as irresponsible and incompetent, these fathers emerged discredited in the wake of the failed war. Bolivia's postwar period is thus a story of the son rebuking and aspiring to replace the father.

The war had exacerbated existing generational and ideological divides between the son and the father, which ultimately broke apart the coalition of formally educated men that had long ruled the country. A generation of students and young professionals had spent their formative years in uniform, as political exiles, or avoiding the draft. These experiences profoundly shaped their visions for Bolivia and their nascent identities as reformers (or even revolutionaries) allied with the masses. Expressing a radical sense of deception, veterans and antiwar activists often worked together in their fight to speak for noncitizens and defy the oligarchy that had led the country into a pointless war. However, they also condemned the war as an imperialist endeavor by Standard Oil—a narrative that served traditional leaders' need for a scapegoat in order to deflect blame from themselves.

Upheaval and unrest characterized the sixteen years between the Chaco War and the 1952 revolution. Three years of war had flung the country into economic, social, and political chaos. Fifty to sixty thousand men—a devastating 2 percent of Bolivia's population—likely died in the conflict, leaving families all over the country mourning their sons, husbands, fathers and brothers.[4] Many of those who had returned did so with mutilated bodies or chronic illnesses.[5] Wartime spending led to crushing debt and hyperinflation; the exchange rate for dollars would increase sevenfold between 1935 and 1939.[6] Rural migrants flooded cities, leading to housing shortages and challenging elite ideas about urbanity and racial identity.[7] Strikes and uprisings proliferated, and the only constitutional transfers of power occurred under provisional governments as traditional elites and reformers overthrew one another's administrations. Paradoxically, the military remained powerful despite the bloody consequences of its strategic and logistic errors during the war. Although explicitly prohibited from political activity, army officers dominated the country's postwar politics.[8]

Whether controlled by civilians or officers, reformers or the old guard, the postwar Bolivian state felt compelled to respond to the demands of veterans. The depth and breadth of wartime mobilization had given viability to a new form of distinction: the good sons who had served the *patria*. Veterans, both indigenous and non, assumed a new authority, using their service to make individual and collective demands on the state and expressing belonging to Bolivia. This profoundly affected Bolivia's social hierarchy, as veteran status gained the potential to compete with long-standing hierarchies of ethnicity, class, and education. Military service did not upend these hierarchies but did become a new way of establishing worth.

THE "REDEMPTION AND REHABILITATION" OF BOLIVIA'S BAD SONS

Beyond leaders' immediate goal of avoiding blame for defeat, the government and the military faced two major postwar challenges: punishing those who had failed to serve in the war and developing a political constituency among those who had. Instituting a documentary regime that would force all men to regularize their military status, Bolivia's leaders proposed to reorganize society along the lines of patriotic service. Although discursively powerful, this task presented practical challenges. The prospect of a police state that would track down, try, and imprison the tens of thousands of men who had evaded or deserted was impractical and expensive. On the other hand, blanket forgiveness would diminish the contributions of the good sons who had defended Bolivia's claims, and it would undercut the viability of ongoing demands for military service.

The initial stance was strict. Immediately after the war's end, military and police units patrolled Bolivia's borders and captured all deserters and *omisos, remisos,* and *emboscados* (whom I will collectively call "evaders") returning from neighboring countries.[9] Yet, only months later, the same administration created a parallel process that gave these bad sons another path to recoup their rights and be accepted back into the Bolivian family. A December 1935 decree offered them six months to surrender to military authorities and be assigned to socially useful labors. Evaders would serve for two years and deserters for three. Per the decree, this process would allow them to redeem their place in the nation by rehabilitating themselves through labor that benefited the *patria.* Those assigned to road brigades would be fed, housed, and clothed by the state but would earn no wages. Those employed by mining companies would have 25 percent of their salary garnished and deposited in the state's infrastructure account. The decree further provided that deserters and evaders unfit for such labors could pay a fine to "redeem their offense."[10]

This decree was a coercive mechanism to blacklist any bad sons who failed to comply. Penalties primarily targeted literate men—the famed *emboscados* who had evaded service. The decree explicitly suspended their citizenship rights until they had rehabilitated their military status, mandating that anyone attempting to enroll in the Civic Register present a demobilization booklet. It also denied them access to government jobs and set forth fines for anyone employing a man who lacked official military documents. In theory, this would aid unemployed veterans by removing deserters and evaders from the formal labor force. Eminently practical, this decree marked an implicit admission that the state did not have the funds, the bureaucratic strength, or the manpower to identify, capture, and judicially process all of Bolivia's bad sons. This compromise would allow the state to collect information about its residents, refill its coffers, improve its infrastructure, and contribute to strategic industries while still insisting that all men owed service to the nation.

The regulations implementing the December 1935 decree set up a hierarchy among bad sons based on the same racialized ideas that had structured mobilization orders during the war. The crafters of these regulations chose to assume that, far from willfully neglecting their duties, Indians were ignorant children needing benevolent guidance. Depicting indigenous peons as subject to the whims of their *patrones* rather than as independent actors, these regulations provided for their term of labor to be shorter than for other offenders.[11] Differentiation based on these assumptions continued throughout the period. Even a 1940 decree instituting a census to inspect military service documents created a tiered system (expressed in racialized class terms) to fine violators: all "indigenous elements" would pay fifty bolivianos, whereas this fine would be doubled for "non-indigenous manual laborers, artisans, and workers" and tripled for professionals and highly educated individuals.[12] These provisions reflected the widespread conviction that indigenous men did not fully belong to the Bolivian nation and therefore could not be held equally responsible for failures in patriotic duty.

However, before the six months provided to present could expire, a general strike in La Paz triggered the overthrow of Salamanca's vice president and successor, Liberal politician José Luis Tejada Sorzano, by Army Chief of Staff Germán Busch.[13] The officer most associated with the war's heroic tradition, Busch had rapidly risen through the ranks from lieutenant to lieutenant colonel for his fearless leadership in the field.[14] Rather than take power himself, Busch ceded to his superior, Colonel David Toro. Most of the traditional parties supported this coup based on the assumption that it would soon lead to elections; however, Toro and then Busch would rule for the next three years.[15] Capitalizing on the popularity of variously defined versions of socialism in postwar Bolivia, they developed an amorphous ideology called military socialism. Although the name associated the army with revolutionary change, their rhetoric emphasized corporatism and putting nationalism above class struggle.[16]

In reckoning with Bolivia's bad sons, the administrations of Toro (1936–1937) and Busch (1937–1939) chose to continue in the same vein as the December 1935 decree. However, rather than letting the decree stand as written, Toro reissued it two weeks after Tejada Sorzano's overthrow. Although

the new decree tinkered with some details, such as the length of service required, the overall idea of compensation through labor or monetary payment
remained. The main difference between the decrees was discursive, as the
language of military socialism pervaded the latter. The preamble set forth a
dual impetus for these measures. Above all, it cited the state's needs: "The Socialist State requires the participation of all Bolivians to bring about postwar
national reconstruction," defined as building infrastructure and increasing
tin production. The second justification, however, departed from Tejada Sorzano's emphasis on literate actors by referring to the many noncitizens who
had deserted and evaded during the war: "It is humane and just to facilitate
the rehabilitation of citizenship rights for those who, lacking civic and moral education, neglected their patriotic duty."[17] This echoed a common trope
that ultimately blamed the sons' ignorance on the fathers (conceived of as
civilian political elites) who had failed to educate them in their duties. Unsurprisingly, the decree ignored the fact that most men thought to lack said
"civic and moral education" were not citizens under the constitution.

Both Liberal President Tejada Sorzano and military socialists Toro and
Busch thus opted for an approach for reckoning with Bolivia's bad sons
whereby the state would benefit from their labor or funds and they would
be able to regain a place of belonging in the nation along with the right to
work, travel, and, if they were literate, vote. On a discursive level, the decrees
employed a religious metaphor of redemption and rehabilitation to describe
this process, likening deserters and evaders to men being saved by God or
restored to communion with the church.

On a pragmatic level, however, these decrees represented an enormous
challenge to the state's bureaucratic and repressive apparatus. To make policing possible, authorities would first have to inspect the host of papers and
passports issued by various officials during the war and reissue them in uniform formats. Bound volumes located in the Ministry of Defense Central
Archive reveal the grinding bureaucratic labor that went into issuing these
documents. For years after the cessation of hostilities, ministry workers
processed petitions and collected documents to provide official booklets
proving military status.[18] Although hidden by these bureaucratic sources,
favoritism and corruption likely marked the process as local authorities and
employers ignored the law and the officials responsible for issuing documents accepted bribes and did favors for friends.

The state also took active measures to increase policing. For example, in
January 1938, a commission of nine soldiers and one local policeman under
a professional NCO set out for the Quillacollo region of Cochabamba to inspect documents in the countryside and arrest evaders and deserters. Over
the course of their two-day expedition, they captured over eighty men.[19] Juan
Condori described the encounter: "I was questioned by a soldier who asked

me about my military status, pointing his rifle at me. . . . I, having taken part in the Chaco Campaign, had no objection to proving my military status."[20] Condori's and others' testimonies indicate that many workers kept their military documents close at hand and that such patrols were not a rarity in rural areas.

During this process of reckoning, thousands of men regularized their military status, taking advantage of the 1935 and 1936 decrees to compensate the state by working in the mines, on road brigades, or on other public works projects. While the literature has portrayed the state as donating this labor to the mining elite,[21] at least four hundred men received booklets for constructing schools for indigenous youth, and many more received them for building Bolivia's roads.[22] For example, Gerónimo Saavedra Esquibel, an *omiso* who should have done his military service in 1930, obtained military documents by working on the road from Santa Cruz to Cochabamba from April 1937 until September 1938.[23] Also listed as *omisos,* Julio Viviani Cartagena and Lino Hurtado Jiménez received booklets for working at the garrison in Riberalta and then on the indigenous school in Casarabe (both in Beni) for one year and five days.[24]

Others paid a fine to receive a Redemption and Rehabilitation Booklet. Under the decrees, they had to pay three bolivianos for each day of labor owed—a total of 2,160 for evaders and 3,240 for deserters. This represented a significant expenditure, given that the average daily wage in the mines in late 1939 was twelve bolivianos per day.[25] In contrast, anyone requesting a duplicate of any type of booklet paid only one hundred bolivianos.[26] Unsurprisingly, middle-class and elite men predominated in the seventy-five successful petitions for this type of booklet that I examined.[27] While this process was primarily a privilege for the wealthy, at least five men categorized as indigenous also took advantage of it.[28]

Strengthening Bolivia's infrastructure and finances, the regularization of military status depended on individuals' need for these documents and on a state strong enough to enforce the policy, even if not entirely effectively. The process also provided the state with information about its residents. Submitting their photographs, demographic and family information, physical description, military training status, and signature or fingerprint, these men joined the thousands of soldiers initiated into the state's documentary regime during the war. Although the state lacked the will and resources to impose its decrees universally or capitalize on most of the information it collected, its agents were significantly more aggressive in their efforts to demand documents. And thousands complied, regularizing their military status through labor or payment, thus "compensating" the state and "redeeming" themselves in its eyes.

This period of redemption and rehabilitation ended along with military socialism in August 1939 when President Busch committed suicide. His conservative chief of staff, General Carlos Quintanilla, quickly declared military rule to prevent the civilian vice president from assuming office. Elections in March 1940 brought to power General Enrique Peñaranda, the candidate favored by an alliance of traditional parties.[29] In keeping with their orientation toward the prewar political system, these administrations abrogated the decrees providing a path to amnesty, mandating that anyone who had not yet taken advantage of these provisions would be subject to the Military Penal Code.[30] Military justice records reflect the reporting and prosecution of wartime deserters after this decree.[31] When Congress passed a general amnesty, Peñaranda vetoed it, insisting on strict adherence to the law.[32] These two presidents likely sought to deflect the blame for defeat onto Bolivia's bad sons and away from themselves (Quintanilla commanded Bolivia's forces in the initial months of the war and Peñaranda for the entire second half). They likely also viewed the choices of evaders and deserters through a more personal lens.

A massacre at the Catavi mines in December 1942 served as a catalyst for the new generation of civilian and military leaders to unite against Peñaranda's government. When Congress next met in August 1943, several young deputies used the forum to protest the massacre and perform their allegiance to the workers they claimed to represent.[33] Belonging to three recently formed parties (the Revolutionary Nationalist Movement [MNR], the Soviet-aligned Party of the Revolutionary Left [PIR], and the Trotsky-influenced Socialist Workers Party of Bolivia [PSOB]), these men had previously worked together as part of the student movement in the 1920s and had been radicalized by the wartime experience, albeit in very different ways.[34] Whereas the future leaders of the PIR and PSOB spent the war years as exiles in Peru and Argentina for opposing Salamanca, many of those who would form the more conservative MNR put aside their differences with the administration, embraced the nationalist cause, and served in the Chaco War.[35]

Political historian Herbert Klein characterizes the ensuing inquiry into the Catavi massacre as "the most intense debate in Bolivian congressional history." The MNR's Víctor Paz Estenssoro and the PIR's Ricardo Anaya decried the massacre as a symptom of an oligarchic state degrading a once-proud army and facilitating the masses' exploitation by anti-national capitalists.[36] Their aggressive questioning attracted the attention of reformist junior officers, who, despite explicit regulations to the contrary, attended the debate in uniform and applauded the deputies' efforts.[37] In fact, the British reported that ferment among officers in the Abaroa and Loa Regiments was so intense during the debate that the army chief of staff moved the units out of La Paz.[38]

These officers likely belonged to a clandestine military lodge that had formed in Paraguay's POW camps. Taking the name Radepa (Razón del Patria, or because of the patria), this group had been spreading since mid-1936 and had supported the military socialist regimes.[39] Although the administration survived the censure vote over Catavi in September, Radepa attempted a coup in November. After this failure, Radepa officers sought an alliance with both the MNR and the PIR. The PIR declined, but the MNR did not, joining with Radepa to successfully overthrow Peñaranda in December 1943 on the anniversary of the Catavi massacre.[40] Although most observers predicted that the MNR would take the lead, the presidency went to a little-known major named Gualberto Villarroel.[41] Radepa and the MNR lacked the support of traditional political parties, and most of the hemisphere refused to recognize their government due to perceived ties to extreme nationalist, fascist, and anti-Semitic ideologies.[42] Coups by other factions of officers threatened the administration on almost a monthly basis, and dozens of senior cadets were dismissed from the Military Academy for mutiny in May 1944.[43]

The return to a reformist military government again affected policy toward Bolivia's bad sons. In 1945, the constituent assembly granted blanket amnesty to all the "omisos, remisos, and deserters from the Chaco Campaign."[44] The law ended ten years of investment by the Bolivian state in regularizing their status though labor, payment, and imprisonment. Although presented as spontaneous and benevolent, this measure responded to a demand for general amnesty made by indigenous activists during a well-publicized meeting in February 1945.[45] This connection reflects the Villarroel administration's efforts to maintain its hold on power by reaching out to the masses.

In some ways, the policies of Villarroel and the military socialists were like the amnesties granted by the Liberals as part of their efforts to establish obligatory military service three decades earlier. In both eras, the government compromised by issuing decrees that attenuated the strict measures of the law. All explained these concessions by citing the failures of the population in general and indigenous ignorance in particular. Yet the 1945 amnesty law responded directly to *demands* made by indigenous activists in contrast to earlier decrees, which had stemmed from petitions professing Indians' ignorance of the laws. Nor was the 1945 amnesty just a practical measure. Whereas prosecutions under Quintanilla and Peñaranda implied that bad sons had failed Bolivia by not sacrificing faithfully in the war, the amnesty represented the MNR and Radepa's alignment with the masses and their indictment of Bolivia's bad fathers for mismanaging the war. These policies thus reveal a disagreement between father and son over who was to blame for Bolivia's loss.

REFORMING BOLIVIA IN THE NAME OF HER VETERANS

The 1945 amnesty would by no means erase the rhetorical power of soldiers' sacrifice on the front lines for the *patria*. Memories and invocations of the Chaco War dominated the public sphere for decades as politicians, military officers, and veterans marshaled the war for their own ends. Wartime sacrifice thus became a central part of public discourse. Using the war to persuade followers to back their plans for Bolivia's future, reformists constructed a narrative of a new generation "forged in the Chaco" that would make "Bolivia a true *patria* for all of her sons."[46]

In the immediate aftermath of the war, the public rejected the military, booing officers and even greeting troops with silence during an October 1935 parade celebrating their return from the Chaco.[47] Yet leaders soon redirected public ire toward the imperialist forces that had supposedly manipulated Bolivia into waging the ill-advised war. Argentine and Paraguayan newspapers had long circulated the idea that Standard Oil, which had concessions in Bolivia, and Royal Dutch Shell, the holder of distribution and exploration rights in Paraguay, had provoked the war over oil fields and pipelines. Because the rumor aligned with their antipathy to capitalism and imperialism, the exile group in Buenos Aires adopted it, and it became a central part of leader Tristán Marof's *La tragedia del altiplano* in 1934. That same year, Huey Long propagated the idea on the floor of the US Senate as part of his crusade against the company that had worked to impeach him after he taxed oil production in Louisiana.[48]

Anti–Standard Oil sentiment was one of the few things about which traditional leaders, reformist-minded nationalists, and more radical leftists agreed. It offered the first a way to deflect responsibility for the war and fulfilled the latter two's expectations about international capital. This convergence allowed the rumor to thrive; many Bolivians needed little convincing that Standard Oil's capitalist ambitions had pushed their nation into a tragic war.[49] In October 1935, President Tejada Sorzano aligned himself with this popular idea by filing a lawsuit alleging that Standard Oil had breached its contract with Bolivia by constructing an illegal pipeline in the 1920s.[50] The nationalization of the company's operations had become a popular demand by the end of 1936, holding a prominent place in the platforms of the largest workers' and veterans' federations.[51] In order to shore up support, President Toro established a state oil company in December 1936 and nationalized Standard Oil's holdings in March 1937, a full year before Mexico's expropriation of foreign-owned oil companies.[52] Oil nationalism would become synonymous with veterans' wartime sacrifice in Bolivia.[53]

Although the nationalists and antiwar leftists worked together to oppose Standard Oil and the massacre of workers, they ultimately had different goals and were competing for the same constituency. Along with a willingness to compromise and ally with other groups, the ability to claim veteran status was one of the main reasons why the reformers of the MNR ultimately prevailed over more radical parties.[54] Most of the workers that both groups sought to represent had served in the war. Leaders thus constructed a heroic narrative of the foot soldiers and noncommissioned officers who had borne the brunt of the fighting. These good son stories, alongside the state's efforts to punish bad sons, created a political atmosphere that favored veterans and gave them the moral authority and leverage to discredit and replace the fathers, whom they depicted as having lost the war despite their sons' heroism. The legacy of the Chaco War thus featured prominently in speeches and debates, especially from reformists like the military socialists, Radepa, and the MNR.

It was not a coincidence that Germán Busch, the most important political actor of the period, was the quintessential good son and hero of the Chaco War. Born in the lowlands to a German father and a Bolivian mother, Busch first gained national attention in 1931 through a daring expedition that strengthened Bolivia's claim on the Chaco by locating and establishing a fort at the lost Jesuit mission of Zamucos. The unit he commanded at the start of the war fought valiantly to break the siege at Boquerón, and he participated prominently in many of the conflict's most significant battles.[55] When he announced his assumption of dictatorial powers in April 1939, Busch invoked the war and his own actions in it throughout the speech, claiming that he did not leave "the Chaco, field of national honor, until the final rifle had quieted." The war, he argued, had "revealed all the nation's weaknesses," which he was working to fix. The speech constructed a community of veterans, claiming that "all those who suffered in the flesh the heroic difficulties of the battlefield" shared an experience with Busch that made them unite with him to achieve "improvement, profound renovation, the purification of the national soul."[56] Employing a military metaphor, he promised that working outside of constitutional norms would allow him to "launch a new campaign to save this collapsing *patria*" that would draw on "the same faith, the same spirit of sacrifice" with which he had defended Bolivia on the battlefield.[57] He thus used the war and his actions in it as proof of his ardent nationalism, to justify his dictatorship, and to speak and act on behalf of all veterans. This speech was one of many discursive acts that created the idea of a Chaco generation and crafted a central place for veterans in postwar Bolivia.

After Busch's suicide, both the traditional and reformist contenders for the presidency, Generals Enrique Peñaranda and Bernadino Bilbao Rioja, sought to associate themselves with the heroic tradition of the war. Having commanded during the disaster, Peñaranda needed to rehabilitate his image. His supporters thus published a pamphlet defending his actions in the Chaco and celebrating him as a self-sacrificing war hero.[58] Bilbao Rioja, on the other hand, more successfully took up Busch's mantle, courting veterans' groups and depicting himself as representing all "authentic veterans of the Chaco."[59] He grew so popular that the traditional parties accused him of plotting a coup and forced him into exile.[60] Once in power, Peñaranda proved incapable of harnessing the veterans' movement. His public speeches mostly avoided references to the war, only bringing it up in relation to practical concerns, such as pensions for widows and the wounded.[61]

Radepa and the MNR attacked Peñaranda's administration by focusing relentlessly on the war and authorizing themselves through frontline service. In the debate over the Catavi massacre in 1943, for example, MNRista Rafael Otazo claimed to speak for the "sentiments of the nation," invoking his service as "a combatant for three years in the Chaco War, without even one day of rest."[62] The MNR/Radepa coup later that year intensified references to veterans. The new administration took concrete steps to strip power from elites who had avoided frontline service. Three months after assuming power, Villarroel issued a decree that limited congressional representation to those in possession of a demobilization booklet, prohibiting reservists on assignment or those with compensation-of-services booklets from serving because "the high responsibility of parliamentary function requires" that citizens "have complied with their obligations to defend the *Patria*."[63]

During the 1944–1945 constituent assembly, MNR representatives repeatedly invoked their wartime service. Alfonso Finot, for example, used the first-person plural to construct himself as part of a collective of veterans that supported Villarroel: "We, the youth, who went to the Chaco campaign.... We left the war hungry and malnourished.... We lost an extensive territory, it is true, but we lost it fighting inch by inch, irrigating those battlefields with the blood of Bolivia's workers and peasants."[64] Also claiming to speak for a community of veterans, his fellow MNRista Rodolfo Palenque asserted that the "Revolution," referring to the December 1943 coup that brought Villarroel to power, was the work of those, like him, "who fought on the front lines during the Chaco campaign."[65] These reformists used the war as shorthand for the fundamental problems they saw in Bolivian society and to portray themselves as the authentic representatives of the masses who had fought.

In the 1940s, the heroic legacy of the Chaco War was firmly the domain of reformist veterans like Radepa and the MNR. Hailing from both the traditional elite and the rising middle class, many of the MNR's young leaders had been radicalized by the wartime experience. Víctor Paz Estenssoro, Hernán Siles Zuazo, Juan Lechín, Augusto Céspedes, and Carlos Montenegro had all served as soldiers or sergeants.[66] They would later attribute their reformist convictions to prolonged contact with the masses during the war. They returned with the impassioned belief that they alone could speak for these actors, modernize the country, and effectively integrate the population. To build a political constituency, they forged a discursive and literal community of veterans, whom they depicted as bound together by the blood sacrificed during the war.

CLAIMS-MAKING BY BOLIVIA'S GOOD SONS

Politicians' efforts both reflected and helped cultivate active communities of Chaco veterans, who served as a moral force and important pressure groups throughout the postwar period. Although organizations formed to channel their voices and individuals invoked their suffering to make claims, most veterans received little financial compensation until decades after the war. While a detailed examination of veterans and their organizations needs further research, this section draws on military justice proceedings, decrees, legislative debates, newspaper coverage, and the secondary literature to offer an analysis of how veterans leveraged the wartime experience.

Most investment in veterans was discursive because the impoverished state could barely afford even minimal compensation for those orphaned, widowed, or permanently disabled by the war. Soldiers had earned wages while on active duty, but most frontline veterans did not become eligible for a pension until after the 1952 revolution.[67] Nor did a pension guarantee financial stability, especially after the inflationary crisis of the late 1930s. The pension for a permanently disabled rank-and-file soldier was only 9.7 bolivianos per month in May 1936, which was less than an adolescent messenger made at the time.[68] Congress attempted to rectify this situation, regularly debating how to raise pensions to keep up with galloping inflation. Agreeing that the wounded and widows deserved more state support for their sacrifice, legislators pontificated about how they were "abandoned in misery" and "dying of hunger and of being forgotten."[69] Between the war's end and the revolution, Congress passed at least twenty-three laws and the executive issued at least sixteen decrees related to Chaco War pensions.[70] But the country was heavily in debt, and no one wanted funds to come from taxing products from their regions.[71]

Qualifying for a pension involved a high level of bureaucratic literacy. Potential beneficiaries had to know they were entitled to a pension; be in possession of the documents needed to prove service, injury, or death; and submit the papers to the proper authorities by the designated date.[72] Pensions thus likely benefitted urban or formally educated sectors disproportionately. Several of the veterans interviewed by historian René Arze Aguirre in the 1980s explained that they had not been able to obtain a pension because they had not understood the benefits available, missed deadlines, lost the necessary documents, or had issues with different versions of names on the requisite paperwork.[73] The press at the time also noted the difficulty of some disabled veterans in obtaining pensions. One 1943 article told the story of Tomás Vitre Tambo, described as a poor and illiterate indigenous veteran from Caquiaviri (Pacajes, La Paz). Vitre Tambo claimed to have been injured after spending only three days on the front lines. Although he eventually lost an eye due to the wound, Vitre Tambo had also lost his documents and, because of the short time he spent on the front lines, could not find anyone to verify his service.[74]

In addition to providing limited pensions, the state attempted to compensate veterans through preferential hiring. Only weeks after assuming power, the Toro regime declared sweeping reform of public employment "as a prize for the effort and civic sacrifice" of those "who had complied with their patriotic duties." The decree declared vacant all public positions at the national, departmental, and municipal levels, with the goal of ending the employment of those who had been illegitimately declared unfit for service or reservists on assignment. It established a committee in each department capital that would be charged with identifying worthy veterans. Several clauses in this decree, however, suggest that it was mostly for show. The preamble stated that ranked preference would apply "given equality of competency and morality." This wording would allow many to retain employment based on hierarchies other than that of wartime service, such as education and administrative experience. The decree also set up a process by which disputes would be adjudicated if those in charge of public offices refused to replace current employees.[75] Even if implemented impeccably, this decree, by its very design, would assist only the formally educated and literate veterans considered competent to hold such positions.

The limited reach of these official measures raises the question of whether the veterans' movement that reformers like the MNR and Radepa claimed to represent was really a national one. Veterans' associations certainly proliferated in the wake of the war, with the most prominent, the Veterans' Legion (LEC), receiving government authorization in September 1935. Although the LEC began as an apolitical mutualist association, it became a major political actor during military socialist rule.[76] Other organizations included Iron Star, Mariscal Santa Cruz, the National Association of Socialist Veterans (ANDES), and the Association of Ex-Prisoners of War (AEP).[77] Most restricted membership to those who could prove service on the front lines, explicitly excluding rearguard service.[78] The leaders of these associations were relatively elite, having served primarily as reserve officers.[79] However, we still lack an understanding of veterans' movements on the ground, including their goals, publications, membership, and accomplishments. Until the completion of such a study, we will not be able to fully evaluate James Malloy's 1970 contention that the postwar ferment had little direct impact on the rural masses.[80]

Evidence from the secondary literature shows that many peasant and labor leaders in the 1940s and 1950s were veterans who spoke of their wartime experience and the ties it provided them as transformative. Based on field-work in the late 1960s, Jorge Dandler concludes that peasant leaders in Cochabamba felt empowered by the war based on the idea that they had proven themselves capable in the trenches. He shows that these leaders used veterans' organizations to forge ties with teachers, landowners, and lawyers who could help them achieve personal and collective goals.[81] He cites the specific case of José Rojas, a former *colono* who had enlisted at the age of sixteen and would later become a powerful peasant union leader in Ucureña.[82] The war also defined the trajectory of labor leaders like Trotskyist Miguel Alandia Pantoja, who had also been held captive in Paraguay.[83]

In addition to serving as an example of veteran leadership, Melitón Gallardo, who eventually led an indigenous movement among *colonos* in Chuquisaca, powerfully demonstrates how veteran status served as a new form of distinction that could begin to destabilize Bolivia's entrenched hierarchies. He remembered his time as a prisoner in Paraguay as transformative and attributed his political awakening to overhearing and then eventually participating in discussions about inequality and internal colonialism with mestizo compatriots in the POW camp. After the war, he experienced limited but direct benefits of veteran status. Although his poor Spanish-language skills prevented him from obtaining public employment in the Sucre Prefecture under the preferential hiring act, he attributed his ability to circulate in the city center, be served at a bar, and secure work at a bakery to his participation in the war.[84]

The 1945 Indigenous Congress sponsored by the Villarroel administration suggests that patron-client relationships forged during the war contributed to the rise of some of the era's indigenous leaders. Attended by over a thousand indigenous delegates, many of whom were veterans, the congress resulted in decrees that outlawed all compulsory non-agricultural labor, mandated that landowners must establish and fund schools for indigenous workers, and called for the establishment of a rural labor code.[85] Although presented as revolutionary, these decrees in many ways represented a continuation of the military socialists' work and even of Bautista Saavedra's efforts in the 1910s to win the support of the Cacique Apoderado movement. All gestured toward rectifying the injustices of land reforms without actually redistributing land or upsetting the racialized social order of the Bolivian countryside. In the same vein, the Villarroel decrees promised education as a path to formal citizenship rather than granting citizenship rights to Indians.

An examination of the indigenous leaders of this event clearly shows that the war provided them access to powerful patrons. Antonio Alvarez Mamani, one of the congress's early organizers, was an educated and bilingual indigenous veteran-turned-activist who had acted as an interpreter for both Busch and Villarroel during the war.[86] Also a veteran, the event's president, Francisco Chipana Ramos, had served as an aide for Busch in the field.[87] Chipana Ramos became an important symbol of the congress, coming to represent

Representativo del indio boliviano

FIGURE 5.1. Francisco Chipana Ramos with Chaco War metal. "Representativo del indio boliviano," *La Calle*, May 13, 1945, Archivo Hemerográfico, Biblioteca y Archivo Histórico de la Asamblea Legislativa Plurinacional, La Paz. Used with permission.

the face of indigenous leadership in the Paceño press.[88] This face was explicitly that of a veteran. Articles in newspapers from across the political spectrum universally invoked Chipana Ramos's wartime service. Printed images also emphasized his veteran status, depicting him, as in figure 5.1, with a medal from the Chaco War pinned to his poncho.[89] The published glosses and translations of his speeches portrayed him as constantly returning to the theme of Indians' wartime service. The excerpt included of his opening speech, for example, ended, "The Revolution has much to teach us. We have chests of bronze, but we know nothing. This is also why, in the Chaco, many of you went from here to there like idiots and died like dogs. Now the president with the new officials will teach us to work the land with machines to live better."[90]

Adopting tropes from *indigenista* discourse, Chipana Ramos's speeches asserted a place for indigenous veterans at the center of the nation, depicting them as proud of having fought for the *patria*. His words portrayed the Villarroel administration as a revolution that was measurably different from the state that had led so many to die "like dogs." His speeches, much like MNRistas' rhetoric in congressional debates, implied an alliance forged in the Chaco between elite reformers and frontline soldiers that had the potential to make Bolivia a true conscript nation for which indigenous soldiers would be proud to fight.

The prevailing message of the published versions of Chipana Ramos's speeches was that fellow delegates should trust Villarroel. He emphasized loyalty, portrayed labor as a patriotic duty, and invested the state with a tutelary role vis-à-vis Indians. Yet his words also insisted on the contractual nature of the event, emphasizing the government's obligation to provide the protection, education, and tools that would allow Indians to prosper. Chipana Ramos presented indigenous-state relations as a paternalistic model of authority in which the state had the active role of protecting and raising its indigenous children. However, this paternalism should not obscure the fact that the delegates who attended Bolivia's first state-sponsored indigenous congress affirmed collective demands as if they were rights-bearing citizens. This congress and the authority with which its delegates spoke were possible because of the mass participation of indigenous men in the Chaco War, which authorized them to speak as good sons of the *patria*. Unlike in the prewar period, the mainstream press in 1945 was willing to present Chipana Ramos as speaking with authority and making claims for Indians' place in the nation as "sons of the same soil."[91]

Evidence suggests that at least some veterans outside of leadership positions also leveraged their wartime service to make demands on the state. Historian Roberto Fernández Terán cites several examples of petitions to the La Paz municipality in which veterans invoked the idea of special rights and privileges. One written in the name of Pedro, Manuel, and Manuel Segundo Mamani stated, "Due to our condition as evacuees, we have the right to the authorities treating us with some more consideration."[92] Based on his work with district court records, Luis Sierra argues that frontline service constituted part of "the definition of honor for residents of indigenous neighborhoods."[93] In keeping with the MNR's claim to represent the masses, *La Calle*, the daily paper associated with the party, regularly printed articles in which less privileged and usually indigenous veterans voiced complaints and demands.[94] One particularly detailed article concerned an unnamed indigenous sergeant from Milluguayo (North Yungas, La Paz), who accused his *patrón*, Don Benjamín Guerra, of evading duty during the war and abusing the sergeant despite the fact that he "fought against the *pilas* and Won [his] rank."[95] Oral histories also depict veterans as commanding respect. Agricultural laborer Cristóbal Arancia remembered that his *patrón* treated him better after he returned from the war, no longer using the whip to force him to work. He described himself as braver and "more of a man." Veterans, he noted, were more willing to rebel and resist.[96]

Veterans drew on the discursive project of the nation as expressed by the leaders who passed the 1907 conscription law and mobilized these soldiers to war as sons of Bolivia. Patriotic discourse had escaped the control of officers and legislators and had been widely appropriated by veterans from across the social spectrum. Bolivia was still a hierarchical society dependent on racialized differences, but a new hierarchy of wartime service had been added to the old ones of education, ethnicity, and social class.

Despite wreaking havoc on Bolivia's military institution, party system, and traditional leaders, the Chaco War strengthened the state. Administering the war's aftermath led to increased contact with the state as veterans, evaders, deserters, widows, and orphans navigated the paperwork needed to vote, travel, work, or receive pensions. Along with the return of veterans to communities throughout the country, this bureaucratic process spread knowledge of the state and helped produce investment from below in military service. Ironically, the government and army's many failures during the war, which had led to the death, mutilation, suffering, and capture of its soldiers, encouraged many veterans and their families to engage with rather than reject the state. These actors had a stake in assuring that those who had evaded service would not escape without penalty. And the bad sons who sacrificed time, labor, or funds to redeem themselves in the eyes of the state were in turn more invested in ensuring that others would do the same. The morass of laws designed to bring Bolivia's bad sons back into the national family without belittling the service of veterans was ultimately consistent with the long-term trend of passing strict laws and then granting concessions in the name of practicality.

New hierarchies of service to the nation emerged as some veterans gained respect, access to jobs, and a sense of entitlement to make individual and collective demands on the state. Compared to the prewar terms *omiso* and *remiso,* these new categories did not correlate as closely with hierarchies of ethnicity, class, and education. This did not, of course, mean the end of racialization or paternalistic views of Indians as children; in fact, many laws and even the 1945 Indigenous Congress were premised on these very ideas. But in the postwar environment, the hierarchy of service could overlie and perhaps even trump other hierarchies. Veterans like Chipana Ramos could claim credibility and authority based on their personal participation in the war and the collective contribution of the many indigenous men who had fought on the front lines. Patriotic service thus authorized new actors to speak more confidently based on an assumption that the central state would listen; in so far as the state fulfilled these expectations, this interaction contributed to a sense of belonging to the nation.

CHAPTER 6

SOLDIERS AND VETERANS BUT STILL NOT CITIZENS

In December 1939, future indigenous activist Luciano Tapia joined the long line of young men snaking around the barracks in La Paz. After spending his early childhood in the mining district of Corocoro and his *ayllu* of Qallirpa, Tapia had joined his grandmother in La Paz as part of the migratory streams in place even before the war. When he was about nine, his father marched off to fight in the Chaco, and his mother placed him in domestic service to help support the family. Although he continued to work, an aunt helped him get a primary education at a Franciscan school. He held various jobs in La Paz, Qallirpa, and mining districts before presenting for military service at the age of seventeen.[1] Yet "such a quantity of young men" showed up with him at the recruitment commission in La Paz that he used what little money he had to travel almost one hundred kilometers to the barracks in Corocoro. Even there, so many men had presented that the officers had their choice of conscripts, selecting only the "most robust and best educated."[2] These men queued up at recruitment centers first and foremost to obtain the military service booklet that, in Tapia's words, "accredited [him] as a Bolivian citizen."[3]

As reflected in Tapia's narrative, military conscription thrived in the postwar period. The armed forces grew from the five thousand troops mandated by the initial protocol with Paraguay in June 1935 to a high of perhaps twenty thousand in 1952.[4] The increased importance of military service documents, the state's capacity to devote more resources to conscription, social pressure from peers and veterans, and individuals' power to use service to make claims on the state combined to make military service something that men did. Strikingly, however, many of the good sons who had served on the front lines and who filled the barracks in the 1940s were still noncitizen soldiers, at least in the sense of holding formal citizenship rights. Despite the increasing acceptance of conscription and the rhetorical emphasis on veterans' sacrifice, postwar Bolivia was by no means a citizenry in arms. Even the reformist administrations of the military socialists and Villarroel were unable to break from deeply entrenched notions of hierarchy, explicitly choosing to retain the literacy provisions that barred the vast majority from voting. Bolivia's illiterate sons owed the duty of military service but were not "ready" for the responsibility of citizenship. A war during which many non-citizen conscripts lost their lives was not enough to immediately overturn these long-held beliefs.

Characterized by racialized hierarchies and gendered abuse, obligatory military service continued to serve assimilationist goals. However, mass participation in a failed war and the circulation of reformist and revolutionary ideologies had fundamentally challenged the discursive structure of political legitimacy, which did begin to affect attitudes and cultural norms in the military. Chaco veterans and conscripts like Tapia expressed a new sense of entitlement in their interactions with the state and used their military status to get ahead in postwar Bolivia. More importantly, at least some officers responded, investigating their petitions, listening to their testimony, expressing interest in conscripts' well-being, and even taking tentative steps to include indigenous actors in the military's pantheon.

POSTWAR CONSCRIPTION

The tremendous effort put toward raising successive armies for war had significantly strengthened the military's bureaucracy and ability to act on a national scale. Widespread mobilization during the war also familiarized a larger subset of the population with the idea of military service, and the presence of so many veterans likely influenced relatives and neighbors to serve. The war had normalized and valorized conscription, transforming it into a routine part of many communities' lives. Recruitment thus massified in the postwar period: around sixteen thousand men a year decided to line up in front of registration tables, submit to medical examinations, and perhaps enter a regiment.[5] This figure represented 60 percent of the male age cohort, which was a dramatic increase from the early years of obligatory military service, when it hovered around 38 percent.[6] In fact, so many men were presenting in the early 1940s that more than half received immediate discharge without training.[7] Evidence suggests, however, that conscripts' demographics in the 1940s were quite distinct from those depicted in the 1950 census, reflecting the effective reach of the state far more than that of the nation as a whole.

The soldiers who populated the ranks of Bolivia's postwar military were the product of a considerably stronger, more bureaucratic, and more centralized conscription process than had existed before the Chaco War. Local civilian authorities no longer played an official role in conscription. Rather than registering for military service in their home communities, young men traveled to designated recruitment centers, where institutional actors controlled registration. Nor could men arrange for medical exemptions through their family doctors; the military instead controlled who would determine their fitness.[8] Registration no longer occurred months before recruitment, thus solving the problem of men registering but then failing to present. The military had also moved to semiannual recruitment in January and July to achieve a more constant level of experienced conscripts and avoid having the ranks depopulated at the end of each year.

For example, on July 4, 1949, Major Julio Olmos officially signed and stamped the final military register sheet for the city of Cochabamba's recruitment center, attesting that 470 men had presented.[9] For the previous four days, his subalterns (officers, NCOs, or even formally educated conscripts) had sat at a registration table to enter the vital data of the men who had fulfilled the legal obligation of presenting for military service. They used a recruitment form to record each man's name, age, marital status, profession, literacy status, height, weight, chest measurement, place of residence, and nearest living relative. In the process, they were supposed to inspect documents proving his identity and age. The registrant was then bathed and had his head shaved before a designated medical professional examined him to determine whether he was fit for military service. The medical committee noted the results as well as a brief physical description of each man on the form. Those declared fit entered a lottery if more had presented than the center's quota; those not exempted by lottery were immediately escorted to their new military units. Upon completion of this process, the data from the recruitment forms were entered onto a preprinted table. Along with the original forms, the set of tables that Olmos signed made its way to the Ministry of Defense to be bound into that year's military register and archived.[10]

Olmos and his colleagues were supposed to follow precise rules in registering men, determining who would serve, and archiving the paperwork that documented the process. Conscription was to be an impersonal process in which young men's connections, appearance, and personality should have held no sway. Officers' performance of this bureaucratic ideal was an important part of Bolivia's aspirations of being a modern state. Conscription was supposed to encompass all men in the national territory, treat them equally, and bring them into a centralized documentary regime in which their information would be stored for easy reference and verification. Yet this bureaucracy still functioned imperfectly. Olmos's fifteen sheets represented a rarity in 1949 in that the complete, signed set was eventually bound into the military register. This occurred for only two other recruitment commissions that year.[11] Evidence from a participant and even a military source also belied this bureaucratic ideal, suggesting that commissions chose to register only those recruits deemed the strongest and most capable, with individual conscripts sometimes able to convince officers that they would make good soldiers.[12]

The fragmentary nature of evidence from military registers prior to 1952 necessarily limits and qualifies what can be drawn from them. As with the

TABLE 6.1. Comparison of Professions in 1949 Military Register with 1950 Census

Professional Category	Percent of Conscripts	Percent in Census
Agriculture	24	69
Mining	0.4	3
Artisans	24	7
Construction	10	3
Transportation	16	2
Service	2	3.4
Commerce	5.5	5
Industry	1.5	1.2
Professionals	4.5	5
Students	12	14

Census data on professions reflect all economically active male age cohorts. Census data on students represent the specific age cohort. Although students and professionals are proportionally represented, presumably many of the students who registered would go on to become professionals, suggesting an overrepresentation of this group. Sources: 1949 Military Register, RT-MDN (20 percent sample); Dirección General de Estadística y Censos, *Censo demográfico* (1950), 87, 148–49, 231–52.

statistics from the Chaco War, the number and demographic profile of those registering and serving in the postwar era remain fuzzy and imprecise. In the absence of more complete data, however, this source can still provide some sense of conscription's reach and demographic profile. It shows a robust system that drew a significant number of conscripts from all of Bolivia's departments except for the newly created Pando. Although the quantity of missing sheets prevents analysis of regional variation, the data on the departments of La Paz and Cochabamba are quite robust. These data show that the percentage of conscripts from La Paz was roughly proportional to the department's population at the time but that conscripts from Cochabamba were significantly overrepresented.[13] This suggests that Cochabamba's history of domination by large estates and long-standing integration into the national economy made the conscription system more effective there, due to either coercive structures or social pressure.[14] Men registering for military service were also far more urban than the Bolivian population as a whole, showing that the borders of the Bolivian state did not match those of the national territory.[15]

The conscripts whose data appear on the 1949 register had a wide variety of educational backgrounds and professions. About a quarter worked in agriculture. More than half claimed skilled or semiskilled professions such as tailor, carpenter, bricklayer, painter, chauffeur, or mechanic. Twelve percent were still in school, and another 5 percent claimed higher-status professions such as employee, telegraph operator, or businessman.[16] Yet this group was

FIGURE 6.1: Conscript Walter Murillo with his mother, Rosa Salcedo Guarachi, 1940. Personal collection of Rosa Marina Murillo, La Paz. Used with permission.

far from representative of the Bolivian population. Men who registered for military service were disproportionately concentrated in certain professions: white-collar professionals, artisans, and workers in the construction and transportation sectors were far more likely to register than those working in agriculture and mining (see table 6.1). These disparities again reflect the urban bias of the conscription system at the time. Although miners were a symbolically important segment of the population, their numbers were always relatively small, never surpassing 4 percent. Among conscripts, the number of miners represented less than half of 1 percent. However, these statistics underrepresent the number of former conscripts working in the mines since some likely became miners after completing their military service. While the division between peasants and miners at first appears stark, it was in fact quite porous, as miners came from and often maintained ties to rural communities.[17]

Where conscripts stand out the most is in literacy rates: the 1949 military register reported that an astounding 82 percent of conscripts were literate, as compared with 26 percent of their male age cohort. Even if these statistics were exaggerated and aspirational, including conscripts with the slimmest of claims to literacy, they indicate that the vast majority of literate Bolivian men registered for service each year.[18] Walter Murillo was likely characteristic of this class of literate conscripts. A student from La Paz, Murillo was the son of a hatmaker. Two of his half brothers had served in the Chaco, and one had perished during the war. Pictured in figure 6.1 with his mother, Rosa Salcedo Guarachi, Murillo presented for service in February 1940 and was assigned to the Bolívar Second Artillery Regiment in Oruro. During his seven and a half months of service, he was promoted to private first class and then to corporal due to his good conduct and topography skills.[19]

Two factors likely account for the overrepresentation of literate men, urban dwellers, Cochabambinos, and certain professional categories. First, men fitting one or more of these categories were more closely tied to the state and thus needed the documents provided by military service more than their counterparts. Second, the military gatekeepers that ultimately determined who registered and served most likely preferred men from these categories. The 1949 military register shows that obligatory military service had grown deep roots in urban environs, drawing people from a range of social classes, including many recent migrants from the provinces.[20] Yet vast swathes of the countryside remained functionally outside of the conscription system, producing just a smattering of soldiers each year. The experience of lining up to register had become a ritual, but this ritual was much more compelling and had more force for the third of the population living in urban areas or with some formal education.[21]

RACIALIZED HIERARCHIES OF SERVICE AND CITIZENSHIP

Outside of anecdotal observations, which continued to represent conscripts as majority indigenous, little evidence exists as to the demographics of the men who actually joined the ranks after registering. Those who did entered an institution shaped by deep-seated ideas about cultural difference and explicitly designed to assimilate non-Spanish-speaking soldiers. Like Liberals before them, postwar reformists expressed faith in the power of the barracks to prepare the masses for citizenship by teaching them Spanish, literacy skills, and patriotic nationalism. And formally educated youth continued to experience privilege, both codified and informal, in conscription procedures and barracks life. However, the postwar ferment did have an effect: the beliefs and conduct of some officers changed in ways that could begin to alter conscripts' experience.

The deepest continuity can be found in the failure of postwar reformists, despite their claims to represent the masses, to expand formal citizenship beyond the thin stratum of literate men. Embracing the social constitutionalism spreading throughout Latin America, the military socialists held a convention in 1938 to rewrite the constitution for the first time since 1880. Veterans and leftists, including future leaders of the MNR and PIR, predominated because many traditional parties declined to participate in the election. A radical departure from previous liberal constitutions, the resulting document stressed the state's responsibilities to its people, limited the rights of foreign companies, guaranteed the right to unionize, and recognized the corporate rights of indigenous communities.[22] Led by Wálter Guevara Arze and Víctor Paz Estenssoro, reformists passionately but unsuccessfully advocated for state control of tin exports and for redistributing land to peasants.[23] Yet when it came to citizenship, *no one* proposed eliminating the literacy requirement, as had recently been done in Mexico, Argentina, and Uruguay.[24] While the constitution did expand the electorate by removing property and income requirements, it still barred all women and most men, including veterans, by requiring that citizens be male, be over twenty-one, have Bolivian nationality, be enrolled in the Civic Register, and be able to read and write.[25] Given that the 1950 census reported 69 percent of the population to be illiterate, this severely limited formal citizenship.[26] As historian Rossana Barragán notes, the idea of society "as a collectivity made up of people with the same rights was still difficult to imagine," even for reformists.[27]

Legislators' comments about military service illustrate why they were reticent to end this legal exclusion. Speakers on the floor of Congress echoed their early twentieth-century predecessors in asserting the power of the barracks to uproot "the Indian from the indifference in which he lives."[28] Implying that indigenous soldiers had few loyalties to the idea of Bolivia, they claimed that the army "must first create the *Patria*, before it could be adequately defended."[29] Most blatant was a comment by United Socialist Party Deputy Desiderio M. Rivera in advocating for the use of armed force to repress a rural uprising in 1941: "It is necessary to protect citizens from possible attacks by Indians."[30] Clearly, he conceived of these Indians as outside the Bolivian family deserving of state protection. Even postwar reformers could not escape long-standing prejudices that defined rural and indigenous people as needing to be improved before they could be citizens.

The *Revista Militar* reinforced this narrative, publishing articles that professed the power of military training to "reincorporate the indigenous class into the productive forces of the nation."[31] According to these articles, indigenous conscripts were motivated solely by the need for a military service booklet, which would "save them once and for all from the domination and cruelty of the Corregidor."[32] In the barracks, however, they gained far more: literacy, Spanish-language skills, and knowledge of their civic duties. They returned to "their yearned-for homes carrying with them ingrained ideas about civilization that [had] prepared them to redeem themselves from their sad situation, then becoming elements for the effective progress of the country."[33] These articles portrayed military officers as the agents of this change. Their "selfless labor" taught indigenous conscripts "the duties of citizenship," making them "useful and beneficial for society."[34] One even wrote of a monolingual Quechua recruit who flowered under the attention of a benevolent officer. By the end of his service, this conscript had become the model citizen: fluent in Spanish, literate, and taking an interest in national issues.[35] These articles conveyed a clear message: the indigenous majority would need to radically modify its way of life before becoming trustworthy citizens and effective defenders of the nation. And the army would accomplish this task.

Much of this message had not changed since 1905 when Lieutenant Colonel Carlos Nuñez del Prado presented the fictional Quilco as having no sense of *patria*, belonging to little more than "his sheep and llamas."[36] Quilco's function in the story was to demonstrate the need to transform the population through obligatory military service. This dream was also explicitly ethnocidal: the army would kill the Indian to save the man, using the barracks to create disciplined soldiers who obeyed authority figures, were patriotic, and shed indigeneity as they came to participate in a unified, homogenous, and modern nation.

Like Quilco's creator, these officers writing in the late 1930s imbued military service with the power to create a unified nation by transforming the lifeways of the indigenous population. But they also show how some officers' thinking was beginning to shift. Instead of using explicitly civilizing terms to depict abject and barbarous Indians, they used the language of nationalist modernization to describe their efforts to form workers and citizens in the barracks. However, officers still drove this process; authority and notions of racialized hierarchy had by no means disappeared. Indeed, one lieutenant in 1942 praised military service for "cementing our nationality upon the indestructible bases of order and culture," implying that conscripts' communities lacked precisely these characteristics. The difference in his formulation, though, was that he asserted that military training would produce "not only men capable of defending the Patria but also efficient citizens" capable of taking up the "weapons of work."[37]

Not surprisingly, hierarchies of race and social class continued to dominate the army that produced these articles. Conscripts from "the better families" served shorter terms and often lived or ate at home rather than in the barracks.[38] And Congress regularly proposed codifying this inequality by providing students and professionals with official reductions in service.[39] Speaking Spanish seems to have been the most important factor in determining a soldier's ability to perform leadership tasks and even routine guard duty.[40] Some deemed less capable found themselves completely segregated from fellow conscripts. José Mamani of the Sucre Infantry Regiment in the mining region of Corocoro reportedly slept on the floor of the officer's club (rather than in the dormitory) and did not attend training.[41] Select units usually excluded illiterate soldiers.[42] These units were uncomfortable places for those who did not fit in. One soldier, identified as an illiterate mestizo assigned to guard the Legislative Palace, reported feeling isolated and being mocked by his more educated fellows.[43]

As in the prewar period, conscripts' labor assignments reflected racialized hierarchies, with indigenous men disproportionately performing manual labor. Typical of soldiers assigned to 1940s sapper units was Pedro Ayadiri Ohari, a twenty-two-year-old agricultural laborer from Pocoata (Potosí). Described in military records as a mostly illiterate Quechua speaker who understood a little Spanish, Ayadiri served eight months as a sapper.[44] US military attachés visiting these road units in the 1940s confirmed this trend, reporting that the "enlisted men are Indians with very slight knowledge of Spanish" who "live under very primitive conditions."[45] The fact that assignment to such units served as punishment for urban soldiers reveals the implied hierarchy.[46] Even conscripts in La Paz faced labor discrimination, as superiors denied military training to the less educated. For example, the commanders of a company garrisoned near the capital explained that they picked "the soldiers least capable of carrying out individual training" to use as "a special group of workers." They classified at least one of these workers as an "uncommunicative indigenous soldier" who did not speak Spanish and was "illiterate and very slow in his mental activity."[47]

Even official regulations continued to differentiate based on paternalistic ideas about race and class. For example, a 1940 decree mandating the inspection of military service documents created a tiered system to fine violators: all indigenous men would pay fifty bolivianos, whereas this fine would be doubled for "non-indigenous manual laborers, artisans, and workers" and tripled for professionals and highly educated individuals.[48] And magistrates in military justice proceedings usually chose to assume that far from willfully neglecting their duties, Indians were ignorant children in need of benevolent guidance. As had occurred during the war, cases in the 1940s often ended with invocations of the offender's "indigenous mentality" or "condition as an illiterate *indígena*" as extenuating factors.[49] These comments reflected a persistent conviction that indigenous men did not fully belong to the Bolivian nation and therefore could not be held equally responsible for failures in patriotic duty.

Some individual officers, however, did exhibit new attitudes toward the indigenous and popular classes. Most surprising was Major Ricardo Herbas's inclusion of indigenous heroes in a 1938 speech to his troops in the Ayacucho Regiment. Before the soldiers took their oath to the flag on Army Day, Herbas reminded them of those that had sacrificed for their "liberty" from Spanish tyranny. In listing Bolivia's "protomartyrs," Herbas opened with Tomás Katari and Túpac Amaru, indigenous leaders of the 1780–1781 rebellions, before moving on to more traditional *criollo* heroes of independence like Pedro Murillo and José Miguel Lanza.[50] This was a substantive shift that indicated an attempt to reconceptualize the relationship between the military and indigeneity. Rather than erasing indigeneity, this particular narrative of the military's heroic deeds expanded to explicitly include indigenous actors.[51] However, in addition to being appropriated, these figures also had to be appropriate, as shown by the exclusion of Túpac Katari (Julián Apaza), the third prominent rebel leader from the 1780s. Of even humbler origin than Tomás Katari, Apaza was strongly associated with the idea of race war and likely seen as too radical for Herbas's list of heroes.[52]

This discursive change was accompanied by substantive ones, at least in military justice proceedings. Many of these investigations look quite different from those of the 1920s, which had focused almost exclusively on officers and literate soldiers. Tribunals in the postwar period regularly gathered and even heeded testimony from indigenous and illiterate conscripts. At least some of the officers acting as magistrates appear to have taken an active interest in actors whom they had ignored prior to the war.[53] They also began investigating desertion and suicide in more depth, probing *why* conscripts had snuck off or killed themselves, specifically whether any officers or military procedures had provoked the incident.[54] While they had begun to ask similar questions about rations, receipt of wages, and abuse during the war, this intensified questioning reflected new ideas about the military's duties to its soldiers. Prosecutors in the 1940s regularly asked witnesses about the conscript's personality, any punishment he had received, any concerns he might have expressed for his family, and his relationship with other members of his regiment.[55] This paternalistic interest in the well-being and grievances of soldiers from the popular classes suggests a narrowing of social distance after the war.

The lack of consistency in military officers' writing about and actions toward conscripts is a reminder that changes in social norms occur through the daily actions of individuals who often disagree with their peers and who themselves can be inconsistent in their beliefs and actions. Change in military discourse and practice came unevenly as reformists tried to break with the past and include new actors but also found themselves chained to deep-seated prejudices. They took a new interest in the masses who had

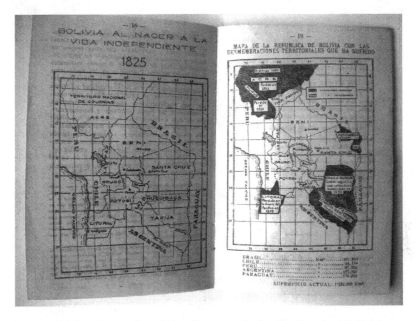

FIGURE 6.2: Maps printed in 1941 military service booklet that show Bolivia's territorial losses. Personal collection of Rosa Marina Murillo, La Paz. Used with permission.

participated in the war but could not break with the idea that these masses would have to transform before being entrusted with the responsibility of formal citizenship. As part of efforts to revive its image after a failed campaign, the army pledged yet again to accomplish this task. Making the population less indigenous thus remained central to the institution's mission. However, the treatment indigenous and illiterate conscripts received in the barracks worked at counter purposes to promises to nationalize and educate this population. Segregating and granting privileges to formally educated soldiers meant that they could not serve as models. Relegating to manual tasks the conscripts perceived as least prepared offered few opportunities for them to learn the skills and civic-mindedness that military service promised to instill.

THE EMBRACE OF MILITARY SERVICE

This vision of the army as a nationalizing force had been a justification for obligatory military service since the turn of the century. In the wake of the disastrous war, however, reformist leaders paired it with the idea of the military as a productive force that would literally build Bolivia. This would eventually lead to major shifts in characterizations of the military and the martial purpose of military service. Yet many aspects of barracks life remained little changed from the prewar period described in chapter 2. Officers and NCOs still routinely used illegal and sometimes horrific physical punishment in response to perceived indiscipline or disrespect. Conscripts continued to develop cliques and intimate friendships while in the ranks and use gendered taunts to influence their fellows. Even as the military strengthened its conscription process and formalized military justice proceedings, it was far from an impersonal, bureaucratic institution. In fact, the personal nature of military service was part of what made it a formative experience in which many men took pride. It was becoming an essential component of manhood in certain communities.

Prior to 1938, the constitution had charged the military with "the conservation of order" and the "defense of independence and national integrity."[56] This martial purpose remained strong in the postwar period, as the military embraced a narrative of a dismembered nation that needed to be defended. Military service booklets issued to conscripts in the 1940s contained a map of Bolivia at independence next to a map that documented "the territorial dismemberment that it had suffered" (see figure 6.2) between 1860 and 1935. The inclusion of these maps along with the lyrics to the national anthem and the slogan "To love the *patria* is a duty! To die for her is a glory!" sought to instill a nationalist spirit in conscripts to protect and revenge their wounded mother.[57]

However, reformist ideology, along with the sense that the military had profoundly failed at its martial tasks, led to an official expansion of its mission to include cooperation "in work on roads, communications, and colonization."[58] During debate over this clause in the 1938 Constitution, legislators emphasized the value of this work and agreed it could be accomplished without compromising the mission of preparing for war. They hoped these tasks would repair the institution's image: "It is necessary to change," stated one representative, "the impression of the people that the Army only consumes and does not produce."[59] A 1939 measure then created farms on state land with the goal of agricultural self-sufficiency for military forces.[60]

Soldiers' productive labor thus gained prominence in the aftermath of the war, both in official discourse and in practice. Military authorities introduced more than seventy different units named for types of manual labor (Agricultural, Colonization, Hydraulic, Engineering, Railroad, Sapper) rather than for programs of military training (Infantry, Artillery, Cavalry).[61] However, even martial units performed nonmartial labor: in 1941, the famed Colorados Infantry Regiment hacked out an eighteen-kilometer stretch between Corocoro and Ballivián.[62] In 1948, more than one thousand conscripts worked on building a new general barracks in La Paz.[63] The same year, conscript Rafael Montero of the Colorados Infantry Regiment described the seventeen months he had spent building a school in Sucre as "treading on mud, making bricks, putting stone over stone."[64]

Although these labors differed little from those performed before and during the war, nonmartial labor was becoming increasingly legible within the nation. The La Paz daily *El Diario*, for example, emphasized use of military labor in infrastructure projects, publishing photographs of soldiers moving earth with their shovels and arguing that their sweat and toil would "surely bring economic expansion to the country."[65] In the aftermath of the Chaco War, work had emerged as a credible terrain in which all Bolivians could come together discursively. Officers in the barracks and halls of government aimed to form Bolivians who understood their labor in the mines, in the fields, and on infrastructure as directly contributing to national interests. But they had not yet succeeded: a 1943 recruitment manual mentioned conscripts' resistance to performing road and agricultural work; it dictated that only *omisos* seeking military service documents after the age of nineteen be assigned to such missions.[66]

Some communities, on the other hand, wholeheartedly embraced the military's productive labors, even attempting to dictate the assignment of conscripts from their region to local projects. In August 1938, for example, three civilian officials in Apolo, a tropical town in northeastern Bolivia at the edge of the Amazon Basin, begged that the detachment of new conscripts from their municipality be assigned to local roadwork rather than sent to the Amazonian province of Beni. They reported significant resistance among the population, especially the women, who had "congregated in front of the barracks" to express feeling "defrauded of their legitimate aspirations for progress."[67] They were not alone: *El Diario* reported in 1947 that hundreds more conscripts than usual had presented in Vallegrande (Santa Cruz) based on the assumption that they would work on a road between their home community and Lagunillas. Resentment developed when they were instead garrisoned at Roboré, more than six hundred kilometers away.[68] These peripheral communities seemed to have viewed military conscription not as service to the nation but rather as a mechanism to mobilize labor to achieve local objectives at the expense of the central state.

The men who presented, however, may have had more than local needs in mind. Increasing numbers of rural people were migrating after the war, and obtaining military service documents had become a necessity for those seeking to travel or work outside of their community. Universities and employers demanded military paperwork, and police regularly stopped people on the streets to inspect their documents.[69] While enforcement was still arbitrary, it was more effective than before the war. Unlike in the 1920s, military justice records from the 1940s contain stories of family members pressuring loved ones to complete service. Juan Prudencio Aczara, for example, reported that when he deserted in 1947, his mother rejected him for abandoning the barracks. Unable to convince him to return, she reported him to local military authorities, who arrested him and took him back to his regiment.[70] Another mother even adopted the military's narrative of making productive citizens. Juana Valencia of La Paz wrote to the regional commander in 1950, asking that her son be re-enrolled after deserting several months earlier. Invoking his alcoholism and lack of respect for her, she expressed her confidence in the army's ability to put him "on a good path" as a "school that forms men healthy in body and soul."[71]

These anecdotes, along with the Tapia memoir that opened this chapter, suggest the increased importance of not only documents but also the experience of military service. Tapia and his fellows did not amass at recruitment centers just because of the state's coercive power to demand military service documents. Tapia *chose* to enter the ranks; if he had not, he would have registered in La Paz and likely been discharged without training due to the excess of recruits. Instead, he used his resources to travel to a place where he thought he would be accepted into a unit. He and Juana Valencia seem to have believed that time in the barracks would provide conscripts with some experience, material advantage, prestige, or skills beyond the documents that protected them from impressment.

Life in the barracks was still profoundly violent and gendered, which was part of what convinced young men to serve. Surviving harsh psychological and physical punishments in a homosocial space supposedly made conscripts into "men." Memoirs and military justice records emphasize the abuse, humiliation, and privation of barracks life. Captain Humberto Fernández, for example, testified that he considered physical punishment a necessary component of readying soldiers for war. He told the military tribunal that he regularly recovered stolen items by ordering NCOs to give "chocolate" to the soldiers.[72] Unique to the Bolivian military, this slang term usually refers to the practice of hitting soldiers with hands or belts, although it can also describe exhausting physical exercise, such as walking in a squatting position.[73] In use by 1931, the term suggests that violence was being presented, perhaps sarcastically, as a gift to the soldier. As Captain Fernández indicated, officers and NCOs performed this violence to toughen up new recruits, implying that they needed the experience to be successful soldiers.

In this case, conscript Lorenzo Espejo Canda testified that the captain had "ordered the NCOs to punish us with their belts, declaring at the same time that he wanted to see some three or four dead; the blows . . . were so strong that they made the soldiers cry."[74] The military justice system dismissed these accusations of abuse, concluding that no proof of whipping existed; the soldiers had just been "given chocolate."[75] Memoirs of military service tell similar stories, describing sleep deprivation, the lack of adequate supplies for keeping recruits warm and dry, gushing blood, and the physical pain of receiving chocolate.[76] While serving as an exposé, such stories also reveal the tellers' pride in having survived and even thrived in such conditions.

Military justice proceedings indicate the prevalence of gendered competition and insults in the barracks. For example, a basketball match between the Pérez Regiment and the Military Academy in 1947 ended in a brawl after a solider allegedly called a cadet a *margarita* (pansy).[77] This questioning of the cadet's masculinity by an educated conscript could not go unanswered and was resolved by physically proving masculinity with violence. Similarly, a conscript claimed that his sergeant had pressured him to participate in a mutiny by asking whether he was a man or a woman.[78] Military justice records also suggest how the idea of masculinity as sexual conquest might have played out in the barracks. Having completed his military service, Alejandro Mamani Choque reenlisted as a corporal. When out drinking with four fellows one night in February 1940, he picked out a woman at the bar and said that "the one who could fuck her" would be deemed "the most handsome" of the group.[79]

Proving manliness was a factor in some men's decision to enter the barracks.[80] When miner Juan Rojas considered deserting in the 1940s, his commanding officer convinced him otherwise: "A man must bear any martyrdom. That is why we were born men." Rojas remembered engaging with this discourse, thinking, "I will leave with honor and will be a good man for my country."[81] Ex-conscripts could define their masculinity in terms of their military service and invoke the militarized masculinity they gained in the barracks to question the patriotism and manliness of elite men. When the *colonos* of Finca de Totorani denounced their landlords in 1941, for example, one of their pieces of evidence was that these men had failed to serve their country in the army.[82]

Many recruits also became less indigenous by donning a uniform. Inspired by the experience of improved social status that his Chaco uniform provided him, Melitón Gallardo decided to permanently change his manner of dress and lessen his accent, noting, "I really liked how people treated me and thought people would never treat me like that if I were to dress as a *jalqa*."[83] Similarly, Luciano Tapia used his military service to shed the overly indigenous name Lusiku Qhispi Mamani.[84] His story and that of Gallardo show how young men could use the barracks to change their names and dress, gain education, and improve their Spanish, partially reworking who they were and how others perceived them.

In their reminiscences of military service, both Tapia and Juan Rojas take care to portray themselves as successful soldiers. Rojas boasted about being entrusted with the keys to the supply room and gaining the trust and respect of his superiors, even eating with them on one occasion. He reported,

FIGURE 6.3. Conscripts of the Bolívar Regiment in Viacha, 1947. *Ultima Hora,* January 10, 1947, Archivo Hemerográfico, Biblioteca y Archivo Histórico de la Asamblea Legislativa Plurinacional, La Paz. Used with permission.

"[By the end of my service] I went in and out of the post as though it were my home; I didn't need to ask permission from anyone."[85] Tapia similarly expressed pride in successfully competing with his more educated fellows to become "one of the best soldiers in [his] company and perhaps in the whole regiment."[86] He portrayed his time in the barracks as transformative: he learned to write, gained leadership skills, and mediated between officers and non-Spanish-speaking conscripts.[87] The pride taken in service is also evident in military justice proceedings from the era. Antonio Rios, identified as an illiterate agricultural worker from rural Tarija, contrasted his status as a conscript with that of Domingo Luna, who had been enrolled as an *omiso.* During a dispute about food, Rios rebuked Luna, telling him that as an *omiso,* he had "no right to raise his voice at Ríos because he [Ríos] was a soldier."[88] Similarly, a conscript promoted to private first class invoked his status as proof of his innocence in a fellow's suicide: someone of such rank obviously had nothing to do with the affair.[89]

Military service was an important experience in these men's lives. The barracks were a place of sociability where men trained, worked, played, and slept side-by-side (often with less than a foot between their cots).[90] Conscripts testifying in military justice proceedings regularly referred to the importance of friendships to their lives during military service. They mocked their superiors when their backs were turned, drank together to celebrate birthdays, and competed on their days off to win the prettiest woman.[91] Most units played soccer on a regular basis, either as an official activity organized by officers or on conscripts' initiative.[92] And former conscripts sometimes returned to their old haunts, regaling current soldiers with their memories of service.[93]

The military and mainstream press publicized the social aspects of barracks life to assuage the fears of middle-class youth that conscription would be a time of abuse and deprivation. An image printed in a conservative La Paz newspaper in 1947 shows a group of new conscripts in Viacha's Bolívar Artillery Regiment eagerly crowding into a photograph (see figure 6.3). They hold up two plates of food as one conscript irreverently mimes licking the plate. Their apparent enthusiasm stands in contrast to their NCO (right), who peers seriously into the camera. The caption described them as "happy, fat, and proud."[94] In addition to providing the documents needed to work, study, and avoid impressment, conscription had become a rite of passage and proof of masculinity. This occurred because of the state's increased enforcement but also because of social pressure exerted by Chaco War veterans and former conscripts on their family and community members to serve.

The experience of military service depended heavily on personal relationships with officers, NCOs, and other conscripts since rules were enforced inconsistently. Soldiers routinely drank in the dormitories, abandoned guard posts, and left without permission to go into town or visit family members. Most suffered no consequences; those who did fall afoul of military justice proceedings expressed surprise at the censure, testifying that everyone else was guilty of similar behavior.[95] For example, conscript Maximiliano Concha admitted to wandering away from guard duty for two hours to buy some medicine at the local pharmacy. He testified to knowing this was wrong but doing it anyway because of the example set by his superiors: "Every week after eating, those subofficials go down to the city and come back days later."[96] Another conscript testified that he had intended to return to the barracks after completing an official errand but then ran into some friends and "went to a cantina to drink for two days."[97] Individual officers and NCOs decided when and how to report and punish these failures in service and acts of indiscipline. This left much room for conscripts to maneuver and negotiate.

A case from the Loa Regiment in September 1946 serves as a particularly striking example of the importance of personal connections. It occurred during a period of instability after President Villarroel had been violently overthrown in July and Radepa officers had been purged.[98] Civilians attacked soldiers on the street and looted their barracks; student leaders of the uprising even commanded uniformed soldiers to protect the embassies.[99] Many conscripts received an early discharge, and those who remained were concentrated in La Paz to be monitored closely and to guard against another coup.[100] Officers watched for conscripts who might have enlisted "for political reasons" to carry out the orders of "agitators."[101]

In this context, a group of conscripts and NCOs planned a mutiny in the Loa Regiment, which had endured much upheaval since July. Deeming the regiment essential to preventing a coup, the high command moved it one hundred kilometers from Corocoro to La Paz and replaced its commanding officers. The new leaders reported that indiscipline had taken hold during the chaos: they alleged that more than half the soldiers regularly missed roll call, leaving the barracks to drink, visit family, or frequent a local brothel.[102] One conscript in the unit was eighteen-year-old René Busch Cabrera, who was widely accepted as the illegitimate son of former President Busch.[103] He testified to receiving preferential treatment by the unit's old commander, who had been "a good friend of my father Germán Busch."[104] Busch, several dozen of his peers, and some of their NCOs believed the new officers' disciplinary methods to be abusive and planned a mutiny in protest.[105] The plot came to light after Busch warned members of the administration about the mutiny so they would know that it was not political but rather related to internal treatment. Some participants even claimed that Busch and two fellow soldiers had met with the president and minister of defense to plead for reassignment and complain of abuse.[106] Before the mutiny could take place, the regimental commander mustered the troops and asked if they were unhappy with their provisions or had received any abusive treatment. Showing off bruises, they requested that he change out their officers.[107] Although the press immediately reported it as an attempt at regime change, the resulting military justice proceeding found no evidence of political involvement.[108] It sanctioned the mutiny's planners with time served and blamed the officers for abusing their authority and using illegal punishments.[109]

These conscripts had power because of the political moment and the personal connections of their leaders. The civilian junta led by Tomás Monje sought to quell unrest in order to ensure that the traditional parties could retake power through elections. In this context, a politically connected conscript like Busch could approach Bolivia's leaders to register discontent with the treatment he and his peers were receiving from their new officers. The fact that the tribunal absolved the conscripts and instead blamed their officers indicates the power that conscripts could wield and that their allegiance mattered. Despite civilian rule, the army continued to be the ultimate arbiter of political power.

For these conscripts, the terms of military service were particularly negotiable. The continuation of a personal, rather than bureaucratic, mode of relations meant that conscripts' experiences were highly dependent on their labor assignments and personal relationships in the barracks. Depending on the political context and individual circumstances, conscripts might have no influence on their conditions of service or they might be able to do almost as they pleased. This made the barracks a site that perpetuated hierarchies based on race and class but also created the possibility for some of those on the lower end of these hierarchies to prove themselves as outstanding soldiers. By the 1940s, conscription had become part of many families' and communities' expectations for young men. It not only provided much-needed paperwork but also offered opportunities for sociability and for proving manliness.

LEVERAGING SERVICE

Military service also gave men a way to authorize themselves as having done their patriotic duty. Military justice records from the late 1930s and early 1940s provide striking examples of individual veterans' taking advantage of the postwar atmosphere to make claims on the state. Petitioners and witnesses in desertion and evasion cases, most of which had their roots in local disputes over land, labor, and political office, deployed the dominant discourse of patriotism to convince the state to punish their personal enemies and rivals. Although men and women from across the social spectrum provided the spark that initiated these investigations, half of the extant cases were initiated by veterans identified as indigenous. The military tribunal devoted significant time and manpower to their claims, making arrests, taking the testimony of multiple witnesses, and even having experts inspect relevant documents.[110] These cases suggest important changes in the postwar period. Not only had the bureaucratic apparatus been strengthened by the war but many of the officers serving as magistrates were willing to heed non-elite, illiterate, and even non-Spanish-speaking actors.

As had occurred in the prewar period, *patrones* often reported as evaders or deserters people they considered rabble-rousers in the hopes of engaging the state's repressive force against them. However, at least once in the postwar period, this strategy backfired due to a veteran's claim of loyal service. This case began in June 1940 when Pacífico Burgoa, the *patrón* of the Jaupani *hacienda* in Puerto Acosta (La Paz), reported one of his *colonos* as a Chaco War deserter. The *indígena* Ramón Sossa, he alleged, was "using the weapon with which he deserted" to "sow panic and anxiety" in the region. Sossa used his interrogation to denounce Burgoa for lying, abusing his *colonos*, and hoarding state property. He claimed that Burgoa's accusation was knowingly false "in retaliation" for leaving work on his farm. "I would like to note," his statement read, "that four years have passed since the day that I . . . presented myself to Sr. Burgoa, giving him my discharge papers; and that only because I abandoned the intense work to which said *señor* has subjugated his *colonos*, has he devised the denunciation." Sossa then accused Burgoa of hoarding military supplies in his home, including weapons, ammunition, and uniforms. Based on this accusation, a local military authority searched Burgoa's residence and questioned five of his *colonos*. Described as an indigenous peasant who could not speak Spanish, sign his name, or even identify his precise age, Sossa was forced to interact with the state by Burgoa.[111] However, he responded in kind, deploying his compliance with wartime mobilization to ask the state to discipline his former *patrón*.

Unlike Sossa, other indigenous veterans actively sought out such engagements, attempting, much as Burgoa had, to use the state opportunistically in intercommunity and even intrafamily disputes. In June of 1939, for example, Antonio Choque-Vara signed a letter in which he identified himself as an indigenous combat veteran from the ex-community of Taracollo-Corocoro (Pacajes, La Paz). The letter set up a contrast between his community's willingness to sacrifice for the *patria* during the war and the evasion and desertion of their rivals: "The *indígenas* from the Ancochualla estancia," his petition stated, "have become our enemies, stripping us of our lands." He claimed that his community could not defend itself because "almost all of [the residents] have died in the Chaco campaign" and those left "are almost all sick or mutilated." He called on the state to arrest seven men with the surnames Mamani, Condori, and Canqui in order to protect those who defended Bolivia during the war from those who had not.[112] Similarly, Rufino Chipana of the Ongora estancia paid a notary (since he was illiterate) to compose and send a letter denouncing six of his indigenous neighbors for desertion. Calling on his authority as "an ex-combatant who fought in the burning sand of the Chaco," his petition accused them of being "cowardly subjects who, in moments of danger for our *patria*, refused [to serve]."[113] While neither Chipana nor Choque-Vara's petitions led to the arrest of the accused, the tribunal made a modest effort to investigate, writing increasingly strongly worded letters ordering local military authorities to track down and arrest the men.[114]

Mateo Torrez Mamani was far more successful in his efforts to draw the state into a dispute with his cousins in May 1945. Like Choque-Vara and Chipana, Torrez Mamani invoked his veteran status to prove his trustworthiness. He even attached his demobilization booklet to a letter reporting the *indígenas* Alejandro, Ezequiel, and Carlos Mamani as deserters. Identifying himself as a semiliterate indigenous rural laborer from the Lluxt'ari community in Calamarca (La Paz), he engaged a notary to petition the local military commander. It opened, "As an ex-combatant in the Chaco (I served in the Twentieth Cavalry Regiment from Cochabamba) who was wounded in the war, I denounce before your authority the crimes of desertion during wartime and the robbery of the army's rifles by [these] indigenous reservists."[115] The tribunal acted decisively on his accusation, sending agents to interview a dozen witnesses and detaining two of the brothers, who claimed that Torrez Mamani was acting out of spite because of a dispute over the hosting of a religious festival.[116] Torrez Mamani likely regretted attaching his demobilization booklet, however, since the tribunal never bothered to return it, despite his pleas that he needed it "to prove [his] condition as having been discharged from the ranks to the patrols that now demand military documents."[117]

Indigenous communities and individuals of course had a long history of petitioning the Bolivian state. As shown in chapter 1, petitioners identified as indigenous reported their fellows as *omisos* as early as 1914.[118] What changed in the postwar period, however, was the entitlement apparent in these petitions. They did not employ a purely denunciatory tone. Nor did they adopt the pathos or tributary logic that Celestino Coico had used in his attempts to avoid military service in 1924. Instead, the petitions of Chipana, Torrez Mamani, and Choque-Vara expressed a credibility and authority derived from the war—not only their own participation in it but that of the tens of thousands of noncitizens, mostly indigenous, who had fought in the hot sands of the Chaco.

Whatever the process of composite or co-authorship that produced these documents, the writers believed that these indigenous veterans had some sort of leverage. Some of these men were not citizens under the constitution, but they acted as if they were, asserting their belonging and using veteran status as a weapon. Their petitions insisted on a process of postwar reckoning that would recognize their contributions and penalize their enemies for their failures.

The postwar period played a key role in making Bolivia a conscript nation. The barracks were becoming places where men from across divides of social class, ethnicity, and education converged and worked out their relationships with each other and with the state. The terms and meanings of military service were negotiated, both individually and collectively, by conscripts and veterans, who expressed a sense of entitlement based on their service. The inclusion of testimony from illiterate and indigenous actors in military justice proceedings signals this change, as does the tone of petitions by veterans without formal citizenship rights. Conscription spread and was embraced from below in part because it provided a space for ongoing negotiations.

So many youth presented for service each year that even the newly expanded army could not accommodate all of them. These men showed up because the state was strong enough to make them do so, but also because of a new awareness of military service due to circular streams of rural-to-urban migration and the return of veterans to their home communities. Even if they did not qualify as citizens, conscripts and their families had begun to associate military service with access to the state and the benefits it might provide. Conscription was becoming a path to manhood and a way to gain skills or connections to patrons who might help a young man ascend the social hierarchy. The prominence of veterans and veterans' issues at the national level helped lend credence to the implicit promise of military service. Despite their strong continuities of racialized hierarchies, the barracks could also be flexible spaces open to negotiation that encouraged a strong sense of belonging.

Although military and civilian reformists saw themselves as profoundly different from the oligarchic state, their patriotic discourse and belief in the transformative power of military service to assimilate the indigenous majority reveals the limitations of their vision for Bolivia. They relied on the army to forge simultaneously the citizens and the nation they imagined. This nation would include all Bolivians, but only on the terms of middle-class reformers. Conscripts would have to learn basic literacy skills, speak Spanish, and put the nation before themselves to become citizens. The conscription process was an important part of the urban conquest of Bolivia's national territory. This conquest was still in its very early stages, as shown by the unrepresentativeness of the 1949 military register. The nation forged in the barracks in the 1940s was still a relatively urban and educated one. This would change in the decade that followed.

CHAPTER 7

WHAT DIFFERENCE DID A REVOLUTION MAKE?

On April 9, 1952, factory workers and other supporters of the MNR took several strategic locations around the city of La Paz with the help of the *carabineros*. During combat, many civilian participants drew on their experience from the Chaco War or obligatory military service.[1] One remembered, "Many of us had been in the barracks and knew perfectly well how to handle weapons."[2] Contrary to the hopes of the insurgents, the remaining units of the army put up a fight even though many conscripts switched sides. But large groups of miners arrived the next day to prevent additional ammunition and army units from reaching the city. By the morning of the eleventh, the MNR was in power and the military's top leaders had fled to Peru.[3]

After participating in the Villarroel administration, the MNR had attempted to take power several times during the six years between Villarroel's overthrow and the 1952 revolution. The first occurred without the clear involvement of army officers in February 1949.[4] Remembered as a civil war, the next attempt was a strong, coordinated effort supported by officers in provincial regiments. They initially took four cities, but units loyal to the government dislodged their forces over the next three weeks. Hundreds of officers were purged as a result, with many going into exile alongside civilian leaders.[5] Although the MNR's exiled candidate, Víctor Paz Estenssoro, won a majority of the vote in the 1951 election, a military junta prevented him from assuming power.

The events of April 1952 at first looked like a typical palace coup. As with previous coups, it depended on the support of a high-ranking army officer—in this case General Antonio Seleme, who controlled the *carabinero* police force.[6] Seleme had approached the MNR in March with an offer to provide arms and the support of the *carabineros* in exchange for the presidency. They agreed, provided he swear loyalty to the party. In preparation, Seleme convinced President Hugo Ballivián to move most army troops out of La Paz to protect against an MNR coup, alleging that the commander favored the party. Seleme sought asylum at the Chilean embassy at a low point in the fighting, which allowed the coup the possibility of becoming a revolution.[7] Víctor Paz thus triumphantly returned from Buenos Aires on April 15 to assume the presidency.

The MNR immediately proclaimed the success of its *national* revolution, emphasizing domestic concerns and disavowing any affiliation with internationalism. The party solidified its revolutionary legacy during its first sixteen months by issuing three far-reaching decrees that distinguished it from previous coups. The first showed how far the party's leaders had come since participating in the 1938 constituent assembly. A July 1952 decree made suffrage universal, ensuring that all veterans and future conscripts could claim citizenship rights. Issued after strong pressure from miners and rural workers, the other two nationalized the three largest tin mines (October 1952) and enacted agrarian reform in favor of small producers (August 1953). These decrees served to build a social base outside of established political actors and to strengthen the MNR coalition. The new administration faced a dilemma, however, over the military. How would it deal with the powerful institution that had dominated Bolivian politics for decades?

REVOLUTIONARY ANTIMILITARISM

The revolution opened space for the expression of a deep wellspring of antimilitary sentiment built up after mass loss of life in the Chaco and decades of repressing strikes and uprisings. During the first years of MNR rule, militias proliferated and Bolivians punished the military for its support of the oligarchic state. However, Paz Estenssoro ultimately chose to reform rather than abolish the institution. In contrast to militias, which represented the interests of particular parts of the nation, maintaining an official military that could incarnate the nation as a whole fit the MNR's rhetoric of a revolution that was national above all else. Thus, rather than eliminating the military, the administration slashed its budget, officer corps, and size to allow its allies among the officers to rebuild the institution in the revolution's image.

On May Day only weeks after the revolution, placards demanding the military's elimination could be seen among the thousands of armed marchers representing the powerful Bolivian Workers Central (COB).[8] Miners, the party's most visible supporters, considered the army an enemy—not surprising given that local units' pay had long been supplemented by mine owners to guarantee loyalty.[9] Public art designed to cement the revolutionary legacy also emphasized antimilitary themes. A 1953 mural in the Presidential Palace by Miguel Alandia, a Chaco veteran who had become a leader of the Trotsky-influenced Revolutionary Workers Party (POR), had virulently antimilitary themes. Entitled *History of the Mine*, the prominently placed eighty-six-square-meter mural celebrated the role of workers and depicted their massacre at the hands of the oligarchic army.[10]

Leaders on the party's left, especially Minister of Mines Juan Lechín and Minister of Peasant Affairs Ñuflo Chávez, advocated for the military to be abolished and replaced by militias, likely because they represented the groups who wielded power in the new militias and who had suffered the most at the hands of the military. But President Paz Estenssoro steadfastly refused.[11] Eliminating the official armed forces would decentralize power too radically. Paz Estenssoro was also surrounded by reformist military officers who likely convinced him that the institution could serve his needs. Then-Captain René Barrientos copiloted the plane that brought the MNR's leader back from Buenos Aires. Also on that flight were two lieutenant colonels who had been with Paz in exile: Armando Fortún Sanjinés and Clemente Inofuentes Gisbert.[12] The new president would go on to appoint Fortún and other discharged members of the Radepa military lodge to his defense ministry and military high command.[13]

Although Paz let the military survive, his administration radically attacked the institution to hobble its political potential and then tried to remake it along revolutionary lines. The new high command purged at least 166 officers from the rolls for political reasons; others chose to abandon their posts for the civilian world or exile.[14] In all, about half the corps likely left during the revolution's first year.[15] The MNR also closed the Military Academy, unceremoniously dismissing all cadets.[16] It slashed military funding, which immediately dropped from 23 percent to 13.7 percent of the national budget before hitting a low of 6.7 percent in 1957.[17] Most dramatic was the reduction in troops, which likely fell by 70 percent (from around eighteen thousand to five thousand).[18] Many military service sheets from 1952 carry a stamp indicating that the conscript had been discharged "with deficient instruction," and recruitment was suspended in July 1952.[19]

In January 1953, the British ambassador characterized the army as "reduced, demoralized, divided."[20] The institution survived on a "starvation diet" during the first years of MNR rule, often even unable to provide conscripts with uniforms and shoes.[21] Gary Prado, whose father served as minister of defense beginning in 1956 and who himself was part of one of the first classes of cadets under the MNR, describes the reuse of uniform fabric and mailing envelopes to illustrate the institution's penury.[22] Yet all military functions did limp along after the revolution: military justice proceedings continued apace, and a substantial number of conscripts recruited in January 1952 served until April 1953, when tables once again appeared throughout the country to register conscripts.[23] A new issue of the *Revista Militar* appeared soon after the revolution, opening with a highly favorable editorial on the new regime.[24]

This much-weakened military could no longer claim a monopoly on armed power associated with the state, as the *carabineros* and militias benefitted from having supported the MNR in 1952. Formed in the early twentieth century, the *carabineros* were a militarized police force under the command

FIGURE 7.1. Peasant militia, c. 1953. Dirección Nacional de Informaciones, *Bolivia: 10 años de revolución,* 56.

of military officers. *Carabinero* troops had to have completed obligatory military service or served in the Chaco War.[25] The MNR expanded this force after 1952, purchased it new equipment, and built a state-of-the-art police academy to reward its collaboration during the revolution.[26]

Militias, however, were the most prominent face of the revolution and distinguished it from the oligarchy's dependence on the army. During the precarious first eighteen months of MNR rule, militias helped thwart repeated coup attempts by right-wing elements, both military and civilian.[27] Militias dwarfed the army, claiming well over ten times as many members in the mid-1950s.[28] However, most militias were organized locally by occupation, such as particular mining camps, factories, or rural communities.[29] Loosely aligned with the MNR, they would be loyal to it only as long as its policies converged with their local interests.

The presence of militiamen at politically important events, like the signing of the agrarian reform decree in 1953, constituted an implicit threat and demonstrated the regime's alignment with the popular classes.[30] The national and international press reinforced this narrative by featuring images like figure 7.1.[31] *Lluch'us* (knit caps), clothing of a handmade woolen textile called *bayeta de la tierra,* and too-large western jackets likely purchased secondhand identify these militiamen as indigenous peasants.[32] Some give the MNR's "V" signal while others proudly hold their Mauser rifles, expropriated from army stores.[33] Images like this portray the radical change in social order represented by Bolivia's militias: men distinctly marked as rural subjects brandish army weapons without overt signs of state discipline like uniforms, evenly spaced lines, and commanding officers. This image would have raised the age-old specter of race war for many elite observers.

The official newspaper, *La Nación,* regularly highlighted the strength of workers' militias. After the declaration of agrarian reform, it also reported the formation of various peasant militias numbering between one and two thousand men each and named for MNR leaders like Paz Estenssoro, Hernán Siles, and Federico Fortún. The naming of these units indicates the partisan nature of their loyalty. Unlike the army, which was supposed to be loyal to the state regardless of which party controlled it, these militias proclaimed a more personal loyalty to the revolution and its leaders. The articles reinforced this, assuring readers of the units' "unconditional support for [President Paz Estenssoro] and the Government of the National Revolution, in whose defense [they] are ready to offer [their] lives."[34]

Humiliated by militias' prominence and power, military leaders sought ways to preserve the armed forces. After the COB approved plans for a national militia in June 1953, Chief of Staff General Armando Fortún offered the institution's expertise to train militiamen, presenting them as a valuable reserve force.[35] Participating militiamen even received military service booklets.[36] Officers thus insinuated themselves into the militias, imposing their own ideas about training and comportment and conducting inspections of the troops. Yet they also had given up exclusive control over this powerful piece of paperwork.

Paz's decision to create a new unit within the army less than a month after taking power reveals his misgivings about both the official military and the militias. Tasked with guarding the president's safety, the Waldo Ballivián Regiment carried the name of the major who had died alongside Villarroel in 1946.[37] The administration later formed a similar unit in Oruro named for José Félix Soria, a labor leader killed during the April 1952 revolution.[38] These units resembled Bautista Saavedra's Republican Guard of the 1920s: they enlisted former conscripts who were paid by the state and wore military uniforms but were loyal to the president rather than the military as an institution. Newspaper reports and military justice records depict the regiment's officers as militia members and troops as peasants, workers, and miners who had previously completed military service and had reenlisted specifically to serve in these partisan units.[39] Testifying in a military justice proceeding about stolen ammunition in 1954, Ballivián soldier Francisco Quispe Cuellar proudly identified himself "as a reenlisted soldier of the Army of the National Revolution."[40] In an important symbolic move, the MNR chose the Waldo Ballivián Regiment, rather than the miners' militias, to take possession of the tin mines nationalized in October 1952.[41]

The decision to use an officially uniformed and paid unit of the army, albeit one whose loyalty was unquestionable, signaled the administration's desire for a middle ground between the old army and the new militias. An "Army of the National Revolution" would have the institutionality of the old army but be loyal to and under the control of the MNR. By September 1953, the government cautiously staged military parades and announced the reopening of the Military Academy. British observers attributed the institution's public reappearance to the "assiduous but cautious efforts" of Fortún and his civilian brother Federico, a close ally of Paz Estenssoro who served as his minister of government.[42] The institution had survived and would adjust to the new realities of post-1952 Bolivia.

SAVING THE MILITARY INSTITUTION

Because Víctor Paz Estenssoro's decision to retain the official military ran contrary to the wishes of many in his coalition, he and his allies launched a major propaganda campaign to rebrand the institution and assure the public of its loyalty to the party. Jerry Knudson's study of the Bolivian press highlights the importance of this question to the regime, noting that it "filled more space in the official newspapers than any other issue."[43] The MNR worked to distinguish the old "massacring army" at the service of the oligarchy from its new army "of workers, peasants, and people of the middle class, organized and educated to defend and serve the aspirations of Bolivia and Bolivians."[44] As militias and carabineros took over primary responsibility for maintaining social order, the MNR increasingly defined its army according to nonmartial objectives that would literally build Bolivia.

In July 1953, the MNR issued a decree reorganizing its purged and reduced military. The lengthy preamble decried the army as "an instrument of oppression in service of the dominant group" that had "practically converted itself into an armed political party." It praised the efforts of Presidents Gualberto Villarroel and Germán Busch in recognizing the need to "transform the economic, social, and political structure of the country." The decree then dedicated the reorganized "National Army" to "the defense of the Patria's economic and political independence" and declared it to be "at the service of the national majority's interests." However, it left the details to the minister of defense, which meant that this reorganization would be mostly rhetorical.[45] The MNR thus adopted the same strategy with the military that it used with other power brokers. Instead of creating its own revolutionary structures and institutions, the party tried to control those already in existence.

More concrete was the decree's authorization of a new Military Academy and an aviation school named for Villarroel and Busch, both of whom were frequently invoked as martyrs in MNR rhetoric.[46] The party tried to institute a quota system for cadets to ensure that the next generation of officers would be loyal to the MNR and have roots in the working and peasant classes.[47] It also reviewed applications to prevent anyone with ties to the opposition from gaining admission.[48]

Table 7.1. Oaths to the Flag

1924 Oath	1953 Oath
"Do you swear before God and the *Patria* to defend your flag even to the sacrifice of your life, never to abandon those who command you during war, and to comply with the orders of your superiors, as befits a good soldier in his duty to God, his *Patria* and his flag?"	"Do you swear before God, the *Patria* and the sacred memory of presidents Busch and Villarroel to defend your flag, which represents the political and economic independence of the Nation; to serve the people, of which you are part, in all of their needs and aspirations; and to comply with the orders of your superiors, as befits a good soldier in his duty to God, his *Patria* and his Flag?"

Sources: Supreme decree of August 4, 1924, in Bolivia, *Gaceta oficial* (1924); "Profundo sentido Revolucionario adquirió la Jura a la Bandera," *La Nación*, August 9, 1953.

In mid-1953, military officers began pledging adherence to the MNR. Gary Prado reports that a rumor spread through the corps that public affiliation with the party was authorized despite the institution's long history of prohibiting party membership as part of its constitutional mandate. Hundreds of officers swore oaths of loyalty to the MNR in June and July of 1953.[49] In a speech addressing the two hundred officers taking this oath at the Presidential Palace on June 30, 1953, President Paz dismissed the army's supposed apolitical history, reminding the public that "officers are always identified with the ruling regime because the army is one of the organizations of the state." He asserted the MNR's identification "with the interests of the national majority" to justify the "public affiliation of officers." Officers enrolling in the MNR were thus "serving the interests of the army, that is to say of the new army."[50] An official military cell of the MNR soon followed, forming on October 31, 1953. Prado ascribes a variety of motives to officers' choice to affiliate. Some, he believed, did so to help the institution by convincing the MNR's left that the military could be revolutionary. Others aligned with the MNR out of genuine attraction to the party's message. A third group was only seeking career advancement.[51] Those who avoided swearing loyalty did indeed find their careers stalled; being promoted to general required "a record of strong party support usually capped by membership" in the party's military cell.[52] After purging the corps of known opposition, the MNR sought to include military leaders in their coalition. For many officers, party membership served both personal and institutional goals.

Professions of loyalty to the revolution also infiltrated conscripts' experience. In 1953, the minister of defense rewrote the oath that each conscript had intoned since 1924 (table 7.1). The new revolutionary oath elevated the "sacred memory of presidents Busch and Villarroel" to equal status with God and the *patria*. It also emphasized "political and economic independence," signaling freedom from both US imperialism and internationalist communism.[53] Although it retained the clause demanding obedience to superiors, rather than emphasizing the soldier's martial sacrifice during war, it constructed him as an active citizen of a nation fundamentally aligned with the interests of the masses. Hierarchy and authority had not disappeared, but the emphasis had profoundly changed.

The discourse surrounding soldiers' labor also underwent a profound shift as the MNR emphasized the productive capacity of its new army. Development projects offered the military a new path forward: the redemptive power of work would revitalize the institution and help it return to the center of the nation. Reconfiguring nonmartial labor as a war tactic, Minister of Defense General Luis Arteaga went so far as to declare that the armed forces' first mission, ahead of preparing for the country's defense, was to "fight the war against misery and the hunger of the people."[54] The use of conscripts for development labor was by no means new. Chapter 2 shows that nonmartial tasks such as road construction and agricultural work had been part of the Bolivian military, especially in frontier units, since at least the 1910s. Additionally, chapter 5 details how soldiers' nonmartial labor gained prominence and legibility under the military socialists. What was different about the MNR era was the prevalence of nonmartial labor and its packaging as a revolutionary innovation to fight poverty.

During the early years of the revolution, the MNR publicized the productive capacity of its new army. Speeches, newspaper articles, and pieces in the Revista Militar reiterated ad nauseam the accomplishments of the MNR's "Productive and Technical Army" and regularly published photographs of soldiers' manual labors.[55] A November 1952 image, for example, highlights the levees constructed by soldiers on the San Jerónimo farm.[56] In another such image, conscripts pose with a bulldozer on the bare altiplano; the caption describes the heroic efforts of the "Revolution's Army" to forge a highway.[57] Units named for productive activities proliferated, and even infantry, cavalry, and artillery regiments dedicated their labor to these tasks. In 1954, 50 percent of the Colorados Regiment spent their days working on the highway between Tarapaya and Potosí; the Eighth Infantry Regiment was repairing La Paz's urban roads; the Eguino Cavalry Regiment was growing foodstuffs behind their barracks; and the Camacho Artillery Regiment was cultivating peas, beans, quinoa, barley, and potatoes on forty-three hectares.[58] Between 1955 and 1961, successive cohorts of conscripts in one regiment built sixty-one kilometers of roads, fifty-five bridges, and seventy drainage systems.[59]

Legal reforms under the MNR formalized the long-standing practice of using conscripts for commercial operations and as contract workers for private companies.[60] These hired-out soldiers did the same labor as those on military farms but brought the state income rather than saving it money. Reformers hoped that codifying this use of military labor would limit opportunities for corruption. As early as 1954, *La Nación* was bragging of the Vergara Artillery Group's help with the cotton harvest at Finca Menonah in Roboré and at the La Algodonera farm in Santa Cruz.[61]

The MNR placed particular emphasis on its use of military labor to integrate the lowlands into the national economy.[62] Between 1955 and 1957, 3,600 conscripts traveled to the lowlands to prepare land for settlement; by 1962, they had cleared over 11,800 hectares.[63] To publicize these efforts, the government published a pamphlet in 1956 that tried to encourage military colonization through the illustrated history of a conscript named Alberto Rodríguez Ríos, who traveled "from his barren land in the Altiplano to the pleasant eastern meadows, where he now owns his own parcel and lives happily with his family."[64] It also sponsored a 1958 documentary film entitled *The Peace Offensive* that highlighted the development of Santa Cruz through military labor and attempted to convince highland soldiers to migrate. *La Nación's* article about the film bragged, "New soldiers no longer march to the 'front'[;] now they are trained in managing the pick and the shovel to make inhospitable lands productive."[65]

While still emphasizing the need to defend frontier regions and the savings for state coffers, politicians and officers began to depict endemic poverty as a battle, thus expanding the list of threats against which Bolivia needed protection. Their argument that national defense must be achieved through economic development not only responded to the specific situation faced by the MNR in the 1950s but also echoed voices emerging throughout Latin America.[66] Phrases that militarized development labor abound after 1952, popping up in military magazine articles, presidential addresses, speeches to soldiers, and even laws. Military labor would "save our *Patria* from economic chaos"; the army must wage "the peaceful and edifying battles of national economic emancipation" in which victory was a road bulldozed or a farm mechanized.[67] The most enthusiastic proponents employed almost laughable rhetoric, insisting that building roads would allow Bolivia to "impose its hegemony on the continent."[68] This discourse not only imbued nonmartial labor with a higher purpose but attempted to mobilize conscripts as actors invested in Bolivia's future. In stark contrast to the martial emphasis that allowed some pre–Chaco War conscripts to object to nonmartial assignments, the MNR glorified this work. It sought not only the labor of conscripts from rural areas and the mines but also their political support. How conscripts perceived their quotidian labor for the *patria* mattered in ways that it had not before 1952, so the messages surrounding this labor had to change as well.

CONSCRIPTS IN THE POSTREVOLUTIONARY ARMY

In keeping with this celebration of nonmartial labor, the MNR's discourse surrounding conscripts emphasized their class status, nationalism, and sacrifice. The party's efforts to cultivate a mass base of support also produced some significant shifts in the conscript population. Not only did miners enter the barracks at higher rates but soldiers from urban centers were no longer overrepresented as conscripts increasingly hailed from rural areas. This change suggests both groups increasingly embraced military service under an administration that claimed to represent them rather than elites. Yet, like their liberal predecessors, the MNR viewed military service as a tool for indigenous assimilation. And barracks culture proved remarkably persistent, showing few shifts from the pre-revolutionary period.

Analysis of the 1955 military register shows an increase in men identifying as miners. Whereas miners constituted only 0.4 percent of conscripts in 1949, they were 2 percent six years later, which was much closer to their national representation of 3 percent of economically active men.[69] This suggests that miners were either more accepting of military service or more willing to identify themselves as miners when registering for service. I suspect the latter. Previous administrations' persecution of miners likely suppressed their official count even if many were still registering. Under the new government, which was still profoundly identified with miners in 1955, men were proud to claim this occupation. Either way, the increase shows changing attitudes toward military service among miners and that many registered despite the option of receiving military service booklets through militia training.

Another change was even more significant. Conscripts registering to serve in the MNR's military were astoundingly less urban than their counterparts just six years before. Those listed as having agricultural professions had risen from 24 percent to 33 percent between 1949 and 1955, which represented the most significant shift in professional categories. Likewise, whereas the city of La Paz had been substantially overrepresented as compared with its provincial towns and countryside in 1949 with 51 percent of the department's registrants claiming residence in the city, in 1955, this number had dropped to 32 percent, which was actually two points lower than reported in the 1950 census.[70] The urban bias of the conscript population had reflected the institutional needs of previous administrations and the social needs of Bolivians before 1952. These needs had changed after the revolution, as formal citizenship expanded and the MNR actively worked to build a social base outside of cities.

Data on conscripts' changing demographics support observations made at the time. In 1956, Colonel Cupertino Ríos expressed surprise at the "extraordinary enthusiasm . . . of the *campesino* class who have come voluntarily from distant provincial cantons" to serve.[71] The president of the state-owned Bolivian Development Corporation noted in 1957 that military service "was completed in an almost religious manner by all social sectors but is even more deeply rooted among the peasants."[72] Similarly, Última Hora printed a photograph in 1958 of long recruitment lines, commenting on "the flood of peasants and people from the provinces."[73] Anthropologists in the 1960s confirmed that military service had become a rite of passage among Aymara communities in the La Paz department. Based on fieldwork in 1961, Carter and Mamani note that the community viewed "attending the barracks and complying with military service" as "acts of prestige."[74] The Buechlers similarly argue that conscription marked indigenous men as adults, that returning soldiers were feted upon returning to the community, and that people gossiped about and criticized those who chose not to serve: "They think that you are not a man."[75]

It is tempting to attribute increased rural conscription to the 1953 agrarian reform and the MNR's reorientation toward peasants and the middle class after 1956.[76] Understanding military service as an act of gratitude, however, ignores rural communities' long history of pressuring the MNR for land, education, and labor laws.[77] The prominent lionization of Busch and Villarroel should also be interpreted as a signal to rural recruits, as these former presidents loomed large in the popular memory of many rural communities.[78] But explanations of the ruralization of conscription must also take into account the patterns of circular migration that had increasingly connected agricultural communities to cities and mining camps since the Chaco War. The migrants who expanded La Paz's population by 133 percent between the war's end and 1950 did not leave their rural communities behind; many retained land rights, returned for celebrations, and maintained a dense web of social and economic networks that spanned both the city and the countryside.[79] As individuals traveled between these environs, they also spread ideas about military service. While the suddenness of the boom in rural conscripts should be attributed to the MNR's politics, it would not have been possible without these long processes of migration and engagement.

Yet the revolution and its expansion of citizenship by no means ended hierarchical ideas about the proper place of recruits from indigenous and peasant communities. Revealing their prejudices about rural life, leaders claimed that military service would teach "discipline in work" and asserted the "significant evolution" of peasants in the barracks, where they learned "to fulfill many needs" that they did not even know they had before being conscripted.[80] However, revolutionary officers also expressed fear that military service would cause conscripts to abandon agriculture to become urban migrants. One 1954 Revista Militar article lamented discharged conscripts' desire to wear "shoes instead of sandals and a tie instead of a scarf" and urged officers to teach recruits that "the duty of a Bolivian does not end in the Barracks but continues in the agricultural sector, giving their parents the joy of producing more barley, quinoa, fava beans, oca, fruits, etc., in the Altiplano, and yucca, beans, pumpkins, corn, fruit in the tropics. (Which is what we need in our markets.)"[81] Rural men needed to change their way of life in order to contribute to a modern Bolivia, yet they also needed to remain in their proper place as food producers. The long-standing contradictions of *indigenismo* trumped revolutionary change.

Like Liberals before them, the MNR understood obligatory military service to be a tool to mold the population into its vision for the nation. Whereas Liberals had viewed this as a neutral process, the MNR explicitly framed it as political indoctrination of revolutionary values. In 1954, the minister of defense bragged to an audience of factory workers that conscripts were being taught "political doctrine" in the barracks.[82] Gary Prado reports that this was not just bravado: the troops' reply to the duty officer's traditional nightly salutation of "Subordination and Determination!" changed from "Viva Bolivia!" to "For the National Revolution!"[83] MNR leaders presented this as empowering: the "new Soldier of the *Patria*, aware of his revolutionary duty, is the vigilant guardian of the awakening of Bolivia" and "part of the liberation of all citizens."[84] And officers claimed they would produce a soldier characterized by *conciencia* (awareness) rather than subordination, familiar with his "duties and rights as a citizen and a defender of the *Patria*."[85] Yet this was still a top-down and authoritarian experience. The party was the principal actor in these formulations, bestowing citizenship upon the masses and awakening them to their oppression. For such citizens, the love of *patria* and party would be inexorably linked; the defense of the latter would protect the former.

In practice, however, the authoritarian nature and internal practice of the military institution remained unchanged. Military justice records reveal that conscripts in the "Revolution's Army" experienced many continuities with the pre-1952 and even the pre-Chaco army. Despite claims that conscripts had a "decent life" and no longer suffered the "bullying of the Corporal," abuse and racialized hierarchy still characterized daily relations between conscripts and with their officers.[86] Testimony about gendered taunts, being overworked, physical violence, and abysmal rations continued apace, suggesting few changes to the culture of barracks life.[87] The allocation of labor assignments also continued along racial lines. Juan Acarapi Mamani, for example, spent his days laboring with a "group of soldiers charged with making roof tiles for the Regiment" rather than participating in military training with the other conscripts in the Castrillo Infantry Regiment.[88]

These continuities in conscripts' experience despite the MNR's explicit statements to the contrary suggest something about the nature of both military service and the Bolivian state. The leeway that officers had in how they treated conscripts and in what information they included in bureaucratic documents points to a Bolivian state that continued to be quite local, with subalterns wielding substantial power and being subject to little direct oversight. While the party viewed military service as a site for indoctrination, the institution's ingrained practices, along with the MNR's own prejudices, stood in the way of radical change.

MILITARY RESURGENCE AFTER 1956

The first four years of revolutionary rule had brought drastic reductions in the military's troops, budget, power, and prestige. Despite this humiliation, however, the military retained its structural position as Bolivia's most coherent and centralized institution with even pretensions of national reach. Its officer corps contained ex-Radepa members who believed in reform, had personal ties to MNR leaders, and had themselves suffered discharge and exile. Others had survived the purges by keeping their heads down and parroting the party line. Although many officers were genuinely enthusiastic about the revolution and the MNR's reformist agenda, they still felt loyalty to the institution that had trained them and were pained to see it so beleaguered. When the MNR began to splinter over economic policy and succession, military officers took advantage of the opening to restore the institution's dignity and eventually regain its position as the main arbiter of high politics. The United States would serve as a willing and powerful partner, as it continued to use aid and advisers to ensure that more conservative forces in the MNR prevailed.[89] However, the US role should not be overstated. It nudged, pressured, and helped create the circumstances that allowed for military revival, but the institution's resurgence should be attributed to officers' deep-seated loyalty and to Paz and Siles's desire to control both their rivals within the party and the forces from below that had been empowered by the revolution.

Although militia members far outnumbered army troops, efforts to coordinate them on a national level foundered. The militias reached their height in terms of numbers and power at the end of Víctor Paz Estenssoro's first term in 1956, when they provided a strong show of support during the June elections.[90] The first held under universal suffrage, these elections brought to power Paz's vice president and fellow MNR founder, Hernán Siles Zuazo, with an overwhelming majority of the vote. Siles faced a difficult task. The MNR's reformist platform in opposition to the oligarchy had allowed it to build a broad coalition in the 1940s that crossed lines of ideology and class. Revolutionary fervor, nationalization of the mines, and agrarian reform had brought many others into the fold. This coalition was becoming increasingly untenable, however, as the MNR could no longer balance the conflicting interests of its supporters in the face of profound economic crisis.

By 1956, Bolivia's economy was in freefall, with the cost of living index up by over 2,000 percent since the revolution. Increased social spending, multiple exchange rates, the indemnification paid for the nationalized tin mines, and outstanding debt from the Chaco War had led to hyperinflation and a flourishing black market.[91] With the threat of food riots looming, most leaders agreed with Paz's decision to set up a stabilization commission in the final days of his presidency. The resulting plan reduced spending and tariffs, increased taxes, ended price controls, froze wages, and unified the exchange rate. An orthodox example of monetarism, this plan was conceived and implemented by US adviser George Jackson Eder. Bolivia's growing dependence on US financial assistance gave Eder an extraordinary amount of control over the terms of stabilization. Starting as a 1.3 million dollar grant of emergency assistance in 1953, US aid had ballooned to 18.2 million in 1954 and 33.5 million in 1955.[92] It made up one-third of Bolivia's budget in the late 1950s, which was likely the highest per-capita aid in the world at the time.[93]

Yet the stabilization package implemented in December 1956 was not just a US imposition. It also served MNR leaders' goal of weakening the power of the labor movement. Primarily represented by COB leaders, the MNR's left wing held a clear majority at the party's January 1956 convention and in the national congress elected later that year.[94] Although labor supported Siles's candidacy, this show of strength seems to have encouraged the party's centrist leaders to reconsider their military policy. Soon after, the MNR's ambassador to the United States, Víctor Andrade, hinted to Assistant Secretary for Inter-American Affairs Henry Holland that both Paz and Siles might be open to rebuilding the military to check the power of labor.[95]

US support for the Bolivian military had actually begun informally soon after the revolution. British observers commented in February 1954 on the importance of US missions to keeping up military pride, and the first of many Bolivian officers attended the School of the Americas in Panama that year.[96] However, it did not become official US policy until this 1956 encounter.[97] Soon after Siles's inauguration, Holland met with him to relay the fear that militias were havens for communists who might overthrow the administration.[98] A favorable military policy became one of the preconditions of US-backed monetary stabilization.[99] US instructors began teaching at Bolivia's Military Academy that same year.[100]

Yet Siles rejected repeated offers of military aid until December 1957.[101] The timing of this decision to accept aid likely resulted from a crisis between Siles and Chief of Staff General Clemente Inofuentes over the nature of the revolution and the role of the armed forces in it. A founder of Radepa, Inofuentes spent time in exile with Paz Estenssoro, wrote pro-MNR pieces for the *Revista Militar* after the revolution, and then served in diplomatic posts until being appointed chief of staff by Siles in 1956.[102] The split between the two came after a confrontation between Siles and the COB in late June 1957 when COB members found themselves particularly affected by the stabilization package's ending of price controls and subsidies. During COB's June congress, members planned to hold a general strike at the end of the month unless the administration raised workers' cost-of-living compensation. Yet Siles also cultivated significant support during the congress and eventually prevailed on the group to call off the strike without meeting their demands.[103]

After this victory, General Inofuentes apparently pressed the president to take strong measures against leftist activities within and beyond the COB. Siles disagreed, put Inofuentes under house arrest, and asked for his resignation. The reaction among the officer corps in La Paz was immediate, and 178 officers sent Inofuentes a letter in which they offered to resign in protest. Inofuentes demurred, citing the need for unity and discipline. This moment revealed the existence of a significant population of officers acting as an interest group to resist the military's subordination to the MNR. Siles reversed his decision and allowed Inofuentes to return to his position, but the conflict led to a September 26 decree that reorganized the armed forces, subordinating the chief of staff to the minister of defense and relegating the position to a technical, rather than political and administrative, role. This reorganization led to Inofuentes's resignation and the appointment of General Miguel Ayllón, who had served as chief of staff right after the revolution.[104]

Mobilizing in opposition to Ayllón, a group of officers led by Colonel Windsor López barricaded themselves in the Miraflores military headquarters on October 3. The administration cut off water, electricity, and telephone service to the barracks and ordered militia leaders to arm themselves in case any army units supported the mutineers.[105] After mediation by the archbishop and papal nuncio, the group surrendered, submitted themselves to military justice, and issued a statement expressing their loyalty to the president and denying any political goals. They attributed their actions to "their desire to impede the promotion of military authorities that they [did] not consider good for the Army."[106] In this they were ultimately successful: Minister of Defense Julio Prado, portrayed by many as a communist, resigned at the end of October, and Siles replaced Ayllón with General Luis Rodríguez Bidegaín after only three and a half months in the position.[107]

This battle over Inofuentes was actually a skirmish over institutionality and the power of the MNR's left wing. Gary Prado, a cadet at the time whose father was minister of defense, reports that a faction of high-ranking officers had coalesced around Inofuentes as a representative of the military's corporate interests and that Siles felt threatened by him.[108] The British ambassador agreed in part. Although judging Inofuentes to be "a sincere personal friend" of and loyal to Siles, he portrayed him as an anticommunist and institutionalist who "regard[ed] the Armed Forces as a law unto themselves."[109] The chief of staff certainly had a strong following among the officer corps in La Paz, as shown by the support he received during the July incident. Later events suggest that Inofuentes was motivated by the antiradicalism and view of the military's role that were characteristic of what would become known as National Security Doctrine.[110] In January 1958, he met with US Ambassador Philip Bonsal to relay his frustration with the continued power of the militias, averring that only the military could keep the country stable.[111] In the swirl of rumors that characterized politics in La Paz, someone reported to the British ambassador that Inofuentes had formed a secret society of army and *carabinero* officers to combat "the Communist or fellow traveling opposition" and had plotted to assassinate Siles in late January.[112] The administration then shipped Inofuentes off as military attaché to Germany, where he died the next year.[113]

This dispute over military leadership and the decision to seek aid soon after reveals Siles's attempt to maintain officers' loyalty. It suggests that, despite purges and oaths, the revolution had not profoundly changed the officer corps. Five years was too short a period to dislodge entrenched institutional culture. Officers continued to envision an exalted role in society for themselves and their institution. Although four classes of cadets had graduated from the revamped Military Academy, they were still junior officers. Additionally, efforts to diversify the officer corps had had minimal impact, as most cadets continued to hail from the middle classes and military families because few members of the targeted groups both met entry qualifications and had a desire to pursue a career in a much-weakened military.[114]

The economic crisis in 1956 created an opening for institutionalists to seek support from the US and pressure Siles to strengthen the institution. Siles's resistance to accepting US military aid indicates his awareness that a strong military constituted a threat to his party and agenda. Yet by late 1957, he needed the military to balance the power of labor in his coalition and ensure the continuation of his economic policies. The strong show of support for Inofuentes in mid-1957 may have convinced him to remove the leader but mollify the institutionalists that he represented. Although clearly guilty of mutiny for their takeover of the barracks in opposition to the new chief of staff, the offending officers were prosecuted only for indiscipline.[115] Siles also gave in to their demands by replacing Ayllón. Post-stabilization, Siles decided that he would need a relatively strong official military and could no longer rely on the workers' militias. This would mean concessions to institutionalists, including the training and arms made possible by US assistance.

In fact, only weeks after the Inofuentes incident, Siles used the military for internal security for the first time since the revolution. At the end of October 1957, the leader of the opposition Bolivian Socialist Falange (FSB) seized oil machinery and attacked government buildings in Santa Cruz to demand that profits from YPFB, the state-run oil company, be shared with the department. After mediation by leading politicians failed, Siles sent about two hundred army troops to surround the city. Backed by the threat of these forces, the papal nuncio and archbishop successfully mediated an end to the standoff and a declaration of loyalty to Siles. The British ambassador highlighted the implications of the military's deployment: "The Army has been used, for the first time since 1952, as the instrument of law and order, which will enhance its morale and prestige." This deployment far from the mines and factories of the altiplano was no coincidence: an observer in London's foreign office guessed that Siles was testing public reaction in "a safe place" and would not "have dared to use them to put down disturbances in Oruro, Cochabamba, or La Paz."[116]

The military would only grow stronger after US weapons began arriving in April 1958, which marked the Bolivian military's reorientation to US arms, training, and tactics. Shipments of semiautomatic rifles, Browning machine guns, and Bazooka rocket launchers to replace European weaponry dating from the Chaco War imbued the officer corps with hope and a renewed pride in their institution.[117] Newsreels produced by the United States Information Service (USIS) worked to spread this pride to the larger population by emphasizing the military's achievements.[118]

The institution became stronger and bolder as Siles repeatedly called on it to resolve domestic issues. Military forces, at first accompanied by peasant militiamen, again suppressed uprisings in Santa Cruz in May 1958, June 1958, and April 1959.[119] More telling was a July 1958 mission to negotiate the release of several officers imprisoned by a local militia in Cochabamba. This test proved the institution's continued weakness (or perhaps meekness); its forces retreated in humiliation after militiamen assaulted General Alfredo Ovando with the butts of their rifles.[120] But training, funding, and the continued use of the military for internal security would provide leading officers like Ovando with increased confidence and power. By March 1959, Siles was willing to send troops to control the riots that had broken out in La Paz after a *Time* article quoted an anonymous embassy official that the US was "wasting money" by pouring so much aid into Bolivia without "a damn thing to show for it" and suggested that the country's territory "be divided amongst its neighbors."[121] The next month, the president successfully used it against workers in the MNR's coalition, deploying the army to secure YPFB installations during a strike.[122]

Several events in 1960 proved the military's return to dominance over its armed rivals. They occurred in the context of a schism within the MNR, which had been provoked by the question of presidential succession. Wálter Guevara Arze, an MNR founder who had become the leader of the party's right wing, made a play to succeed Siles. In an attempt to avoid the split this would cause, the left advocated for Víctor Paz Estenssoro to return from his diplomatic post and seek the presidency again. However, Paz's offer of the vice presidency to Juan Lechín cemented the divide, leading Guevara Arze to run under the banner of a splinter party. The Authentic Revolutionary Nationalist Movement (MNRA) thus siphoned off the MNR's right and some of the center.[123]

Guevara Arze's candidacy was one of the issues spurring the armed conflict that broke out among rival peasant unions in Cochabamba in October 1959. Siles repeatedly used army troops in attempts to control this dispute, which is known as the Ch'ampa Guerra. Military intervention was overtly partisan in this case, as the forces prevented Guevara Arze from announcing his candidacy among his allies in Cliza but allowed Víctor Paz to campaign freely.[124] Over the course of this civil war, the army took on the role of mediator and imposed martial law to manage the violence. Characterized primarily by the assassination of rival peasant leaders, the conflict dragged on until September 1963, when General René Barrientos brokered a peace agreement between the two sides, launching his own political career and reinforcing the military's role as peacekeeper.[125]

Militiamen had also been purged from the ranks of the official army. In contrast to post-revolution characterizations of the Waldo Ballivián Regiment, the minister of defense in 1960 could claim (and, importantly, wanted to claim) that the unit had "not one militiaman in its ranks."[126] When a unit of *carabineros* attacked the Ballivián barracks in an attempt to overthrow Siles in March 1960, Ballivián troops quickly repelled them. After retreating to the north of the city, the *carabineros* were efficiently defeated by Ballivián troops, the Ingavi Cavalry Group, and the air force's shelling and machine-gun fire.[127] This event marked the army's superior firepower and its eclipse of the previously favored *carabineros*. The military's prominent role in Paz's August 1960 inauguration ceremony definitively signaled the institution's triumphant return and how much had changed since its reduced and demoralized showing during Siles's inaugural parade just four years before.[128]

When confronted with political turmoil, officers in the MNR's military continued to violate the institution's official norms in favor of its habitual practice: acting outside of the official chain of command to do what they thought necessary to protect the institution. They were not subordinated to civilian authorities and again felt empowered to play kingmaker in Bolivian politics. The resurgence of Bolivia's military after its humiliation in 1952 closely tracks with the fracturing of the MNR's coalition. Facing economic and diplomatic pressure after the initial set of revolutionary decrees, Siles came to rely on the "Revolution's Army" to maintain his rule. Yet the revolution and MNR rule had not fundamentally changed the institution. Siles and Paz convinced themselves that the postrevolutionary military was different since they controlled it and its high command was dominated by reformists who had been discharged for supporting Radepa or the MNR. In a 1959 speech, Víctor Paz even stated that the MNR "had never been divorced from the Army because military elements had been part of its ranks from the earliest times."[129] Yet despite purges and oaths of loyalty, institutional inertia and ingrained habits continued to dominate Bolivia's military. Even the most steadfast MNRistas like Generals Fortún and Inofuentes did what officers had done for the previous century: put the institution first.

The revolution had brought the military a significant increase in rural recruits as part of the process of incorporating them into the voting population explicitly as supporters of the MNR. Along with the military's newly valorized focus on nonmartial productive labor, this meant that the institution was increasingly oriented toward and supported by the rural communities that supplied its soldiers and benefited from its productive labor. Although the embedding of military service in rural areas had its origins in the mass mobilization of the Chaco War and decades of migration, it came to fruition only after the agrarian reform. Although conscripts' daily routines had not changed drastically and the MNR still aimed to improve through military service a population deemed too rural, too illiterate, and too indigenous, the postrevolutionary state actively courted these men as revolutionary citizens. Conscripts were no longer seen as noncitizen soldiers.

EPILOGUE

THE MILITARY'S RESTORATIVE REVOLUTION OF 1964

Facing profound challenges from both the right and the left during his second term, the increasingly authoritarian Víctor Paz Estenssoro came to rely on the military to remain in power. The United States became a key ally in this endeavor, pouring twelve million dollars into the Bolivian armed forces, sending advisers, and using training at the School of the Americas to indoctrinate over 1,100 Bolivian military personnel in anticommunist counterinsurgency.[1] Histories covering the 1960–1964 period read like a laundry list of strikes, states of siege, crises, and requests to the United States for tear gas, riot gear, weapons, and ammunition.[2] Miners and leaders on the MNR's left definitively broke from Paz during this period, cementing the party's shift from a broad-based coalition to one that relied on rural areas, the military, and US assistance. While Bolivia was not yet a military dictatorship, the influence of National Security Doctrine was already apparent as the administration and the military focused on the interrelated goals of development and fighting internal enemies.

Funds from the Kennedy administration's new civic action program began flowing to Bolivia in 1961. Encouraging the use of local military forces in development projects like schools and water sanitation systems to combat communism, civic action gave an official term (and, more importantly, additional funding) to the Bolivian military's long history of performing nonmartial productive labor. By 1964, a fifth of the military's manpower hours were dedicated to such projects.[3] This role helped forge the military's image as an institution above politics and devoted to the development of rural Bolivia.[4]

Paz and the MNR reinforced the military's centrality to a redefined revolutionary project permeated by ideas that would become associated with National Security Doctrine. After asserting the institution's identification with Bolivia's majority classes, the party's governing program from August 1960 stated that the primary role of the armed forces was "defending the State against internal enemies."[5] It placed this priority above the defense of

Bolivia's sovereignty, reflecting the administration's reliance on the military to maintain its increasingly tenuous hold on power. The MNR platform then highlighted the institution's achievements in agricultural and industrial production, colonization, and roadwork. The 1961 Constitution reinforced this productive role, as did the 1963 Organic Law of the Armed Forces.[6] Historian Thomas Field writes of this moment as the "culmination of a piecemeal process whereby the development goals of the national revolution were turned over to the Bolivian armed forces."[7]

The principal face of the military in the 1960s was Air Force General René Barrientos Ortuño, who had fought for the MNR in the 1949 civil war and had flown Paz Estenssoro back from exile in 1952. A native son of Tarata (Cochabamba), Barrientos used his position, charisma, and Quechua-language abilities to build extensive patron-client ties in rural areas by directly identifying himself with civic action projects and playing a personal role in mediating disputes, especially the Ch'ampa Guerra.[8] When Paz decided to run again in 1964, General Barrientos openly campaigned to be his vice president. Paz ultimately nominated longtime ally Federico Fortún and attempted to informally exile Barrientos to a diplomatic position in London. However, he added Barrientos to the ticket instead after a highly publicized (and likely staged) assassination attempt just hours before the general was to depart the country.[9] Barrientos had maneuvered himself and the military back into the center of Bolivian politics. His history as a steadfast MNRista, however, suggests that the armed forces had never really lost that role.

On the other hand, the increasingly positive image of the institution and of military service in rural areas marked an important shift. Bolivia's demographics meant that rural agriculturalists would be the clear majority of voters after the turn to universal suffrage in 1952 and therefore a key interest group to cultivate. As Paz stated in a 1959 speech, the idea that a military unit would be used to "rob peasants of their communal land" had become "inconceivable" in postrevolutionary Bolivia.[10] In fact, the prominent face of the military in development projects, combined with the widespread participation of rural men in conscription and the changes wrought by the agrarian reform, led to the forging of the Military-Peasant Pact (PMC) shortly before Paz's reelection in May 1964. The PMC's crafters worked to link it explicitly to the revolutionary legacy and display the numerical power of the peasantry: with thirty thousand peasants in attendance, it was signed on the anniversary of the April 9 revolution in front of the Ucureña (Cochabamba) monument commemorating the 1953 agrarian reform. Yet its content reflected National Security Doctrine and the course taken by the MNR over twelve years of rule. In it, Barrientos, representing the military, and forty-eight peasant organizations pledged to work together to support Barrientos's candidacy for the vice presidency, guarantee social peace, combat extreme doctrines, ensure economic diversification, and defend the social, political, and economic interests of the signees.[11]

Only months later, pro-Barrientos officers commanding military regiments in La Paz and Cochabamba overthrew President Paz Estenssoro on November 3, 1964. Although this event has been narrated as another instance of US support for military intervention in the region, Thomas Field has convincingly shown that the US State Department viewed Barrientos as too unpredictable and actually supported Paz Estenssoro right up until he boarded a plane for exile, even approving a last-minute request to provide arms for his militiamen.[12] In fact, except for the Trotskyist Revolutionary Workers Party (POR), all of the major players in Bolivia had been pressuring the military and Barrientos to intervene for months.[13] In the words of James Dunkerley, the right and left united in 1964 to oppose "the ramshackle remnants of a party that no longer possessed any popularity beyond that generated through state patronage."[14] Barrientos could thus term his coup the Restorative Revolution. As Bridgette Werner has shown, his administration then worked to strengthen its identification with rural areas through the PMC, using the MNR's method of indirect rule through patron-client ties.[15] Military dictators would control Bolivia with only brief interruptions for the next seventeen years.

Obligatory military service long outlived the MNR, just as it had every other twentieth-century administration. Liberals planted the seeds of conscription, the Chaco War allowed them to take root, and the revolution deepened those roots. Military service had become embedded in the lives and culture of Bolivia's lower classes. In elaborating his life history as part of a collaborative process with US scholars, mining labor leader Félix Muruchi Poma recounted the essential nature of military service to men of his social class in the 1960s: "We perceived the army as a rite of passage; we always knew who had gone. . . . Lots of soldiers got a small tattoo to identify their division, and it provided them something that connected them to broader society." Muruchi describes a complex process of coercion and consent that persuaded him and his peers to join the "tremendous line that snaked more than three blocks around the base" on enlistment day. He points to "the pressure to prove [their] manhood," a "sense of camaraderie," and how military service allowed men to "participate fully in fiestas," to be able to marry, and to obtain the discharge papers without which "everything was more difficult."[16]

With the intensification of the Cold War and the embrace of National Security Doctrine, Muruchi and his fellow conscripts were joining an institution increasingly oriented toward a global geopolitical project that labeled members of their communities communists and used military force to control them. Although this ideological bent was new, the Bolivian military had a long history of repressing the indigenous and mining communities that provided it with soldiers. At the behest of supposedly fearful landlords in the early twentieth century, military forces had repeatedly marched into rural indigenous areas to prevent uprisings and a so-called race war. And mining companies regularly had called on these same forces to break strikes and intimidate their workforce.[17] The Chaco War and the 1952 revolution had drawn more men into the institution but had by no means changed its orientation toward internal repression.

The striking disjuncture between the institution's actions and the interests of its conscripts is precisely the paradox that this book has sought to explain. This is indeed the story of a state successfully using military service to create and strengthen itself through establishing bureaucratic structures and spreading a sense of national identity. Liberal governments, the MNR, and the military regimes dreamed that obligatory military service would indoctrinate the population into their visions for society. But the men who presented for military service were not unaware of the ways the institution served elite interests. Like soldiers throughout the world, they still forged meaning out of the experience and made it their own. However, the enduring weakness of the Bolivian state made the extent of this co-creation distinct. This weakness paradoxically strengthened the institution of obligatory military service because it could not effectively be imposed from above and instead depended on the investment of conscripts and their communities. Their contributions to the institution and the ways that they shaped it cannot be dismissed as complicit submission.

Conscription was not only the state's attempt to impose a documentary regime; it also comprised the decisions made by local authorities about how to implement the law, the punishments and encouragements that conscripts received from officers, the multilingual interactions that occurred in the barracks, and the subtle teasing and exclusions perpetuated by conscripts on their fellows. It included the patriotic tunes played by the regimental band, the feeling of wielding a rifle and wearing a uniform, the food eaten during communal meals, and the stories that conscripts told about their experiences when they returned to their homes. Beginning in the 1940s and strengthening after the revolution, rural Bolivians' enthusiasm for conscription shows that they came to see military service as useful in their lives—as a tool for social ascent and forging patronage networks. It had become hegemonic through a process of coercion and consent that was negotiated from below. Understanding military service as a terrain for negotiating the relationship between the state and society shows that these men and their families helped produce Bolivia rather than simply being overrun by it. Conscription has endured because governments of all stripes continued to dream of a conscript nation and conscripts of all stripes appropriated it, investing it with their own meanings.

NOTES

INTRODUCTION: CONSCRIPTION'S DEEP ROOTS

1. Evo Morales inaugural address, January 21, 2006, https://www.pagina12.com.ar/diario/especiales/18-62330-2006-01-30.html. All translations are my own unless otherwise noted.

2. Bolivia, *Nueva Constitución*, 5. On the translation of *buen vivir*, see Eisenstadt, LeVan, and Maboudi, *Constituents before Assembly*, 133–34.

3. For a discussion of the debates surrounding military service in the Constituent Assembly, see Cabezas Fernández, "Ciudadanía y estado," 49–54.

4. Bolivia, *Nueva Constitución*, Article 108. See also Articles 142, 234, and 249.

5. Bolivia, *Nueva Constitución*, Article 234.

6. For one of the earliest assessments, see Van Doorn, "Decline of the Mass Army."

7. Flynn, *Conscription and Democracy*, 248. While complicating this teleology of conscription's inevitable decline with case studies from Nordic countries, Pertti Joenniemi acknowledges the common assumption that "the traditional system of drafting" is now seen as "hopelessly outdated." Joenniemi, *Changing Face*, 3.

8. Alejandra Sánchez Bustamente, "Reclutamiento militar empieza con largas filas," *La Razón*, January 30, 2017; Jorge Quispe, "Se reclutaron 122 mujeres para servicio militar 2018," *La Razón*, February 28, 2018.

9. Cruz Quispe, *Subordinación y constancia*, 16, 29.

10. "Tramite libreta de redención a partir de los 23 años," Ministerio de Defensa, accessed May 1, 2018, http://www.mindef.gob.bo/mindef/sites/default/files/tramites.pdf; Guiomara Calle and Paulo Cuiza, "Hombres trans tropiezan con la obtención de la libreta militar," *La Razón*, March 17, 2017; Paulo Cuiza, "FFAA amplía el periodo de registro y el número de cupos para el servicio premilitar 2017–2018," *La Razón*, September 12, 2017.

11. Goudsmit, "Praying for Government," 208.

12. Law 954 of June 9, 2017, http://www.gacetaoficialdebolivia.gob.bo/; Rubén Ariñez, "Este jueves se abre el reclutamiento para el servicio militar con 10 unidades para mujeres," *La Razón*, January 30, 2018. Women received voluntary training for auxiliary roles from 1943 to 1946. Although voluntary pre-military service for both genders was part of a 1966 law, no women received training. The first female officers

graduated from the Military Academy in 1982. Female secondary students have had the option of participating in pre-military service since 1997. Quintana T., *La conquista ciudadana*, 37–48.

13. Dunkerley, "Evo Morales," 139.

14. A. Cuervas and C. Corz, "Viceministro anuncia que presidenciables deben hablar idioma nativo y haber hecho efectivo servicio militar," *La Razón*, April 4, 2017. The quotation goes on to refer specifically to former presidents Jorge Quiroga (2001–2002), Jaime Paz (1989–1993), and Gonzalo Sánchez de Lozada (1993–1997, 2002–2003). Quiroga also ran against Morales in 2014.

15. Eichler, *Militarizing Men*, 4–5. See also Gillis, *Militarization of the Western World*, 1–5.

16. Galindo de Ugarte, *Constituciones bolivianas*, 610–11. Leonard Smith has convincingly argued that "the concept of an 'apolitical' army is fundamentally inconsistent with an army of citizen-soldiers," so "authority and obedience will be thus constantly subject to questioning and negotiation from below." Smith, *Between Mutiny and Obedience*, 11.

17. Galindo de Ugarte, *Constituciones bolivianas*, 103, 108.

18. For a discussion of the meaning and limits on citizenship during this period, see Gotkowitz, *Revolution for Our Rights*, 27–30, 117–20.

19. Centeno, *Blood and Debt*, 43–44.

20. Klein, *Concise History of Bolivia*, 183.

21. On the connection between claims-making and citizenship, see Cooper, *Citizenship, Inequality, and Difference*.

22. Centeno, *Blood and Debt*.

23. Alonso, *Thread of Blood*; Deas, "Man on Foot"; Ferrer, *Insurgent Cuba*; Foote and Horst, *Military Struggle and Identity Formation*; Guardino, "Gender, Soldiering, and Citizenship"; Hunefeldt, "Power Constellations in Peru"; Kraay, *Race, State, and Armed Forces*; Kraay and Whigham, *I Die with My Country*; Mallon, *Peasant and Nation*; Morgan, *Legacy of the Lash*; Neufeld, *Blood Contingent*; Rugeley and Fallaw, *Forced Marches*; Rath, *Myths of Demilitarization*.

24. Best, "Militarization of European Society," 14–17; Cohen, *Citizens and Soldiers*, 42–59; Leonhard and von Hirschhausen, "Does the Empire Strike Back?," 202–9; Ralston, *Importing the European Army*. For some examples of work on non-European states outside Latin America, see Altinay, *Myth of the Military-Nation*; Conway, *Masculinities, Militarisation*; Jaundrill, *Samurai to Soldier*; Mann, *Native Sons*; Zürcher, *Arming the State*.

25. Loveman, *For la Patria*, 73.

26. Frevert, *Nation in the Barracks*; Karsten, *Recruiting, Drafting, and Enlisting*; Krebs, *Fighting for Rights*; Sanborn, *Drafting the Russian Nation*; von Hagen, *Soldiers in the Proletarian Dictatorship*; Zürcher, *Arming the State*, 8–11.

27. Eichler, "Militarized Masculinities," 82–83. See also Ahlbäck, *Manhood and the Making of the Military*; Moon, *Militarized Modernity*; Eichler, *Militarizing Men*;

Geva, *Conscription, Family, and the Modern State*; Sanborn, *Drafting the Russian Nation*, 132–64.

28. Frevert, *Nation in the Barracks*, 2–5; Lynn, *Battle*, 183–88.

29. Beattie, *Tribute of Blood*, 207–84; Carey Jr., *Our Elders Teach Us*, 183–86; Rath, *Myths of Demilitarization*, 56–61; Rouquié, *Military and the State*, 94–97. Conscription also had these internal purposes in other parts of the world; see Best, "Militarization of European Society," 14–17; Frevert, *Nation in the Barracks*; Sanborn, *Drafting the Russian Nation*.

30. Adams, "Race and Ethnicity," 107–12; Foote, "Monteneros and Macheteros," 100–102; McCann, *Soldiers of the Pátria*, 185.

31. Centeno, *Blood and Debt*, 66.

32. Most studies (including this one) are on the national level but suggest significant variation in different states/departments and between rural and urban areas.

33. Ablard, "'Barracks Receives Spoiled Children,'" 300–311, 325.

34. Maldonado Prieto, "El servicio militar en Chile"; Passmore, *Wars inside Chile's Barracks*, 77–79; Sater and Holger, *Grand Illusion*, 102–9.

35. Méndez G., "Las paradojas del autoritarismo," 29–30. See also González-Cueva, "Conscription and Violence in Peru"; Méndez G., "Militares populistas"; Hurtado Meza, "Ejército cholificado."

36. Ortiz B., "La influencia militar"; Selmeski, "Guerreros y ciudadanos," 72.

37. Rath, *Myths of Demilitarization*, 54–80.

38. Ablard, "'Barracks Receives Spoiled Children,'" 301.

39. Beattie, *Tribute of Blood*, 120–22, 177–203, 268–81; Rath, "Modernizing Military Patriarchy," 815–17. On labor see Ablard, "'Barracks Receives Spoiled Children,'" 306; Selmeski, "Sons of Indians," 168.

40. Ablard, "'Barracks Receives Spoiled Children,'" 320; Gill, "Creating Citizens, Making Men"; Selmeski, "Sons of Indians," 167–75; Rath, "Modernizing Military Patriarchy," 816.

41. Gill, "Creating Citizens, Making Men."

42. Carey Jr., "Mayan Soldier-Citizens," 179; Beattie, *Tribute of Blood*, 207–37; McCann, *Soldiers of the Pátria*, 174–86.

43. Quotations from Beattie, *Tribute of Blood*, 252, 261. See also Smallman, *Fear & Memory*, 32–49.

44. Bastos, *Etnicidad y fuerzas armadas*, 59–90; Carey Jr., *Our Elders Teach Us*, 177–85.

45. Carey Jr., "Mayan Soldier-Citizens."

46. Carey Jr., *Our Elders Teach Us*, 180–83. See also Carey Jr., "Who's Using Whom?."

47. Carey Jr., *Our Elders Teach Us*, 191–93.

48. Díaz Arguedas, *Historia del ejército, La guerra con el Paraguay,* and *Fastos militares de Bolivia*; Rodríguez, *Autopsia de una guerra*; Vergara Vicuña, *Historia de la Guerra del Chaco*; Pol, *La campaña del Chaco*; Zook, *Conduct of the Chaco War*; Wil-

de Cavero, *Historia militar de Bolivia*; Querejazu Calvo, *Masamaclay*; Farcau, *Chaco War*; Pereira Fiorilo, *Historia secreta de la Guerra del Chaco*. For histories focused on the military's role in politics, see Nunn, *Yesterday's Soldiers*; Lowenthal and Fitch, *Armies and Politics in Latin America*; Rouquié, *Military and the State*; Loveman, *For la Patria*.

49. James Dunkerley's 1979 pioneering dissertation, which was finally published in Spanish in 1987, tracks elite debates over military service, explains conscription laws, and provides some statistical data with the overarching purpose of understanding the institutional origins of dictatorship in the 1970s. Juan Ramón Quintana's 1998 sociological study is the most comprehensive work to date on conscription. It provides a more robust historical overview that relies upon, but also goes beyond, Dunkerley. The heart of Quintana's work, however, is the analysis of data from 1980 to 1995, including several surveys of troops in the tenth division. Looking at the 1910s, a chapter in Luis Oporto's monograph shows that young men turned to mining jobs to avoid military service. Based on prefectural and judicial archives, oral histories, and newspaper accounts, René Arze's 1987 study of rural unrest during the Chaco War suggests that soldiering may have shifted local notions of belonging from one of "community and *ayllu*" to a "national consciousness." Also addressing the 1930s, an article by Roberto Fernández investigates officers' ideological construction of the indigenous citizen-soldier. Dunkerley, *Orígenes del poder militar*; Quintana Taborga, *Soldados y ciudadanos*; Oporto Ordoñez, *Uncía y Llallagua*; Arze Aguirre, *Guerra y conflictos sociales*; Fernández Terán, "Transformaciones y prácticas de poder."

50. Quotations from Quintana Taborga, *Soldados y ciudadanos*, 46, 71. Two pieces by anthropologists offer a complex understanding of contemporary military service in Bolivia, exploring not only violence and assimilation but also indigenous men's motivations for serving. Canessa, "The Indian within," 136–40; Gill, "Creating Citizens, Making Men."

51. On this fluidity, see Gotkowitz, *Revolution for Our Rights*, 13; Ari, *Earth Politics*, 14; Luykx, *Citizen Factory*, xli, 20–24; Grieshaber, "Fluctuaciones en la definición del indio." Previous generations of scholars either took indigeneity as an ontological category or argued that ethnic and racial terms served to mask class relationships.

52. For historical works see Gotkowitz, *Revolution for Our Rights*; Kuenzli, *Acting Inca*; Ari, *Earth Politics*; Barragán, *Asambleas constituyentes*. Contributions by anthropologists include Lazar, *El Alto, Rebel City*; Postero, *Now We Are Citizens*; Albro, *Roosters at Midnight*; Canessa, *Intimate Indigeneities*.

53. Quotations from Lazar, *El Alto, Rebel City*, 126, 141. See also Bigenho, *Sounding Indigenous*, 29–60; Goldstein, *Spectacular City*, 134–78; Van Vleet, *Performing Kinship*, 99–128.

54. Albro, *Roosters at Midnight*, 102.

55. Bigenho, *Sounding Indigenous*, 44–45.

CHAPTER 1: CONSCRIPTION WITHOUT CITIZENSHIP

1. Lt. Col. Carlos Nuñez del Prado, "Grandezas y pequeñeces—El centinela," *Revista Militar* 14 (1905): 135–46. Quotation from 135. The *Revista Militar* began publishing in 1901.

2. This view of the armed forces as a nationalist guardian above partisan politics was developing across Latin America. See Loveman, *For la Patria*; Loveman and Davies Jr., *Politics of Antipolitics*; Nunn, *Yesterday's Soldiers*.

3. Nuñez del Prado, "Grandezas y pequeñeces," 136–37. In the Bolivian and Latin American historiography, "patria" is often translated as "fatherland." Following Brian Loveman, however, I choose not to translate the term, which comes from the root for "father" but is gendered female. Loveman, *For la Patria*, xviii.

4. Nuñez del Prado, "Grandezas y pequeñeces," 136–37.

5. Nuñez del Prado, "Grandezas y pequeñeces," 137–38.

6. Nuñez del Prado, "Grandezas y pequeñeces," 141–42.

7. Nuñez del Prado, "Grandezas y pequeñeces," 146.

8. Nuñez del Prado, "Grandezas y pequeñeces," 145.

9. Rates of participation in the Bolivian military during the twentieth century were on a par with other Latin American countries but far lower than in European countries. Centeno, *Blood and Debt*, 225.

10. Dunkerley, "Reassessing Caudillismo," 15.

11. Dunkerley, "Reassessing Caudillismo," 13–17.

12. Dunkerley, *Orígenes del poder militar*, 34–42; quotation from 29. See also Sater, *Andean Tragedy*, 20–22.

13. Gotkowitz, *Revolution for Our Rights*, 36.

14. Klein, *Concise History of Bolivia*, 107–9.

15. Klein, *Concise History of Bolivia*, 146–56; Larson, *Trials of Nation Making*, 219–21; Langer, *Economic Change and Rural Resistance*, 20–28; Gotkowitz, *Revolution for Our Rights*, 26–35; Dunkerley, *Orígenes del poder militar*, 46.

16. Díaz Arguedas, *Historia del ejército*, 23–25, 57, 177; Dunkerley, *Orígenes del poder militar*, 57.

17. Laws of August 6, 1875, and September 20, 1892.

18. Langer, *Economic Change and Rural Resistance*, 27–30; Hylton, "Reverberations of Insurgency," 75; Platt, "Andean Experience of Bolivian Liberalism," 299.

19. Kuenzli, *Acting Inca*, 33–39; Larson, *Trials of Nation Making*, 231–42; Gotkowitz, *Revolution for Our Rights*, 36–38; Dunkerley, *Orígenes del poder militar*, 68–76; Hylton, "Reverberations of Insurgency"; Condarco Morales, *Zárate, el temible Willka*; Mendieta Parada, *De Tupac Katari a Zárate Willka*.

20. Kuenzli, *Acting Inca*, 33–39; Hylton, "Reverberations of Insurgency," 91–92, 182–83, 234–38.

21. Kuenzli, *Acting Inca*, 33–55; Hylton, "Reverberations of Insurgency," 241–79.

22. Klein, *Orígenes de la revolución nacional boliviana*, 43–50.

23. Díaz Arguedas, *Historia del ejército*, 162.

24. Dunkerley, *Orígenes del poder militar*, 86. For provisions that prohibited recruitment, see ministerial order of June 28, 1838, which was reiterated on March 12, 1860, and December 30, 1881. Flores Moncayo, *Legislación boliviana del indio*, 104, 186, 283.

25. Dunkerley, *Orígenes del poder militar*, 82–84; Scheina, "Acre War, 1903," 7–9.

26. Galindo de Ugarte, *Constituciones bolivianas*, 610–11.

27. Circular no. 45, February 26, 1908, in Ministerio de Guerra, *Boletín militar*, 4:94.

28. The French mission under Sever instituted a new rank system and a uniform dress code, reorganized the Military Academy, and abolished the *fuero militar*, which had provided immunity for military members in civilian judicial processes. Brockmann, *El general y sus presidentes*, 34; Bieber, "La política militar alemana," 87.

29. Chile contracted with Prussian Captain Emilio Körner in 1886, and a contingent of thirty-six officers joined him there in 1895. French Captain Paul Clément arrived in Peru in 1896 with a staff of four officers. By 1914, thirty-one French officers had worked in Peru. Argentina contracted retired Prussian Colonel Alfred Arent in 1899 along with three officers. Nunn, *Yesterday's Soldiers*, 3, 100–104, 112, 117, 123.

30. Article 2, supreme decree of February 24, 1908, in Bolivia, *Anuario de leyes* (1908). The text of many laws and resolutions are also available at www.gacetaoficial debolivia.gob.bo/.

31. See Minister of War circular of June 7, 1905 and supreme decrees of September 27, 1905; December 17, 1905; February 7, 1906; and April 13, 1906.

32. Law of January 16, 1907, in Bolivia, *Anuario de leyes* (1907). The next major law governing conscription was issued on December 20, 1963.

33. In departmental capitals, this table would be manned by the *mayor de plaza* and two high-ranking officers. In provincial seats, the commission would consist of the subprefect, *corregidor* (administrator of province), and a military officer. The *corregidor* and one officer would register men at the canton level; in the absence of an officer, the second seat could be filled by a civilian named by the subprefect.

34. Law of January 16, 1907; "Reglamento del servicio militar," April 6, 1907, in Ministerio de Guerra, *Boletín militar*, 3:121–48.

35. Law of January 16, 1907; "Reglamento del servicio militar," 121–48. The daily wage for mineworkers in 1907 was two bolivianos. Smale, *"I Sweat the Flavor of Tin,"* 53.

36. The law called for the lottery to choose people who would serve. However, those who did not serve were called "sorteados." Scholars generally assume that these lotteries were rigged. See Oporto Ordoñez, *Uncía y Llallagua*, 124.

37. Law of January 16, 1907; "Reglamento del servicio militar," 121–48.

38. "La nueva ley militar," *El Comercio*, January 20, 1907.

39. Law of January 16, 1907; "Reglamento del servicio militar," 121–48.

40. Minister of War to Prefects, January 21, 1907, in Ministerio de Guerra, *Boletín militar*, 3:21–28.

41. Minister of War Ministerial Resolution, March 25, 1907, in Ministerio de Guerra, *Boletín militar*, 3:84.

42. General Jacques Sever, Circular no. 61, March 26, 1907, in Ministerio de Guerra, *Boletín militar*, 3:86. In December 1905, Bolivia conferred the rank of brigadier general on French Colonel Jacques Sever, who served as chief of staff from 1906 until the mission contract expired in 1909. Ministerio de Guerra, *Escalafón militar de 1906*, 6; Díaz Arguedas, *Historia del ejército*, 64.

43. Twenty-third extraordinary session, January 5, 1907, in Bolivia, *Redactor de la H. Cámara de Diputados*, 3:1460.

44. Sanjinés Goitia, *El militar ingeniero*, 350.

45. Scott, *Seeing Like a State*, 183.

46. Muñoz Reyes, *Geografía de Bolivia*, 91–98; Oficina Nacional de Inmigración, Estadística, y Propaganda Geográfica, *Censo general*, 2:iv.

47. Oficina Nacional de Inmigración, Estadística, y Propaganda Geográfica, *Censo general*, 2:iv.

48. Oficina Nacional de Inmigración, Estadística, y Propaganda Geográfica, *Censo general*, 2:iv, xxxviii–xlii, xciv–ci, cxxi.

49. Oficina Nacional de Inmigración, Estadística, y Propaganda Geográfica, *Censo general*, 2:xiii–xiv, ci–cii; Klein, *Concise History of Bolivia*, 1–9.

50. Oficina Nacional de Inmigración, Estadística, y Propaganda Geográfica, *Censo general*, 2:lxxxii–xcii.

51. Oficina Nacional de Inmigración, Estadística, y Propaganda Geográfica, *Censo general*, 2:lxxvii–lxxix.

52. Oficina Nacional de Inmigración, Estadística, y Propaganda Geográfica, *Censo general*, 2:lix–lx.

53. The territorial figure also included 66,170 kilometers attributed to the Littoral department. The 1904 treaty would cede an additional 120,000 kilometers. Oficina Nacional de Inmigración, Estadística, y Propaganda Geográfica, *Censo general*, 1:11–14.

54. Oficina Nacional de Inmigración, Estadística, y Propaganda Geográfica, *Censo general*, 1:35–36.

55. Oficina Nacional de Inmigración, Estadística, y Propaganda Geográfica, *Censo general*, 1:15, 2:18.

56. Oficina Nacional de Inmigración, Estadística, y Propaganda Geográfica, *Censo general*, 2:42–44.

57. The additional 9.43 percent were listed as "not reported." These included people whose racial identity was not reported by census takers and a 5 percent augmentation used to estimate those missed by census takers. Oficina Nacional de Inmigración, Estadística, y Propaganda Geográfica, *Censo general*, 2:30–35.

58. Grieshaber, "Fluctuaciones en la definición del indio."

59. Oficina Nacional de Inmigración, Estadística, y Propaganda Geográfica, *Censo general*, 2:35–36.

60. Oficina Nacional de Inmigración, Estadística, y Propaganda Geográfica, *Censo general*, 2:17.

61. For how liberal education reforms aimed to control and modernize the indigenous population, see Choque Canqui and Quisbert Quispe, *Educación indigenal en Bolivia*; Choque et al., *Educación indígena*; Larson, "Capturing Indian Bodies."

62. Ministerio de Guerra, *Memoria de guerra* (1910), 7.

63. Ministerio de Guerra, *Memoria de guerra* (1915), 12. The minister of war ceased reporting on the number of conscripts who presented and served after 1913. Congress set the army size for 1915 at 3,576. Law of November 9, 1914, in Bolivia, *Anuario de leyes* (1914).

64. Brockmann, *El general y sus presidentes*, 34. See also Annual Report for 1911, January 24, 1912, FO 371/10016, National Archives (TNA).

65. Ministerio de Guerra, *Memoria de guerra* (1910), 40.

66. Ministerio de Guerra, *Memoria de guerra* (1911), 14–15.

67. Ministerio de Guerra, *Memoria de guerra* (1912), 22.

68. Díaz Arguedas, *Historia del ejército*, 763; Sanjinés Goitia, *El militar ingeniero*, 352; Bieber, "La política militar alemana," 97–100; Dunkerley, *Orígenes del poder militar*, 94.

69. Ministerio de Guerra, *Memoria de guerra* (1908), xxvi–xxvii.

70. Ministerio de Guerra, *Memoria de guerra* (1911), 21; *Memoria de guerra* (1912), 32.

71. Yearly reports submitted by the minister of war to Congress reflect these discharge dates. Only in 1916 were the conscripts chosen for three months of training discharged immediately after the lottery. Ministerio de Guerra, *Memoria de guerra* (1916), 36.

72. Ministerio de Guerra, *Boletín militar* (1907–1909).

73. Ministerio de Guerra, *Boletín militar* (1908), 4:307.

74. Ministerio de Guerra, *Boletín militar* (1907), 3:484.

75. Oporto Ordoñez, *Uncía y Llallagua*, 120–24.

76. Oficina Nacional de Inmigración, Estadística, y Propaganda Geográfica, *Censo general*, 2:27–29. This finding supports the minister of war's 1916 estimate that only 30 percent of each cohort registered. Ministerio de Guerra, *Memoria de guerra* (1916), 61.

77. Supreme decree of December 16, 1908, in Bolivia, *Anuario de leyes* (1908).

78. Prefect of La Paz to Quartermaster of Caupolicán, January 2, 1909, Prefecture-Exped box 170, d. 247, Archivo de La Paz (hereafter ALP).

79. Ministerial resolution, December 28, 1912, in Ministerio de Guerra, *Anexos* (1913), 20.

80. Ministerio de Guerra, *Memoria de guerra* (1910), 10; *Memoria de guerra* (1916), 21; *Memoria de guerra* (1918), 15; ministerial resolution, December 28, 1912, in Ministerio de Guerra, *Anexos* (1913), 20.

81. Minister of War to Prefects, no. 304, June 16, 1916, Prefecture-Admin box 149, ALP.

82. Subprefect of Ingavi quoted in Prefect of La Paz to Minister of War, no. 41, January 6, 1913, Prefecture-Admin box 147, ALP.

83. *Corregidor* of Canton Cohoni quoted in Prefect of La Paz to Minister of War, no. 272, January 29, 1913, Prefecture-Admin box 147, ALP.

84. *Corregidor* of Italaque to Prefect of La Paz, September 8, 1913, Prefecture-Admin box 147, ALP.

85. For examples, see Luis Zalles C., Prefect of La Paz to Police Intendant, no. 2637, October 22, 1909, Prefecture-Exped box 170, d. 273; Prefect of La Paz to Police Intendant of Larecaja, no. 13, January 3, 1911, Prefecture-Exped box 181, d. 163; Minister of War memorandum to Prefects, no. 173, August 15, 1913, Prefecture-Admin box 147; Minister of War to Prefect of La Paz, no. 212, March 13, 1914, Prefecture-Admin box 148, all in ALP. See also Ministerio de Guerra, *Memoria de guerra* (1910), 13; Minister of War Col. Julio La Faye memorandum to Prefects, no. 118, February 3, 1912, in Ministerio de Guerra, *Anexos* (1912), 33.

86. Minister of Industry José S. Quinteros to Prefects, July 14, 1913, quoted in C. Morales to Subprefects, July 21, 1913, vol. 165, Archivo de la Prefectura de Oruro (hereafter APDO), document and translation courtesy of Robert Smale.

87. Oporto Ordoñez, *Uncía y Llallagua*, 126.

88. Juan Postigo to Prefect of La Paz, March 31, 1909, Prefecture-Exped, box 170, d. 584, ALP. See also petition by Francisco Cirón, December 30, 1909, Prefecture-Exped box 169, d. 37, ALP.

89. I compiled this statistic based on records in Prefecture-Admin boxes 147, 148, ALP; Prefecture-Exped boxes 164 (d. 47), 170 (d. 116, 247, 349, 414, 416, 470), 178 (d. 33, 52, 145), 181 (d. 158), 182 (d.126), 189 (d. 26), 190 (d. 4), ALP.

90. Petition from Martín Poma, José Valencia, Pedro Villca, Juan Alejo, Bonifacio Condori, Gumercindo Flores, Tiburcio Poma, Blas Ticona, and Dámazo Ticona signed by Tomás Alba to Prefect of La Paz, December 27, 1912, Prefecture-Exped box 190, d. 4, ALP.

91. Quartermaster of Viacha to Prefect of La Paz, January 26, 1909, Prefecture-Exped box 170, d. 230, ALP.

92. Ministerio de Guerra, *Memoria de guerra* (1910), 50.

93. Constantino Morales, Prefect of Oruro, to the Minister of Government and Development, June 20, 1913, vol. 172, APDO. Document courtesy of Robert Smale.

94. Eduardo Diez de Medina, Prefect of Oruro, "Informe Departamental 1914," "Ministerio de Instrucción y Agricultura, Comensado en 14 de Octubre de 1913, Termina en . . . ," vol. 191, APDO. Document and translation courtesy of Robert Smale.

95. This extends Tristan Platt's argument that a pact existed between the state and indigenous communities whereby they paid tribute in exchange for state protection from landowner encroachment. Platt, *Estado boliviano*.

96. This supports the argument of political scientist George Gray Molina that an enduring characteristic of the Bolivian state is an "indirect form of rule that involves multiple local agents or partners" and that developed as a "structural feature of po-

litical accommodation under weak elites." Gray Molina, "State Society Relations," 112–13. See also Migdal, *Strong Societies and Weak States; State in Society.*

97. "La nueva ley militar," *El Comercio,* January 20, 1907.

98. On Latin American versions of eugenics, see Stepan, *Hour of Eugenics.* For a discussion of the Bolivian case, see Zulawski, *Unequal Cures.*

99. Twenty-fourth extraordinary session of the 1906 Legislature, January 7, 1907, in Bolivia, *Redactor de la H. Cámara de Diputados,* 1477.

100. Minister of War José S. Quinteros memo to Prefects, January 21, 1907, in Ministerio de Guerra, *Boletín militar,* 3:21–28.

101. Memorandum from Minister of War to Prefects, no. 12, quoted in Prefect of Oruro V. E. Sanjines to Subprefects, June 6, 1907. Document courtesy of E. Gabrielle Kuenzli.

102. I compiled this statistic based on records in Prefecture-Admin boxes 147, 148, 149, 208, ALP; Prefecture-Exped box 178, d. 120, ALP.

103. This, of course, implied that anyone classified as indigenous in this matrix was a rural laborer.

104. Ministerio de Guerra, *Memoria de guerra* (1912), 10; *Memoria de guerra* (1913), 17, 70; *Memoria de guerra* (1914), 63.

105. See Ari, *Earth Politics;* Gotkowitz, *Revolution for Our Rights.*

106. Correspondence between Isidro Quispe, Prefect of La Paz, and Minister of War, February 21–March 13, 1908; Minister of War to Prefect of La Paz, March 13, 1908, Prefecture-Exped box 164, d. 32, ALP.

107. Ministerio de Guerra, *Memoria de guerra* (1912), 6.

108. Quotation from Ministerio de Guerra, *Memoria de guerra* (1910), 8. See also *Memoria de guerra* (1910), 50; *Memoria de guerra* (1912), 3.

109. Article 16, law of September 23, 1910, in Bolivia, *Anuario de leyes* (1910); Article 3, law of December 4, 1911, in Bolivia, *Anuario de leyes* (1911).

110. Ministerio de Guerra, *Memoria de guerra* (1911), 36; *Memoria de guerra* (1913), 11; *Memoria de guerra* (1914), 17–18; *Memoria de guerra* (1918), 19.

111. Ministerio de Guerra, *Memoria de guerra* (1914), 7; *Memoria de guerra* (1915), 15; *Memoria de guerra* (1921), 65.

112. Ministerio de Guerra, *Memoria de guerra* (1921), 65. The first two terms refer to relationships of ritual kinship. For more on this system, see chapter 4.

113. Real Academia Española, *Diccionario de la lengua española,* 22nd ed. (2001), s.v. "omiso," http://www.rae.es; Charlton T. Lewis and Charles Short, *Latin Dictionary* (Oxford: Clarendon Press, 1879), s.v. "omissus," Database of Latin Dictionaries.

114. Luis Oporto makes a similar point about local authorities using military service to enact revenge, citing a 1905 memorandum to prefects. Oporto Ordoñez, *Uncía y Llallagua,* 131.

115. I compiled this statistic based on records in Prefecture-Admin boxes 147, 148, 149, ALP; Prefecture-Exped boxes 170, 190, 196, 222, 235, 237, 244, ALP.

116. Prefect of La Paz to Minister of War, no. 868, April 8, 1913; Minister of War to Prefect of La Paz, no. 881, April 11, 1913, both in Prefecture-Admin box 147, ALP.

117. Minister of War to Prefect of La Paz, no. 129, June 16, 1920, Prefecture-Admin box 148, ALP.

118. Gotkowitz, *Revolution for Our Rights*, 53, 63, 217. See also Abercrombie, *Pathways of Memory*, 86–90; Platt, "Andean Experience of Bolivian Liberalism," 284–87.

119. Thirty-seventh ordinary session, September 27, 1917, in Bolivia, *Redactor de la H. Cámara de Diputados*, 1:491–502.

120. Minister of War to Prefect of La Paz, no. 754, April 17, 1912, Prefecture-Admin box 147, ALP.

121. The first clear attempt to use conscription to promote interregional mixing occurred in 1925 when the chief of staff distributed conscripts from Santa Cruz among altiplano regiments in order to "strengthen feelings of solidarity" and "combat the regionalism [that is] so pernicious in the country." Ministerio de Guerra, *Memoria de guerra* (1925), 11.

122. Ministerio de Guerra, *Memoria de guerra* (1913), 60. See also thirty-seventh ordinary session, September 27, 1917, in Bolivia, *Redactor de la H. Cámara de Diputados*, 1:491–502.

123. Ministerio de Guerra, *Memoria de guerra* (1915), 18. See also memorandum no. 201 from Minister of War Néstor Gutiérrez to Prefect of Chuquisaca, November 18, 1913, in Ministerio de Guerra, *Anexos* (1913), 85–87; *Memoria de guerra* (1916), 36; *Memoria de guerra* (1917), 65.

124. Twenty-second ordinary session, September 10, 1917, in Bolivia, *Redactor de la H. Cámara de Diputados*, 1:237–42.

125. Deputy Sánchez A. quoted in twenty-second ordinary session, September 10, 1917, in Bolivia, *Redactor de la H. Cámara de Diputados*, 241.

126. Ministerial Resolution, January 22, 1907, in Ministerio de Guerra, *Boletín militar*, 3:38–39.

127. Deputy Sánchez A. quoted in fiftieth session, October 13, 1917, in Bolivia, *Redactor de la H. Cámara de Dipudatos*, 2:244. See also eleventh session, August 18, 1916, in *Redactor de la H. Cámara de Dipudatos*, 1:211–12; twenty-second, thirty-seventh, and fiftieth ordinary sessions, September 10, September 27, and October 13, 1917, in *Redactor de la H. Cámara de Dipudatos*, 1:237–42, 491–502, 2:241–49; law of November 24, 1917, in Bolivia, *Anuario de leyes* (1917).

128. Bourdieu, *Distinction*.

129. "Bolivia: Combat Estimate," January 10, 1928, RG 165, NM 84-77, box 557, folder S-C Intelligence Reference Pubs, National Archives and Records Administration (hereafter NARA).

130. Coico's ex-community is also identified as Guaruruni and Guayruru. When the 1874 Disentailment Law officially abolished indigenous communities, many community members began referring to themselves as ex-*comunarios* and their land as an ex-community. See Larson, *Trials of Nation Making*, 219.

131. Celestino Coico to Minister of War, January 7, 1924, Prefecture-Exped box 260, d. 106, ALP.

132. Although an 1882 law formally abolished tribute at the national level, it (under the new name of "contribución territorial de indígenas") would remain a significant part of departmental budgets for several decades. Gotkowitz, *Revolution for Our Rights*, 29–30.

133. Bacilio Pillco to Prefect of La Paz, November 14, 1911, Prefecture-Exped box 182, d. 126, ALP.

134. Burns, *Into the Archive*, 39.

135. President of Recruitment Commission of La Paz to Minister of War, January 8, 1924, Prefecture-Exped box 260, d. 106, ALP.

136. Celestino Coico to Minister of War, January 14, 1924, Prefecture-Exped box 260, d. 106, ALP.

137. Celestino Coico to Minister of War, January 18, 1924, Prefecture-Exped box 260, d. 106, ALP.

138. Commander of Northern Military Zone to Minister of War, January 19, 1924, Prefecture-Exped box 260, d. 106, ALP.

139. Coico's name is spelled Cuyo in this set of documents, yet the match in circumstances, community, and the assistance of "Molina" indicate that they refer to the same man.

140. Statement of Celestino Cuyo, February 8, 1924, quoted in Col. Hermógenes Ibañez, Commander of Northern Military Zone, to Prefect of La Paz, no. 8, February 13, 1924, Prefecture-Admin box 208, ALP.

141. Col. Hermógenes Ibañez, Commander of Northern Military Zone, to Prefect of La Paz, no. 10, February 15, 1924, Prefecture-Admin box 208, ALP.

142. The war ministry stopped reporting the number of men registered and presented after 1912.

143. For one of many reports of this practice, see report that the *corregidor* of Yanacachi (Sud Yungas, La Paz) was charging *indígenas* twenty bolivianos "not to require them to present for military service." Col. Hermógenes Ibañez, Commander of Northern Military Zone, to Prefect of La Paz, no. 3, January 19, 1924, Prefecture-Admin box 208, ALP.

144. Rodolfo Baldivia G., Subprefect of Muñecas, quoted in Prefect of La Paz to Minister of War, no. 632, March 6, 1913, Prefecture-Admin box 147, ALP.

CHAPTER 2: LIFE AND LABOR IN THE BARRACKS

1. Richter, *En el puesto del deber*, 15–18, 21.

2. Richter, *En el puesto del deber*, 19.

3. Díaz Machicao, *Saavedra*, 110–11.

4. Richter, *En el puesto del deber*, 26, 33–35, 41; Richter, *Catecismo del soldado*; Bretel and Sanjinés, *Catecismo del soldado*.

5. Richter, *Catecismo del soldado*, 28–31.

6. Lt. Simón B. Aguirre statement, March 8 and 19, 1921, MOT-71-002A; Pando Regiment Commander to Second Division Commander, September 21, 1931,

ABA-01-003; Ricardo Pacheco statement, November 4, 1921, INS-59-003; Lt. Col. Alberto Sotomayor statement, October 1, 1931, ABA-01-004, all in Tribunal Permanente de Justicia Militar, Archivo Histórico Militar (hereafter TPJM-AHM).

7. Richter, *Catecismo del soldado*, 23–28.

8. Minister of War Muñoz to Minister of Justice and Public Instruction, no. 356, October 7, 1909; Germán Zegarra at Ministry of War to Minister of Justice and Public Instruction, no. 349, December 31, 1909, Ministerio de Educación box 307, ALP.

9. Minister of War Fermín Prudencio to Prefect of La Paz, no. 128, June 14, 1920, Prefecture-Admin box 148, ALP.

10. Ministerio de Guerra, *Memoria de guerra 1925*, 43–44.

11. "Reformas a la ley del servicio militar," *La Reforma*, March 15, 1921; "La reorganización del ejército," *La Reforma*, March 24, 1921; Gen. Gonzalo Jáuregui, "Las razas indígenas en Bolivia y su educación en los cuarteles," *Revista Militar* 55 (1926): 533–37; Capt. Alfredo F. Peñaranda, "El soldado Andrés Quispe," *Revista Militar* 54 (1926): 483–89; "Dos mil jóvenes conscriptos desfilan por las calles," *El Diario*, January 14, 1927.

12. See, for example, Ricardo Pacheco statement, November 4, 1921, INS-59-003, TPJM-AHM.

13. Ministerio de Guerra, *Memoria de guerra* (1914), 55.

14. Saturnino Alsuarás statement, May 15, 1932, ABA-01-006, TPJM-AHM.

15. Legrand, *Un civil en campo militar*, 36.

16. On conscripts' preparing meals, see Julio Rendón and Ricardo Pacheco statements, November 4–5, 1921, INS-59-003; Francisco Vargas statement, November 23, 1931, ABA-01-004, TPJM-AHM. For wage garnishments, see Ministerio de Guerra, *Memoria de guerra* (1910), 19; Minister of War Circular to Commanders, no. 221, May 21, 1914, in Ministerio de Guerra, *Anexos* (1914), 95–98; Eighty-eighth ordinary session, November 23, 1914, in Bolivia, *Redactor de la H. Cámara de Diputados*, 4:420.

17. For examples of allegations, see Hilario Chavez to Prefect of La Paz, April 8, 1908, Prefecture-Exped box 164, d. 21; Santiago Mollo, Cecilio Antonio, Pablo Lardon, Leandro Callisaya, and Rafael Choquehuanca to Minister of War, January 22, 1909, Prefecture-Exped box 168, d. 123; Andrés Aruquipa, Santos Choque, Luis Aruquipa and Martín Cadena to Minister of the Interior, June 27, 1922, Prefecture-Exped box 247, d. 25, ALP.

18. Justo Fernandez and Francisco Vargas statements, November 23, 1931, ABA-01-004. See also Valentín Gazon statement, April 25, 1932, SED-94-004, TPJM-AHM.

19. Roberto Camacho statement, May 15, 1932, ABA-01-006, TPJM-AHM.

20. Acting Chief of Staff Col. Carlos M. de Villegas, no. 181, December 15, 1910, and General Order no. 283, January 12, 1911, in Ministerio de Guerra, *Anexos* (1911), 43–45, 49–51; Richter, *Catecismo del soldado*, 81–83.

21. Richter, *Catecismo del soldado*, 42.

22. Richter, *Catecismo del soldado*, 34.

23. See MOT-71-001 (1920), SED-94-001 (1920), INS-59-003 (1921), INS-59-004 (1930), MOT-71-002A (1921), MOT-71-004 (1930), ABA-01-007 (1932), SED-04-004 (1932), TPJM-AHM; Prefecture-Exped box 175, d. 61 (1909), ALP.

24. The army repeatedly attempted to solve this problem, establishing short-lived NCO schools in 1900, 1916, and 1927. In 1919, selected conscripts in the first year of service formed a separate battalion in order to receive NCO instruction and then spent the second year serving as NCOs in regiments around the country. Ministerio de Guerra, *Memoria de guerra* (1916), 38; *Memoria de guerra* (1919), 15; *Memoria de guerra* (1926), 58; *Memoria de guerra* (1928), 5, 42; Díaz Arguedas, *Historia del ejército*, 162. For an example of gaps in training, see the testimony of Ricardo Pacheco, a private first class responsible for training new conscripts, who claimed ignorance of military law due to poor instruction by his own NCOs. Ricardo Pacheco statement, November 4, 1921, INS-59-003, TPJM-AHM.

25. Humberto Marquez statement, May 15, 1932, ABA-01-006, TPJM-AHM.

26. Peñaranda, "El soldado Andrés Quispe," 483–89; Saturnino Alsuarás, I. Carras Echavez, and Humberto Marquez statements, May 15, 1932, ABA-01-006, TPJM-AHM.

27. The prefecture records for the department of La Paz report on 111 conscripts who deserted from various army units between 1911 and 1921. Of these, 18 percent (twenty men) were classified as indigenous; 37 percent (forty-one men) were listed as *mestizo*, and 7 percent (eight men) were categorized as white. Statistics compiled based on records in Prefecture-Admin boxes 147, 148, 149, 208; Prefecture-Exped box 178, d. 120, ALP.

28. Peñaranda, "El soldado Andrés Quispe," 483–89; Richter, *Catecismo del soldado*, 61.

29. For an explanation of how this system functioned in 1920, see Quiroga Ochoa, *En la paz y en la guerra*, 61. Correspondence regarding individual desertions also mentions godfathers' negligence as a factor. See March 28, 1914, letter, Prefecture-Admin box 148, ALP.

30. Commander of Uyuni Garrison Capt. Justiniano Céspedes to Minister of War and Prefect of La Paz, no. 35, April 15, 1914, Prefecture-Admin box 148.

31. Valentín Murillo and Concepción Mamani statements, March 13 and April 22, 1921, DES-15-007, TPJM-AHM.

32. Hugo Tapia statement, September 12, 1930, MOT-71-004, TPJM-AHM. Known as an indigenous neighborhood, Chijini was associated with sex work during this era. See Sierra, "Indigenous Neighborhood Residents," 63–65; Zulawski, *Unequal Cures*, 144.

33. Vicente D. Torres statement, December 17, 1909, Prefecture-Exped box 175, d. 61, ALP.

34. Manuel Guzmán statement, September 8, 1930, MOT-71-004; Cabo Cecilio Valderrama statement, July 24, 1920, SED-94-001; Sub. Lt. Sergio Rivera statement, October 27, 1927, ABA-01-002, TPJM-AHM.

35. Ministerio de Guerra, *Memoria de guerra* (1912), 34; *Memoria de guerra* (1916), 61. The Murillo Regiment also reported 132 literacy students in 1914. See *Memoria de guerra* (1914), 74.

36. Sarg. Humberto del Castillo statement, October 8, 1931, ABA-01-004, TPJM-AHM. See also the mention of literacy classes by Zenón Castillo, July 15, 1930, INS-59-004, TPJM-AHM.

37. Ministerio de Guerra, *Memoria de guerra* (1916), 57–59.

38. Ministerio de Guerra, *Memoria de guerra* (1926), 57; *Memoria de guerra* (1927), 63.

39. Lt. C. Bleichner, "Las escuelas primarias en nuestro ejército," *Revista Militar* 47–48 (1925): 995–98.

40. Peñaranda, "El soldado Andrés Quispe," 483–89.

41. Richter, *Catecismo del soldado*, 6, 15.

42. Richter, *Catecismo del soldado*, 1.

43. Military justice tribunals viewed this oath to be of importance, as judges asked most conscripts who testified whether or not they had participated, apparently using this indicator to determine whether a conscript should have been familiar with military laws. The first evidence of this oath dates from 1910. Ministerio de Guerra, *Memoria de guerra* (1910), 65.

44. Minister of War to Prefect of La Paz, no. 904, July 29, 1913, Prefecture-Admin box 147; Gen. Adalid Tejada Fariñas, Commander of Northern Military Zone, to Prefect of La Paz, August 4, 1919, Prefecture-Admin box 148; Minister of War Pedro Gutierrez to Prefect of La Paz, no. 31, July 5, 1925, Prefecture-Admin box 149, all in ALP. See also Richter, *En el puesto del deber*, 15–18, 21.

45. "Desde Sorata," *Revista Militar* 9 (1922): 665–68.

46. Supreme decree of August 4, 1924, in Bolivia, *Gaceta oficial* (1924).

47. Legrand, *Un civil en campo militar*, 34–35, 93.

48. Capt. Humbero Eguino statement, October 15, 1919, FAS-42-003; Rodolfo Cordero statement, December 11, 1931, HOM-45-005, both in TPJM-AHM; Alberto Villegas statement, December 18, 1922, Prefecture-Exped box 251, d. 7, ALP.

49. Vicente D. Torres, Dalio Fernandez, and Aparicio Morales statements, January 15 and 28, 1910, Prefecture-Exped box 175, d. 61, ALP.

50. See chapter 4 for a discussion of the role of *madrinas* during the Chaco War.

51. Richter, *Catecismo del soldado*, 9.

52. Annual athletic tournaments began in 1924. See Ministerio de Guerra, *Memoria de guerra* (1924), 22; *Memoria de guerra* (1928), 13. The *Revista Militar* published the results. For evidence of soccer matches, see Capt. Enrique Vidaurre, "La infantería boliviana," *Revista Militar* 26 (1924): 97–103; Daniel Ramos statements, April 29, 1921, and March 19, 1921, MOT-71-002A, TPJM-AHM.

53. Capt. Luis Emilio Aguirre, Cabo Enrique Murillo, Cabo Walter Candia, and Frucuoso Jemio statements, March 12 and April 14–26, 1921, MOT-71-002A, TPJM-AHM.

54. Reg. Pando Commander to Second Division Commander, September 21, 1931, ABA-01-003, TPJM-AHM.

55. Richter, *Catecismo del soldado*, 11. A November 9, 1923, supreme decree explicitly prohibited alcohol from all garrisons in order to maintain morale, discipline, and health. See Ministerio de Guerra, *Memoria de guerra* (1924), 7. See also statements by Hugo Tapia, Alfredo Ponce, Manuel Guzmán, and Alberto Salazar, September 8–12, 1930, MOT-71-004, TPJM-AHM.

56. Ricardo Pacheco and Cornelis Schneider statements, October 4, 1921, INS-59-003; Domingo Delgado statement, April 28, 1932, SED-94-004, TPJM-AHM.

57. Antonio Rosell statement, March 19, 1921, MOT-71-002A, TPJM-AHM; Hernán Quiroga statement, December 20, 1922, Prefecture-Exped box 251, d. 7, ALP.

58. Gen. Gonzalo Jáuregui, "Las razas indígenas en Bolivia y su educación en los cuarteles," *Revista Militar* 55 (1926): 533–37.

59. Ricardo Pacheco statement, November 4, 1921, INS-59-003, TPJM-AHM.

60. Bacilio Pillco to Prefect of La Paz, July 10, 1911, Prefecture-Exped box 182, d. 126, ALP.

61. See Canessa, "Indian within," 138–40.

62. Ministerio de Guerra, *Memoria de guerra* (1911), 23; Dirección de Sanidad Militar, "Morbosidad general correspondiente al año 1913," in Ministerio de Guerra, *Anexos* (1914), 162.

63. Subprefect of Sicasica to Prefect of La Paz, June 18, 1921, Prefecture-Exped box 245, d. 13, ALP; Lt. Víctor Ballivián statement, May 10, 1932, ABA-01-006, TPJM-AHM; Mariano Alvarez, Ermógenes Martínez, and Ildefonso Cruz to Prefect of La Paz, June 7, 1921, Prefecture-Exped box 245, d. 13, ALP. Local authorities eventually investigated this second claim of rape, questioning more than thirty colonos, including the victim, who denied the incident.

64. See 1935 case against Sublieutenant Mario Quiroga C. for rape of a minor, which was marked "does not correspond to Military Justice," VIO-107-003, TPJM-AHM. Rape is not mentioned in the 1905 military penal code or in any modifications up to 1948. Ministerio de Guerra, *Códigos militares*; Salinas Mariaca and Silva, *Códigos de justicia militar*. In her work on slander lawsuits, Laura Gotkowitz (drawing on a case from 1884) notes that "'india' was the term used when slanderers referred to victims of rape. In all such cases, the insulted woman was blamed for permitting a man to force her to have sex with him." Gotkowitz, "Trading Insults," 98. More work is needed on the meanings and prosecution of rape in early twentieth-century Bolivia in order to interpret the omission of this offense from the military penal code. Were sexual offenses (especially against low-status women) ignored as a necessary by-product of military life? Was rape seen as an indelicate matter and therefore omitted from the written record?

65. Bernardino Fernández statements, April 11 and March 19, 1921, MOT-71-002A, TPJM-AHM.

66. Sub-Lt. Olmos to Bolivar Artillery Regiment Commander, July 14, 1930, INS-59-004, TPJM-AHM.

67. Abelino Romay statement, July 14, 1930, INS-59-004, TPJM-AHM.

68. Ministerial resolution, December 17, 1913, in Ministerio de Guerra, *Anexos* (1914), 20; Ministerio de Guerra, *Memoria de guerra* (1914), 31; *Memoria de guerra* (1925), 12.

69. Ministerio de Guerra, *Anexos* (1910), xlvii–xlviii.

70. Ministerial resolution, December 24, 1907, Ministerio de Guerra, *Boletín militar*, 3:581–89.

71. "Servicio militar," *El Diario*, October 14, 1917.

72. Peñaranda, "El soldado Andrés Quispe," 489.

73. Legrand, *Un civil en campo militar*, 99.

74. Lt. Roberto Carrasco V., "¿Idealismos?" *Revista Militar* 33 (1924): 733–36.

75. For an excellent overview of military labor, see Zürcher, *Fighting for a Living*.

76. Quotation from Commander of Sucre Regiment, October 25, 1927, ABA-01-002. For other references to work, see Sarg. José Alvarez, Capt. Humberto Eguino, and Cabo Felix Portocarreo statements, October 15, 1919, FAS-42-003; Sub. Lt. Manuel Heguegone, Moises Rivas statements, November 17–18, 1920, MOT-71-001; Sub. Lt. Emilio Orihuela statement, October 2, 1931, ABA-01-004; Rodolfo Cordero statement, December 11, 1931, HOM-45-005; Dgte Lucio Benavides statement, April 26, 1932, SED-94-004; Saturnino Alsuarás statement, May 15, 1932, ABA-01-006, all in TPJM-AHM.

77. These tasks fell under the army's mission to "conserve order," which was first included in the 1851 Constitution. See Galindo de Ugarte, *Constituciones bolivianas*, 608.

78. "Otra sublevación indigenal en Cochabamba," *El Diario*, April 6, 1919. For a few examples see Prefect of La Paz to Minister of War, nos. 101, 189, 743, January 11, January 21, and March 26, 1913, Prefecture-Admin box 147, ALP.

79. Prefecture-Admin boxes 147, 148, 149, 208, ALP.

80. Prefect of La Paz to Minister of War, no. 1073, reply no. 751, April 13, 1912, Prefecture-Admin box 147, ALP; "Informaciones sobre los succsos de Corocoro," *El Diario*, January 16, 1919; Smale, "*I Sweat the Flavor of Tin*," 88–91.

81. Minister of War to Prefect of La Paz, nos. 83 and 101, January 20 and March 8, 1920, Prefecture-Admin box 148, ALP.

82. Minister of War to Prefect of La Paz, no. 159, December 4, 1920, Prefecture-Admin box 148, ALP. See also Minister of War to Prefect of La Paz, no. 884, April 22, 1913, Prefecture-Admin box 147, ALP.

83. Minister of War to Prefect of La Paz, no. 1730, January 30, 1915, Prefecture-Admin box 148, ALP. See also Minister of War to Prefect of La Paz, no. 1851, December 19, 1916, Prefecture-Admin box 149, ALP.

84. Richter, *Catecismo del soldado*, 24–26.

85. Vicente Ledezma statement, November 19, 1920, MOT-71-001, TPJM-AHM. See also Aniceto Montesinos statement, November 19, 1920, INS-59-002, and Cornelis Schneider, Ricardo Pacheco, and José Siñani statements, November 4–5, 1921, INS-59-003, TPJM-AHM.

86. Humberto Marquez statement, May 15, 1932, ABA-01-006, TPJM-AHM.

87. Juan Chuquimia statement, October 8, 1931, ABA-01-004, TPJM-AHM.

88. Assistants' monthly salary was set at a minimum of eight bolivianos. Legal copy of Reglamento de régimen interno no. 6, October 2, 1931, ABA-01-004, TP-JM-AHM. I suspect that these rules were followed only loosely and perhaps disappeared altogether for those garrisoned far from urban centers.

89. Víctor Zambrana Flores statement, November 6, 1921, INS-59-003, TPJM-AHM.

90. Liberal administrations created the first ministry of colonization in 1904 and then assigned this duty to the minister of war in 1910. The ministries would remain conjoined until 1929. See law of October 18, 1894 and supreme decree of December 23, 1910, both in Bolivia, *Anuario de leyes* (1894, 1910).

91. Ministerio de Guerra, *Memoria de guerra* (1910), 9, 28–31; *Memoria de guerra* (1912), 45; *Memoria de guerra* (1913), 60, 70; *Memoria de guerra* (1914), 71, 74, 81–83, 97; *Memoria de guerra* (1915), 31, 64; *Memoria de guerra* (1917), 71, 76–77; *Memoria de guerra* (1918), 93, 104, 113; *Memoria de guerra* (1919), 63, 73, 77; *Memoria de guerra* (1921), 52, 82, 122, 157; *Memoria de guerra* (1922), 22; *Memoria de guerra* (1923), 67; *Memoria de guerra* (1925), 37; *Memoria de guerra 1928*, 107, 128–29.

92. My. Marcelino Guzmán y B., "La vida del oficial en fronteras," *Revista Militar* 16 (1923): 312–19; My. Julio Bretel, "Misión del oficial en fronteras," *Revista Militar* 6 (1922): 414–23; Sub. Lt. Emilio Orihuela statement, October 2, 1931, ABA-01-004, TPJM-AHM.

93. Capt. José Angel Rivero to Delegado Nacional, June 2, 1913, in Arauz, *Informe que eleva*, 191.

94. See, for example, the report of seven deaths in the Montes Battalion in 1908. Ministerio de Guerra, *Boletín militar*, 4:257.

95. Gregorio Valencia and Esteban Valcarcel to Prefect of La Paz, July 15 and 22, 1909, Prefecture-Exped box 169, d. 81 and 91, ALP.

96. Ministerio de Guerra, *Memoria de Guerra* (1926), 68.

97. "¡Obras son amores . . . !" *Revista Militar* 75 (1928): 177–79.

98. Jaime Mendoza, "Una valiosa opinión acerca del camino carretero al Chaco," *Revista Militar* 79 (1928): 433–35.

99. For examples, see *Revista Militar* 50 (1926): cover; My. Julio Bretel, "Misión del oficial en fronteras," *Revista Militar* 6 (1922): 423; "De nuestras fronteras," *Revista Militar* 10 (1922): 696; "De nuestras fronteras," *Revista Militar* 11 (1922): 780; *Revista Militar* 44 (1925): 732; *Revista Militar* 47–48 (1925): cover; *Revista Militar* 59 (1926): cover; "De nuestra guarnición del sudeste," *Revista Militar* 66 (1927): 492.

100. For examples, see *Revista Militar* 27 (1924): 204; *Revista Militar* 47–48 (1925): 1024.

101. "El ejército y la vialidad nacional," *El Diario*, 25 December 1930.

102. Prefect of La Paz to Minister of War, no. 1849, 16 August 1913, Prefecture-Admin box 147, ALP.

103. INS-59-003, TPJM-AHM.

104. Except for a brief period in 1915 when all ranks of the military earned 30 percent less, soldiers earned eighty cents a day between 1910 and 1919, but half of that was immediately diverted to pay for communal meals. See Ministerio de Guerra, *Memoria de guerra* (1910), 19; Minister of War Circular to Commanders, no. 221, May 21, 1914, in Ministerio de Guerra, *Anexos* (1914), 95–98; Eighty-eighth ordinary session, November 23, 1914, in Bolivia, *Redactor de la H. Cámara de Diputados*, 4:420; Minister of War circular, no. 247, December 14, 1914, in Ministerio de Guerra, *Anexos* (1915), 36; *Memoria de guerra* (1919), 24.

105. Sub. Lt. J. N. B., "La necesidad de prepararnos para una probable prueba y las ventajas del servicio militar obligatorio," *Revista Militar* 91 (1929): 404.

106. Seventeen soldiers to Second Division Commander, September 21, 1931, ABA-01-004, TPJM-AHM.

107. Klein, *Concise History of Bolivia*, 162–68; Malloy, *Bolivia, the Uncompleted Revolution*, 20–22; Spencer, "Oil, Politics, and Economic Nationalism in Bolivia," 31.

108. See supreme decree of March 6, 1918; supreme resolution of 30 July 1919, both in Bolivia, *Anuario de leyes* (1918, 1919).

109. Ministerio de Guerra, *Memoria de guerra* (1916), 35; *Memoria de guerra* (1917), 64, 71; *Memoria de guerra* (1922), 18; *Memoria de guerra* (1925), 6; *Memoria de guerra* (1928), 3, 88–91, 160.

110. Ministerio de Guerra, *Memoria de guerra* (1928), 22–24.

111. Minister of War to Chief of Staff, January 26, 1931, ABA-01-004, TPJM-AHM.

112. Lt. Col. Alberto Sotomayor statement, October 1, 1931, ABA-01-004, TPJM-AHM.

113. Ignacio Torres and Sarg. Manuel Flores statements, November 18, 1906, and November 28, 1907, Prefecture-Exped box 189, d. 177, ALP.

114. Respective quotations from José Siñani statement, November 17, 1921, INS-59-003, and Soldiers to Minister of War, November 1, 1920, MOT-71-001.

115. Sub. Lt. Manuel Heguigarre statement, November 17, 1920, MOT-71-001, TPJM-AHM.

116. Seventeen soldiers to Second Division Commander, September 21, 1931, ABA-01-004, TPJM-AHM.

117. *Postillonaje* was quite common despite its abolition in 1904. That same year, a law established the *prestación vial* road tax, which could be paid in cash or labor, depending on region and/or social status. See Gotkowitz, *Revolution for Our Rights*, 304–05n301. For a general overview of extractive labor practices, see Larson, *Trials of Nation Making*, 249.

118. Adapted from an Incaic labor system, the *mita* was an infamous colonial-era form of corvée labor most commonly associated with the extraction of silver from Potosí.

119. Ricardo Pacheco statement, November 4, 1921, INS-59-003, TPJM-AHM.

120. Col. Fausto D. González, "Contribución del ejército nacional a la educación del indio," *El Diario*, June 19, 1930, 9.

121. Richter, *Catecismo del soldado*, 4–5.

122. Ninth ordinary session, August 17, 1915, in Bolivia, *Redactor de la H. Cámara de Diputados*, 1:249–50.

123. Ministerio de Guerra, *Memoria de guerra* (1916), 33. For a later version of the text, see Salinas Mariaca and Silva, *Códigos de justicia militar*, 207–18.

124. Article 27, Military Penal Code, 1905, published in Ministerio de Guerra, *Códigos militares*, 190.

125. Foucault, *Discipline and Punish*.

126. For descriptions see Cabo Félix Portocarrero statement, October 15, 1919, FAS-42-003; Antonio Mamani statement, October 29, 1927, ABA-01-002, both in TPJM-AHM.

127. Sub-Lt. Olmos to Commander of Bolivar Artillery Regiment, July 14, 1930, INS-59-004, TPJM-AHM.

128. See FAS-42-002 (1917); FAS-42-003 (1919); MOT-71-001 (1920); INS-59-003 (1921); ABA-01-002 (1927); INS-59-004 (1930); MOT-71-004 (1930); ABA-01-004 (1931); ABA-01-007 (1932); SED-94-004 (1932); ABA-01-005 (1932); ABA-01-006 (1932), all in TPJM-AHM; Prefecture-Exped box 251, d. 7 (1922), ALP.

129. Quartermaster Colonel Raimundo González Flor to Surgeon of Quartermaster's Corps, Dr. Luís Martínez Lara, October 14, 1919; Pablo Carreón, Manuel Mollo, and Ramon Venegas statements, October 14–15, 1919, FAS-42-003, both in TPJM-AHM.

130. Sub. Lt. N. Pereira to Colonel Commander Abaroa Regiment, May 17, 1917, FAS-42-002, TPJM-AHM.

131. Lt. Leonicio Menacho statement, September 23, 1931, ABA-01-003, TPJM-AHM.

132. Pacífico Arce statement, June 10, 1932, ABA-01-006, TPJM-AHM.

133. Ricardo Pacheco statement, November 4, 1921, INS-59-003, TPJM-AHM.

134. Quartermaster Colonel Raimundo González Flor to Surgeon of Quartermaster Corps, Dr. Luís Martínez Lara, October 14, 1919, FAS-42-003; Manuel Valdez statement, May 6, 1932, ABA-01-005, both in TPJM-AHM.

135. See FAS-42-002 (1917); FAS-42-003 (1919); MOT-71-001 (1920); INS-59-003 (1921); ABA-01-002 (1927); INS-59-004 (1930); MOT-71-004 (1930); ABA-01-004 (1931); ABA-01-007 (1932); SED-94-004 (1932); ABA-01-005 (1932); ABA-01-006 (1932), all in TPJM-AHM; Prefecture-Exped box 251, d. 7 (1922), ALP.

136. See Gotkowitz, *Revolution for Our Rights*, 149, 156; Ari, *Earth Politics*, 68, 71; Smale, "*I Sweat the Flavor of Tin*," 88, 164.

137. Scott, *Weapons of the Weak*.

138. Not one of the 238 conscripts who testified in twenty-five military justice cases from 1916 until the start of the Chaco War in 1932 were described as indigenous, and at least 220 (92 percent) were literate enough to affix their signatures to their depositions. Of the remaining eighteen deponents, fifteen were described as illiterate or had their statements signed by another party. I do not have the signature

page for the final three witnesses. Data compiled from boxes 1, 15, 42, 45, 59, 69, 71, 94, TPJM-AHM. I did not have the opportunity to review the additional thirteen cases in the archive that date from the period and involved conscripts.

139. Víctor Zambrana statement, November 6, 1921, INS-59-003, TPJM-AHM.

140. On governmentality, see Burchell, Gordon, and Miller, *Foucault Effect*.

141. On habitus, see Bourdieu, *Outline of a Theory*.

142. Leovegildo Ortuno and José Siñani statements, November 5 and 17, 1921, INS-59-003, TPJM-AHM.

143. Julio Rendón statement, November 4, 1921, INS-59-003, TPJM-AHM.

144. Seventeen soldiers to 2nd Commander, September 21, 1931, ABA-01-004, TPJM-AHM.

145. Carter and Mamani, *Irpa Chico*, 373.

CHAPTER 3: CLIENTELISM AND CONSCRIPT INSUBORDINATION

1. This analysis is indebted to Leonard Smith's work on mutinies.

2. Population figure estimated from the 1928 census of La Paz (142,549), cited in Pando Gutiérrez, "Reseña demográfica de la ciudad de La Paz," 57.

3. Dunkerley, "Reassessing Caudillismo," 16.

4. Dunkerley, "Reassessing Caudillismo," 15–17.

5. Klein, *Parties and Political Change*, 45–46.

6. Klein, *Parties and Political Change*, 46–48; Dunkerley, *Orígenes del poder militar*, 99–100.

7. Fourth, sixth, eighth, and ninth ordinary sessions, August 11, 13, 16, and 17, 1915, in Bolivia, *Redactor de la H. Cámara de Diputados*, 38, 128, 180–90, 236–73.

8. Ninth ordinary session, August 17, 1915, in Bolivia, *Redactor de la H. Cámara de Diputados*, 236–73.

9. Soldiers at the time would have associated raw food with animals and cooked food with humans. Personal communication from Waskar Ari, March 7, 2011.

10. Klein, *Parties and Political Change*, 46–49; Dunkerley, *Orígenes del poder militar*, 99–101.

11. Irurozqui Victoriano, "A bala, piedra y palo," 287–303; Klein, *Parties and Political Change*, 50–51; Dunkerley, *Orígenes del poder militar*, 101.

12. Dunkerley, *Orígenes del poder militar*, 102–103.

13. Gallo, *Taxes and State Power*, 129; Quintana Taborga, *Policía y democracia*, 32; Céspedes, *El dictador suicida*, 68–69.

14. "Las masas republicanas provocan el más grave conflicto; Conscriptos muertos y heridos," *El Diario*, December 6, 1917.

15. "Los conscriptos mal vestidos, mal comidos y maltratados," *La Verdad*, April 20, 1920.

16. Smale, "I Sweat the Flavor of Tin," 83–85.

17. Choque Canqui and Quisbert Quispe, *Líderes indígenas aymaras*, 130–33; Grieshaber, "Resistencia indígena," 121.

18. Smale, *"I Sweat the Flavor of Tin,"* 88–91; Dunkerley, *Orígenes del poder militar*, 102.

19. Session of February 12, 1920, in Bolivia, *Redactor de de la H. Cámara de Diputados*, 4:11–14.

20. Session of February 12, 1920, in Bolivia, *Redactor de de la H. Cámara de Diputados*, 4:10–12.

21. Choque Canqui and Quisbert Quispe, *Líderes indígenas aymaras*, 130–70.

22. Brockmann, *El general y sus presidentes*, 61; Gómez, *Bautista Saavedra*, 11–12.

23. Gómez, *Bautista Saavedra*, 11–12, 23–25; Parker, *Bolivians of To-Day*, 257–58.

24. El Internacional, *Las verdaderas crónicas*, 2–17; Dunkerley, *Orígenes del poder militar*, 103–104.

25. El Internacional, *Las verdaderas crónicas*, 32.

26. El Internacional, *Las verdaderas crónicas*, 43–54, quotation from 58.

27. El Internacional, *Las verdaderas crónicas*, 56–57, 64–67.

28. El Internacional, *Las verdaderas crónicas*, 67–72.

29. Built in the early eighteenth century, La Merced belonged to the Mercedarios until this religious order closed in 1912. Simbrón García, *Imagínatelapaz*, 95.

30. "Guardia republicana," *La Razón*, September 25, 1920.

31. Brockmann, *El general y sus presidentes*, 62.

32. Sarg. Miguel Carreón statement, November 24, 1920, and Sarg. Emilio Miranda to Magistrate Judge, December 4, 1920, MOT-71-001; Tomás Fuentes statement, March 19, 1921, and Cabo Domingo Peña confession, July 18, 1921, all in MOT-71-002A, all in Tribunal Permanente de Justicia Militar, Archivo Histórico Militar (TPJM-AHM).

33. Díaz Machicao, *Saavedra*, 60.

34. Dunkerley, *Orígenes del poder militar*, 110.

35. Sgto. Miguel Carreon statement, November 23, 1920, MOT-71-001, TPJM-AHM.

36. José Méndez, Juan Bustillos, Ignacio Hidalgo, Teófilo Claros, and Moises Rivas statements, November 5, 18, and 19, 1921, MOT-71-001, TPJM-AHM.

37. Moises Rivas statement, November 18, 1921, MOT-71-001, TPJM-AHM.

38. Macario Coronel, Teófilo Vargas, Pedro Calderón, and Sarg. Miguel Carreón statements, November 19 and 24, MOT-71-001, TPJM-AHM.

39. Macario Coronel, Teofilo Vargas, and Pedro Calderón statements, November 19, 1920, MOT-71-001, TPJM-AHM.

40. Letter to Minister of War, November 1, 1920; Commander Campero Regimento to Lt. Delfín Arias, November 4, 1920; Raul Camargo, Teófilo Vargas, Jab Mendez, Daniel Araujo, and Macario Coronel statements, November 5, 1920, MOT-71-001, all in TPJM-AHM.

41. All sixteen Campero conscripts who testified in the proceedings were literate. Those eventually indicted claimed professions of student, telegraph operator, and carpenter and came from diverse cities and towns in the departments of La Paz, Potosí, and Cochabamba. MOT-71-001, TPJM-AHM.

42. Dunkerley, *Orígenes del poder militar*, 110; Díaz Machicao, *Saavedra*, 62, 80; Klein, *Parties and Political Change*, 65–67.

43. Dunkerley, *Orígenes del poder militar*, 111; Díaz Machicao, *Saavedra*, 74.

44. Dunkerley, *Orígenes del poder militar*, 110, 226n114.

45. Díaz Machicao, *Saavedra*, 83.

46. Kundt served on the Galician front and then took command of the Twenty-Fourth Infantry Regiment and later the Fortieth Reserve Infantry Brigade. Several scholars assert that Kundt participated in the outlawed *Freikorps* and the Kapp Putsch, a March 1920 coup attempt in opposition to the Treaty of Versailles. Brockmann, however, finds no evidence to support these claims. The date of Kundt's return is also of some dispute. Dunkerley has him returning to his post (rather than as a civilian) in April; Díaz Machicao states that he returned to the country on August 9. Brockmann shows that he left Germany in May. Citing primary sources from 1929, Hancock determines that Kundt had returned by June. Bieber, citing primary sources from 1920, confirms that Kundt was already in Bolivia by September. And one US military attaché reported that he returned in July 1920, while another had the date as early as 1919. See Lt. Col. Guy S. Norvell memo, October 31, 1923, and Jesse S. Cottrell to Secretary of State, no. 1106, September 13, 1926, RG 165, NM 84-77, box 187, folder 6000-6420, NARA; Brockmann, *El general y sus presidentes*, 45–53, 64–66; Farcau, *Chaco War*, 87; Dunkerley, *Orígenes del poder militar*, 115; Hancock, *Ernst Röhm*, 97; Bieber, "La política militar alemana," 91; Díaz Machicao, *Saavedra*, 62.

47. Haggard telegram, July 29, 1920, quoted in Dunkerley, *Orígenes del poder militar*, 115.

48. "Bolivia, Estimate of Political-Military Situation," c. 1930, RG 165, NM 84-77, box 187, folder 3020, NARA.

49. MOT-71-002A (March 1921), TPJM-AHM.

50. MOT-71-002A (March 1921), TPJM-AHM.

51. Major José Ferrufino and legislators Aurelio Balderrama and José Almaraz were those named. Díaz lists them among the Genuines in July 1921. Ex-sergeant Tomás Fuentes and ex-soldier Saturnino Quiroga statements, May 18, 1921; confession of Saturnino Quiroga, July 19, 1921, all from MOT-71-002A, TPJM-AHM. Díaz Machicao, *Saavedra*, 107.

52. Max Terán and cabo Mariano Parra statements, April 19 and 27, 1921, MOT-71-002A, TPJM-AHM.

53. Confession of Corporal Domingo Peña, July 18, 1921, MOT-71-002A, TPJM-AHM.

54. Cabos Luis Gallardo, Max Terán, Daniel Cardenas, and Mariano Parra statements, April 25 and 27, 1921, TPJM-AHM. See also Dunkerley, *Orígenes del poder militar*, 110, 226n114.

55. Capt. Luis Emilio Aguirre statement, March 12, 1921, MOT-71-002A, TPJM-AHM.

56. See, for example, "Sobre el motín militar del Loa," *La Reforma*, March 11, 1921; "La verdad sobre los sucesos de 3 de marzo," *El Tiempo*, March 27, 1921; debate on May 18, 1921, in Bolivia, *Redactor de la H. Convención Nacional*, 5:7–30.

57. Dunkerley, *Orígenes del poder militar*, 116. Supreme decree of September 1, 1921, MOT-71-002A, TPJM-AHM.

58. Gallo, *Taxes and State Power*, 124; Ministerio de Guerra, *Memoria de guerra* (1923), 36; *Memoria de guerra* (1924), 19; *Memoria de guerra* (1925), 12; *Memoria de guerra* (1926), 20; *Memoria de guerra* (1927), 33. Report prepared by the Department of State, November 5, 1929, RG 165, NM 84-77, box 187, folder 6000-6420, NARA. Later, US military attachés reported that the line army's numbers had returned to around seven thousand by the end of Saavedra's term in 1925. "Country: Bolivia," c. 1934, RG 165, NM 84-77, box 187, folder 6000-6420, NARA.

59. Interview with Col. Julio Sanjinés cited in Brill, "Military Civic Action in Bolivia," 64–65.

60. Dunkerley, *Orígenes del poder militar*, 114.

61. Dunkerley mentions a 1925 mutiny among a battalion of military engineers reported by a US diplomat. If the case was formally investigated and prosecuted, the records have yet to be found. Dunkerley, *Orígenes del poder militar*, 114. I have found records of only three cases for rebellion, sedition, mutiny, or insubordination from this period. One 1922 case prosecuted two subaltern officers for attempted rebellion. A mutiny case in December 1923 briefly investigated two NCOs, and a January 1927 case pursued a colonel for attempted rebellion in a frontier unit. See MOT-71-003 and REB-77-007, TPJM-AHM, and Prefecture-Exped box 251, d. 7, Archivo de La Paz (ALP).

62. Choque Canqui and Ticona Alejo, *Jesús de Machaqa*, 38–63, 68, 74, 77, 94–97.

63. Smale, *"I Sweat the Flavor of Tin,"* 110–43. Quotation from 137.

64. Díaz Machicao, *Saavedra*, 131; Dunkerley, *Orígenes del poder militar*, 116.

65. Díaz Machicao, *Saavedra*, 166–69. See also Lt. Col. Andrés Valle to Prefect of La Paz, February 20, 1924, Prefecture-Admin box 208, ALP; "El incendio crimin [*sic*] al del cuartel de la Guardia Republicana," *La República*, Feburary 19, 1924; "Más sobre el incendio del cuartel de la Guardia Republicana," *La República*, Feburary 22, 1924; "En torno al incendio del cuartel de la Guardia Republicana," *La República*, March 7, 1924.

66. Brockmann, *El general y sus presidentes*, 74–76; Díaz Machicao, *Saavedra*, 169–73; Dunkerley, *Orígenes del poder militar*, 117–18.

67. Hylton, "Tierra común"; Arze Aguirre, *Guerra y conflictos sociales*, 11–25; Harris and Albó, *Monteras y guardatojos*, 59–71; Montes Ruiz, *La máscara de piedra*, 339–42. Quotation from Arze Aguirre, *Guerra y conflictos sociales*, 25.

68. Banzer's nephew, Hugo, rose to the rank of general and was twice president of Bolivia, as a military dictator from 1971 to 1978 and through elections from 1997 to 2001. On the Banzer family, see Sivak, *El dictador elegido*, 87–91.

69. During a period of turmoil over the presidential succession in 1925, a disaffected lieutenant colonel openly accused Kundt of committing atrocities during World War I and of corrupt dealings in his arms purchases for Bolivia. Although Kundt was acquitted, his reputation was badly damaged. He soon traveled to New York to investigate purchases for the army and then to Germany for a vacation. In his absence, 150 officers signed a petition in September 1926 to block his return. Siles ceded to their wishes but continued to pay Kundt according to his contract, assigning him to purchase arms and travel as a Bolivian emissary. When a border skirmish with Paraguay necessitated the mobilization of troops to the Chaco in December 1928, Siles used the opportunity to recall Kundt and reinstate him as chief of staff. See Brockmann, *El general y sus presidentes*, 96–102; Hancock, *Ernst Röhm*, 699; Dunkerley, *Orígenes del poder militar*, 124–26.

70. Aramayo, "Intellectual Origins," 169; Brockmann, *El general y sus presidentes*, 135–45.

71. Dunkerley, *Orígenes del poder militar*, 129–30; Díaz Machicao, *Guzmán, Siles, Blanco Galindo*, 114–21; Brockmann, *El general y sus presidentes*, 145–48.

72. Nunn, *Yesterday's Soldiers*, 288–89.

73. Quoted in Díaz Machicao, *Guzmán, Siles, Blanco Galindo*, 123.

74. Brockmann, *El general y sus presidentes*, 149–68.

75. Díaz Machicao, *Guzmán, Siles, Blanco Galindo*, 125.

76. Dunkerley, *Orígenes del poder militar*, 240–41n241.

77. Díaz Machicao, *Guzmán, Siles, Blanco Galindo*, 139–46; Dunkerley, *Orígenes del poder militar*, 132–33; Klein, *Parties and Political Change*, 114–15.

78. Dunkerley, *Orígenes del poder militar*, 135.

79. For parallel mutinies by French citizen soldiers, see Smith, *Between Mutiny and Obedience*.

80. Citing a British diplomat, Dunkerley interprets the aviation mutiny as "the work of the Silista rump, particularly strong in the Air Force." Dunkerley, *Orígenes del poder militar*, 432n424.

81. Alberto Salazar, Manuel Guzmán, Carmelo Menacho, Joaquín Aguirre, Luis Barrientos, Hernán Badani, Hugo Leclere, Saturnino Fuentelaz, Alfredo Ponce, Julio Lizarazu, Sof. Enrique Toro Gorea, and Major Jordán statements, September 10–13 and 19, 1930, MOT-71-004, TPJM-AHM.

82. Hugo Tapia statement, September 12, 1930, MOT-71-004, TPJM-AHM.

83. "Una relación de los hechos ocurridos en la escuela de aviación, hecha por los actuantes," *El Diario*, September 26, 1930.

84. Sub-Lieutenant Juan Antonio Rivera to the Director of Aviation School, September 9, 1930, MOT-71-004, TPJM-AHM.

85. Carmelo Menacho, Hugo Leclere, Antonio Rivera, and Sergeant Feliciano Quiroz statements, September 10–11, 1930, MOT-71-004, TPJM-AHM.

86. Sub-Lieutenant Juan Antonio Rivera to the Director of Aviation School, September 9 1930; Alberto Salazar, Carmelo Menacho, Luis Barrientos, Hugo Le-

clere, Raímundo Ríos, and Saturnino Fuentelás statements, September 10–11, 1930, MOT-71-004, TPJM-AHM.

87. Major Jorge Jordán to President of Military Tribunal, September 10, 1930, MOT-71-004, TPJM-AHM.

88. Alberto Salazar, Carmelo Menacho, Joaquín Aguirre, Luis Barrientos, Hernán Badini, Hugo Leclere, Antonio Rivera, Raimundo Ríos, Carlos García, and Saturnino Fuentelás statements, September 10–11, 1930, MOT-71-004, TPJM-AHM.

89. "Una relación de los hechos ocurridos en la escuela de aviación, hecha por los actuantes," *El Diario*, September 26, 1930.

90. Carmelo Menacho, Hernán Badini, and Hugo Leclere statements, September 10–11, 1930, MOT-71-004, TPJM-AHM.

91. Quotation from Daniel Saavedra statement; see also Victorino Guzmán and Senobio Acero statements, September 12, 1930, MOT-71-004, TPJM-AHM.

92. Antonio Bayá statement, September 13, 1930, MOT-71-004, TPJM-AHM.

93. Conclusions of the Military Tribunal, October 22, 1930, MOT-71-004, TPJM-AHM.

94. Dunkerley, *Orígenes del poder militar*, 133.

95. Díaz Machicao, *Guzmán, Siles, Blanco Galindo*, 150–52; Dunkerley, *Orígenes del poder militar*, 132–35; Klein, *Parties and Political Change*, 116, 121.

96. Díaz Machicao, *Salamanca, la Guerra del Chaco, Tejada Sorzano*, 26–43, 51; Klein, *Parties and Political Change*, 131–42; Dunkerley, *Orígenes del poder militar*, 107.

97. "Anoche se amotinó el Regimento Colorados," *La Razón*, September 11, 1931.

98. Díaz Arguedas, *Historia del ejército*, 263. Dunkerley cites a British diplomat's report that radical propaganda was found on some of the soldiers. Dunkerley, *Orígenes del poder militar*, 137.

99. Seventeen soldiers to Commander of the Second Division, September 21, 1931, ABA-01-004, TPJM-AHM.

100. Conclusions of Examining Magistrate, October 21, 1931, ABA-01-004, TPJM-AHM.

101. Col. Alberto Sotomayor statement, October 1, 1931; Sarg. Huberto del Castillo statement, October 8, 1931, ABA-01-004, TPJM-AHM.

102. Dunkerley, "Reassessing Caudillismo," 16.

103. See boxes 59, 71, 77–78, and 94, TPJM-AHM; Prefecture-Admin boxes 140 and 147–49; Prefecture-Exped boxes 141, 163, 168, 175, 189, 190, 243–45, and 251, ALP.

104. Twenty-second ordinary session, September 10, 1917, in Bolivia, *Redactor de la H. Cámara de Diputados*, 237–42; Gen. Gonzalo Jáuregui, "Las razas indígenas en Bolivia y su educación en los cuarteles," *Revista militar* 55 (1926): 533–37.

CHAPTER 4: MOBILIZATION FOR THE CHACO WAR

1. Studies of the war have mostly focused on Bolivia's failures of leadership, strategy, and logistics. An exception is Ann Zulawski's 2007 chapter on public health

during the Chaco War, which draws on oral histories, memoirs, and the published work of physicians and public health professionals to offer a detailed rendering of troops' suffering due to disease, dehydration, and inadequate medical care. Zulawski, *Unequal Cures*, 52–85.

Excellent scholarship exists on the wartime experience of the Chaco region's indigenous groups and the devastation wrought on their communities. Capdevila et al., *Los hombres transparentes*; Horst, "Crossfire, Cactus, and Racial Constructions"; Langer, *Expecting Pears*, 260–63; Pifarré, *Historia de un pueblo*.

Too few have followed in the footsteps of two Bolivian social historians whose research raised important questions about the societal conflicts that accompanied wartime conscription in the highlands. Published decades ago, the works of René Arze and Carlos Mamani highlighted how violent recruitment by an internally colonial state combined with long-standing land conflicts to destabilize the countryside. Arze Aguirre, *Guerra y conflictos sociales*; Mamani Condori, *Taraqu, 1866–1935*, 97–139.

2. Calculated based on an average army size of 7,500 noted by US military attachés between 1926 and 1928. See Combat Estimate, August 25, 1926, and January 10, 1928, RG 165, NM 84-77, box 557, folder Bolivia; Jesse S. Cottrell to Secretary of State, September 13, 1926, RG 165, NM 84-77, box 187, folder 6000-6420, all in NARA.

3. Cote, "War for Oil," 747–52; Chesterton, *Grandchildren of Solano López*, 147n143; Wood, *United States and Latin American Wars*, 65–67.

4. Aramayo, "Intellectual Origins," 171–72; Klein, *Concise History of Bolivia*, 174–75. For Bolivia's attempts to secure an export pipeline for its oil production, see Cote, *Oil and Nation*, 79.

5. The summary of the war in this and the preceding paragraph is drawn from Brockmann, *El general y sus presidentes*; Dunkerley, *Orígenes del poder militar*; Querejazu Calvo, *Masamaclay*; Zook, *Conduct of the Chaco War*.

6. Wood, *United States and Latin American Wars*, 25, 39, 84–85.

7. Quintana Taborga, *Soldados y ciudadanos*, 45; Querejazu Calvo, *Masamaclay*, 59, 123–24; Klein, *Concise History of Bolivia*, 183; Dunkerley, *Orígenes del poder militar*, 172.

8. Quintana Taborga, *Soldados y ciudadanos*, 54. Dunkerley, in turn, cites Zook, who cites Vergara Vicuña, who offers no citation. Dunkerley, *Orígenes del poder militar*, 167, 257n162; Zook, *Conduct of the Chaco War*, 149; Vergara Vicuña, *Historia de la Guerra del Chaco*, 307.

9. Farcau, *Chaco War*, 230; Querejazu Calvo, *Masamaclay*, 484.

10. Díaz Arguedas, *Los elegidos de la gloria*; Díaz Arguedas, *La guerra con el Paraguay*, 398–99; Vergara Vicuña, *Historia de la Guerra del Chaco*, 307.

11. Ann Zulwaski presents 1933 statistics from the Villamontes hospital to convincingly support the long-affirmed contention that far more soldiers fell due to disease than to wounds. These sources also indicate that only 2.6 percent of those hos-

pitalized died on site and that 54 percent were evacuated to hospitals in the interior. Zulawski, *Unequal Cures*, 61–64. Farcau estimates that the sick and wounded alone were approximately double those who died—or one hundred thousand. Farcau, *Chaco War*, 230.

12. See Dunkerley, *Orígenes del poder militar*, 167; Quintana Taborga, *Soldados y ciudadanos*, 54; Zook, *Conduct of the Chaco War*, 240.

13. Bolivia conducted national censuses in 1900 and 1950. Based on unclear sources, published estimates of the population in 1932 range from two to three million inhabitants. However, since the 1950 census reported a population of only 2.7 million, the 3 million figure should be dismissed as inaccurate. To calculate these figures, I took the high and low numbers for the recruited and war dead from table 3 and used estimates of 2 million and 2.5 million for the population. To put these numbers in context, the recruitment rate for the US Civil War was approximately 10 percent, and European nations lost about 3 percent of the population in World War I. Woodworth, *Atlas of the Civil War*; Ambrosius, *Social and Economic History*, 6.

14. Zook, *Conduct of the Chaco War*, 149.

15. Brockmann cites a *New York Times* article for the total mobilized in this period. Enumerating particular detachments but offering no citations, Querejazu offers similar numbers. Brockmann, *El general y sus presidentes*, 247; Querejazu Calvo, *Masamaclay*, 63–64. The number of dead is widely cited; see, for example, Klein, *Parties and Political Change*, 178.

16. Widely cited, these numbers trace back to uncited material in Díaz Arguedas, *Los elegidos de la gloria*, 454.

17. Zook, *Conduct of the Chaco War*, 232; Querejazu Calvo, *Masamaclay*, 416–25; Klein, *Parties and Political Change*, 182.

18. Céspedes, *Sangre de mestizos*, 201.

19. Querejazu Calvo, *Masamaclay*, 129.

20. Klein, *Parties and Political Change*, 188.

21. Respective quotations from Gotkowitz, *Revolution for Our Rights*, 104; Gustafson, "Flashpoints of Sovereignty," 226.

22. Aramayo, "Intellectual Origins," 120, 234–56; Klein, *Parties and Political Change*, 188–98. Although Aramayo has traced the roots of these ideas back to the 1920s, his revisionist account has not yet penetrated the academic and popular literature.

23. Cuadros Sánchez, *Los orígenes de la Revolución Nacional*, 37, 165.

24. Zook, *Conduct of the Chaco War*, 24.

25. Ari, *Earth Politics*, 15, 136; Gotkowitz, *Revolution for Our Rights*, 193.

26. See, for example, Rivera Cusicanqui, *Oppressed but Not Defeated*.

27. Grieshaber, "Fluctuaciones en la definición del indio."

28. The Central Archive of the Ministry of National Defense holds over seventy bound volumes related to mobilization and demobilization; those hospitalized, evacuated, and killed; and those who deserted or fell prisoner during the war. But these

lists and correspondence contain only names and, occasionally, residence and next of kin, so they lack direct data on soldiers' origin and social status. See volumes 1–54, labeled variously as "Regimientos," "Reclutamientos," or "Destacamentos," and volumes 28–45, labeled variously as "Muertos," "Fallecidos," "Heridos," "Desaparecidos," "Prisioneros," "Desertores," "Evacuados," or "Licenciados," Archivo Central del Ministerio de Defensa Nacional (hereafter AC-MDN).

29. See folders Notas al Ministerio de Defensa, Prisioneros Bolivianos, and Tribunal Militar Guerra del Chaco, Archivo del Museo Militar del Ministerio de Defensa Nacional (hereafter AMM).

30. Monsignor Juan Sinforiano Bogarín, the archbishop of Asunción, fielded thousands of requests from Bolivian families for information about prisoners. See Guerra del Chaco 901.9, Prisioneros de Guerra I–III, and Asuntos relativos a la Guerra del Chaco 1932–1936, Archivo del Arzobispado de la Santísima Asunción (hereafter AAA). For more on Bogarín's role, see Shesko, "'Same as Here, Same as Everywhere,'" 26–27.

31. Alberto Aramayo Zalles to Juan Sinforiano Bogarín, 7 November 7, 1935, Guerra del Chaco 901.9, Prisioneros de Guerra II, AAA.

32. See series of thirty-six letters and telegrams exchanged between Juan Sinforiano Bogarín, Daniel Beltrán, and Julio Beltrán from February 1934 to March 1938 in Guerra del Chaco 901.9, Prisioneros de Guerra I–III, and Asuntos relativos a la Guerra del Chaco, AAA.

33. "Información telegramas," n.d., folder Prisioneros bolivianos, d. 232–34; telegrams, September 17 and 20, 1933, folder Prisioneros bolivianos—Remitidos a Asuncion, d. 495–501, 514–25; telegrams, September 19, 1933, folder Telegráficos varios; lettter from Minister of War to Minister of Foreign Relations transcribing telegrams, September 19, 1933, folder Prisioneros bolivianos, d. 510–511, all in AMM.

34. See table 4.4.

35. Dirección General de Estadística y Censos, *Censo demográfico, 1950*, 133.

36. Two additional men were too young to have previously served, and the other twenty-two were not asked about their prior service.

37. Early support for the war was not universal, especially among leftist intellectuals. See Aramayo, "Intellectual Origins," 174–229.

38. Selaya P., *Documentos y memorias*, 48; Herbas Cabrera, *El cristo de Tarairí*, 25; Pozo Trigo, *Relatos y anecdotas*, 19; Granier Chirveches, *Diario de campaña*, 35; Böhrt Gastelú, *Deber cumplido*, 29.

39. Petition of Julio Ríos and Eduardo Canedo to military tribunal, January 31, 1933, DES-16-021, TPJM-AHM.

40. Personal communications of March 16 and April 18, 2019, with Marina Murillo, granddaughter of Eulogio Murillo.

41. See documents in Prefecture-Admin box 208, ALP.

42. See fifty-four bound volumes of mobilization records labeled by regiment, AC-MDN.

43. List of soldiers attached to General Federico Velsaco to Commander of the First Division, no. 3131–32, September 5, 1932, Regimientos de Infantería 1 al 23, tomo 1, AC-MDN.

44. Carter and Mamani, *Irpa Chico*, 373.

45. Arze Aguirre, *Guerra y conflictos sociales*, 139, 153, 168, 178, 185, 213, 251.

46. Arze Aguirre, *Guerra y conflictos sociales*, 153, 163.

47. Arze Aguirre, *Guerra y conflictos sociales*, 173–74, 178–79.

48. Subprefect of Achacachi, quoted in Prefect of La Paz to Chief of Staff, no. 237, July 29, 1932. See series of ten transcribed telegrams from various subprefects of the La Paz department noting the enthusiasm with which named reservists had reported for duty in Prefect of La Paz to Chief of Staff, nos. 219, 227, 234, 237, 238, and 241, July 25–August 5, 1932, Prefecture-Admin box 208, ALP.

49. Petition of *indígenas comunarios* transcribed in Prefect of La Paz to Director of Military Mail, no. 161, September 13, 1933, Prefecture-Admin box 208, ALP.

50. Previous research on *madrinas* in Bolivia uses newspaper coverage and select interviews to highlight their role as fundraisers and advocates for Bolivia's rights in the Chaco, and in communicating with and providing for soldiers and their families. Durán Jordán and Seoane Flores, *El complejo mundo*, 69–74, 81. Historian Bridget Chesterton has shown that upper-class Paraguayan *madrinas* during the Chaco War garnered respect for their role in boosting soldiers' morale and providing them with supplies such as toothpaste, cigarettes, and yerba mate (tea). Analyzing a set of letters between several *madrinas* and their *ahijados* (godsons), she argues that although the wartime situation facilitated cross-class relationships, *madrinas* employed a tone of formality to maintain social distance from their *ahijados*. Chesterton, "Composing Gender and Class."

51. Ramón Carrión and Ortíz, *Madrina de guerra*, 24.

52. Although derived from the Catholic model, *compadrazgo* in Bolivia goes far beyond the spiritual sponsorship of children by godparents. A key part of Bolivian social structure, it creates inter- and intra-class ties of mutual obligation. Through *compadrazgo* relationships, individuals serve as godparents not only to children but also to adults for weddings, festivals, sports teams, and even the purchase of consumer goods. See Crandon-Malamud, *From the Fat of Our Souls*, 112; Albó et al., *Para comprender las culturas rurales*, 67–68; Albro, *Roosters at Midnight*, 62–66; Leinaweaver, *Circulation of Children*, 5–8.

53. Böhrt Gastelú, *Deber cumplido*, 33, 44.

54. Pozo Trigo, *Relatos y anecdotas*, 17–20.

55. Letter from Quintín Cuba in Acantonamiento Posta Ybyravo to Archbishop of Asunción, November 7, 1935, Asuntos relativos a la Guerra del Chaco, AAA. See also Letter from Bishop Rodríguez in Villarrica to Archbishop of Asuncion, January 14, 1936, Prisioneros de Guerra II, Guerra del Chaco 901.9, AAA.

56. Unsigned letter to "my dear husband," written in Santa Cruz and addressed to Luis Mercado, November 26, 1932, DES-16-010, TPJM-AHM.

57. Fernández Terán mentions that *madrinas* often wrote letters to soldiers for illiterate family members. Fernández Terán, "Prensa, radio e imaginario boliviano," 218.

58. Jose Castedo in Charagua to Srta. Yolanda Landibar in Santa Cruz, December 13, 1932, DES-16-010, TPJM-AHM.

59. Letter from Raquel Villavicencio in La Paz to Archbishop of Asunción, December 13, 1934, Guerra del Chaco 901.9, Asuntos relativos a la Guerra del Chaco, AAA.

60. Alicia Aramayo de Cariaga in Tupiza to Archbishop of Asunción, December 8, 1933, Guerra del Chaco 901.9, Prisoneros de Guerra III, AAA.

61. Ambrosio Chambi statement, December 19, 1932, DES-16-009, TPJM-AHM.

62. Ramón Julio Choque statement, December 23, 1932, DES-16-009, TPJM-AHM.

63. Law of January 16, 1907, in Bolivia, *Anuario de leyes* (1907); "Reglamento del servicio militar," April 6, 1907, in Ministerio de Guerra, *Boletín militar*, 3:121–48.

64. See series of ten letters between the Prefect of La Paz and the Commander of the Second Division regarding reports by various subprefects and *corregidores* that men were resisting calls for mobilization, nos. 67, 1654, 1735, 1741, 1814, 1815, 26, 100, 104, 116, La Paz, March 2, 9, 13, 15, 16, 20, 23, and 31, 1933, Prefecture-Admin box 208, ALP.

65. Quotation from Albó, "Andean People," 795. See also Gotkowitz, *Revolution for Our Rights*, 104–105; Hylton and Thomson, *Revolutionary Horizons*, 69.

66. Carter and Mamani, *Irpa Chico*, 280, 373–74.

67. Rivera Cusicanqui et al., *La mujer andina*, 43.

68. See, for example, Manuel Ramírez, Nicolás Castro Mansilla, Ramón Julio Choque Gutierrez, and Mariano Chambi Pérez statements, December 16 and 23, 1932, DES-16-009; Emilio Tapia statement, January 12, 1933, DES-16-016, TPJM-AHM.

69. See, for example, Prefect of La Paz to Minister of War, nos. 464 and 389, September 15, 1933, and September 4, 1934, Prefecture-Admin box 149, ALP.

70. Prefect of La Paz to Commander of the Second Division, no. 125, April 10, 1933, Prefecture-Admin box 208, ALP. See also Arze Aguirre, *Guerra y conflictos sociales*, 40.

71. Arze Aguirre, *Guerra y conflictos sociales*, 41. Although Arze dates the decision to institute a quota system to April, a March letter makes reference to it. See Corregidor of Italaque to Prefect of La Paz, March 28, 1934. Another letter refers to a mobilization of indígenas in June 1933. See Prefect of La Paz to Minister of War, no. 207, April 19, 1934, both in Prefecture-Admin box 208, ALP.

72. Commander of Second Division to Prefect of La Paz, no. 1405, April 27, 1935, Prefecture-Admin box 209, ALP.

73. Arze Aguirre, *Guerra y conflictos sociales*, 42–43.

74. Although we still know little about how the quota system worked, evidence from a limited number of cases demonstrates that it functioned in some communi-

ties. See INC-60-007 (1934), INC-60-008 (1934), INC-60-021 (1936), and DES-21-018 (1942), TPJM-AHM.

75. Taller de Historia Oral Andina and Rivera Cusicanqui, "Indigenous Women and Community Resistance," 157.

76. Conclusions of the auditor de guerra, December 15, 1934, INC-60-008, TPJM-AHM.

77. Reservists from Inquisivi referenced in Commander of Second Division to Prefect of La Paz, no. 3291–31, December 14, 1932; *comunarios* from Callapa transcribed in Prefect of La Paz to Auxiliary Chief of Staff, no. 141, July 30, 1934; Nicolás Kapa from Callapa quoted in Director General of Military Police to Prefect of La Paz, no. 305, October 10, 1934, all in Prefecture-Admin box 208, ALP. *Comunarios* of Charazani referenced in PO of Minister of War to Prefect of La Paz, no. 9, April 27, 1933; Charaña indigenous authorities paraphrased in message from police quoted in Prefect of La Paz to Minister of War, no. 389, September 4, 1934, both in Prefecture-Admin box 149, ALP. Reservist from Calacoto paraphrased in Chief of Military Police to Prefect of La Paz, no. 421, March 26, 1935, Prefecture-Admin box 209, ALP. See also Arze Aguirre, *Guerra y conflictos sociales*, 44–49, 65, 69–70.

78. Subprefects of Inquisivi and Pelechuco quoted in Prefect of La Paz to Commander of Second Division, nos. 341 and 344, October 30, 1933; Sub. Lt. J. Soria of Recruitment transcribed in Auxiliary Chief of Staff to Prefect of La Paz, no. 6104, August 21, 1934, both in Prefecture-Admin box 208, ALP.

79. Prefect of La Paz to Commander of Second Division, no. 339, October 13, 1933; subprefect of Larecaja quoted in Prefect of La Paz to Commander of Second Division, November 16, 1933, Prefecture-Admin box 208; Prefect of La Paz to Commander of Second Division, no. 57, November 17, 1933, Prefecture-Admin box 208; *corregidor* of Mocomoco paraphrased in Prefect of La Paz to Minister of War, no. 502, November 7, 1934, Prefecture-Admin box 149; Prefect of La Paz to Commander of Second Division, no. 19, March 11, 1935, Prefecture-Admin box 209, ALP. See also Arze Aguirre, *Guerra y conflictos sociales*, 66.

80. FAD-35-004 (1932), FAD-35-005 (1933), FAD-35-007A (1933), FAD-35-013 (134), FAD 35-014 (1934), FAD-35-017 (1934), FAD-35-018 (1935), ABA-01-009 (1933), DESA-14-002 (1933), INT-61-007 (1934), INT-61-008 (1934), TPJM-AHM. Commander of the Second Division to Prefect of La Paz, no. 4499, October 7, 1933; General Staff to Prefect of La Paz, no. 7136, October 10, 1934, both in Prefecture-Admin box 208, ALP. General Staff to Prefect of La Paz, February 9, 1935; Director General of Military Police to Prefect of La Paz, no. 289, March 2, 1935; Commander of Second Division to Prefect of La Paz, no. 1346, April 23, 1935, all in Prefecture-Admin box 209, ALP. See also Arze Aguirre, *Guerra y conflictos sociales*, 68.

81. Subprefect of Larecaja quoted in Prefect of La Paz to Commander of Second Division, November 16, 1933, Prefecture-Admin box 208, ALP.

82. See chapter 1. Quotation from Ministerio de Guerra, *Memoria de Guerra* (1910), 8.

83. Law of October 23, 1933, in Bolivia, *Gaceta oficial* (1933).

84. Supreme decree of October 10, 1934, in Bolivia, *Gaceta oficial* (1934).

85. See Prefect of La Paz to Minister of War, nos. 438, 439, 441, 443, 450, 479, 484, 486, 488, and 491, October 13 to November 7, 1934, Prefecture-Admin box 149, ALP.

86. Supreme decree of December 14, 1933, in Bolivia, *Gaceta oficial* (1933).

87. Brockmann, *El general y sus presidentes*, 294–95; Granier Chirveches, *Diario de campaña*, 166.

88. Supreme decree of January 27, 1934, in Bolivia, *Gaceta oficial* (1934).

89. The government also made concessions on tin quotas and the proportion of foreign exchange that had to be sold to the government. Gallo, *Taxes and State Power*, 42–44, 149.

90. A May 10, 1934, decree refers to this decree as being issued on September 25, 1933. Despite these measures, many miners fought on the front lines, and the companies still had to import laborers from Peru and Chile. Dunkerley, *Orígenes del poder militar*, 168.

91. Minister of War to Prefect of La Paz, no. 20, 26 September 26, 1933, Prefecture-Admin box 149, ALP.

92. Supreme decrees of February 15, April 12, May 10 and 11, October 5, and November 19, 1934, in Bolivia, *Gaceta oficial* (1934).

93. Receipt of Empresa Minera Negro Pabellón, February 12, 1935, Reservistas en Comisón 7; list of employees and workers of the Oruro Mining Company, June 17, 1935, Reservistas en Comisón 6, both in AC-MDN.

94. As early as September 1933, prefectural correspondence refers to indigenous laborers on roads as having the status of reservists on assignments and being exempt from impressment. Prefect of La Paz to Minister of War, no. 464, September 15, 1933, Prefecture-Admin box 149, ALP.

95. Román Machuca, boleto de licencia, March 3, 1934, Reservistas en Comisión 5, 1934–1935, AC-MDN.

96. Reservistas en Comisión 5, 1934–1935, AC-MDN.

97. The extent of mobilization in particular regions and communities (and among particular social classes) remains a question for future research, especially for departments other than La Paz.

98. Felipe Arias, Hipolito Lismet, Juan Ticona, and Saúl Chávez statements, September 19–20, 1932, DES-16-023; José Cerna statement, November 25, 1932, DES 16-001; Carlos Escobar and Francisco Rocha statements, January 10, 1933, DES-16-015; Julio Ríos statement, January 30, 1933, DES-16-021, all in TPJM-AHM.

99. Carlos Escobar statement, January 10, 1933, DES-16-015, TPJM-AHM.

100. Santiago Vaca and Eugenio Mariscal statements, September 20, 1932, DES-16-023; Pastor Vargas statement, November 25, 1932, DES-15-021; Martín Vargas, José Villca, Juan Chaña, Juan Chuquimia, Francisco Aguirre, Delfín Armijo, and Antonio Llanos statements, November 25, 1932, DES-16-001; Juan Yugar and Pablo

Meneces statements, December 27, 1932, DES-16-011; Santiago Vaca and Eugenio Mariscal statements, September 20, 1932, DES-16-023, all in TPJM-AHM.

101. Manuel Farfán statement, December 16, 1932, DES-16-007, TPJM-AHM.

102. Benedicto Calisaya statement, December 3, 1932, DES-16-003, TPJM-AHM.

103. Examples include claims to measles, tachycardia, gonorrhea, and wounds. See Valentín Ferrufino statement, December 26, 1932, DES-16-011; Ponciano Cerdo statement, December 28, 1932, DES-16-001; Julio Carrillo statement, January 10, 1933, DES-16-015; José Manuel Códova statement, January 12, 1933, DES-16-016, all in TPJM-AHM.

104. Saúl Chávez statement, September 19, 1932, DES-16-023, TPJM-AHM.

105. Joshua Sanborn's work indicates that the Soviet military was able to stem desertion only through an effective family policy. In that case, soldiers who deserted because their families were not being cared for were treated with more compassion since the state was seen to have violated its contract with its defenders. Sanborn, *Drafting the Russian Nation*, 150.

106. Rosendo Cuentas statement, November 27, 1932, DES-15-021, DES-16-001, TPJM-AHM.

107. Quiroga Ochoa, *En la paz y en la guerra*, 82–86.

108. Manuel Fernandez statement, December 28, 1932, DES-16-011; Arturo Jurrico and Julio Palacio statements, January 18–19, 1933, DES-16-017, both in TPJM-AHM.

109. Farcau, *Chaco War*, 74, 109; Granier Chirveches, *Diario de campaña*, 223–28; Tovar Villa and Kundt, *Campaña del Chaco*, 85–86; Zook, *Conduct of the Chaco War*, 132.

110. See Edmundo Checa statement, December 23, 1932, DES-16-009; Juan de Dios López, Federico Paniagua, Eugenio Apaza, and Manuel Fernández statements, December 27–28, 1932, DES-16-011; Salvador Aiza statement, January 4, 1933, DES-16-013; José Manuel Córdova statement, January 12, 1933, DES-16-016; Juan Taboada, Julio Palacio, and Arturo Jurrico statements, January 18–19, 1933, DES-16-017; Eduardo Canedo, Julio Ríos, and Aparicio Alánes statements, January 30, 1933, DES-16-021, all in TPJM-AHM.

111. José Manuel Cordova statement, January 12, 1933, DES-16-016, TPJM-AHM.

112. Ministerio de Guerra, *Códigos militares*, 246.

113. Report on First Company expenses, 124th Oruro Detachment, June 10 and July [unreadable], 1933, Contraloría General de la República, Cajas Blancas 69, d. 254, ALP.

114. See reports on detachments June 1933–February 1934, Contraloría General de la República, Cajas Blancas 69, d. 254, 279, 280, ALP; volumes listing mobilized soldiers, Regimentos de Infantería 1 al 23, vol. 1, Reclutamientos de La Paz-Cochabamba-Sucre-Oruro 11, AC-MDN.

115. Destacamentos del 353–58, Evacuados, Omisos, Desertores 52, AC-MDN.

116. Number of military justice proceedings compiled based on boxes 15–18, TPJM-AHM. Number of executions compiled based on DES-16-026 and DES-16-027, TPJM-AHM; lists of executed soldiers compiled on August 31, 1933, April 18, 1934, May 10, 1934, July 1, 1934, and June 25, 1935, telegram from Second Corps Commander to Campaign Commander, March 8 and 13, 1934, Commander of Ninth Division to Campaign Commander, nos. 82–34, 126–34, and 139–34, March 1, March 29, and April 4, 1934, all in I.C.E Y II.C.E. Fallecidos Heridos Desertores e Izquierdistas 28, 1933–1934, AC-MDN.

117. General Hans Kundt telegram, April 17, 1933, DES-16-026, TPJM-AHM

118. Gonzalo Zambrana statement, March 20, 1933, DES-16-026, TPJM-AHM.

119. Report of the Consejo de Revisión en Campaña, May 8, 1933, DES-16-026, TPJM-AHM.

120. Quiroga Ochoa, *En la paz y en la guerra*, 94–95.

121. See lists compiled on August 31, 1933, April 18, 1934, May 10, 1934, July 1, 1934, and June 25, 1935, I.C.E Y II.C.E. Fallecidos Heridos Desertores e Izquierdistas, tomo 28, 1933–1934, AC-MDN.

122. General Hans Kundt to Departmental Chief of Staff in Cochabamba, September 29, 1933, I.C.E Y II.C.E. Fallecidos Heridos Desertores e Izquierdistas 28, 1933–1934, AC-MDN.

123. General Hans Kundt to Interim Chief of Staff, March 9, 1933, AC-MDN.

124. Recommendation of the military prosecutor, March 6, 1933, DES-16-023, TPJM-AHM.

125. Recommendation of the military prosecutor, October 2, 1932, DES-15-016, TPJM-AHM.

126. Recommendation of My. Alcibiades Antelo, November 25, 1932, DES-16-023, TPJM-AHM.

127. Valentín Mamani statement, September 20, 1932, DES-16-023, TPJM-AHM.

128. Manuel Ramírez statement, December 16, 1932, DES-16-009, TPJM-AHM.

129. Foilán Navarro statement, December 29, 1932, DES-16-008, TPJM-AHM. Writing about the Soviet military, Joshua Sanborn notes that many deserters promised to use violence against the nation's enemies in order to avoid punishment. He reports that the Soviet military officially accepted these promises, allowing soldiers to expiate their sins by performing well on the front line. He argues that violence thus became a central facet of citizenship through which men could recover their lost belonging in the nation. Sanborn, *Drafting the Russian Nation*, 182.

130. See twenty-four similar statements in DES-16-011, DES-16-012, DES-16-013, DES-16-015, DES-16-021, TPJM-AHM.

131. Julio Rivas petition, January 18, 1933, DES-16-013, TPJM-AHM.

132. Juan Cusi statement, January 5, 1933, DES-16-012, TPJM-AHM.

133. General Peñaranda report, October 2, 1934, DES-16-023, TPJM-AHM.

134. The Bolivian state has a long history of positioning itself as the defender of the indigenous population. See Flores Moncayo, *Legislación boliviana del indio.*

CHAPTER 5: GOOD SONS AND BAD FATHERS IN THE POSTWAR PERIOD

1. Petition of Julio Barrera Acuña, August 15, 1940, Reservistas en Comisión, tomo 28, AC-MDN.

2. Ministerial resolution and supporting documents, Ministry of Defense, March 1, 1940, Reservistas en Comisión, tomo 30, AC-MDN.

3. Nor was he alone. Gaspar Caihuara also invoked indigeneity to explain his failure to serve, stating that he had left the country prior to the war to seek work in Argentina in his "condition as an *indígena*" so that he could provide for his family. Ministerial resolution and supporting documents, Ministry of Defense, January 27, 1940, Reservistas en Comisión, tomo 30, AC-MDN.

4. Based on population estimate of 2.5 million. Klein, *Concise History of Bolivia,* 182–83.

5. See, for example, Antonio Choque-Vara to Chief of Staff, June 28, 1939, DES-21-004, TPJM-AHM.

6. Gómez D'Angelo, "Mining in the Economic Development," 91.

7. Sierra, "Indigenous Neighborhood Residents."

8. The army's organic law of 1927 stated that members of the military had to resign their position in order to engage in political activity, including voting, holding office, and taking administrative positions. Bolivia, *Compilación penal militar,* 15–16; Cleven, *Political Organization of Bolivia,* 155.

9. General Quintanilla to Prefect of La Paz, June 18, 1935, Prefecture-Admin box 209, ALP.

10. Supreme decree of December 9, 1935, in Bolivia, *Gaceta oficial* (1935).

11. Campaign Commander to Prefects, December 24, 1935, Prefecture-Admin box 209, ALP.

12. Supreme decree of April 8, 1940, in Bolivia, *Gaceta oficial* (1940).

13. Álvarez España, *Los gráficos en Bolivia,* 94–100; Barcelli S., *Medio siglo de luchas sindicales,* 134, 138–40; Díaz Machicao, *Salamanca,* 275–76.

14. Busch is often referred to as a major because that was his rank when he came to prominence during the war. On Busch's actions and promotions during the war, see Farcau, *Chaco War,* 160; Zook, *Conduct of the Chaco War,* 138.

15. Gallego Margaleff, *Los orígenes del reformismo militar,* 71–72, 95–97, 101.

16. Aramayo, "Intellectual Origins," 355–68; Klein, "David Toro," 32–34; Gallego Margaleff, *Los orígenes del reformismo militar,* 97–99; Dunkerley, *Orígenes del poder militar,* 179–80. On postwar socialisms in Bolivia, see Young, *Blood of the Earth,* 23–24.

17. Supreme decrees of May 30 and August 26, 1936, in Bolivia, *Gaceta oficial* (1936).

18. Reservistas en Comisión tomo 5 through tomo 29, AC-MDN; Desmovilización, tomo 1 through tomo 11, Registro Territorial, Ministerio de Defensa Nacional (hereafter RT-MDN).

19. Sarg. Serafín Bueno statement, May 10, 1938, MUE-69-008, TPJM-AHM.

20. Juan Condori statement, February 14, 1938, MUE-69-008, TPJM-AHM.

21. Quintana Taborga, *Soldados y ciudadanos*, 58.

22. Ministerial resolutions, Ministry of Defense, September 20 and November 4, 1940, Reservistas en Comisión, tomo 29; Ministerial resolutions, Ministry of Defense, October 7 and December 12, 1940, Reservistas en Comisión, tomo 30, AC-MDN. For more on these schools, see Choque Canqui and Quisbert Quispe, *Educación indigenal en Bolivia*; Larson, "Capturing Indian Bodies."

23. Ministerial resolution and supporting documents, Ministry of Defense, October 18, 1940, Reservistas en Comisión, tomo 28, AC-MDN.

24. Ministerial resolution and supporting documents, Ministry of Defense, November 11, 1940, Reservistas en Comisión, tomo 28, AC-MDN.

25. The average daily wage reported for workers from five factories in La Paz in December 1939 ranged from 6.50 to 17 bolivianos, depending on the factory. A mine worker from the four biggest mines earned an average daily wage of 12 bolivianos in October 1939. When Congress set minimum daily wages for industrial and mining workers in 1941, those wages ranged from 7 to 9 bolivianos for children, 10 to 12 bolivianos for women, and 15 to 18 bolivianos for men. Capriles Rico and Arduz Eguía, *El problema social*, 29, 49, 169–170. A mass-market paperback book cost 10 bolivianos in 1940. See Aramayo Alzerreca, *Peñaranda y otras entrevistas*.

26. See Ministerial resolution and supporting documents regarding petition of Juan Condori Lopez for duplicate copy of his Indigenous Quota Card, June 7, 1941, Reservistas en Comisión, tomo 28, AC-MDN.

27. Seventy-five petitions from 1939 to 1943 interspersed through volumes 28–30 of Reservistas en Comisión, AC-MDN.

28. In addition to the two cases cited below, see paperwork of Benigno Ticona from the ex-community of Senani (Sud Yungas), August 23, 1940; Santiago Apaza Pari from Cantón Ocobaya (Sud Yungas), August 7, 1940; paperwork of Cirilio Vargas Gutierrez from Totora (Cochabamba), November 12, 1940, Reservistas en Comisión, tomo 28, all in AC-MDN.

29. Aramayo, "Intellectual Origins," 370–81; Klein, *Parties and Political Change*, 292–334.

30. Supreme decrees of March 25 (under Quintanilla) and May 25, 1940 (under Peñaranda), in Bolivia, *Gaceta oficial* (1940).

31. DES-21-008 (1940), DES-21-011 (1940), DES-21-015 (1941), DES-21-016 (1942), DES-21-018 (1942), DES-21-022 (1944), TPJM-AHM.

32. Adrián Barrientos Franco speech, fourteenth ordinary session, August 24, 1943, in Bolivia, *Redactor de la H. Cámara de Diputados*, 1:300.

33. Bolivia, *Redactor de la H. Cámara de Diputados* (1944); Klein, *Parties and Political Change*, 360–66.

34. Aramayo, "Intellectual Origins," 139.

35. See footnote 66 of this chapter for MNR leaders' service. For details on the exile experience, see chapter 5.

36. Klein, *Parties and Political Change*, 360–66, quotation from 360. For Víctor Paz Estenssoro's comments on the army during the debate, see Mitchell, *Legacy of Populism*, 21.

37. Prado Salmón, *Los militares y la revolución nacional*, 57.

38. Chargé J. Dalton Murray to Foreign Office, no. 84, October 23, 1943, FO 371/33610, National Archives (hereafter TNA).

39. Prado Salmón, *Los militares y la revolución nacional*, 16–22.

40. Klein, *Parties and Political Change*, 365–68. See also Chargé J. Dalton Murray to Foreign Office, November 26, 1943, FO 371/33610, TNA.

41. Prado Salmón, *Los militares y la revolución nacional*, 72. The British Chargé at the time reported it as an MNR coup. J. Dalton Murray to Foreign Office, December 20, 1943, FO 371/33610, TNA.

42. Prado Salmón, *Los militares y la revolución nacional*, 68–93; Dorn, *Truman Administration and Bolivia*, 28–48; Klein, *Concise History of Bolivia*, 201–3.

43. Chargé J. Dalton Murray to Foreign Office, no. 48, July 24, 1944, FO 371/37832; Minister T. Ilfor Rees to Foreign Office, no. 53, June 14, 1946, FO 371/551881, both in TNA; García Prada, *El ejército y la revolución*, 83–88; Prado Salmón, *Los militares y la revolución nacional*, 84–90.

44. Supreme decree of July 30, 1945, in Bolivia, *Gaceta oficial* (1945). The constituent assembly later determined that all remaining deserters and evaders would receive a free rehabilitation booklet after presenting their baptismal certificates to military authorities. See law of October 17, 1945, in Bolivia, *Gaceta oficial* (1945).

45. "Fué solemne la reunión de representantes a la Asamblea Indígena-Departmental," *El Diario*, March 6, 1945, 8.

46. Prado Salmón, *Los militares y la revolución nacional*, 25, 15.

47. Aramayo, "Intellectual Origins," 321.

48. Cote, *Oil and Nation*, 79–80, 84–90; Klein, *Parties and Political Change*, 194–96.

49. Although no evidence has been found to support a direct role of Standard Oil in the war, anger at the company was by no means unfounded. Standard Oil had repeatedly lied about oil production, violated the terms of its contract, and refused to refine oil for Bolivia's war efforts. Cote, "War for Oil," 741–42, 747–52; Klein, "American Oil Companies," 54–58, 64–65. For an excellent discussion of how "resource myths and rumors . . . gained acceptance because they resonated with deeply felt grievances and goals" in Bolivia, see Young, *Blood of the Earth*, 174–75.

50. Klein, *Parties and Political Change*, 217.

51. Cote, *Oil and Nation*, 96; Klein, *Parties and Political Change*, 255–56.

52. Klein, "American Oil Companies," 60–67. For the alternative theory that Argentina's diplomatic machinations during the Chaco peace process influenced the decision to nationalize, see Philip, *Oil and Politics*, 196–98; Cote, *Oil and Nation*, 105–6.

53. Young, *Blood of the Earth*, 26, 165; Cote, *Oil and Nation*, 124–25.

54. Carlos Aramayo argues, "The fact that Marxist and socialist intellectuals did not participate on the frontlines hampered their effectiveness." Aramayo, "Intellectual Origins," 182.

55. Durán S., *Germán Busch*, 5, 27–28; Céspedes Toro and Busch Becerra, *Diario de guerra*, 37–39, 142.

56. Speech reproduced in Durán S., *Germán Busch*, 58–59.

57. Quoted in Díaz Machicao, *Historia de Bolivia*, 95.

58. Guerrero, *Peñaranda*.

59. Díaz Machicao, *Historia de Bolivia*, 133.

60. Díaz Machicao, *Historia de Bolivia*, 135–36.

61. See 1940, 1941, and 1942 speeches by Peñaranda for the opening of Congress in Bolivia, *Mensaje del Presidente*.

62. Rafael Otazo V. speech twenty-ninth ordinary session, September 10, 1943, in Bolivia, *Redactor de la H. Cámara de Diputados*, 2:806.

63. Supreme decree of March 29, 1944, in Bolivia, *Gaceta oficial* (1944). This decree applied only to men of mobilization age during the war.

64. Alfonso Finot speech, first ordinary session, August 5, 1944, in Bolivia, *Redactor de la H. Convención Nacional*, 1:117–18.

65. Rodolfo Palenque speech, first ordinary session, August 5, 1944, in Bolivia, *Redactor de la H. Convención Nacional*, 1:139.

66. For these leaders' wartime service, see Lora, *History of the Bolivian Labour Movement*, 297; Cajías, *Historia de una leyenda*, 33–37; Knudson, *Roots of Revolution*, 37; Foster, *Latin American Government Leaders*, 15–17; "Siles Zuazo, Hernán," 265; Weston Jr., "Ideology of Modernization," 89–90; Montenegro and Baptista Gumucio, *Montenegro el desconocido*, 21. Wálter Guevara Arze also saw frontline service but in the relatively safe position of secretary and then observer. He lost a brother in the war. Baptista Gumucio, *Fragmentos de memoria*, 67–73.

67. In 1941, Congress granted substantial pensions to Acre War veterans who had also fought on the front lines in the Chaco. In 1949, it gave the survivors of Alihuatá and Kilometer 7 *benemérito de la patria* (meritorious hero of the nation) status, which came with a rank-based pension. See laws of April 4, 1941, and November 22, 1949, in Bolivia, *Gaceta oficial* (1941, 1949). Víctor Paz Estenssoro granted *benemérito* status to all honorably discharged frontline Chaco soldiers in 1955 but with the provision that "the honorary distinction does not carry with it pecuniary benefits of any type." See supreme decrees of June 11 and November 10, 1955, in Bolivia, *Gaceta oficial* (1955). Congress updated this law the next year, offering veterans preferential land grants through the agrarian reform and job security for those holding public

employment but clarifying that they would receive no financial benefits as long as the "national veterans' account does not have sufficient resources." See law of December 21, 1956, in Bolivia, *Gaceta oficial* (1956).

68. "Los mutilados de la vista piden que suministre el material protéxico [*sic*]," *El Diario*, May 28, 1936. This was before foreign exchange controls were lifted in 1937. Based on the exchange rate at the time, this was the equivalent of 0.194 pounds sterling or about 1 US dollar. M. Epstein, ed., *Statesman's Yearbook*, 735, 745. Working as a messenger for a Spanish club in La Paz at around this time, Luciano Tapia earned a salary of fifteen bolivianos a month, plus room and board. Tapia, *Ukhamawa jakawisaxa*, 117.

69. Respective quotations from Rodolfo Palenque speech, first ordinary session, August 5, 1944, in Bolivia, *Redactor de la H. Convención Nacional*, 1:138; Antonio Anze Jimenez speech, fifteenth ordinary session, September 4, 1947, in Bolivia, *Redactor de la H. Cámara de Dipudatos*, 1:333.

70. Supreme decrees of February 6, 1936, March 24, 1936, June 12, 1936, July 13, 1937, August 19, 1937, October 5 and 6, 1937, February 1, 1938, March 5, 1938, July 3, 1940, May 19, 1941, April 28, 1949, December 27, 1950, January 11, 1951, February 13, 1951, and February 14, 1952; laws of February 18, 1937, September 2, 1938, October 7, 1940, November 8, 1940, December 3, 1940, April 19, 1941, June 12, 1941, November 27, 1941, December 6, 1941, November 8, 1944, December 31, 1944, January 16, 1945, August 12, 1947, November 8 and 22, 1947, December 8, 1947, January 3, 1949, November 17, 1949, November 22, 1949, November 28, 1949, January 5, 1950 (two on same date), and November 15, 1950. This count excludes the many laws that granted pensions to individual beneficiaries. See gacetaoficialdebolivia.gob.bo/.

71. See debate over funding pensions in eighty-sixth and eighty-seventh ordinary sessions, December 14 and 15, 1948, in Bolivia, *Redactor de la H. Cámara de Diputados*, 5:375–407, 438–45. The eventual funding structure is in the law of January 3, 1949, in Bolivia, *Gaceta oficial* (1949).

72. See supreme decree of February 6, 1936, in Bolivia, *Gaceta oficial* (1936); law of September 5, 1907, in Bolivia, *Anuario de leyes* (1907); Bolivia, *Compilación penal militar*, 34.

73. Arze Aguirre, *Guerra y conflictos sociales*, 146–47, 230.

74. "Clama un ciego porque le permitan probar su calidad de ex-soldado," *La Calle*, August 18, 1943.

75. The committee was to consist of a military commander, a veterans' representative, and a member of the local press. Supreme decree of June 12, 1936, in Bolivia, *Gaceta oficial* (1936).

76. Gallego Margaleff, *Los orígenes del reformismo militar*, 76; Young, *Blood of the Earth*, 22–23, 26, 28.

77. Gallego Margaleff, *Los orígenes del reformismo militar*, 76, 191; Prado Salmón, *Los militares y la revolución nacional*, 24.

78. Klein, *Parties and Political Change*, 209.

79. Prado Salmón, *Los militares y la revolución nacional*, 24.

80. Malloy, *Bolivia*, 75.

81. Dandler, "Politics of Leadership," 76.

82. Dandler, "Politics of Leadership," 92. For more on Rojas, see Gordillo, *Campesinos revolucionarios*.

83. John, *Bolivia's Radical Tradition*, 28.

84. Ari, *Earth Politics*, 120–22.

85. Gotkowitz, *Revolution for Our Rights*, 194–224.

86. Alvarez Mamani and Ranaboldo, *El camino perdido*, 61–66. See also Kohl, "Peasants Speak."

87. Dandler, "Politics of Leadership," 106–7.

88. Chipana Ramos appeared in 22 percent (thirteen out of fifty-eight) of the newspapers' photographic depictions of the congress.

89. For examples, see "Con grandiosa sencillez se inauguró ayer el Primer Congreso de Indígenas," *La Calle*, May 11, 1945; "Chipana Ramos el presidente indígena," *La Razón*, May 12, 1945; "Representativo del indio boliviano," *La Calle*, May 13, 1945; "Apuntes al vuelo en la clausura del congreso indigenal," *El Diario*, May 16, 1945.

90. "Con grandiosa sencillez se inauguró ayer el Primer Congreso de Indígenas," *La Calle*, May 11, 1945.

91. C.R.L., "Fruto del congreso ha sido humanizar el trabajo campesino y levantar la dignidad humana, nos dice el Ministro Monroy," *La Noche*, May 16, 1945, 5.

92. Quoted in Fernández Terán, "Prensa, radio e imaginario boliviano," 244.

93. Sierra, "Indigenous Neighborhood Residents," 167.

94. *La Calle* was founded in 1936 by Augusto Céspedes and Armando Arce as a Socialist Party organ and became associated with the MNR after the party's founding in 1941. It cost 50 percent less than the other daily papers in order to reach the masses. Knudson, *Bolivia*, 29, 39–41.

95. Capitalization in original. "No por ser sargento del ejército sino por indio lo han agredido en Milluguayo (Yungas)," *La Calle*, February 20, 1937.

96. Arze Aguirre, *Guerra y conflictos sociales*, 148.

CHAPTER 6: SOLDIERS AND VETERANS BUT STILL NOT CITIZENS

1. Tapia, *Ukhamawa jakawisaxa*, 17, 27, 65, 87, 97, 122–58.

2. Tapia, *Ukhamawa jakawisaxa*, 163. Similarly, miner Juan Rojas described arriving hours before dawn to queue up on recruitment day in January 1945. Nash, *I Spent My Life*, 56.

3. Tapia, *Ukhamawa jakawisaxa*, 171.

4. Corbett, "Military Institutional Development," 203; Alexander and Parker, *History of Organized Labor*, 113.

5. This estimate is drawn from the military registers for 1946 to 1952. Although none of the sets of registration sheets is complete for these years, I used averages per

registration location for the years in which the sets were complete or mostly complete to arrive at this number. The actual number of registrants is likely higher. Annual military registers, 1946–1952, RT-MDN. An army publication confirmed that conscription in 1942 produced over 15,554 recruits. Ejército Nacional—Ministerio de Defensa Nacional, *Prescripciones*, 30.

6. Percentage calculated based on Dirección General de Estadística y Censos, *Censo demográfico, 1950*, 46–55. Registration percentage for 1908 to 1912 from the Ministry of War reports are cited in table 1.1 and the male age cohorts are noted in the 1900 census. Oficina Nacional de Inmigración, Estadística, y Propaganda Geográfica, *Censo general*, 2:27.

7. Ejército Nacional—Ministerio de Defensa Nacional, *Prescripciones*, 31.

8. Ejército Nacional—Ministerio de Defensa Nacional, *Prescripciones*.

9. 1948–1949 Military Register, 148th sheet, RT-MDN.

10. I developed this narrative of conscription in the 1940s from the physical military register and conscription forms, both located in RT-MDN; Ejército Nacional—Ministerio de Defensa Nacional, *Prescripciones*; and Tapia, *Ukhamawa jakawisaxa*, 163.

11. The only other complete sets are from Cochabamba in January and Corocoro in July. Many other sets are missing a sheet here or there. Others are more fragmentary or completely absent. Only the last sheet from the city of Oruro made it, and the results of commissions' work in the cities of Potosí and Santa Cruz do not appear in the register. And only a few sheets include information on the lottery and to which units the new conscripts were sent. 1948–1949 Military Register, RT-MDN.

12. Tapia, *Ukhamawa jakawisaxa*, 163–64. Instructions for recruitment in 1943 explicitly prohibited commissions from picking the best conscripts, indicating that this practice was likely widespread. Ejército Nacional—Ministerio de Defensa Nacional, *Prescripciones*, 41.

13. La Paz produced 33.6 percent of conscripts as compared to 34.5 percent of men in the relevant age cohort reported in the 1950 census. Cochabamba had only 15 percent of men in the relevant age cohort but contributed 29 percent of conscripts. 1948–1949 Military Register, RT-MDN; Dirección General de Estadística y Censos, *Censo demográfico*, 46–55.

14. Gotkowitz, *Revolution for Our Rights*, 9–12; Larson, *Cochabamba*; Jackson, *Regional Markets*.

15. Precise rural/urban analysis is made difficult by the fact that recruiters sometimes entered the nearest canton rather than a specific community or hacienda for rural registrants. I thus analyzed the capital city of departments to make this claim. Because of the missing sheets for 1949, I cannot do a national-level analysis. The data for the departments of Cochabamba and La Paz are complete, however. They show that 51 percent of registrants from La Paz were from the capital city (as compared to 34 percent in the census) and that 28 percent of registrants from Cochabamba were from the departmental capital (as compared to 16.5 percent in the census). 1949

Military Register, RT-MDN; Dirección General de Estadística y Censos, *Censo demográfico*, 3–4.

16. Statistics based on a 20 percent sample of the extant military register sheets from each recruitment site for 1949 (both January and July recruitment). For example, one of several commissions in the city of Cochabamba recorded the names of 1,022 men on 32 sheets. I randomly sampled 7 of these sheets for a total of 205 names. 1949 Military Register, RT-MDN.

17. Smale, *"I Sweat the Flavor of Tin,"* 28–32. For an example, see Tapia, *Ukhamawa jakawisaxa,* 17–38. Miner and activist Félix Muruchi reports that in the 1960s many miners lied about their profession when enlisting because of the stigma against them as leftists. Kohl, Farthing, and Muruchi, *From the Mines,* 45–46.

18. Extrapolation from the 20 percent sample indicates that around 13,200 men listed as literate registered in 1949. The 1950 census reports that around 13,400 men belonging to the relevant age cohort were literate. 1949 Military Register, RT-MDN. Census literacy statistics calculated from Dirección General de Estadística y Censos, *Censo demográfico,* 112–13.

19. Military service booklet of Walter Murillo Salcedo, 1940, personal collection of Rosa Marina Murillo, La Paz, Bolivia.

20. On migration see Sierra, "Indigenous Neighborhood Residents," especially 127, 165–70, 192–96. For an overview of the artisans and other workers in Bolivia's cities and rural towns, see Lehm A. and Rivera Cusicanqui, *Los artesanos libertarios.*

21. The 1950 census reported that 28 percent of men had at least a first-grade education and that 34 percent lived in urban areas. Dirección General de Estadística y Censos, *Censo demográfico,* 116–21.

22. Gotkowitz, *Revolution for Our Rights,* 114–30; Klein, *Parties and Political Change,* 276–91.

23. Klein, *Parties and Political Change,* 284–85.

24. Gotkowitz, *Revolution for Our Rights,* 117–20. Rossana Barragán reports that the assembly "never questioned" the principal of restricted voting. Barragán, *Asambleas constituyentes,* 130. For statistics on voting requirements in Latin America, see Hartlyn and Valenzuela, "Democracy in Latin America," 132.

25. Galindo de Ugarte, *Constituciones bolivianas,* 108.

26. Averanga Mollinedo, *Aspectos generales de la población boliviana,* 137.

27. Barragán, *Asambleas constituyentes,* 132.

28. Minister of Foreign Relations Tomás Manuel Elio speech, August 31, 1943, in Bolivia, *Redactor de la H. Cámara de Diputados,* 1:474.

29. General Angel Rodriguez, *Ultima Hora,* May 9, 1944. Translated and quoted in "Digest of Clippings from Bolivia," box 49, folder 39—Bolivia General, Papers of Robert Jackson Alexander, Rutgers University Libraries (hereafter RUL/MC974).

30. Thirty-sixth ordinary session, September 20, 1941, in Bolivia, *Redactor de la H. Cámara de Diputados,* 2:17.

31. Quotation from Lt. Acio, "El ejército, como redentor del indio," *Revista Militar* 13–14 (1938): 84. A series of articles with such arguments was published between February and October of 1938. Similar articles were also published during the Peñaranda and Villarroel administrations.

32. Lt. Acio, "El ejército, como redentor del indio." *Corregidors* administer cantons.

33. My. Ricardo Goitia, "El factor indio, dentro de las filas del Ejército," *Revista Militar* 19–20 (1938): 568.

34. Lt. Col. Roberto Olmos, "La labor actual del Ejército," *Revista Militar* 21–22 (1938): 789, 791.

35. Lt. Luis Ramos Arce, "El official piscólogo," *Revista Militar* 21–22 (1938): 769–71.

36. Lt. Col. Carlos Nuñez del Prado, "Grandezas y pequeñeces—El centinela," *Revista Militar* 14 (1905): 136–46.

37. Lt. Guillermo García, "Instructores e instruidos," *Revista Militar* 57–58 (1942): 95–101.

38. Lt. Col. Clarence W. Bennett, US Military Attaché, report on morale and welfare, May 3, 1941, and report on military posts, April 28, 1941, RG-165, NM-84–77, box 187, folder 6000-6420; Lt. Col. Clarence W. Bennett, US Military Attaché, report on current events, November 4, 1942, RG-165, NM 84-77, box 188, folder 8000-9940; memo on foreign military publications, February 12, 1943, RG-165, NM 84-77, box 176, folder 2810, all in NARA. Military justice records support these assertions; see Primo A. Rodriguez statement, September 13, 1939, DEL-14-003; Francisco Toledo statement, June 12, 1951, DES-24-013, both in TPJM-AHM.

39. Forty-second ordinary session, September 27, 1941, in Bolivia, *Redactor de la H. Cámara de Diputados*, 2:127–29; twenty-first ordinary session, September 1, 1942, in Bolivia, *Redactor de la H. Cámara de Diputados*, 1:332–39; twentieth ordinary session, September 10, 1947, in Bolivia, *Redactor de la H. Cámara de Diputados*, 1:432–42.

40. Sof. Saturnino Torrico statement, October 22, 1940, DES-21-007, TPJM-AHM.

41. Maj. Jorge Mauri and Sra. Jacinto Torres Zeballos statements, April 23, 1947, DES-22-015, TPJM-AHM.

42. Maj. José Pinto, commander of Abaroa Regiment, to president of military tribunal, February 27, 1940, MUE-69-013, TPJM-AHM.

43. See, for example, Mario Dueñas statement, April 19, 1947, DES-22-014, TPJM-AHM.

44. Zapadores Hoja de Servicio no. 039933, August 28, 1944, RT-MDN.

45. Military Attaché Report: Bolivia, June 9, 1944, RG 165, NM 84-77, box 191, folder MA Reports vol. 2; Military Attaché Report: Bolivia, June 17, 1942, box 189, folder 971-9965, both in NARA.

46. See, for example, conclusions of examining magistrate, April 19, 1947, DES-22-014, TPJM-AHM.

47. My. Hugo Arteaga and Capt. Walter Castellón statements, April 20, 1948, ACC-07-007, TPJM-AHM.

48. Supreme decree of April 8, 1940, in Bolivia, *Gaceta oficial* (1940).

49. Respective quotations from conclusions of auditor de guerra, May 6, 1947, DES-23-005, and conclusions of examining magistrate, March 12, 1946, ABG-05-010, both in TPJM-AHM.

50. My. Ricardo Herbas speech to Regimiento Ayacucho and Escuadrón Divisionario, published in "El día del ejército en caiza," *Revista Militar* 19–20 (1938): 723. For more on Herbas, see his response to a pro-Toro tract in which he details his own actions in the Chaco and against Toro at El Palmar. Herbas P., *Una página de la historia?*.

51. As E. Gabrielle Kuenzli has shown, this appropriation of the pre-colonial indigenous past was typical in the liberal period. Kuenzli, *Acting Inca*, 56–85. However, it seems not to have extended to the military; I have found no references in military publications to indigenous heroes prior to 1938.

52. On the differences among these three leaders, see Serulnikov, *Subverting Colonial Authority*; Thomson, *We Alone Will Rule*; Walker, *Tupac Amaru Rebellion*.

53. Conclusion based on the 512 conscripts who gave testimony in the 139 cases from 1937 to 1952 that I examined. Fifteen percent of witnesses whose literacy status was identified were completely illiterate as compared to only 7 percent prior to the war. In addition to signing their names, 17 percent from the later period self-identified as literate when asked during testimony. Sixty-five percent were not asked about their literacy status but could at least sign their names. The remaining 2 percent said they could read or write "a little." Of the small number (forty-four) of those identified by race, 43 percent were labeled as indigenous. See boxes 2–3, 5, 7, 21–25, 34, 39, 42, 50–52, 56, 59, 69, 71, 74, 86, 88, 94, and 97. For the most salient examples, see MUE-69-011 (1939), ABG-05-004 (1942), ABG-05-005 (1943), and ACC-07-007 (1948), TPJM-AHM.

54. Conclusion based on fifty-seven desertion and suicide cases between 1937 and 1951, boxes 5, 21–25, and 96, TPJM-AHM.

55. See, for example, the case of deserter Juan Nuñez Lopez, DES-23-004 (1947), TPMJ-AHM.

56. Art. 87 (b), Constitución política de la República de Bolivia, 1868 and 1880, in Galindo de Ugarte, *Constituciones bolivianas*, 608.

57. Military service booklet of Hugo Murillo, 1941, personal collection of Rosa Marina Murillo, La Paz, Bolivia.

58. Art. 169 (b), Constitución política de la República de Bolivia, October 30, 1938. This clause remained unchanged until 1961. See Galindo de Ugarte, *Constituciones bolivianos*, 608–9.

59. One hundred and twenty-eighth session, October 24, 1938, in Bolivia, *Redac-*

tor de la H. Convención Nacional, 5:325.

60. Ley de zapadores, October 29, 1939. See also "Las granjas agrícolas del ejército nacional," *Revista Militar* 31–32 (1939): 883.

61. Index of service sheets, RT-MDN.

62. Commander of 1st Military Region to Prefect of La Paz, no. 210, May 3, 1941, Prefecture-Admin 209, ALP.

63. "El año militar," *Revista Militar* 135–37 (1949): 107–9.

64. Capt. Hugo Suarez Guzman, "Crónica sobre la construcción de Escuela Modelo Ricardo Mujia en Sucre," *Revista Militar* 154 (1950): 35–47.

65. "El camino de Padcaya a Fortín Campero," *El Diario,* June 12, 1936, 8.

66. Ejército Nacional—Ministerio de Defensa Nacional, *Prescripciones,* 31.

67. Prefect of La Paz to Jefe del Estado Mayor General, August 10 and 17, 1938, transcribing telegrams from the municipal mayor and subprefect, Prefecture-Admin box 209, ALP.

68. "Conscriptos enrolados," *El Diario,* February 4, 1947, 6.

69. For examples, see PER-74-001 (1940), SUP-97-004 (1942), ROB-86-006 (1942), ABA-03-003 (1944), and HER-52-002 (1945), TPJM-AHM. See also the notice printed in newspapers that warned residents of the La Paz department to carry with them at all times their military service documents, or, in the case of minors, documents proving their age. "Aviso militar," *La Calle,* March 18, 1943.

70. Juan Prudencio Aczara statement, April 18, 1947, DES-22-013, TPJM-AHM.

71. Juana Valencia to commander of first military region, October 31, 1950, DES-24-001, TPJM-AHM.

72. Captain Humberto Fernández Gavizo statement, October 29, 1942, PER-74-005, TPJM-AHM.

73. "Chocolate" is used as both a noun and a verb by witnesses in military justice proceedings. Definition of "chocolate" from Nash, *I Spent My Life,* 63; García Prada, *El ejército y la revolución,* 156; Prado Salmón, *Defendete,* 33, 124. Testimony regarding this punishment in DES-24-008 (1931), PER-74-005 (1942), and DES-24-013 (1951), TPJM-AHM.

74. Lorenzo Espejo Canda statement, October 29, 1942, PER-74-005, TPJM-AHM.

75. Conclusions of magistrate, November 10, 1942, PER-74-005, TPJM-AHM. For other examples of physical punishments from this era, see FAS-42-012 (1938), MUE-69-014 (1939), PER-74-005 (1942), ADA-03-001 (1944), MOT-71-005 (1946), HOM-24-008 (1950), and DES-24-013 (1951), TPJM-AHM.

76. Tapia, *Ukhamawa jakawisaxa,* 166–68; Nash, *I Spent My Life,* 57.

77. Lt. Jamie Dalenz Tapia report transcribed in Col. Hugo Ballivián to Commander of Armed Forces, July 29, 1947, FDI-42-005, TPJM-AHM. Referring to the white gloves that cadets wore, civilians used the term "margarita" to insult them. Prado confirms that cadets also used the insult to question their peers' masculinity. Prado Salmón, *Defendete,* 39.

78. Nemecio Villarroel Caballero statement, August 19, 1946, SED-94-012, TPJM-AHM.

79. Cabo Alejandro Mamani Choque statement, March 15, 1940, INS-59-015, TPJM-AHM.

80. For an in-depth exploration of masculinity and military service in post-1952 Bolivia, see Gill, "Creating Citizens, Making Men."

81. Nash, *I Spent My Life*, 63. Gill, "Creating Citizens, Making Men," 536.

82. Gotkowitz, *Revolution for Our Rights*, 151.

83. Quoted in and translated by Ari, *Earth Politics*, 120–21. *Jalqa* refers to an ethnic group that emerged in the second half of the nineteenth century from the intermixing of Aymara and Uru communities. Ari describes the physical markers of *jalqa* identity as being "long braids, colorful poncho, sheep's wool pants, and llama sandals." *Earth Politics*, 64, 119.

84. Tapia, *Ukhamawa jakawisaxa*, 172. Gill describes the hispanicization of surnames as a common practice among recruits in the 1980s and 1990s. Gill, "Creating Citizens, Making Men," 537.

85. Nash, *I Spent My Life*, 65–66, 70–72. Quotation from 72.

86. Tapia, *Ukhamawa jakawisaxa*, 164.

87. Tapia, *Ukhamawa jakawisaxa*, 163–73.

88. Ramón Caucota Bejarano statement, November 11, 1950, HOM-50-002, TPJM-AHM.

89. Dámasco [illegible: _aíbo] Lupe statement, July 4, 1938, SUI-97-004, TPJM-AHM.

90. Cabo Teófilo Negrete statement, April 30, 1938, MUE-69-007, TPJM-AHM.

91. For examples, see ABA-03-001 (1944), ABG-05-004 (1941), and INS-59-015 (1940), TPJM-AHM.

92. Lt. Col. Clarence W. Bennett, US Military Attaché, "Duties of Division G-1," June 25, 1942, RG 165, NM 84-77, box 191, folder Misc. Bolivia, NARA; Lt. Vicente Antezana report, February 3, 1951, DES-24-012; Dgte. Wálter Lea Plaza Pérez statement, August 26, 1951, HOM-50-005, both in TPJM-AHM.

93. Ernesto Laredo Torrico statement, December 18, 1950, HOM-50-001, TPJM-AHM.

94. *Ultima Hora*, January 10, 1947.

95. For examples, see INS-59-015 (1940), PER-74-001 (1940), ABG-05-002 (1941), ABA-02-009 (1942), PER-74-002 (1942), HUR-56-006 (1942), ABG-05-007 (1943), ABG-05-008 (1945), DES-22-013 (1947), and DES-22-013 (1947), TPJM-AHM.

96. Cabo Maximiliano Concha Avenado statement, January 15, 1942, ABG-05-003, TPJM-AHM.

97. Reinaldo Rodoy Tudela statement, October 2, 1951, DES-25-007, TPJM-AHM.

98. Prado Salmón, *Poder y fuerzas armadas*, 42; Klein, *Parties and Political Change*, 383. For a narrative of the coup and subsequent discharges, see DES-22-005, TPJM-AHM.

99. Written declaration of Alejandro Esperella y P., October 22, 1946, DES-22-005, TPJM-AHM; Dorn, *Truman Administration and Bolivia*, 52.

100. Capt. Simón La Rosa statement, September 23, 1946, MOT-71-005; DES-22-005 (1946), both in TPJM-AHM.

101. Quotations from Sub. Lt. Gustavo Monje Maldonado statement, June 12, 1951, DES-24-013, TPJM-AHM. See also Alberto Ferreira Cossio statement, October 8, 1946, MOT-71-005, TPJM-AHM.

102. Capt. Simón La Rosa and Sub. Lt. Froilán Cadima statements, September 23, 1946; conclusions of examining magistrate, September 23, 1946, MOT-71-005, both in TPJM-AHM.

103. René Busch Cabrera statement, October 11, 1946, MOT-71-005, TPJM-AHM. The constituent assembly convened under Villarroel received a petition on November 20, 1945, from Justina Cabrera asking them to grant her son René Busch Cabrera a scholarship to pursue his studies. Bolivia, *Informes de Comisiones*, 2:768.

104. René Busch Cabrera statement, October 11, 1946, MOT-71-005, TPJM-AHM.

105. Jorge Raznatovich statement, September 23, 1946, MOT-71-005, TPJM-AHM.

106. Federico Orozsa, Sarg. René Michel Portocarreo, and René Busch Cabrera statements, September 22 and 26 and October 11, 1946; conclusions of examining magistrate, September 23, 1946, all in MOT-71-005, TPJM-AHM.

107. Alberto Ferreira Cossio and René Busch Cabrera statements, October 8 and 11, 1946, MOT-71-005, TPJM-AHM.

108. "Ha sido debelado con toda energía un movimiento de insubordinación en el Loa," *El Diario*, September 24, 1946.

109. Conclusions of auditor de guerra, December 6, 1946 MOT-71-005, TPJM-AHM.

110. See boxes 19–22, TPJM-AHM.

111. Pacífico Burgoa to Chief of Military District in Puerto Acosta (La Paz), June 14, 1940; Ramón Sossa statement, November 25, 1940; Military Tribunal President to the Chief of Military District, November 25, 1940, all in DES-21-008, TPJM-AHM.

112. Antonio Choque-Vara to Chief of Staff, June 28, 1939, DES-21-004, TPJM-AHM.

113. Rufino Chipana letter, February 5, 1944, DES-21-022, TPJM-AHM.

114. See letters dated July 25 and December 22, 1939, and July 4 and September 16, 1940, DES-21-000; telegrams and letters dated March 6 and December 18, 1944, and April 4, 1945, DES-21-022, both in TPJM-AHM.

115. Mateo Torrez Mamani to Commander of 1st Military Zone, May 29, 1945, DES-22-003, TPJM-AHM.

116. Carlos Mamani statement, June 26, 1945, DES-22-003, AMH-TPJM.

117. Mateo Torrez Mamani to military tribunal, October 5, 1945, TPJM-AHM.

118. See José Valdéz to Prefect of La Paz, June 14, 1914, Prefecture-Exped box 196, d. 25, ALP.

CHAPTER 7: WHAT DIFFERENCE DID A REVOLUTION MAKE?

1. Dunkerley, *Rebellion in the Veins*, 3–4; Murillo, *La bala no mata sino el destino*, 136–40.

2. Max Aguirre Calderón quoted in Dávila and Silva J., *Historia oral de los barrios paceños*, 21.

3. Brill, "Military Civic Action," 76–78; Lehman, *Bolivia and the United States*, 91–92; Dunkerley, *Rebellion in the Veins*, 38–39.

4. This attempt is narrated and analyzed in First Secretary David Muirhead to Foreign Office, no. 21, February 24, 1949, FO 371/74501, TNA.

5. Dorn, *Truman Administration and Bolivia*, 100–101; Prado Salmón, *Los militares y la revolución nacional*, 98; Seleme Vargas, *Memorias del Gral. Antonio Seleme Vargas*, 38–39; Corbett, *Latin American Military*, 27. Reports on the progress of the civil war are given in three communications from First Secretary David Muirhead to Foreign Office, September 7, 14, and 16, 1949, FO 371/74502, TNA. Detailed narrations of the events in Cochabamba and Potosí are available in C. Fraser Elliott to L. B. Pearson, September 1, 1949, FO 371/74502, and First Secretary David Muirhead to Foreign Office, no. 146E, September 9, 1949, FO 371/74512, TNA.

6. Seleme had been Paz Estenssoro's commander in the Chaco. Mitchell, *Legacy of Populism*, 32.

7. Brill, "Military Civic Action," 73–78.

8. Dunkerley, *Rebellion in the Veins*, 48.

9. Dunkerley, *Rebellion in the Veins*, 15.

10. Andrade, "História, arte e política," 147–54; Montoya, "La revolución nacional."

11. Prado Salmón, *Poder y fuerzas armadas*, 43–44, 47; Dunkerley, *Rebellion in the Veins*, 49–50.

12. Prado Salmón, *Poder y fuerzas armadas*, 40; Field Jr., *From Development to Dictatorship*, 215n269.

13. Prado Salmón, *Poder y fuerzas armadas*, 41. Within weeks of coming to power, the MNR reinstated fifty-three officers who had been forcibly retired due to suspected or real ties to Radepa or the party. See Corbett, *Latin American Military*, 27; Mitchell, *Legacy of Populism*, 52.

14. The figure of 166 comes from Prado, based on specific general orders. Prado Salmón, *Poder y fuerzas armadas*, 40, 44–45, 51. Citing an interview with General

Ovando, Brill estimates that one to two hundred were dismissed. Brill, "Military Civic Action," 81. Knudson gives a figure of three hundred based on a 1955 interview with Víctor Paz. Knudson, *Press and Revolution*, 320.

15. Knudson, *Press and Revolution*, 320.

16. Prado Salmón, *Poder y fuerzas armadas*, 47–48.

17. Wilkie, *Bolivian Revolution*, 22.

18. Corbett, *Latin American Military*, 29; Alexander and Parker, *History of Organized Labor*, 113.

19. 1952 military register; seventy-three service sheets sampled from Sucre Second Infantry, Pérez Third Infantry, Campos Sixth Infantry, Montes Seventh Infantry, Warnes Tenth Infantry, Camacho First Artillery, Bolivar Second Artillery, Veraga Third Artillery, Ballivián Second Cavalry, Riberalta Battalion, First Detachment Andino, Sixth Agricultural Detachment, Second Military Shipyard, and Monte Punco Sapper Company, 1952, all in RT-MDN.

20. Ambassador John Garnett Lomax to Foreign Office, no. 12, January 20, 1953, FO 371/103625, TNA.

21. Corbett, *Latin American Military*, 31–32.

22. Prado Salmón, *Poder y fuerzas armadas*, 66, 69, 73, 97.

23. 1953 military register; seventy-three service sheets sampled from Sucre Second Infantry, Pérez Third Infantry, Campos Sixth Infantry, Montes Seventh Infantry, Warnes Tenth Infantry, Camacho First Artillery, Bolivar Second Artillery, Veraga Third Artillery, Ballivián Second Cavalry, Riberalta Battalion, First Detachment Andino, Sixth Agricultural Detachment, Second Military Shipyard, and Monte Punco Sapper Company, 1952, all in RT-MDN; military justice proceedings from TPJM-AHM.

24. "El nuevo regimen gubernamental," *Revista Militar* 174–75 (1952): 5–6.

25. Quintana Taborga, *Policía y democracia*, 38–45.

26. Dirección Nacional de Informaciones, *Bolivia: 10 años de revolución*, 239; Prado Salmón, *Poder y fuerzas armadas*, 49.

27. For narration of coup attempts in January, July, and November 1953, see Gordillo, *Campesinos revolucionarios*, 59, 69–72, 74; Prado Salmón, *Poder y fuerzas armadas*, 50–51. For an additional attempt in June 1953 by the Bolivian Socialist Falange (FSB), some retired officers, and some leading *carabineros*, see Ambassador John Garnett Lomax to Foreign Office, no. 54, June 29, 1953, FO 371/103626, TNA.

28. See estimates ranging from thirty thousand to seventy thousand in Marquis of Salisbury to Foreign Office enclosing memo by Victor Cecil, November 6, 1953, FO 371/103626; Ambassador J. Garnett Lomax report on labor affairs in November 1953, n.d., LAB 13/1082, TNA; Blasier, "United States and the Revolution," 94.

29. Dunkerley, *Rebellion in the Veins*, 49.

30. "Milicias armadas mineras vigilan el orden público de la ciudad," *La Nación*, August 4, 1953.

31. Knudson, *Press and Revolution*, 316.

32. On *bayeta de la tierra*, see Ari, *Earth Politics*, 228.

33. Lora, *History of the Bolivian Labour Movement*, 284. Although dating from the Chaco War, these rifles were in current use by the Bolivian army. My thanks to Professors Kyle Sinisi and Paul Johstono for assistance in identifying the rifles.

34. Quotation from "El presidente posesionó al comando del Regimiento Campesino Villarroel," *La Nación*, May 20, 1954. For other examples see "Milicias armadas mineras vigilan el orden público de la ciudad," *La Nación*, August 4, 1953; "Ayer realizó concentración el reg. Campesino Hernando Siles," *La Nación*, August 18, 1953; "Dos nuevos regimientos campesinos," *La Nación*, April 15, 1954; "Nuevo Regimiento de campesinos," *La Nación*, June 10, 1954; "Prestó juramento de lealtad el Regimiento Campesino de Sorata," *La Nación*, June 29, 1954. The article about the Hernando Siles Regiment clarified that it was named in honor of Vice President Hernán Siles's father, who had been president from 1926 to 1930 and had done much for the Murillo Province.

35. Prado Salmón, *Poder y fuerzas armadas*, 52–54. *La Nación* reported that the COB accepted this proposal in "Coordinarán actividades milicias obreras y el ejército nacional," August 14, 1953.

36. Prado Salmón, *Poder y fuerzas armadas*, 75.

37. "El regimiento Ballivián nacido de la revolución, celebra su aniversario," *La Nación*, May 10, 1954.

38. "Una síntesis de la labor del Reg. Félix Soria en ciudad de Oruro," *La Nación*, June 3, 1954; "Se formó un ejército de la revolución a semejanza de ejército rojo de Rusia," *El Diario*, October 26, 1957. On its namesake, see Cajías, *Historia de una leyenda*, 148–49.

39. Testimony of soldiers from unit recorded in HUR-56-10 (1954), TP-JM-AHM; Ambassador J. Garnett Lomax report on labor affairs in August 1953, n.d., LAB 13/1082, TNA; "Solemnemente fue celebrado el aniversario del Reg. Escolta Mayor Waldo Ballivián," *Revista Militar* 158–59 (1953): 186–87; "Me encuentro feliz porque podré defender bien a nuestro gobierno," *La Nación*, May 9, 1954; "Se formó un ejército de la revolución a semejanza de ejército rojo de Rusia," *El Diario*, October 26, 1957.

40. Testimony of Francisco Quispe Cuellar, April 30, 1954, HUR-56-10, TPJM-AHM.

41. "Guardia militar en los edificios comerciantes de las tres empresas," *La Nación*, October 31, 1952.

42. Ambassador J. Garnett Lomax report on labor affairs in August 1953, n.d., LAB 13/1082, TNA. See also Ambassador John Garnett Lomax to Foreign Office, Annual Review for 1953, January 5, 1954, FO 371/109218, TNA.

43. Knudson, *Press and Revolution*, 298.

44. Víctor Paz Estenssoro, "Mensaje del Presidente Constitucional de la Rep. de Bolivia," *Revista Militar* 188–94 (1952): 18.

45. Supreme decree n. 3468 of July 24, 1953, in Bolivia, *Gaceta oficial* (1953).

46. Supreme decree n. 3468 of July 24, 1953.

47. Supreme decree n. 3468 of July 24, 1953; Knudson, *Press and Revolution*, 307–8.

48. Prado Salmón, *Poder y fuerzas armadas*, 61.

49. Prado Salmón, *Poder y fuerzas armadas*, 54–55.

50. Quoted in Prado Salmón, *Poder y fuerzas armadas*, 55–56.

51. Prado Salmón, *Poder y fuerzas armadas*, 55, 57.

52. Brill, "Military Civic Action," 120.

53. "Profundo sentido Revolucionario adquirió la Jura a la Bandera," *La Nación*, August 9, 1953.

54. *El Diario*, June 4, 1953, quoted in Barrios Morón, "El nacionalism militar boliviano," 41.

55. Quotation from Capt. Remberto Iriarte Paz, "El Ejército nacional de Bolivia con mando y técnica," *Revista Militar* 178–82 (1952): 7.

56. *Revista Militar* 178–82 (1952): 90.

57. "El camino Coroico-Caranavi estará a cargo del ejército de la revolución," *La Nación*, November 11, 1952, 5.

58. "El Regimiento Colorados realiza eficaz labor de beneficio público," *La Nación*, May 8, 1954; "Varias obras públicas ejecutaron unidades del Ejército," *La Nación*, June 21, 1954; "Actividad territorial y desarrollo de la exposición agrícola ganadera de Challapata," *Revista Militar* 199–200 (1954): 70.

59. Lt. Col. Hugo Antezana, "El camino al Ichilo," *Revista Militar* 246–48 (1961): 81–85.

60. Arts. 23 and 58, law of December 20, 1963, in Bolivia, *Gaceta oficial* (1963).

61. "La Región Militar no. 5 ayuda al autoabastecimiento," *La Nación*, May 19, 1954; "Activa labor de la Región Militar No. 5 en el Oriente," *La Nación*, June 7, 1954.

62. For examples see Víctor Paz Estenssoro, "Mensaje del Presidente Constitucional de la Rep. de Bolivia," *Revista Militar* 188–94 (1952): 18–19; "Historia de un soldado-colono," *La Nación*, July 28, 1956; "Historiando algo con respeto a la película 'Ofensiva de Paz,'" *La Nación*, August 15, 1958.

63. Joaquin de Lemoine, "Proyecto de Migraciones Internas," July 3, 1957, 34 Bolivia—General, RUL/MC974; Dirección Nacional de Informaciones, *Bolivia: 10 años de revolución*, 147.

64. "Historia de un soldado-colono."

65. "Historiando algo con respeto a la película 'Ofensiva de Paz.'" The film was directed by Víctor Paz's brother-in-law, the filmmaker Waldo Cerruto. From 1952 until 1956, Cerruto served as director of the Instituto Cinematográfico Bolivano, a semiautonomous institution overseen by the government and charged with making cultural and educational materials for Bolivian and international audiences. Sánchez H., *Art and Politics*, 31–33.

66. Loveman and Davies Jr., *Politics of Antipolitics*, 7–8.

67. Respective quotations from "Actividades del ejército de la Revolución Nacional," *Revista Militar* 184–85 (1953): 111; Col. Clemente Inofuentes, "Necesitamos un ejército que sea síntesis del anhelo popular," *Revista Militar* 184–85 (1953): 67.

68. My. Elka, "La vialidad y el ejército nacional," *Revista Militar* 174–75 (1952): 15.

69. Data drawn from 20 percent sample of extant military register sheets from each recruitment site. Only seven men identified as miners in the 1949 sample. In 1955, that number was sixty-six. 1955 military register, RT-MDN.

70. Data drawn from 20 percent sample of extant military register sheets from each recruitment site for 1955. This increase corresponded with a decrease in artisans (from 24 percent to 20 percent) and men working in transportation (from 16 percent to 12 percent). Other indicators were surprisingly static. Again, around sixteen thousand men registered from all the departments except Pando, the exact same percentage (83) was recorded as being literate, and other professional categories changed no more than one percentage point. 1955 military register, RT-MDN.

71. Quoted in and translated by Knudson, *Press and Revolution*, 311.

72. Joaquin de Lemoine, "Proyecto de Migraciones Internas," July 3, 1957, Bolivia—General, RUL/MC974.

73. "Comenzó hoy el reclutamiento de los conscriptos de la categoría de 1959," *Última Hora*, May 12, 1959.

74. Carter and Mamani, *Irpa Chico*, 373.

75. Buechler and Buechler, *Bolivian Aymara*, 34–36, 49, 80. Quotations from 35.

76. Kevin Young argues that the MNR gained support for its austerity measures by reorienting its "revolutionary identity" to focus on peasants, the middle class, and the army rather than miners and urban workers. Young, *Blood of the Earth*, 91, 107.

77. Albó, "And from Kataristas to MNRistas?," 383–85; Gotkowitz, *Revolution for Our Rights*, 269–71.

78. Dandler and Torrico, "Bolivia, 1945–1947," 358–75; Gotkowitz, *Revolution for Our Rights*, 130.

79. The population expanded from 150,000 in 1935 to 350,000 in 1950. Sierra, "Indigenous Neighborhood Residents," especially chapter 4. Statistic from 176.

80. "El camino Coroico-Caranavi estará a cargo del ejército de la revolución," *La Nación*, November 12, 1952.

81. Lt. Col. Ristell, "El año militar podrá comenzar el 1.º de julio y terminar el 31 de mayo de cada año," *Revista Militar* 199–200 (1954): 34.

82. Col. Armando Prudencio, "El ejército vuelve a ser el mejor amigo del pueblo," *Revista Militar* 197–98 (1954): 173.

83. Prado Salmón, *Poder y fuerzas armadas*, 74.

84. Respective quotations from Army Chief of Staff General Armando Fortún Sanjinés, "El segundo aniversario de la Revolución de abril y la tecnificación de las FF.AA.," *La Nación*, April 9, 1954; *La Nación*, July 5, 1955, quoted in and translated by Knudson, *Press and Revolution*, 310–11.

85. My. Alberto Candia Almaraz, "Ejército, como factor básico de la estructuración de la patria," *Revista Militar* 183 (1953): 27.

86. Quoted in and translated by Knudson, *Press and Revolution*, 310–11.

87. For the most salient examples, see MUE-71-009 (1953), HER-52-012 (1953), HOM-50-008 (1953), and SED-94-013 (1954), TPJM-AHM.

88. Juan Acarapi Mamani statement, May 1, 1953, MUE-71-009, TPJM-AHM. Félix Muruchi similarly reports that peasant recruits in his unit were assigned to farm labor and denied training. Kohl, Farthing, and Muruchi, *From the Mines to the Streets*, 45.

89. For a detailed analysis of US support for the Bolivian military during the Kennedy era, see Field Jr., *From Development to Dictatorship*.

90. Ambassador John Garnett Lomax to Foreign Office, no. 35, June 21, 1956, FO 371/120453, TNA; Knudson, *Press and Revolution*, 317.

91. Dunkerley, *Rebellion in the Veins*, 86; Young, *Blood of the Earth*, 66–67.

92. Blasier, "United States and the Revolution," 390.

93. Blasier, *Hovering Giant*, 143–44. Blasier notes that perhaps Israel received a higher level of aid.

94. Lora, *History of the Bolivian Labour Movement*, 302, 307.

95. Lehman, *Bolivia and the United States*, 148. For more details of this encounter, see Lehman, "US Foreign Aid," 614–15.

96. Air Attaché to Lima Group Captain R.B. Ward 1953 report on Bolivian Air Force, February 5, 1954, FO 371/109228, TNA. Corbett asserts that seven officers attended in 1954, while Prado Salmón writes that twelve participated as observers. Corbett, "Military Institutional Development," 404; Prado Salmón, *Poder y fuerzas armadas*, 99. Early relations between the US military and the MNR need further research. Kirkland's account of military attachés picks up the story in 1958. Kirkland, *Observing our Hermanos de Armas*.

97. Lehman, *Bolivia and the United States*, 148–49; Kirkland, "United States Assistance," 37–38; Siekmeier, *Bolivian Revolution and the United States*, 81.

98. Kirkland, "United States Assistance," 39.

99. Dunkerley, *Rebellion in the Veins*, 114.

100. Hudson and Hanratty, *Bolivia*, 227.

101. Lehman, "US Foreign Aid," 627–28.

102. Arze Cuadros, *Bolivia, el programa del MNR*, 130; Aramayo, "Intellectual Origins," 267; Prado Salmón, *Poder y fuerzas armadas*, 75–76; Corbett, *Latin American Military*, 27, 30. See series of articles published under Inofuentes's byline in the *Revista Militar* from 1953 to 1955.

103. Lora, *History of the Bolivian Labour Movement*, 303–4, 309.

104. British Embassy in La Paz to Foreign Office, August 12, 1957, FO 371/126789; Ambassador J. Thyne Henderson to Selwyn Lloyd in Foreign Office, no. 77, October 14, 1957, FO 371/126803, both in TNA; supreme decree no. 4743 of September 26, 1957, in Bolivia, *Gaceta oficial* (1957); Prado Salmón, *Poder y fuerzas armadas*, 41.

105. Narrative drawn from Ambassador J. Thyne Henderson to Selwyn Lloyd in Foreign Office, no. 77, October 14, 1957, FO 371/126803; British Embassy in La Paz to Foreign Office, November 11, 1957, FO 371/126789, both in TNA; "Un pequeño grupo de jefes y oficiales desconoció al nuevo comandante en jefe," *El Diario*, October 4, 1957; Prado Salmón, *Poder y fuerzas armadas*, 77–80.

106. "Con la rendición incondicional de jefes y oficiales del cuartel general se puso fin al impasse militar," *El Diario*, October 5, 1957.

107. Ambassador J. Thyne Henderson to H. A. Hankey in Foreign Office, October 29, 1957, FO 371/126789, TNA; Prado Salmón, *Poder y fuerzas armadas*, 80. See also supreme decrees 4747 of October 3, 1957 and 4870 of February 21, 1958 appointing new chiefs of staff, in Bolivia, *Gaceta oficial* (1957, 1958).

108. Prado Salmón, *Poder y fuerzas armadas*, 76.

109. First quotation from British Embassy in La Paz to Foreign Office, August 12, 1957, FO 371/126789; second quotation from Ambassador J. Thyne Henderson to Selwyn Lloyd in Foreign Office, no. 77, October 14, 1957, FO 371/126803, both in TNA.

110. On National Security Doctrine, see Pion-Berlin, "National-Security Doctrine," 386–92; Fitch, *Armed Forces and Democracy*, 106–12.

111. Kirkland, "United States Assistance," 40.

112. Quotation from Ambassador J. Thyne Henderson to Selwyn Lloyd in Foreign Office, no. 8, January 24, 1958, FO 371/132453. For narrative, see P. H. Scott to Selwyn Lloyd in Foreign Office, no. 73, August 26, 1958, TNA; supreme decree no. 5145, February 14, 1959, in Bolivia, *Gaceta oficial* (1959).

113. P. H. Scott to Selwyn Lloyd in Foreign Office, no. 73, August 26, 1958, TNA; supreme decree no. 5145, February 14, 1959.

114. On the failure to achieve quotas, see Brill, *Military Intervention in Bolivia*, 29–30.

115. Ambassador J. Thyne Henderson to Selwyn Lloyd in Foreign Office, no. 77, October 14, 1957, FO 371/126803, TNA.

116. Ambassador J. Thyne Henderson to Selwyn Lloyd in Foreign Office, no. 85, November 4, 1957, FO 371/126803, TNA.

117. Prado Salmón, *Poder y fuerzas armadas*, 99–101.

118. Young, *Blood of the Earth*, 97.

119. Prado Salmón, *Poder y fuerzas armadas*, 83–91.

120. Kirkland, "United States Assistance," 40.

121. "Chaos in the Clouds," *Time*, March 2, 1959, 25. The final and most incendiary part of the quotation was apparently included only in the international version of the article. However, it did appear in the translated version in *El Diario*: "Texto de la publicación efectuada por 'Time,'" March 1, 1959. Lehman, *Bolivia and the United States*, 114–15, 150, 250n111.

122. "Fuerzas regulares del ejército supervigilan las instalaciones de YPFB en La Paz y Santa Cruz," *Última Hora*, April 17, 1959.

123. Malloy, *Bolivia*, 241.

124. Mitchell, *Legacy of Populism*, 72, 77; Prado Salmón, *Poder y fuerzas armadas*, 93–97. For detailed analysis of the Ch'ampa Guerra, see Gordillo, *Campesinos revolucionarios*, chapter 3; Werner, "'To Make Rivers of Blood Flow,'" chapters 4–5; Dandler, "La 'Champa Guerra.'"

125. Gordillo, *Campesinos revolucionarios*, 115–16, 135–40; Werner, "'To Make Rivers of Blood Flow,'" 116, 162–76, 205.

126. "El reclutamiento de abril próximo abarcará a conscriptos de todas las clases sociales," *El Diario*, March 9, 1960.

127. Prado Salmón, *Poder y fuerzas armadas*, 98–99; Quintana Taborga, *Policía y democracia*, 51–54.

128. Prado Salmón, *Poder y fuerzas armadas*, 101; Lehman, *Bolivia and the United States*, 150. On the 1956 parade, see Knudson, *Press and Revolution*, 90.

129. Paz Estenssoro, *Las Fuerzas Armadas*, 12.

EPILOGUE: THE MILITARY'S RESTORATIVE REVOLUTION OF 1964

1. Barber and Ronning, *Internal Security*, 145; Kohl, "National Revolution to Restoration," 22–23; Siekmeier, *Bolivian Revolution and the United States*, 181.

2. Field Jr., *From Development to Dictatorship*; Dunkerley, *Rebellion in the Veins*, 103–19.

3. Brill, "Military Civic Action in Bolivia," 88, 125.

4. Field Jr., *From Development to Dictatorship*, 87.

5. Movimiento Nacionalista Revolucionario, *Programa de gobierno*, 115–16.

6. Brill, "Military Civic Action," 90.

7. Field Jr., *From Development to Dictatorship*, 139.

8. Field Jr., *From Development to Dictatorship*, 80; Brill, "Military Civic Action," 104, 112, 209; Dunkerley, *Rebellion in the Veins*, 114–16. Field reports that Barrientos's Quechua was poor until he began taking lessons in 1961. See 215n70.

9. Field Jr., *From Development to Dictatorship*, 137–38, 227n138; Dunkerley, *Rebellion in the Veins*, 116–19.

10. Paz Estenssoro, *Las Fuerzas Armadas*, 6.

11. Soto S., *Historia del Pacto Militar Campesino*, 14; Werner, "'To Make Rivers of Blood Flow,'" 234.

12. Field Jr., *From Development to Dictatorship*, 146–48, 164–88.

13. Field Jr., *From Development to Dictatorship*, 140–70, 193; Dunkerley, *Rebellion in the Veins*, 118.

14. Dunkerley, *Rebellion in the Veins*, 118.

15. Werner, "'To Make Rivers of Blood Flow,'" 229–30.

16. Kohl, Farthing, and Muruchi, *From the Mines to the Streets*, 42–46.

17. See chapters 2 and 3.

BIBLIOGRAPHY

MANUSCRIPT SOURCES

La Paz, Bolivia

Archivo Central del Ministerio de Defensa Nacional (AC-MDN)
Registro Territorial—Ministerio de Defensa Nacional (RT-MDN)
Tribunal Permanente de Justicia Militar—Archivo Histórico Militar (TPJM-AHM)
Archivo de La Paz (ALP)
Biblioteca y Archivo Histórico del Asamblea Legislativo Plurinacional (BAH-ALP)
Biblioteca Arturo Costa de la Torre, Gobierno Autónomo Municipal La Paz (GAMLP)

Asunción, Paraguay

Archivo del Museo Militar del Ministerio de Defensa Nacional (AMM)
Archivo Alfredo Seiferheld en custodia del Museo Andrés Barbero (AAS)
Archivo del Arzobispado de la Santísima Asunción (AAA)
Biblioteca Nacional de Asunción (BNA)

United States

National Archives and Records Administration, Washington D.C. (NARA)
Papers of Robert Jackson Alexander—Special Collections and University Archive, Rutgers University Libraries, New Brunswick, NJ (RUL/MC974)

United Kingdom

The National Archives (TNA)

PERIODICALS

Bolivia

La Calle
El Comercio
El Diario
La Nación
La Noche
El Tiempo

La Razón
La Reforma
La República
Revista Militar
Última Hora
La Verdad

PUBLISHED PRIMARY AND SECONDARY SOURCES

Abercrombie, Thomas Alan. *Pathways of Memory and Power: Ethnography and History Among an Andean People.* Madison: University of Wisconsin Press, 1998.

Ablard, Jonathan D. "'The Barracks Receives Spoiled Children and Returns Men': Debating Military Service, Masculinity and Nation-Building in Argentina, 1901–1930." *The Americas* 74, no. 3 (2017): 299–329.

Adams, Richard N. "Race and Ethnicity in the Guatemalan Army, 1914." In *Military Struggle and Identity Formation in Latin America: Race, Nation, and Community during the Liberal Period,* edited by Nicola Foote and René D. Harder Horst, 107–35. Gainesville: University Press of Florida, 2010.

Ahlbäck, Anders. *Manhood and the Making of the Military: Conscription, Military Service and Masculinity in Finland, 1917–39.* Burlington, VT: Ashgate, 2014.

Albó, Xavier. "Andean People in the Twentieth Century." In *The Cambridge History of the Native Peoples of the Americas,* edited by Frank Salomon and Stuart B. Schwartz, 765–871. New York: Cambridge University Press, 1999.

Albó, Xavier. "And from Kataristas to MNRistas? The Surprising and Bold Alliance between Aymaras and Neoliberals in Bolivia." Translated by Charles Roberts. In *Indigenous Peoples and Democracy in Latin America,* edited by Donna Lee Van Cott, 55–82. New York: St. Martin's Press, 1994.

Albó, Xavier, Kitula Libermann, Armando Godinez, and Francisco Pifarré. *Para comprender las culturas rurales en Bolivia.* La Paz: MEC; CIPCA; UNICEF, 1989.

Albro, Robert. *Roosters at Midnight: Indigenous Signs and Stigma in Local Bolivian Politics.* Santa Fe, NM: School for Advanced Research, 2010.

Alexander, Robert J., with the collaboration of Eldon M. Parker. *A History of Organized Labor in Bolivia.* Westport, CT: Praeger, 2005.

Alonso, Ana María. *Thread of Blood: Colonialism, Revolution, and Gender on Mexico's Northern Frontier.* Tuscon: University of Arizona Press, 1995.

Altinay, Ayşe Gül. *The Myth of the Military-Nation: Militarism, Gender, and Education in Turkey.* New York: Palgrave Macmillan, 2004.

Álvarez España, Waldo. *Los gráficos en Bolivia.* La Paz: n.p., 1977.

Alvarez Mamani, Antonio, and Claudia Ranaboldo. *El camino perdido: Biografía del dirigente campesino kallawaya Antonio Alvarez Mamani.* La Paz: SEMTA, 1988.

Ambrosius, Gerold. *A Social and Economic History of Twentieth-Century Europe.* Cambridge: Harvard University Press, 1989.

Andrade, Everaldo de Oliveira. "História, arte e política: o muralismo do boliviano Miguel Alandia Pantoja." *História (São Paulo)* 25, no. 2 (2006): 147–61.

Aramayo, Carlos Roy. "The Intellectual Origins of the Modern Bolivian Political System, 1918–1943." Ph.D. diss., Yale University, 2008.

Aramayo Alzerreca, Carlos. *Peñaranda y otras entrevistas*. La Paz: Imp. Artística, 1940.

Arauz, Rodolfo. *Informe que eleva al Ministerio de Guerra y Colonización el Delegado Nacional en el Territorio de Colonias*. Riberalta: n.p., 1913.

Ari, Waskar. *Earth Politics: Religion, Decolonization, and Bolivia's Indigenous Intellectuals*. Durham, NC: Duke University Press, 2014.

Arze Aguirre, René Danilo. *Guerra y conflictos sociales: El caso rural boliviano durante la campaña del Chaco*. La Paz: CERES, 1987.

Arze Cuadros, Eduardo. *Bolivia, el programa del MNR y la revolución nacional: Del movimiento de reforma universtaria al ocaso del modelo neoliberal (1928–2002)*. La Paz: Plural Editores, 2002.

Averanga Mollinedo, Asthenio. *Aspectos generales de la población boliviana*. 3rd updated ed. La Paz: Libería Editorial Juventud, 1998.

Baptista Gumucio, Mariano. *Fragmentos de memoria Walter Guevara Arze*. La Paz: Editorial Garza Azul, 2002.

Barber, Willard F., and C. Neale Ronning. *Internal Security and Military Power: Counterinsurgency and Civic Action in Latin America*. Columbus: Ohio State University Press, 1966.

Barcelli S., Agustín. *Medio siglo de luchas sindicales revolutionarias en Bolivia, 1905–1955*. La Paz: Editorial del Estado, 1957.

Barragán, Rossana. *Asambleas constituyentes: Ciudadanía y elecciones, convenciones y debates (1825–1971)*. La Paz: Muela del Diablo Editores, 2006.

Barrios Morón, J. Raúl. "El nacionalism militar boliviano: Elementos para la reformulación estratégica." *Nueva Sociedad* 81 (January–February 1986): 36–45.

Bastos, Santiago. *Etnicidad y fuerzas armadas en Guatemala: Algunas ideas para el debate*. Guatemala City: FLASCO Guatemala; Sede Académica Guatemala, 2004.

Beattie, Peter M. *The Tribute of Blood: Army, Honor, Race, and Nation in Brazil, 1864–1945*. Durham, NC: Duke University Press, 2001.

Best, Geoffrey. "The Militarization of European Society, 1870–1914." In *The Militarization of the Western World*, edited by John Gillis, 13–29. New Brunswick: Rutgers University Press, 1989.

Bieber, León E. "La política militar alemana en Bolivia, 1900–1935." *Latin American Research Review* 29, no. 1 (1994): 85–106.

Bigenho, Michelle. *Sounding Indigenous: Authenticity in Bolivian Music Performance*. New York: Palgrave, 2002.

Blasier, Cole. *The Hovering Giant: U.S. Responses to Revolutionary Change in Latin America*. Pittsburgh, PA: University of Pittsburgh Press, 1976.

Blasier, Cole. "The United States and the Revolution " In *Beyond the Revolution: Bolivia since 1952*, edited by James M. Malloy and Richard S. Thorn, 53–109. Pittsburgh, PA: University of Pittsburgh Press, 1971.

Böhrt Gastelú, Roberto. *Deber cumplido: Páginas de la Guerra del Chaco*. La Paz: Offset Prisa Publicidad, 1993.

Bolivia. *Anuario de leyes y disposiciones supremas*. La Paz: Various Publishers, 1840–1923.

Bolivia. *Compilación penal militar, precedida por la Ley orgánica del ejército*. La Paz: n.p., 1948.

Bolivia. *Informes de Comisiones de la H. Convención Nacional de 1945*. Vol. 2. La Paz: Ed. América, 1945.

Bolivia. *Gaceta oficial*. La Paz: Various Publishers, 1924–1964.

Bolivia. *Mensaje del Presidente de Bolivia, Gral. Enrique Peñaranda H. al H. Congreso Ordinario*. La Paz: n.p., 1940–1943.

Bolivia. *Nueva Constitución Política del Estado*. La Paz: Asamblea Constituyente, 2008.

Bolivia. *Redactor de la H. Cámara de Diputados*. La Paz: Various Publishers, 1893–1960.

Bolivia. *Redactor de la H. Convención Nacional*. 5 Vols. La Paz: Editorial Universo, 1938–1939.

Bourdieu, Pierre. *Distinction: A Social Critique of the Judgement of Taste*. Translated by Richard Nice. Cambridge: Harvard University Press, 1984.

Bourdieu, Pierre. *Outline of a Theory of Practice*. New York: Cambridge University Press, 1977.

Bretel, A., and G. Sanjinés. *Catecismo del soldado*. 7th ed. La Paz: Gisbert y Cía, 1952.

Brill, William H. "Military Civic Action in Bolivia." Ph.D. diss., University of Pennsylvania, 1965.

Brill, William H. *Military Intervention in Bolivia: The Overthrow of Paz Estenssoro and the MNR*. Washington, D.C.: Institute for the Comparative Study of Political Systems, 1967.

Brockmann, Robert. *El general y sus presidentes: Vida y tiempos de Hans Kundt, Ernst Röhm y siete presidentes en la historia de Bolivia, 1911–1939*. La Paz: Plural Editores, 2007.

Buechler, Hans C., and Judith-Maria Buechler. *The Bolivian Aymara*. New York: Holt, Rinehart and Winston, 1971.

Burchell, Graham, Colin Gordon, and Peter Miller, eds. *The Foucault Effect: Studies in Governmentality*. Chicago: University of Chicago Press, 1991.

Burns, Kathryn. *Into the Archive: Writing and Power in Colonial Peru*. Durham, NC: Duke University Press, 2010.

Cabezas Fernández, Marta. "Ciudadanía y estado: Servicio militar obligatorio en la Bolivia contemporánea." *Íconos* 52 (2015): 43–57.

Cajías, Lupe. *Historia de una leyenda: Vida y palabra de Juan Lechín Oquendo, líder de los mineros bolivianos*. La Paz: Ediciones Gráficas "EG," 1988.

Canessa, Andrew. "The Indian within, the Indian without: Citizenship, Race, and Sex in a Bolivian Hamlet." In *Natives Making Nation: Gender, Indigeneity, and the State in the Andes*, edited by Andrew Canessa, 130–55. Tuscon: University of Arizona Press, 2005.

Canessa, Andrew. *Intimate Indigeneities: Race, Sex, and History in the Small Spaces of Andean Life*. Durham, NC: Duke University Press, 2012.

Capdevila, Luc, Isabelle Combès, Nicolás Richard, and Pablo Barbosa. *Los hombres transparentes: Indígenas y militares en la Guerra del Chaco (1932–1935)*. La Paz: Instituto Latinoamericano de Misionología, U.C.B., Itinerarios, CERHIO, 2010.

Capriles Rico, Remberto, and Gastón Arduz Eguía. *El problema social en Bolivia: Condiciones de vida y de trabajo*. La Paz: Editorial Fenix, 1941.

Carey Jr., David. "Mayan Soldier-Citizens: Ethnic Pride in the Guatemalan Military." In *Military Struggle and Identity Formation in Latin America: Race, Nation, and Community during the Liberal Period*, edited by Nicola Foote and René D. Harder Horst. Gainesville: University Press of Florida, 2010.

Carey Jr., David. *Our Elders Teach Us: Maya-Kaqchikel Historical Perspectives. Xkibe'ij Kan Qate' Qatata'*. Tuscaloosa: University of Alabama Press, 2001.

Carey Jr., David. "Who's Using Whom?: A Comparison of Military Conscription in Guatemala and Senegal in the First Half of the Twentieth Century." *Comparative Social Research* 20 (2002): 171–99.

Carter, William E., and Mauricio Mamani. *Irpa Chico: Individuo y comunidad en la cultura aymara*. La Paz: Librería-Editorial Juventud, 1982.

Centeno, Miguel Angel. *Blood and Debt: War and the Nation-State in Latin America*. University Park: Pennsylvania State University Press, 2002.

Céspedes, Augusto. *El dictador suicida: 40 años de historia de Bolivia*. Santiago, Chile: Editorial Universitaria, 1956.

Céspedes, Augusto. *Sangre de mestizos: Relatos de la Guerra del Chaco*. Santiago, Chile: Nascimento, 1936.

Céspedes Toro, Jaime, and Germán Busch Becerra. *Diario de guerra de Germán Busch Becerra y la epopeya de Boquerón*. La Paz: Hanns-Seidel Stiftung; FUNDEMOS, 2000.

Chesterton, Bridget María. "Composing Gender and Class: Paraguayan Letter Writers during the Chaco War, 1932–1935." *Journal of Women's History* 26, no. 3 (2014): 59–80.

Chesterton, Bridget María. *The Grandchildren of Solano López: Frontier and Nation in Paraguay, 1904–1936*. Albuquerque: University of New Mexico Press, 2013.

Choque Canqui, Roberto, and Cristina Quisbert Quispe. *Educación indigenal en Bolivia: Un siglo de ensayos educativos y resistencias patronales*. La Paz: Unidad de Investigaciones Históricas Unih-Pakaxa: IBIS, 2006.

Choque Canqui, Roberto, and Cristina Quisbert Quispe. *Líderes indígenas aymaras: Lucha por la defensa de tierras comunitarias de origen*. Unidad de Investigaciones Históricas UNIH-PAKAXA, 2010.

Choque Canqui, Roberto, and Esteban Ticona Alejo. *Jesús de Machaqa: La marka rebelde— Sublevación y masacre de 1921*. 2nd ed. La Paz: CEDOIN; CIPCA, 1996.

Choque, Roberto, Vitaliano Soria, Humberto Mamani, Esteban Ticona, and Ramón Conde. *Educación indígena: Ciudadanía o colonización?* La Paz: Ediciones Aruwiyiri Taller de Historia Oral Andina, 1992.

Cleven, N. Andrew. *The Political Organization of Bolivia*. Washington, D.C.: Carnegie Institution of Washington, 1940.

Cohen, Eliot A. *Citizens and Soldiers: The Dilemmas of Military Service*. Ithaca, NY: Cornell University Press, 1985.

Condarco Morales, Ramiro. *Zárate, el temible Willka: Historia de la rebelión indígena de 1899 en la República de Bolivia*. Revised 2nd ed. La Paz: n.p., 1983. First published 1966.

Conway, Daniel. *Masculinities, Militarisation and the End Conscription Campaign: War Resistance in Apartheid South Africa*. Johannesburg, South Africa: Wits University, 2012.

Cooper, Frederick. *Citizenship, Inequality, and Difference: Historical Perspectives*. Princeton, NJ: Princeton University Press, 2018.

Corbett, Charles D. *The Latin American Military as a Socio-Political Force: Case Studies of Bolivia and Argentina*. Coral Gables, FL: Center for Advanced International Studies, University of Miami, 1972.

Corbett, Charles D. "Military Institutional Development and Sociopolitical Change: The Bolivian Case." *Journal of Interamerican Studies and World Affairs* 14, no. 4 (1972): 399–435.

Cote, Stephen. *Oil and Nation: A History of Bolivia's Petroleum Sector*. Morgantown: West Virginia University Press, 2016.

Cote, Stephen. "A War for Oil in the Chaco, 1932–1935." *Environmental History* 18, no. 4 (2013): 738–58.

Crandon-Malamud, Libbett. *From the Fat of Our Souls: Social Change, Political Process, and Medical Pluralism in Bolivia.* Berkeley: University of California Press, 1991.

Cuadros Sánchez, Augusto. *Los orígenes de la Revolución Nacional: La Guerra del Chaco y sus secuelas, 1932–1943: Relato de un combatiente y "estratega" de la clase de tropa.* La Paz: Editorial Los Amigos del Libro, 2003.

Cruz Quispe, Adela. *Subordinación y constancia: El cuartel, el sistema militar y los jóvenes de la Ciudad de El Alto.* La Paz: CEADL, 2002.

Dandler, Jorge. "Politics of Leadership, Brokerage, and Patronage in the Campesino Movement of Cochabamba, Bolivia (1935–54)." Ph.D. diss., University of Wisconsin, 1971.

Dandler, Jorge. "La 'Champa Guerra' de Cochabamba: Un proceso de disgregación política." In *Bolivia: La fuerza histórica del campesinado,* edited by Fernando Calderon and Jorge Dandler, 240–71. La Paz: UNRISD; CERES, 1984.

Dandler, Jorge, and Juan A. Torrico. "From the National Indigenous Congress to the Ayopaya Rebellion: Bolivia 1945–1947." Translated by Steve J. Stern and Hunter Fite. In *Resistance, Rebellion, and Consciousness in the Andean Peasant World, 18th to 20th Centuries,* edited by Steve J. Stern, 334–78. Madison: University of Wisconsin Press, 1987.

Dávila, Amanda, and Jitka Silva J. *Historia oral de los barrios paceños.* Vol. 1. La Paz: Ediciones Casa de la Cultura, Gobierno Municipal, 1998.

Deas, Malcolm. "The Man on Foot: Conscription and the Nation-State in Nineteenth-Century Latin America." In *Studies in the Formation of the Nation State in Latin America,* edited by James Dunkerley, 77–93. London: Institute of Latin American Studies, 2002.

Díaz Arguedas, Julio. *Fastos Militares de Bolivia.* La Paz: Escuela Tipografica Salesiana, 1943.

Díaz Arguedas, Julio. *Historia del ejército de Bolivia, 1825–1932.* La Paz: n.p., 1940.

Díaz Arguedas, Julio. *La guerra con el Paraguay: Resúmen histórico-biográfico, 1932–1935.* La Paz: n.p., 1942.

Díaz Arguedas, Julio. *Los elegidos de la gloria.* La Paz: Imprenta Intendencia General de Guerra, 1937.

Díaz Machicao, Porfirio. *Guzmán, Siles, Blanco Galindo, 1925–1931.* La Paz: Gisbert y Cia, 1955.

Díaz Machicao, Porfirio. *Historia de Bolivia: Toro, Busch, Quintanilla, 1936–1940.* La Paz: Gisbert y Cia, 1957.

Díaz Machicao, Porfirio. *Saavedra, 1920–1925.* La Paz: Alfonso Tejerina, 1954.

Díaz Machicao, Porfirio. *Salamanca, la Guerra del Chaco, Tejada Sorzano, 1931–1936.* La Paz: Gisbert y Cia, 1955.

Dirección General de Estadística y Censos. *Censo demográfico, 1950.* La Paz: Editorial Argote, [1955?].

Dirección Nacional de Informaciones. *Bolivia: 10 años de revolución.* La Paz: n.p., 1962.

Dorn, Glenn J. *The Truman Administration and Bolivia: Making the World Safe for Constitutional Oligarchy.* University Park, PA: Pennsylvania State University Press, 2011.

Dunkerley, James. "Evo Morales, the 'Two Bolivias' and the Third Bolivian Revolution." *Journal of Latin American Studies* 39, no. 1 (2007): 133–66.

Dunkerley, James. *Orígenes del poder militar: Historia política e institucional del Ejército Boliviano hasta 1935.* Translated by Rose Marie Vargas. La Paz: Quipus, 1987.

Dunkerley, James. "Reassessing Caudillismo in Bolivia, 1825–79." *Latin American Research Review* 1, no. 1 (1981): 13–25.

Dunkerley, James. *Rebellion in the Veins: Political Struggle in Bolivia, 1952–82.* London: Verso, 1984.

Durán Jordán, Florencia, and Ana María Seoane Flores. *El complejo mundo de la mujer durante la Guerra del Chaco*. La Paz: Ministerio de Desarrollo Humano, 1997.

Durán S., Juan Carlos. *Germán Busch y los orígenes de la Revolución Nacional: Fragmentos para una biografía*. La Paz: Honorable Senado Nacional, 1997.

Eichler, Maya. "Militarized Masculinities in International Relations." *Brown Journal of World Affairs* 21, no. 1 (2014): 81–93.

Eichler, Maya. *Militarizing Men: Gender, Conscription, and War in Post-Soviet Russia*. Stanford, CA: Stanford University Press, 2010.

Eisenstadt, Todd A., A. Carl LeVan, and Tofigh Maboudi. *Constituents before Assembly: Participation, Deliberation, and Representation in the Crafting of New Constitutions*. Cambridge: Cambridge University Press, 2019.

Ejército Nacional—Ministerio de Defensa Nacional. *Prescripciones para el reclutamiento del año 1943*. La Paz: Intendencia Central del Ejército, 1942.

Epstein, M., ed. *The Statesman's Yearbook*. London: MacMillan, 1937.

Farcau, Bruce W. *The Chaco War: Bolivia and Paraguay, 1932–1935*. Westport, CT: Praeger, 1996.

Fernández Terán, Roberto. "Prensa, radio e imaginario boliviano durante la Guerra del Chaco (1932–1935)." In *La música en Bolivia: De la prehistoria a la actualidad*, edited by Wálter Sánchez Canedo, 209–48. Cochabamba, Bolivia: Fundación Simón I. Patiño, 2002.

Fernández Terán, Roberto. "Transformaciones y prácticas de poder en el ejército boliviano: Hacia la construcción del ciudadano soldado (1932–1940)." *Análisis Político* 3, no. 5 (1999): 51–60.

Ferrer, Ada. *Insurgent Cuba: Race, Nation, and Revolution, 1868–1898*. Chapel Hill: University of North Carolina Press, 1999.

Field Jr., Thomas C. *From Development to Dictatorship: Bolivia and the Alliance for Progress in the Kennedy Era*. Ithaca, NY: Cornell University Press, 2014.

Fitch, J. Samuel. *The Armed Forces and Democracy in Latin America*. Baltimore, MD: Johns Hopkins University Press, 1998.

Flores Moncayo, José. *Legislación boliviana del indio: Recopilación, 1825–1953*. La Paz: Ministerio de Asuntos Campesinos, Departamento de Publicaciones del Instituto Indigenista Boliviano, 1953.

Flynn, George Q. *Conscription and Democracy: The Draft in France, Great Britain, and the United States*. Westport, CT: Greenwood Press, 2002.

Foote, Nicola. "Monteneros and Macheteros: Afro-Ecuadorian and Indigenous Experiences of Military Struggle in Liberal Ecuador, 1895–1930." In *Military Struggle and Identity Formation in Latin America: Race, Nation, and Community during the Liberal Period*, edited by Nicola Foote and René D. Harder Horst, 83–106. Gainesville: University Press of Florida, 2010.

Foote, Nicola, and René D. Harder Horst, eds. *Military Struggle and Identity Formation in Latin America: Race, Nation, and Community during the Liberal Period*. Gainesville: University Press of Florida, 2010.

Foster, David William. *Latin American Government Leaders*. 2nd ed. Tempe: Center for Latin American Studies, Arizona State University, 1975.

Foucault, Michel. *Discipline and Punish: The Birth of the Prison*. Translated by Alan Sheridan. 2nd ed. New York: Vintage Books, 1997. First published 1974.

Frevert, Ute. *A Nation in the Barracks: Modern Germany, Military Conscription and Civil Society*. Translated by Andrew Boreham and Daniel Brückenhaus. New York: Berg, 2004.

Galindo de Ugarte, Marcelo. *Constituciones bolivianas comparadas, 1826–1967.* La Paz: Editorial Los Amigos del Libro, 1991.

Gallego Margaleff, Ferran. *Los orígenes del reformismo militar en América Latina: La gestión de David Toro en Bolivia.* Barcelona, Spain: PPU, 1991.

Gallo, Carmenza. *Taxes and State Power: Political Instability in Bolivia, 1900–1950.* Philadelphia, PA: Temple University Press, 1991.

García Prada, Hernán. *El ejército y la revolución de abril de 1952.* Cochabamba: n.p., 1999.

Geva, Dorit. *Conscription, Family, and the Modern State: A Comparative Study of France and the United States.* New York: Cambridge University Press, 2013.

Gill, Lesley. "Creating Citizens, Making Men: The Military and Masculinity in Bolivia." *Cultural Anthropology* 12, no. 4 (1997): 527–50.

Gillis, John, ed. *The Militarization of the Western World.* New Brunswick, NJ: Rutgers University Press, 1989.

Goldstein, Daniel M. *The Spectacular City: Violence and Performance in Urban Bolivia.* Durham, NC: Duke University Press, 2004.

Gómez, Eugenio. *Bautista Saavedra.* La Paz: Biblioteca de la Sesquicentenario de la República, 1975.

Gómez D'Angelo, Walter. "Mining in the Economic Development of Bolivia, 1900–1970." Ph.D. diss., Vanderbilt University, 1973.

González-Cueva, Eduardo. "Conscription and Violence in Peru." *Latin American Perspectives* 27, no. 3 (2000): 88–102.

Gordillo, José M. *Campesinos revolucionarios en Bolivia: Identidad, territorio y sexualidad en el Valle Alto de Cochabamba, 1952–1964.* La Paz: Plural Editores, 2000.

Gotkowitz, Laura. *A Revolution for Our Rights: Indigenous Struggles for Land and Justice in Bolivia, 1880–1952.* Durham, NC: Duke University Press, 2007.

Gotkowitz, Laura. "Trading Insults: Honor, Violence, and the Gendered Culture of Commerce in Cochabamba, Bolivia, 1870s-1950s." *Hispanic American Historical Review* 83, no. 1 (2003): 83–118.

Goudsmit, Into A. "Praying for Government: Peasant Disengagement from the Bolivian State." *Bulletin of Latin American Research* 25, no. 2 (2006): 200–219.

Granier Chirveches, Juan. *Diario de campaña: Fragmento de una vida patriótica en la Guerra del Chaco, 1932–1935.* La Paz: Ah! Publicidad, [2005?].

Gray Molina, George. "State Society Relations in Bolivia: The Strength of Weakness." In *Unresolved Tensions: Bolivia Past and Present,* edited by John Crabtree and Laurence Whitehead, 109–24. Pittsburgh, PA: University of Pittsburgh Press, 2008.

Grieshaber, Erwin P. "Fluctuaciones en la definición del indio: Comparación de los censos de 1900 y 1950." *Historia Boliviana* 5, no. 1–2 (1985): 45–65.

Grieshaber, Erwin P. "Resistencia indígena a la venta de tierras comunales en el departamento de La Paz, 1881–1920." *Data: Revista del Instituto de Estudios Andinos y Amazónicos* 1 (1991): 113–45.

Guardino, Peter. "Gender, Soldiering, and Citizenship in the Mexican-American War of 1846–1848." *The American Historical Review* 119, no. 1 (2014): 23–46.

Guerrero, Julio C. *Peñaranda: Semblanza de un hombre ejemplar.* La Paz: Intendencia Central del Ejército, 1940.

Gustafson, Bret. "Flashpoints of Sovereignty: Territorial Conflict and Natural Gas in Bolivia." In *Crude Domination: An Anthropology of Oil,* edited by Andrea Behrends, Stephen P. Reyna, and Günther Schlee, 220–40. New York: Berghahn Books, 2011.

Hancock, Eleanor. *Ernst Röhm: Hitler's SA Chief of Staff.* New York: Palgrave Macmillan, 2008.

Harris, Olivia, and Xavier Albó. *Monteras y guardatojos: Campesinos y mineros en el norte de Potosí.* 2nd ed. La Paz: CIPCA, 1986. First published 1975.

Hartlyn, Jonathan, and Arturo Valenzuela. "Democracy in Latin America since 1930." In *The Cambridge History of Latin America: Latin America since 1930,* edited by Leslie Bethell, 99–162. New York: Cambridge University Press, 1994.

Herbas Cabrera, Carlos. *El cristo de Tarairí: "Dos hermanos en la guerra" (diario de campaña): Bolivia con el Paraguay, 1932–1935, una contribución a la historia.* Oruro, Bolivia: Editorial Universitaria, 1977.

Herbas P., Ricardo. *Una página de la historia de Bolivia?* 2nd ed. La Paz: Editorial Voluntad, [1939?].

Horst, René D. Harder. "Crossfire, Cactus, and Racial Constructions: The Chaco War and Indigenous People in Paraguay." In *Military Struggle and Identity Formation in Latin America: Race, Nation, and Community during the Liberal Period,* edited by Nicola Foote and René D. Harder Horst, 286–306. Gainesville: University Press of Florida, 2010.

Hudson, Rex A., and Dennis M. Hanratty, eds. *Bolivia: A Country Study.* 3rd ed. Washington, D.C.: Research Division, Library of Congress, 1991.

Hunefeldt, Christine. "Power Constellations in Peru: Military Recruitment around the War of the Pacific in Puno." In *Power, Culture, and Violence in the Andes,* edited by Christine Hunefeldt and Misha Kokotovic, 50–84. Brighton, UK: Sussex Academic Press, 2009.

Hurtado Meza, Lourdes. "Ejército cholificado: Reflexiones sobre la apertura del ejército peruano hacia los sectores populares." *Íconos* 26 (2006): 59–72.

Hylton, Forrest. "Reverberations of Insurgency: Indian Communities, the Federal War of 1899, and the Regeneration of Bolivia." Ph.D. diss., New York University, 2010.

Hylton, Forrest. "Tierra común: Caciques, artesanos e intelectuales radicales y la rebelión de Chayanta." In *Ya es otro tiempo presente: Cuatro momentos de insurgencia indígena,* by Forrest Hylton, Felix Patzi Paco, Sergio Serulnikov, and Sinclair Thomson, 134–98. La Paz: Muela del Diablo Editores, 2003.

Hylton, Forrest, and Sinclair Thomson. *Revolutionary Horizons: Past and Present in Bolivian Politics.* New York: Verso, 2007.

El Internacional. *Las verdaderas crónicas de la revolución* [La Paz?]: Tip. "El Illimani," [1920?].

Irurozqui Victoriano, Marta. *"A bala, piedra y palo": La construcción de la ciudadanía política en Bolivia, 1826–1952.* Seville, Spain: Diputación de Sevilla, 2000.

Jaundrill, D. Colin. *Samurai to Soldier: Remaking Military Service in Nineteenth-Century Japan.* Ithaca, NY: Cornell University Press, 2016.

Joenniemi, Pertti, ed. *The Changing Face of European Conscription.* Aldershot, UK: Ashgate, 2006.

Jackson, Robert H. *Regional Markets and Agrarian Transformation in Bolivia, Cochabamba, 1539–1960.* Albuquerque: University of New Mexico Press, 1994.

John, S. Sandor. *Bolivia's Radical Tradition: Permanent Revolution in the Andes.* Tuscon: University of Arizona Press, 2009.

Karsten, Peter, ed. *Recruiting, Drafting, and Enlisting: Two Sides of the Raising of Military Forces.* New York: Garland Publishing, 1998.

Kirkland, Robert O. *Observing Our Hermanos de Armas: U.S. Military Attachés in Guatemala, Cuba, and Bolivia, 1950–1964.* New York: Routledge, 2003.

Kirkland, Robert O. "United States Assistance to the Bolivian Military, 1958–1964." *MACLAS Latin American Essays* 12 (1998): 37–47.

Klein, Herbert S. "American Oil Companies in Latin America: The Bolivian Experience." *Inter-American Economic Affairs* 18, no. 2 (1964): 42–72.

Klein, Herbert S. *A Concise History of Bolivia.* 2nd ed. New York: Cambridge University Press, 2011.

Klein, Herbert S. "David Toro and the Establishment of 'Military Socialism' in Bolivia." *Hispanic American Historical Review* 45, no. 1 (1965): 25–52.

Klein, Herbert S. *Orígenes de la revolución nacional boliviana: La crisis de la generación del Chaco.* Translated by Rodolfo Medrano. 3rd ed. La Paz: Empresa Editora "Urquizo," 1995.

Klein, Herbert S. *Parties and Political Change in Bolivia, 1880–1952.* London: Cambridge University Press, 1969.

Knudson, Jerry W. *Bolivia: Press and Revolution, 1932–1964.* Lanham, MD: University Press of America, 1986.

Knudson, Jerry W. *Roots of Revolution: The Press and Social Change in Latin America.* Landham, MD: University Press of America, 2010.

Kraay, Hendrik. *Race, State, and Armed Forces in Independence-Era Brazil.* Stanford, CA: Stanford University Press, 2001.

Kraay, Hendrik, and Thomas L. Whigham, eds. *I Die with My Country: Perspectives on the Paraguayan War, 1864–1870.* Lincoln: University of Nebraska Press, 2004.

Krebs, Ronald R. *Fighting for Rights: Military Service and the Politics of Citizenship.* Ithaca, NY: Cornell University Press, 2006.

Kohl, Benjamin, Linda Farthing, and Félix Muruchi. *From the Mines to the Streets: A Bolivian Activist's Life.* Austin: University of Texas Press, 2011.

Kohl, James V. "National Revolution to Restoration: Arms and Factional Politics in Bolivia." *Inter-American Economic Affairs* 39, no. 1 (1985): 3–30.

Kohl, James V. "Peasants Speak: Antonio Mamani Alvarez: A Call to Bolivian Indians." *The Journal of Peasant Studies* 4, no. 4 (1977): 394–97.

Kuenzli, E. Gabrielle. *Acting Inca: National Belonging in Early Twentieth-Century Bolivia.* Pittsburgh, PA: University of Pittsburgh Press, 2013.

La Paz, 450 años, 1548–1998. 2 vols. La Paz: Alcaldía Municipal de La Paz, 1998.

Langer, Erick D. *Economic Change and Rural Resistance in Southern Bolivia, 1880–1930.* Stanford, CA: Stanford University Press, 1989.

Langer, Erick D. *Expecting Pears from an Elm Tree: Franciscan Missions on the Chiriguano Frontier in the Heart of South America, 1830–1949.* Durham, NC: Duke University Press, 2009.

Larson, Brooke. "Capturing Indian Bodies, Hearths and Minds: The Gendered Politics of Rural School Reform in Bolivia, 1910–1952." In *Proclaiming Revolution: Bolivia in Comparative Perspective,* edited by Merilee S. Grindle and Pilar Domingo. Cambridge, MA: David Rockefeller Center for Latin American Studies, Harvard University, 2003.

Larson, Brooke. *Cochabamba, 1550–1900: Colonialism and Agrarian Transformation in Bolivia.* Expanded ed. Durham, NC: Duke University Press, 1998. First published 1988.

Larson, Brooke. *Trials of Nation Making: Liberalism, Race, and Ethnicity in the Andes, 1810–1910.* New York: Cambridge University Press, 2004.

Lazar, Sian. *El Alto, Rebel City: Self and Citizenship in Andean Bolivia.* Durham, NC: Duke University Press, 2008.

Legrand, Mario. *Un civil en campo militar: Grandes maniobras del Ejército Boliviano, Comentarios y observaciones del enviado especial de "El Diario," de La Paz.* La Paz: Arnó Hermanos, 1930.

Lehm A., Zulema, and Silvia Rivera Cusicanqui. *Los artesanos libertarios y la ética del trabajo*. La Paz: Ediciones del THOA, 1988.

Lehman, Kenneth Duane. *Bolivia and the United States: A Limited Partnership*. Athens: University of Georgia Press, 1999.

Lehman, Kenneth Duane. "US Foreign Aid and Revolutionary Nationalism in Bolivia, 1952–1964: The Pragmatics of a Patron-Client Relationship." Ph.D. diss., University of Texas at Austin, 1992.

Leinaweaver, Jessaca B. *The Circulation of Children: Kinship, Adoption, and Morality in Andean Peru*. Durham, NC: Duke University Press, 2008.

Leonhard, Jörn, and Ulrike von Hirschhausen. "Does the Empire Strike Back? The Model of the Nation in Arms as a Challenge for Multi-Ethnic Empires in the Nineteenth and Early Twentieth Century." *Journal of Modern European History* 5, no. 2 (2007): 194–220.

Lora, Guillermo. *A History of the Bolivian Labour Movement, 1848–1971*. Translated by Christine Whitehead. Edited by and abridged by Laurence Whitehead. New York: Cambridge University Press, 1977.

Loveman, Brian. *For la Patria: Politics and the Armed Forces in Latin America*. Wilmington, DE: SR Books, 1999.

Loveman, Brian, and Thomas M. Davies Jr., eds. *The Politics of Antipolitics: The Military in Latin America*. 2nd revised and expanded ed. Lincoln: University of Nebraska Press, 1989.

Lowenthal, Abraham, and J. Samuel Fitch, eds. *Armies and Politics in Latin America*. New York: Holmes and Meier, 1986.

Luykx, Aurolyn. *The Citizen Factory: Schooling and Cultural Production in Bolivia*. Albany: State University of New York Press, 1999.

Lynn, John A. *Battle: A Cultural History of Combat and Culture*. Boulder, CO: Westview Press, 2003.

Maldonado Prieto, Carlos. "El servicio militar en Chile: Del ejército educador al modelo voluntario." In *El servicio militar en América Latina: Procesos y tendencias*, edited by Juan Ramón Quintana, et. al., 49–69. Lima, Peru: CEAPAZ, 2001.

Mallon, Florencia E. *Peasant and Nation: The Making of Postcolonial Mexico and Peru*. Berkeley: University of California Press, 1995.

Malloy, James M. *Bolivia, the Uncompleted Revolution*. Pittsburgh, PA: University of Pittsburgh Press, 1970.

Mamani Condori, Carlos B. *Taraqu, 1866–1935: Masacre, guerra y "renovación" en la biografía de Eduardo L. Nina Qhispi*. La Paz: Ediciones Aruwiyiri, 1991.

Mann, Gregory. *Native Sons: West African Veterans and France in the Twentieth Century*. Durham, NC: Duke University Press, 2006.

McCann, Frank D. *Soldiers of the Pátria: A History of the Brazilian Army, 1889–1937*. Stanford: Stanford University Press, 2004.

Méndez G., Cecilia. "Las paradojas del autoritarismo: Ejército, campesinado y etnicidad en el Perú, siglos XIX al XX." *Íconos* 26 (2006): 17–34.

Méndez G., Cecilia. "Militares populistas: Ejército, etnicidad y ciudadanía en el Perú." In *Repensando la subalternidad: Miradas críticas desde/sobre América Latina*, edited by Pablo Sandoval, 561–98. Lima, Peru: SEPHIS; IEP, 2009.

Mendieta Parada, Pilar. *De Tupac Katari a Zárate Willka: Alianzas, pactos, resistencia y rebelión en Mohoza (1780–1899)*. La Paz: Instituto de Estudios Bolivianos, 2000.

Migdal, Joel S. *State in Society: Studying How States and Societies Transform and Constitute One Another.* New York: Cambridge University Press, 2001.

Migdal, Joel S. *Strong Societies and Weak States: State-Society Relations and State Capabilities in the Third World.* Princeton: Princeton University Press, 1988.

Ministerio de Guerra. *Boletín militar del Ministro de Guerra.* La Paz: Intendencia de Guerra, 1907–1909.

Ministerio de Guerra. *Códigos militares de la República de Bolivia.* La Paz: Imprenta de El Comercio de Bolivia, 1905.

Ministerio de Guerra. *Escalafón militar de 1906.* La Paz: Intendencia de Guerra, 1908.

Ministerio de Guerra. *Anexos a la memoria de guerra.* La Paz: Various Publishers, 1910–1919.

Ministerio de Guerra. *Memoria de guerra.* La Paz: Various Publishers, 1908–1928.

Mitchell, Christopher. *The Legacy of Populism in Bolivia: From the MNR to Military Rule.* New York: Praeger, 1977.

Montenegro, Carlos, and Mariano Baptista Gumucio. *Montenegro el desconocido.* La Paz: Ultima Hora, 1979.

Montes Ruiz, Fernando. *La máscara de piedra: Simbolismo y personalidad aymaras en la historia.* La Paz: Editorial Quipus, 1984.

Montoya, Víctor. "La revolución nacional en los murales de un pintor boliviano." *Fuentes* 5, no. 17 (2011): 42–46.

Moon, Seungsook. *Militarized Modernity and Gendered Citizenship in South Korea.* Durham, NC: Duke University Press, 2005.

Morgan, Zachary R. *Legacy of the Lash: Race and Corporal Punishment in the Brazilian Navy and the Atlantic World.* Bloomington: University of Indiana Press, 2014.

Movimiento Nacionalista Revolucionario. *Programa de gobierno Movimiento Nacionalista Revolucionario, tercer gobierno de la revolución nacional, 1960–64: Aprobado por la VIII Convención del M.N.R.* La Paz: n.p., 1960.

Muñoz Reyes, Jorge. *Geografía de Bolivia.* 2nd ed. La Paz: Libería Editorial Juventud, 1980.

Murillo, Mario. *La bala no mata sino el destino: Una crónica de la insurrección popular de 1952 en Bolivia.* La Paz: Plural, 2012.

Nash, June C. *I Spent My Life in the Mines: The Story of Juan Rojas, Bolivian Tin Miner.* Updated ed. New York: Columbia University Press, 1992. First published 1979.

Neufeld, Stephen B. *The Blood Contingent: The Military and the Making of Modern Mexico, 1876–1911.* Albuquerque: University of New Mexico Press, 2017.

Nunn, Frederick M. *Yesterday's Soldiers: European Military Professionalism in South America, 1890–1940.* Lincoln: University of Nebraska Press, 1983.

Oficina Nacional de Inmigración, Estadística, y Propaganda Geográfica. *Censo general de la población de la República de Bolivia según el empadronamiento de 1o. de septiembre de 1900.* 2 vols. Cochabamba, Bolivia: Editorial Canelas S.A., 1973. First published 1902–1904.

Oporto Ordoñez, Luis. *Uncía y Llallagua: Empresa minera capitalista y estrategias de apropiación real del espacio (1900–1935).* La Paz: IFEA, Plural Editores, 2007.

Ortiz B., Cecilia. "La influencia militar en la construcción política del indio ecuatoriano en el siglo XX." *Íconos* 26 (2006): 73–84.

Pando Gutiérrez, Jorge. "Reseña demográfica de la ciudad de La Paz." In *La Paz en su IV centenario, 1548–1948.* La Paz: Comité pro Cuarto Centenario de la Fundación de La Paz, 1948.

Parker, William Belmont, ed. *Bolivians of To-Day*. New York: Hispanic Society of America, 1922.

Passmore, Leith. *The Wars inside Chile's Barracks: Remembering Military Service under Pinochet*. Madison: University of Wisconsin Press, 2017.

Paz Estenssoro, Víctor. *Las fuerzas armadas y la revolución nacional*. La Paz: Imprenta Militar, 1959.

Pereira Fiorilo, Juan. *Historia secreta de la Guerra del Chaco: Bolivia frente al Paraguay y Argentina*. La Paz: H. Cámara de Diputados, Federación de Entidades Empresariales Privadas de Cochabamba, 1999.

Philip, George. *Oil and Politics in Latin America: Nationalist Movements and State Companies*. New York: Cambridge University Press, 1982.

Pifarré, Francisco. *Historia de un pueblo*. La Paz: Centro de Investigación y Promoción del Campesinado, 1989.

Platt, Tristán. "The Andean Experience of Bolivian Liberalism 1825–1900: Roots of Rebellion in 19th-Century Chayanta (Potosí)." In *Resistance, Rebellion, and Consciousness in the Andean Peasant World, 18th to 20th Centuries*, edited by Steve J. Stern, 280–323. Madison: University of Wisconsin Press, 1987.

Platt, Tristán. *Estado boliviano y ayllu andino: Tierra y tributo en el norte de Potosí*. Lima, Peru: Instituto de Estudios Peruanos, 1982.

Pion-Berlin, David. "The National-Security Doctrine, Military Threat Perception, and the 'Dirty War' in Argentina." *Comparative Political Studies* 21, no. 3 (1988): 382–407.

Pol, Hugo René. *La campaña del Chaco, glosas y reflexiones militares, zona de separación, 1937–primavera 1938*. La Paz: n.p., 1945.

Postero, Nancy Grey. *Now We Are Citizens: Indigenous Politics in Postmulticultural Bolivia*. Stanford, CA: Stanford University Press, 2007.

Pozo Trigo, Carlos. *Relatos y anécdotas de la Guerra del Chaco: Memorias de un ex-combatiente*. La Paz: Servigraf, 2000.

Prado Salmón, Gary. *"Defendete, Gary Prado": Anecdotario*. Santa Cruz, Bolivia: Reflejos SRL, 1994.

Prado Salmón, Gary. *Los militares y la revolución nacional: Análisis crítico*. Santa Cruz, Bolivia: Gary Prado Producciones, 2010.

Prado Salmón, Gary. *Poder y fuerzas armadas, 1949–1982*. Cochabamba, Bolivia: Los Amigos del Libro, 1984.

Querejazu Calvo, Roberto. *Masamaclay: Historia política, diplomática y militar de la Guerra del Chaco*. 2nd ed. La Paz: Empresa Industrial Gráfica E. Burillo, 1975. First published 1965.

Quintana Taborga, Juan Ramón. *La conquista ciudadana: La experiencia del Servicio Premilitar de mujeres en Villazón-Potosí, 1997*. La Paz: Ministerio de Defensa Nacional, Unidad de Análisis de Políticas de Defensa, 1998.

Quintana Taborga, Juan Ramón. *Policía y democracia en Bolivia: Una política institucional pendiente*. La Paz: PIEB, 2005.

Quintana Taborga, Juan Ramón. *Soldados y ciudadanos: Un estudio crítico sobre el servicio militar obligatorio en Bolivia*. La Paz: PIEB, 1998.

Quiroga Ochoa, Ovidio. *En la paz y en la guerra al servicio de la patria, 1916–1971*. La Paz: Libería y Editorial Gisbert & Cía. S.A., 1974.

Ralston, David B. *Importing the European Army: The Introduction of European Military Techniques and Institutions into the Extra-European World, 1600–1914*. Chicago: University of Chicago Press, 1996.

Ramón Carrión, Manuel de, and Carmen Ortíz. *Madrina de guerra: Cartas desde el frente*. Madrid, Spain: La Esfera de los Libros, 2003.

Rath, Thomas. "Modernizing Military Patriarchy: Gender and State-Building in Postrevolutionary Mexico, 1920–1960." *Journal of Social History* 52, no. 3 (2019): 807–30.

Rath, Thomas. *Myths of Demilitarization in Postrevolutionary Mexico, 1920–1960*. Chapel Hill: University of North Carolina Press, 2013.

Richter, Alfredo. *Catecismo del soldado*. La Paz: Imp. Artística de Carlos Diez de Medina, 1909.

Richter, Alfredo. *En el puesto del deber, julio de 1920*. La Paz: Imp. Artística, [1921?].

Rivera Cusicanqui, Silvia. *Oppressed but Not Defeated: Peasant Struggles among the Aymara and Qhechwa in Bolivia, 1900–1980*. Translated from the Spanish. Geneva: United Nations Research Institute for Social Development, 1987.

Rivera Cusicanqui, Silvia, Filomena Nina Huarcacho, Franklin Maquera Cespedes, and Ruth Flores Pinaya, eds. *La mujer andina en la historia*. La Paz: Ediciones del THOA, 1990.

Rodríguez, Angel. . . . *Autopsia de una guerra (campaña del Chaco) (con opiniones técnicas de cinco generales de América)*. Santiago, Chile: Ediciones Ercilla, 1940.

Rouquié, Alain. *The Military and the State in Latin America*. Translated by Paul Sigmund. Berkeley: University of California Press, 1987.

Rugeley, Terry, and Ben Fallaw, eds. *Forced Marches: Soldiers and Military Caciques in Modern Mexico*. Tucson: University of Arizona Press, 2012.

Salinas Mariaca, Ramón, and Carlos Manuel Silva, eds. *Códigos de justicia militar de Bolivia*. La Paz: n.p. 1948.

Sanborn, Joshua A. *Drafting the Russian Nation: Military Conscription, Total War, and Mass Politics, 1905–1925*. DeKalb: Northern Illinois Press, 2003.

Sánchez H., José. *The Art and Politics of Bolivian Cinema*. Lanham, MD: Scarecrow Press, 1999.

Sanjinés Goitia, Julio. *El militar ingeniero*. La Paz: Editorial Los Amigos del Libro, 1975.

Sater, William F. *Andean Tragedy: Fighting the War of the Pacific, 1879–1884*. Lincoln: University of Nebraska Press, 2007.

Sater, William F., and H. Herwig Holger. *The Grand Illusion: The Prussianization of the Chilean Army*. Lincoln: University of Nebraska Press, 1999.

Scheina, Robert L. *Latin America's Wars: The Age of the Professional Soldier, 1900–2001*. Washington, D.C.: Brassey's Inc., 2003.

Scott, James C. *Seeing Like a State: How Certain Schemes to Improve the Human Condition Have Failed*. New Haven, CT: Yale University Press, 1998.

Scott, James C. *Weapons of the Weak: Everyday Forms of Peasant Resistance*. New Haven, CT: Yale University Press, 1985.

Selaya P., Salustio. *Documentos y memorias de la Guerra del Chaco*. La Paz: Urquizo Ltda., 1972.

Seleme Vargas, Antonio. *Memorias del Gral. Antonio Seleme Vargas: Mi actuación en la Junta Militar de Gobierno con el pronunciamiento revolucionario del 9 de abril de 1952*. La Paz: n.p., 1969.

Selmeski, Brian R. "Guerreros y ciudadanos: Estereotipos raciales y cargos militares de los conscriptos indígenas ecuatorianos." In *El servicio militar en América Latina: Procesos y tendencias*, edited by Juan Ramón Quintana, et. al., 70-84. Lima, Peru: CEAPAZ, 2001.

Selmeski, Brian R. "Sons of Indians and Indian Sons." In *Highland Indians and the State in Modern Ecuador*, edited by A. Kim Clark and Marc Becker, 155–78. Pittsburgh, PA: University of Pittsburgh Press, 2007.

Serulnikov, Sergio. *Subverting Colonial Authority: Challenges to Spanish Rule in Eighteenth Century Southern Andes.* Durham, NC: Duke University Press, 2003.

Shesko, Elizabeth. "'Same as Here, Same as Everywhere': Social Difference among Bolivian Prisoners in Paraguay." In *The Chaco War: Environment, Ethnicity, and Nationalism,* edited by Bridget María Chesterton, 21–41. New York: Bloomsbury Academic, 2016.

Siekmeier, James F. *The Bolivian Revolution and the United States, 1952 to Present.* University Park, PA: Pennsylvania State University Press, 2011.

Sierra, Luis Manuel. "Indigenous Neighborhood Residents in the Urbanization of La Paz, Bolivia, 1910–1950." Ph.D. diss., Binghamton University, 2013.

"Siles Zuazo, Hernán." *Men in the News . . .: Personality Sketches from the New York Times* 2 (1960): 264–65.

Simbrón García, Gonzalo. *Imagínatelapaz: Cuando el pasado era presente.* La Paz: Gente de Oficio Editores, 2009.

Sivak, Martín. *El dictador elegido: Biografía no autorizada de Hugo Banzer Suárez.* La Paz: Plural Editores, 2001.

Smale, Robert L. *"I Sweat the Flavor of Tin": Labor Activism in Early Twentieth Century Bolivia.* Pittsburgh, PA: University of Pittsburgh Press, 2010.

Smallman, Shawn C. *Fear and Memory in the Brazilian Army and Society, 1889–1954.* Chapel Hill: University of North Carolina Press, 2002.

Smith, Leonard V. *Between Mutiny and Obedience: The Case of the French Fifth Infantry Division during World War I.* Princeton, NJ: Princeton University Press, 1994.

Soto S., César. *Historia del Pacto Militar Campesino.* Cochabamba, Bolivia: Ediciones CERES, 1994.

Spencer, Jayne. "Oil, Politics, and Economic Nationalism in Bolivia, 1899–1942: The Case of the Standard Oil Company in Bolivia." Ph.D. diss., University of California, Los Angeles, 1996.

Stefanoni, Pablo, and Hervé do Alto. *Evo Morales, de la coca al palacio: Una oportunidad para la izquierda indígena.* La Paz: Malatesta, 2006.

Stepan, Nancy. *The Hour of Eugenics: Race, Gender, and Nation in Latin America.* Ithaca, NY: Cornell University Press, 1991.

Taller de Historia Oral Andina, and Silvia Rivera Cusicanqui. "Indigenous Women and Community Resistance: History and Memory." In *Women and Social Change in Latin America,* edited by Elizabeth Jelin, 151–83. London: Zed Books, 1990.

Tapia, Luciano. *Ukhamawa jakawisaxa (Asi es nuestra vida): Autobiografía de un aymara.* La Paz: HISBOL, 1995.

Thomson, Sinclair. *We Alone Will Rule: Native Andean Politics in the Age of Insurgency.* Madison: University of Wisconsin Press, 2002.

Tovar Villa, Raúl, and Hans Kundt. *Campaña del Chaco, el General Hans Kundt, Comandante en Jefe del Ejército en Bolivia.* La Paz: Editorial Don Bosco, 1961.

Van Doorn, Jacques. "The Decline of the Mass Army in the West: General Reflections." *Armed Forces and Society* 1, no. 2 (1975): 147–57.

Van Vleet, Krista E. *Performing Kinship: Narrative, Gender, and the Intimacies of Power in the Andes.* Austin: University of Texas Press, 2008.

Vergara Vicuña, Aquiles. *Historia de la Guerra del Chaco.* 3 Vols. La Paz: Litografías e Imprentas Unidas, 1940–1944.

Von Hagen, Mark. *Soldiers in the Proletarian Dictatorship: The Red Army and the Soviet Socialist State, 1917–1930.* Ithaca, NY: Cornell University Press, 1990.

Walker, Charles. *The Tupac Amaru Rebellion.* Cambridge, MA: Belknap Press of Harvard University Press, 2014.

Werner, Bridgette K. "'To Make Rivers of Blood Flow': Agrarian Reform, Rural Warfare, and State Expansion in Post-Revolutionary Bolivia, 1952–1974." Ph.D. diss., University of Wisconsin-Madison, 2018.

Weston Jr., Charles H. "An Ideology of Modernization: The Case of the Bolivian MNR." *Journal of Inter-American Studies* 10, no. 1 (1968): 85–101.

Wilde Cavero, Manuel Fernando. *Historia militar de Bolivia.* La Paz: n.p., 1963.

Wilkie, James W. *The Bolivian Revolution and U.S. Aid since 1952: Financial Background and Context of Political Decisions.* Los Angeles: University of California, 1969.

Wood, Bryce. *The United States and Latin American Wars, 1932–1942.* New York: Columbia University Press, 1966.

Young, Kevin A. *Blood of the Earth: Resource Nationalism, Revolution, and Empire in Bolivia.* Austin: University of Texas Press, 2017.

Zook, David H., Jr. *The Conduct of the Chaco War.* New York: Bookman Associates, 1960.

Zulawski, Ann. *Unequal Cures: Public Health and Political Change in Bolivia, 1900–1950.* Durham, NC: Duke University Press, 2007.

Zürcher, Erik-Jan, ed. *Arming the State: Military Conscription in the Middle East and Central Asia 1775–1925.* New York: I.B. Tauris, 1999.

Zürcher, Erik-Jan, ed. *Fighting for a Living: A Comparative History of Military Labour, 1500–2000.* Amsterdam: Amsterdam University Press, 2013.

INDEX

Abaroa Cavalry Regiment, 36, 44, 68, 76, 117

Acre, 20, 54

agrarian reform, 152–55, 161, 163, 169, 171, 213n67

agriculture, 100–103, 161–62

Alandia, Miguel, 124, 152

alcohol, 25, 46, 49, 79–81, 104, 142–46, 190n55

amnesty, 28, 31, 75, 77, 84, 117–18

Andrade, Víctor, 164

anticommunism, 77, 81, 158, 164–66

antiguos, 45, 73–74, 83

Argentina, 117, 135, 210n3; Chaco War, 88, 213n52; military, 10, 20, 180n29

arms purchases, 26, 154, 166–67, 170, 199n69

army size, 4, 27–28, 75, 88–89, 129, 153, 182n63

artillery units, 31, 35, 44–45, 52, 60, 145, 158–59

artisans, 17, 28, 32–33, 36, 77, 114, 132–33

Arze Aguirre, René, 95, 100, 122, 178n49, 201n1

authority, ideas about, 7, 42, 59–63, 65, 79–80, 83

Aymara speakers, 16, 19, 44, 91, 98; acceptance of military service by, 30, 57, 63, 95, 161

Ayllón, Miguel, 165–66

Baldivieso, Pastor, 34, 61, 73

Ballivián Cavalry Regiment, 44, 49, 60, 76

Banzer, Carlos, 77

Banzer, Hugo, 198n68

barracks: conditions of, 42–44, 54, 61, 67;

life in, 43–51, 79–80, 136–37, 140, 142–47, 162, 173

Barrientos Ortuño, René, 153, 168, 171–72, 230n8

Beni, 24, 93, 116, 141

Bogarín, Juan Sinforiano, 91, 97, 203n30

brass bands, 14–15, 42, 47, 51, 173

Brazil, 11–12, 20, 53

bureaucracy, 43, 56, 61–62, 114–15, 127, 130–31, 162–63; outside Bolivia, 10–12; state capacity, 18–19, 109; state formation, 4, 12–13. *See also* conscription system, pensions

Busch, Germán, 8, 114–16, 120, 124, 146, 156–57, 161

Busch, René, 146, 222n103

Cacique Apoderado movement. *See* indigenous activists

Calle, La, 127, 215n94

Camacho Infantry Regiment, 44, 49, 77, 158

Campero Infantry Regiment, 36, 44, 58, 69–71, 75, 83, 196n41

carabineros, 8, 151, 153–54, 156, 166, 168, 224n27

Catavi massacre, 117–18, 121

caudillismo, 16, 18, 20–21, 64–65, 82

cavalry units, 31, 35–36, 44–45, 53, 76, 158, 168; soldiers in, 49, 60, 148

Centeno, Miguel Ángel, 9–10

Central Obrero Boliviana (COB), 152, 155, 164–65

census, 29; of 1900, 23–25, 32, 91, 93, 181n57; of 1950, 132, 135, 160, 202n13, 216–17

Céspedes, Augusto, 90, 109, 121, 215n94

Chaco, 24, 54, 81, 87–89, 120, 199n69, 201n1

Chaco War, 7–8; army size and composition, 89–96, 110; causes, 87–88; compensation by evaders and deserters, 111–18, 212n44; military justice during, 105–9; mobilization, 92–96, 98–103, 109; political impact of, 118–21, 126–27, 130, 152; prisoners of war, 89, 91–92, 97, 117, 123–24; rearguard service, 86, 89, 101, 112, 123. *See also* desertion, draft evasion, madrinas, veterans

Ch'ampa Guerra, 168, 171

Chayanta, 49, 77, 84

Chile: commercial ties to, 18, 103, 207n90; embassy of, 151; military of, 10, 18, 20, 180n29; territorial losses to, 24, 53

Chipana Ramos, Francisco, 124–28

Chuquisaca, 24, 95, 97, 124

citizenship: citizen-soldiers, 9–11, 21, 58, 61–65, 78–79, 83–84, 95; constitutional definition of, 8, 135, 152; elite views on, 124, 130, 139; hierarchy and, 40, 158, 161–62; military service and, 47, 51, 113–15, 121, 134–36, 150; noncitizen soldiers, 6–8, 32, 62, 92, 129, 149, 169; popular understandings of, 39, 126, 129, 142; scholarship on, 13, 176n16, 178n49, 209n129

civil war of 1899, 6, 16, 19

civic action, 170–71

class structure, 111, 136–37; elites and military service, 21, 34, 91–92, 95, 102–3; masking of, 13, 31, 36; middle classes and military service, 64, 79–80, 145; mixing in barracks, 44, 49, 96, 134; place of military service in, 4–5, 17, 35–37, 113, 127–28, 136–37, 147–50; popular classes, 28, 84, 91, 138, 172; social mobility, 10, 62–63, 124, 143

Cochabama, 172; conscripts from, 44, 49, 60, 80, 91, 94, 107

Cochabama (department), 24, 71, 116, 167–68, 171; conscripts from, 27, 71,

104, 108, 196n41; recruitment in, 115, 131–32, 216–17

Coico, Celestino, 37–41, 149

colonialism, internal, 3, 13, 90–91, 124, 201n1

colonization projects, 23, 53–56, 140, 159, 171, 192n90

colonos, 33, 77, 143, 147–48; enrollment of, 29; as soldiers, 16, 98, 101, 124

Colorados Infantry Regiment, 56–57, 69, 81–84, 140, 158

comunarios, 30, 37–40, 77, 101, 148, 185n130

Congress, Bolivian, 98, 102, 117, 121–22, 135–36, 164, 213n67

conscription system, 4–5, 26–31, 40–41, 130–134, 160–61; exemptions, 18, 21, 26–28, 33–34, 37–41, 99–102, 130; law governing, 20–21, 36–38, 180n32; outside Bolivia, 9–12; role of local authorities in, 28–31, 35, 93, 95–96, 110, 115, 173. *See also* bureaucracy

constitution, 3, 71; citizenship provisions, 8, 115, 135; constituent assembly of 1945, 118, 121 212n44; convention of 1920, 71; convention of 1938, 135, 140; military's mandate, 140, 171, 191n77; prohibition on military in politics, 6, 20, 157

corregidor, 24, 28–30, 35, 76–77, 95, 101, 180n33

coup d'états, 7–8, 17, 20, 82, 151–52; attempted, 71, 76, 154; of 1920, 42, 64–65, 68–74, 83; of 1930, 77–79; of 1936, 114; in 1940s, 118, 120–21, 146; of 1964, 172

desertion, 18, 35, 42, 45–47, 61, 142–43; in Chaco War, 86, 89, 93, 104–10, 147–48

Diario, El, 57, 67, 80, 141

discharge: of cadets, 76, 118, 153; of conscripts 21, 26, 38, 49–51, 73–74, 80, 84; importance of paperwork, 147–49, 172; of officers, 82, 151, 153, 163, 223n14; without training, 93, 130, 142

discipline, 36, 50, 58, 61–62, 79–82. *See also* punishment

Disentailment Law of 1874, 18, 67, 185n130
draft evasion, 93, 102–3, 141; capture of
    evaders, 30, 99–100; inability to punish,
    26–28, 41; invoked by politicians, 6;
    invoked by soldiers, 98, 144; *omiso* as
    social category, 21, 33–36, 102–3, 128;
    reporting, 34–35, 101, 127, 147. *See also*
    Chaco War
draft lottery, 17, 21, 27–28, 39, 101, 131,
    180n36
Dunkerley, James, 18, 82, 89, 172, 178n49,
    198n61

economy, 56, 65, 78, 88, 159, 163–66
education: military as providing, 25–26,
    143; rural schools, 77, 116, 124, 170. *See
    also* literacy
elections, 18–19, 78, 117, 135, 146, 151,
    163–64; military interference in, 20, 51,
    66–71, 81–82
exile, 66, 75, 78, 117–20, 151–53, 163–64,
    171–72

Falange Socialista Boliviana (FSB), 166,
    224n27
familial metaphors, 112–120. *See also patria*
Fortún, Armando, 153, 155–56, 169
Fortún, Federico, 155–56, 171
France, 4, 20, 26, 72, 180nn28–29

Gallardo, Melitón, 124, 143
gender, 3–5, 11, 45, 59, 130, 162. *See also*
    masculinity, women
Germany, 4, 26, 72, 88, 166, 197n46, 199n69
Guevara Arze, Wálter, 135, 167–68, 213n66

haciendas, 29, 82, 60, 98, 100–101, 127,
    147–48
honor, 10–11, 22–23, 35–36, 41, 57–62,
    127, 143
hygiene, 25, 43, 45, 58

Indigenous Congress of 1945, 124–26, 128
indigenous activists, 13, 67–68, 77, 124, 118,
    124, 129
indigenous communities, 25, 33, 135; Chaco
    War and, 93–96, 100–101, 148–49; con-
    scription in, 28–31, 37–40, 51, 57–58,
    63, 161; repression of, 44, 52, 76–77, 68,
    82, 135, 171–73
indigenous population: assimilation of,
    3, 31–32, 40–41, 130, 135–39, 143,
    160–63; beliefs about, 17, 25, 28,
    90–91, 135–37; definition of, 13, 25,
    32, 38; as soldiers, 30, 46–47, 49, 51,
    90–91, 137
infantry, 35, 44–45, 54
Inofuentes, Celmente, 153, 164–66, 169
insubordination, 50, 65, 69–71, 74, 78–84,
    95
impressment, 4, 7, 16, 18, 21, 62; during
    Chaco War, 86, 90, 95, 98–101; in
    Guatemala, 11
Iturralde, Abel, 66–68
izquierdistas, 106

Katari, Túpac (Julián Apaza), 3, 138
Katari, Tómas, 138
Klein, Herbert, 90, 117
Kundt, Hans: 1911 mission, 26; Chaco War,
    88–89, 98, 106–7; political involvement
    of, 72–73, 76–79, 197n46, 199n69

labor, 43, 61, 82–84; as compensation,
    113–18; discrimination, 62, 101, 137,
    162; martial vs. nonmartial, 51–58,
    140–41, 158–59, 169–70
labor movements, 76–77, 123–24, 155, 164,
    166. See also *Central Obrero Boliviana*
land tenure, 18–19, 67, 77, 124, 135; 1953
    agrarian reform, 152–55, 161, 163,
    169, 171
La Paz: conscripts from, 94, 134; migration
    to, 161; mutinies in, 70–75, 78–84, 146;
    strategic importance of, 64, 114, 117,
    145, 151, 167, 172
La Paz (department), 23–24; barracks in,
    43–44; and Liberalism, 18–20; recruit-
    ment in, 28–41, 95–96, 129, 132–34,
    142, 160–61
Lara, Jesús, 90, 109
Lechín, Juan, 121, 152, 168
liberalism, 10, 18–20, 32, 40, 62, 76

literacy: classes, 46–47, 136; discrimination based on, 45, 57, 60, 64–65, 137–39; rates, 23–25, 32–36, 93, 134–35, 217n18, 227n70. *See also* education, citizenship

Loa Infantry Regiment, 44, 46, 48–50, 66, 117; mutinies of, 72–76, 83–84, 145–46

Long, Huey, 119

Marof, Tristán (Gustavo Navarro), 119

Marxist doctrines, 8, 90, 117, 213n54. *See also* anticommunism, military socialism

masculinity, 10–11, 49–50, 59, 96–98, 142–45, 220n77. *See also* gender

Mexico, 11, 119, 135

migration, 112, 129, 134, 141, 149, 161–62, 169

Military Academy (*Colegio Militar*), 19, 156, 164, 166, 180n28; cadets, 69, 76, 78, 81, 118, 143, 153, 220n77; closure of, 8, 153

military justice, 50, 58–61, 117, 137–38, 142–49, 165, 189n43. *See also* Chaco War

Military-Peasant Pact (PMC), 171–72

military service booklet, 4–5, 26, 47, 51, 139–42, 155, 160; need for, 21, 29, 32, 37–40, 98, 129, 136; in postwar, 115–16, 121, 148–49

military socialism, 114–18, 120, 123–24, 129, 135

militias, 9, 152–56, 160, 163–68, 172

mining: industry, 19, 102–3; miners, 113, 151–52, 170; miners as soldiers, 105, 143, 172; recruitment of miners, 28–29, 93, 132–34, 155, 160, 217n17, 227n69; repression of miners, 52, 66–67, 76, 117, 152, 172–73

Ministry of War, 23, 26–41, 44, 52, 56, 73–75, 192n90

Ministry of Defense, 103, 115, 131, 153

Montenegro, Carlos, 121

Montes, Ismael, 20, 65–67, 71, 78

Morales, Evo, 3, 5–6

Movimiento Nacionalista Revolucionario (MNR), 8–9, 90, 117–21, 135, 151–69, 170–73

Muñoz, Andrés, 26, 30

Murillo Infantry Regiment, 46, 49, 67, 73–75, 189n35

Muruchi, Félix, 172, 217n17, 228n88

mutinies, 50, 56–57, 64–65, 70–75, 78–84, 146, 198n61; by cadets, 118; by officers, 165–66. *See also* Chaco War

Nación, La, 155, 159

National Security Doctrine, 166, 170–72

national identity, 6, 15, 23, 32, 47–48, 178n49

nationalism, 4, 8–10, 90, 114, 119

nationalization of industry, 119, 152, 155, 163–64, 213n52

noncommissioned officers, 31, 36, 44–45, 49–50, 115, 144; schools for, 20, 69, 78, 118n24. *See also* mutinies, punishment

Nuñez del Prado, Carlos, 16–17, 136

oath to flag, 5, 47, 51, 138, 157, 189n43

obedience, 17, 45, 48–50, 58, 62, 80, 158

occupations of conscripts, 32, 60, 64, 80, 132–33, 160, 227n70

officers, 18, 20, 138; as patrons, 63, 70, 75, 124; political participation of, 6, 20, 66, 78, 85, 112, 156–57; social class of, 53, 156, 166; professionalization of, 20, 26, 43, 65, 82. *See also* coup d'états, discharge, Military Academy, punishment, *Revista Militar*

omisos. See draft evasion

Oruro, 23–24; conscripts from, 57, 61, 95, 98; military units in, 46, 73–74, 77, 134, 155; recruitment in, 30

Ovando, Alfredo, 167, 224n14

pact with state, 3–4, 30, 39–40, 42–43, 183n95

Pando, 24, 132, 227n70

Pando, José Manuel, 19–20, 65

parades, 119, 156, 168

Paraguay, 12, 87–88, 119, 204n50. *See also* Chaco War, prisoners of war

patria, 16, 98, 112–13, 179n3; invoked by officers, 23, 47–48, 78; invoked by politicians, 29, 119–21, 135–36, 140, 156–57, 159, 162; invoked by soldiers, 56–58, 66–67, 79, 94–95, 107–9, 126, 148

patriotism, 16–17, 22, 42, 62; in Chaco War, 94–97, 99, 107–9, 111; discourse, 113–15, 123, 127–28; military service as proof of, 5–6, 143, 147

Partido de la Izquierda Revolucionaria (PIR), 90, 117–18, 135

Partido Liberal, 16–23, 31–32, 53–56, 65–71, 76–81, 114–15, 162

Partido Obrero Revolucionario (POR), 90, 152, 172

Partido Republicano, 42, 64–71, 78

Partido Republicano Genuino, 71, 74, 76–78, 81, 197n51

Partido Socialista Obrero Boliviano (PSOB), 117

paternalism, 28, 47, 77

Paz Estenssoro, Víctor, 8; 1938 convention, 135; 1964 coup, 172; candidacy, 151, 168, 171; Catavi massacre, 117; exile, 153, 164, 166, 171; military policy, 152–57, 163–64, 168–71, 224n14; militias, 155; stabilization, 164; veteran policy, 213n67; wartime service 121, 223n6

peasantry: in MNR discourse, 90, 121, 135, 156, 160–61, 171; leaders, 10, 123–24, 168. See also *colonos*, indigenous communities, militias

Plaza Murillo, 64, 69, 71–73, 77

Peñaranda, Enrique, 89, 98, 108–9; 117–18, 120–21

pensions, 20, 121–23, 127, 213n67, 214n71

Pérez Infantry Regiment, 44, 73, 78, 143

Peru, 10, 18, 20, 117, 151, 180n29, 207n90

police, 29, 39, 68–69, 77, 113, 115, 141

Potosí, 23–24, conscripts from, 46, 49, 95, 98, 104–5, 137

Prado, Julio, 165

Prado Salmón, Gary, 153, 157, 162, 165, 220n77

pride in military service, 6, 12, 21, 57, 96, 140–44

promotions, 20–21, 36, 45, 62, 70, 134, 144

punishment, 11, 50, 58–62, 70, 79–80; accusations of abuse, 66, 79–82, 146–47; chocolate, 142–43, 220n73; corporal, 16–17, 22, 42, 140; firing squad, 106, 109

Quartermasters Corps, 19, 26, 64

Quechua speakers, 44, 48–49, 107, 136–37, 171

Quintana, Juan Ramón, 89, 178n49

Quintanilla, Carlos, 117–18

racial divisions, 11–13, 32, 62, 86, 127, 134–39, 162; fear of race war, 10, 19, 51, 138, 154, 173. See also indigenous population

railroad companies, 34, 98, 103

rape, 49, 190nn63–64

rations, 43–44, 66–67, 76, 104, 144–45, 138, 162

Razón, La, 67, 69, 81

Razón de Patria (Radepa), 117–18, 120–21, 145, 153, 163–64, 169

Republican Guard, 69–70, 72–73, 75–76, 155

remisos. See draft evasion

Revista militar, 16, 46–48, 54, 135, 153, 158, 161, 164

revolution of 1952, 8–9, 151–52; class alignment of, 156, 160–61, 163; military policy of, 152–60, 166–71. *See also* citizenship, MNR

Richter, Alfredo, 35, 42–43; *Soldier's Catechism*, 55, 45, 47–48, 58, 61–62

roadwork, 54–58, 101, 113, 116, 137, 140–41, 158–59

Royal Dutch Shell, 62, 119

rural resistance, 52, 54, 75–77, 101, 135

Saavedra, Bautista, 69, 78, 124; 1920 coup, 68–70; and conscripts, 70–71, 73, 83; and military, 69, 72–76, 81, 155, 198n58; Republican Party, 65, 67–68, 71

Salamanca, Daniel: Chaco War, 82, 86, 88, 93, 98, 102–3; partisan politics, 65–66, 71, 78, 81, 117

San Pedro Prison, 72–73

Santa Cruz, 24, 76; conscripts from, 35, 79, 90, 97, 106; military labor in, 141, 159; recruitment in, 103, 141, 185n121; uprisings in 76, 166–67

School of the Americas, 164, 170

Seleme, Antonio, 151, 223n6

Sever, Jacques, 20, 23, 180n28, 181n42

sex, 49, 104

sexual dominance, 59–60, 143

Siles, Hernando, 75–79, 88, 199n69, 225n34

Siles Zuazo, Hernán, 121, 155, 163–68

Standard Oil, 87, 112, 119, 212n49

state formation. *See* bureaucracy

strikes, 77, 81, 112, 114, 165, 170; military repression of, 8, 51–52, 67–68, 75, 152, 167, 173

Sucre, 18–19, 61, 124, 141

Sucre Infantry Regiment, 44, 46, 48, 137

Tapia, Luciano, 129–30, 142–44, 214n68

Tarija, 24, 76, 96; conscripts from, 27, 35, 90, 144, 103–4

Tejada Sorzano, Luis, 81, 114–15, 119

Toro, David, 8, 77, 114–15, 119, 123, 219n50

tribute, 18, 20, 25, 38, 183n95, 186n132

Ugarte, Rafael de, 66

uniforms, 26, 43, 47, 55, 57–58, 143, 153

United Kingdom, 73, 117, 153, 156, 164–67, 171, 212n41

United States of America, 119; aid to Bolivia, 163–64, 166–67, 170, 228n96; diplomats' observations, 37, 73, 137; imperialism, 158; support for Barrientos, 172

venereal disease, 49

veterans, 12, 111–14, 119–30, 145, 147–50, 152, 213n67

Villamontes, 101, 104, 201n11

Villarroel, Gualberto, administration, 8, 118, 121, 124, 126, 129, 145; memory of, 155–57, 161, 225n34

wages (*socorros*), 43–44, 55, 73–74, 79–82, 104, 122, 138

Waldo Ballivián Regiment, 155, 168

War of the Pacific (1879–1883), 18, 24

women, 5, 10–11, 135, 141–42, 175n12; indigenous, 49, 100; *madrinas*, 48, 96–98, 204n50, 205n57; widows, 121–22, 127

Zook, David, 89–90